EXTREME PUNISHMENT

The Chilling True Story of Acclaimed Law Professor Dan Markel's Murder

Praise for this book:

"Empathetic, engrossing, and impeccably researched, *EXTREME PUNISHMENT* is the single best piece of reporting I've read on the Dan Markel case. Like the best true crime books, it says as much about the law and society as it does about Dan's murder and the subsequent trials. A genuine revelation."

—Matthew Shaer, Creator and Host of Wondery's *Over My Dead Body* podcast

"*EXTREME PUNISHMENT* is a rich, detailed, well-researched telling of the murder of Dan Markel. But it's not the crime that will keep you turning the pages in what will become a classic on the shelves of true crime enthusiasts. What makes this book special is the people involved in this twisted story, the wildly exciting characters you soon realize are just like you and your next-door neighbors. Maybe even your in-laws. Perhaps even your ex-spouse."

—Rod Kackley, award-winning journalist and author of 32 books, including *THE MURDER OF KELSEY BERRETH* and *THE MURDER OF THORA CHAMBERLAIN*

"Steve Epstein's sharp new true-crime rips the lid off the whole sensational story about a wrecked relationship gone horribly awry. Top notch."

—Ron Franscell, *New York Times* bestselling author of *THE DARKEST NIGHT* and *SHADOWMAN*

More praise:

"*EXTREME PUNISHMENT* is a compelling and masterfully told story illuminating the lives of real people caught up in a shocking murder. The startling and complex twists in a war between two families and the unpredictable turns of real courtroom drama will satisfy any true crime lover and anyone else with a passionate interest in human relationships. This outstanding book is a 'can't-put-it-down' to the last page. A must-read."

—Jennifer Zedalis, Senior Legal Skills Professor, Director of
Trial Practice, and Assistant Director of the Criminal Justice
Center, University of Florida Levin College of Law

"A truly fascinating and addicting read. In *EXTREME PUNISHMENT*, Steve Epstein meticulously provides insight into the myriad of personalities and entanglements surrounding the tragic murder of Dan Markel. He has taken a most complex case and synthesized it brilliantly into a riveting and obsessive read."

—John D. Singer, Co-founder of Singer Deutsch LLP
and preeminent NYC and California
employment attorney and legal commentator

"*EXTREME PUNISHMENT* is the book those of us who have been mesmerized by the search for justice in Dan Markel's murder have been waiting for. Steve Epstein takes the reader through all the twists and turns of this remarkable case and provides richly textured insights into the lives of the people involved in, and affected by, this American tragedy."

—Paul Caron, Dean of Pepperdine University
Caruso School of Law and Founder of TaxProf Blog,
a leading source of information about Dan Markel's murder

EXTREME
PUNISHMENT

**The Chilling True Story of
Acclaimed Law Professor
Dan Markel's Murder**

STEVEN B. EPSTEIN

Black Lyon Publishing, LLC

EXTREME PUNISHMENT
Copyright © 2022 by **Steven B. Epstein**

Our books may be ordered through your local bookstore or by visiting the publisher:

www.BlackLyonPublishing.com

Black Lyon Publishing, LLC
PO Box 567
Baker City, OR 97814

ISBN: 979-8-9865124-3-3
Library of Congress Control Number: 2022944717

Published and printed in the United States of America.

For every parent who has endured the horror
and unrelenting anguish of burying a child.

Foreword

ON FRIDAY, JULY 18, 2014, my friend Dan Markel was murdered. I learned of Dan's death that Saturday morning. I was on a bus traveling up to the Berkshires for a relaxing summer weekend with family when I started receiving a flurry of text and email messages from our many mutual friends, all to the same effect: "Did you hear what happened to Dan?"

We were frantically calling, texting, and emailing each other, trying to figure out what had happened. All we knew was that Dan, just 41 at the time, had died, apparently of gunshot wounds. The initial details were sketchy, the theories constantly changing. Was it a burglary gone bad? A suicide? An unhinged attack, maybe by a vengeful law student taught by Dan or an angry reader of his high-profile legal blog?

It was all so shocking. Who would want to kill our friend, a respected law professor? And it was all so shockingly sad. Dan was the father of two young boys, and it was heartbreaking to think of them growing up without their dad.

As more information emerged over the course of the weekend, it became clear that Dan was the victim of a well-planned, targeted killing. As Tallahassee Police Chief Michael DeLeo declared on Monday, "There is no evidence that this was a random act."

Dan was a prominent legal scholar and a leading expert on theories of punishment. His murder made headlines both here and abroad. Writing in the *New York Times,* John Schwartz described Dan as "an internationally known criminal law professor" and "a leader in the world of online legal scholarship," based on his co-founding PrawfsBlawg, one of the most important and influential blogs in the legal world.

Dan was the rare professor whose work was known beyond the ivory tower, thanks to his writing for such mainstream publications as the *Times*, *The Atlantic*, and *Slate*. In fact, he had submitted an opinion piece to the *Times* just a week or two before he was killed, as a mutual friend who was an editor there mentioned to me when we commiserated about Dan's tragic death.

Dan and I had been friends for years, long before he was a renowned legal academic. We first met in the mid-1990s, when we both worked in the editorial department of the *Harvard Crimson*, one of the nation's oldest college newspapers. We became friends through editing each other's columns and spending Sunday nights working on unsigned "staff editorials" that represented the institutional views of the *Crimson*. We didn't see eye to eye on many matters, but we liked and respected each other a great deal. I found Dan to be a polished writer and powerful thinker, even if a bit liberal for my taste at the time. (I chalked some of this up to his being from Canada, about which he occasionally got teased around the building.)

After college, we both found our way to law school, and we reconnected a decade or so later as early entrants into the field of legal blogging. Dan co-founded PrawfsBlawg in 2005, and I launched a widely read blog about the legal profession called Above the Law in 2006. Although we were not close, we kept up with each other through our writing and on social media, and we would see each other at legal conferences or meet up for coffee or drinks if we found ourselves in the same city.

On one of these occasions, when I was living in Washington, D.C., Dan introduced me to his fiancée Wendi. Before we met up, he raved about her, telling me how much I would like her. The three of us went out to coffee at Kramerbooks in Dupont Circle, and we had a delightful time. Dan and I spent much of the time—too much time, in hindsight—talking shop about legal blogging. But even if Wendi didn't get to say much, I left with a positive impression of her and of them as a couple. They seemed well matched—attractive, accomplished, both in the field of law—and very much in love.

The last time I saw Dan was at a legal conference in San Francisco. He took such joy in talking about ideas and connecting with people, so conferences were his happy place. At that conference, I introduced Dan to my husband Zach, a fellow scholar of criminal law. At the time, Zach hosted a podcast about punishment, and he wanted to have Dan on as a guest, given his importance in the field. Alas, the episode never happened—which makes me think of all the things that Dan will never get to do, from attending his sons' *bar mitzvahs* to playing with grandchildren.

Dan will be remembered as a brilliant scholar, talented writer, loving father, devoted son, and loyal friend. He was extremely generous with his time and insights to anyone who asked for his help—a true *mensch*.

That said, Dan was not always easy to get along with. He was brilliant, and he knew it. He had opinions, which he did not hesitate to share. To those of us who could take his bluntness, Dan was an invaluable source of honest perspectives and feedback—but his bluntness could rub people the wrong way at times.

At the end of the day, though, Dan was a law professor, and his debates were academic ones with fellow scholars. He lived in Tallahassee's Betton Hills, a safe, upscale neighborhood populated by fellow lawyers, doctors, and other well-to-do professionals. He focused on his research, his teaching, and his two sons; he led no double life. Who would want to kill him—and why?

The story of who killed Dan and why is the book you are now reading. It is an important story, given Dan's stature as a scholar and the universal themes that it implicates. It is a riveting story, given the heroic efforts of investigators and prosecutors to bring Dan's murderers to justice. And it is above all a tragic story, given the void that Dan's killing has left not just in the world of legal scholarship, but in the world of his friends and family—especially his two sons, whom he adored beyond all measure.

For those of us who were Dan's friends and family, this is a difficult story to read. I know that I and many others who knew Dan are grateful to Steve Epstein for telling this story with sensitivity, eloquence, and grace. Given who Dan was and how he was killed, in such a shocking and cold-blooded way, it is not surprising that parts of this story have been told before— on multiple television programs, a hit podcast, and many news outlets around the world. Meticulously researched and beautifully written, *Extreme Punishment* is now the definitive account of Dan's life and death, the standard against which all future tellings will be measured.

It would be hard to imagine someone better situated than Steve to write this book. First, Steve is a former law professor. The world of legal academia is a specific and insular world; as someone who lived in it during the mid-1990s, Steve knows it well. He has a firsthand understanding of Dan's professional life, which was deeply important to him, and reveals important connections between Dan's work as a scholar of justice and the long-running quest for justice following his murder.

Second, Steve is an experienced and talented author. He has published two acclaimed true-crime books, *Murder on Birchleaf Drive*, about the murder of Michelle Young, and *Evil at Lake Seminole*, about the murder of Mike Williams—which also took place in Tallahassee.

Third, as you will learn, an ugly divorce lies at the epicenter of the plot to murder Dan, and the story culminates with the trials of some of Dan's murderers. Steve is now a matrimonial and trial lawyer with more than three decades of experience, which gives him special insight into the legal battles at the beginning and end of this story.

I wish nobody had to tell this tale. But since it is being told— and should be told, to honor Dan's legacy—I am thankful to Steve for doing so with such thoughtfulness, understanding, and skill.

As a professor of criminal law, Dan Markel spent nearly every day thinking and writing about justice, defined as giving each their due. In *Extreme Punishment*, Steve has given Dan his due, bearing witness not only to Dan's horrific death, but to his extraordinary and inspiring life as a scholar, teacher, father, son, and friend. My fervent hope is that by the time you read this book, some measure of justice will have been visited upon the individuals—all of the individuals—who brought Dan's life to such an untimely and tragic end.

David Lat

Founding Editor, Above the Law
Founder, Original Jurisdiction
Summit, New Jersey
October 2022

PART ONE
In Broad Daylight

1.

Friday, July 18, 2014
10:50 a.m.

JIM AND SHARON GEIGER sat side-by-side on one of two plush loveseats neatly arranged around a glass-topped coffee table. Soft pastel paintings hanging from the walls of their elegantly decorated living room conveyed a peaceful, tranquil ambience. The white-draped bow window stretching across the front wall—opposite from where they were seated—provided a glimpse of the green shrubbery and freshly mown grass comprising the Geigers' expansive front yard.

Nearing their golden wedding anniversary, Jim and Sharon were as smitten as when they'd fallen in love in their early twenties, when both were schoolteachers. Their home exuded the same warmth as it did when they first moved into the one-story brick structure in 1977—with two kids in tow. Betton Hills was a fairly young neighborhood back then, with fewer than 80,000 people calling Tallahassee "home."

The quiet, tree-canopied subdivision sat some three miles northeast of the 25-story state capitol building, which was still under construction when Jim and Sharon arrived. By Florida standards, "Tally," as it was affectionately nicknamed by locals, was more of a sleepy, southern town than a bustling city like Miami or Tampa.

Jim eventually formed his own company, running it for more than 20 years before handing the reins over to his younger colleagues. Now 72, he still served as chairman of the board, reporting to work most every day. He and Sharon had traveled the world together, visiting nearly 60 countries and 46 American states. In just nine days, Oregon would make it 47, the itinerary for their two-week getaway to the Pacific Northwest having been meticulously planned out for months.

During the 37 years the Geigers had lived in Betton Hills, Tally's population had more than doubled. Though the neighborhood had certainly changed—oversized two-story houses owned by doctors, lawyers, and other professionals now sprinkled throughout the neighborhood—much remained the same. Many of their neighbors who were young adults when Jim and Sharon arrived in the 1970s remained in the same homes, now grandparents just like them. It was still a quiet, peaceful neighborhood, serious crime virtually unheard of, though an occasional home or car break-in would cause a stir every now and again.

Trescott Drive, where the Geigers resided, ran in a semi-circle dissecting the entire subdivision, beginning at Betton Road at the south and running clockwise for a mile and a half to Centerville Road at the east. Their home was just a short walk from Betton Road.

In November 2007, the Geigers had been invited to a house-warming party for an attractive young couple who'd just moved in next door. Wendi Adelson and Dan Markel, they learned, were lawyers who'd recently joined the faculty at nearby Florida State University. As they approached their new neighbors' front door that evening, Jim and Sharon were surprised to see a large pile of shoes on the front porch. A box of light-blue hospital booties sat nearby, intended for guests who preferred to wear their shoes once inside.

"We just had brand new oak floors installed," Dan explained as he politely asked Jim and Sharon to remove their shoes if they didn't mind. "We really don't want them getting scuffed up." That somewhat awkward initial meeting set the tone for the two couples' interactions over the ensuing years. Not having much in common, they kept mainly to themselves, the 2007 party the only occasion either pair would spend time in the other's home.

The Geigers would sometimes see Wendi through their living-room window as she jogged along Trescott Drive in the mornings. By the fall of 2009, they'd more often spot her pushing a baby stroller containing the couple's first child, Benjamin, born that July. By late 2010, the stroller had become a doublewide, baby Lincoln now seated next to his big brother. Wendi was friendly and gracious whenever they stumbled into one another, her bright smile and piercing blue eyes always disarming.

The Geigers' sightings of Wendi pushing a stroller, however, didn't last very long. They learned from neighbors that Wendi and Dan had separated in September 2012, with Wendi moving across town. Jim and Sharon hadn't seen her since and rarely saw the boys out and about. They'd occasionally see Dan driving by but hadn't exchanged more than a few words with him in years. Their interactions had become so infrequent that, by July 2014, Jim had even forgotten his neighbor's last name.

On this hot and muggy Friday morning—typical mid-summer weather for North Florida—Jim had decided to take the day off. Two of his and Sharon's granddaughters were spending a few days with them to provide a much-needed respite to their daughter Kim, a single mom in Gainesville, about 150 miles away. Though Sharon had a doctor's appointment scheduled that morning, all four planned to meet up for an afternoon movie after Jim took the girls for some pizza.

Before Sharon headed off for her appointment, she and Jim were working their way through Google search results on Sharon's iPad as they tried to figure out how to create email lists. Septuagenarians though they were, the Geigers did their level best to stay current with evolving technology.

Their tutorial was suddenly interrupted by a loud popping noise—which startled them—as if a firecracker had exploded in their front yard. Jim sprang up from the loveseat and hustled over to the window, hoping to determine from which direction the noise had come. Out of the corner of his eye, as he peered to his right—in the direction of Dan's property—he detected a small, light-colored car at the far end of the driveway. At first, the car appeared still, but a split second later it quickly backed out into the street, lurched forward, and began racing toward Betton Road.

As he watched it speed away, Jim sensed something was amiss. He suspected that whoever was driving the small car had broken into Dan's home—or had attempted to—and was now fleeing the scene. He decided to investigate. "I'm going next door to check it out," he told Sharon, hurrying toward the front door.

While walking briskly across his front yard toward Dan's house, Jim could see that the white door to his neighbor's two-car garage was raised. Peering inside, he glimpsed the rear of a black car and noticed its motor running. A sense of relief washed over him. Logically, Jim thought, there couldn't have been a burglary attempt if Dan was in his car about to back down the driveway. He abruptly reversed course just before reaching the vehicle and returned home.

After telling Sharon what he'd seen, Jim stood at their living-room window, transfixed, waiting to see the black car back down the driveway. His sight line, however, was somewhat restricted, with Dan's garage not visible at all.

Another five minutes passed. But still no car. Jim was now pretty sure something was wrong after all. "He should have backed out by now," he told his wife, who was still fiddling with her iPad on the loveseat. "Something doesn't seem right. I'm going to head back over there to see what's going on."

As he neared his neighbor's garage a second time, Jim found the garage door still up and the black car still running inside. This time, he decided to enter the garage and walk up to the driver's side to make sure everything was okay. He expected to find nothing more ominous than Dan talking on his cellphone. But that isn't even close to what Jim Geiger found.

As he came within a foot or two of the driver's-side door, Jim felt and heard crunching beneath his shoes, which was startling enough. He then noticed that the door's window was shattered, a large portion missing entirely. The only glass that remained intact was fractured in a spiderweb pattern, surrounding two-thirds of a quarter-sized hole in the upper-right-hand-corner of the frame. Small, jagged shards were scattered on the garage's concrete floor — what Jim had sensed crunching beneath his feet. In that brief instant, he realized a gunshot had blown through the glass window.

"Oh my God!" he thought to himself, his relaxing day off with his grandkids suddenly thrown into a tailspin. Standing beside the car door, he cocked his head to peer through the shattered window.

What he observed was utterly horrifying. His neighbor Dan Markel was slumped over — behind the steering wheel — the left side of his head covered with a thick layer of blood. More glass shards surrounded him inside the car. It was obvious he'd been shot, though unclear whether his head wound had been self-inflicted or the result of an assault. Jim wondered whether Dan had become so despondent over his divorce with Wendi that he'd opted for suicide.

"Danny, what happened?" he shouted through the broken window. No response. He could see Dan's head rocking ever so slightly from his left shoulder to his right, suggesting he was still alive, but perhaps unconscious.

"Danny, Danny, what happened?" Jim hollered more loudly this time. Still nothing. He realized further attempts to arouse his neighbor would be futile. His heart now pumping furiously, he reached into his pocket for his cellphone, but then remembered he'd left it on the coffee table.

Jim rushed back home a second time, this time in a frenzied panic. Sharon could see the terrified expression on her husband's face and asked him what happened. Not wanting to alarm his granddaughters, Jim held his right index finger up to his temple, his thumb pointed upwards, to demonstrate that Dan had been shot, telling his wife he needed to call for help right away. He tried mashing 911 on his phone as he raced out the front door, inadvertently dialing 9119 instead. He corrected his mistake. A dispatcher came on the line as Jim stood amid a pile of shattered glass beside the driver's-side door of Dan's Honda Accord. The call connected at 11:02 a.m.

"What's the address of your emergency?" a male voice asked.

"It's right next door to my house, which is 2122 Trescott Drive," Jim answered, fairly calm despite the alarming circumstances.

"Okay, and tell me exactly what happened," the dispatcher instructed.

"We heard a loud bang and a car pulled away from next door," Jim explained, his cadence accelerating as he spoke. "I came over and looked in. The garage door was up, and I thought the gentleman was backing out and I went back to my house, but he never backed out. And I came back over and his win— his driver's-side window is shattered and he's spattered and can't answer. He's inside. I don't know if somebody tried to shoot him or if he shot himself or what. I don't know."

The dispatcher asked where the incident had occurred. "Right next door," Jim replied, indicating he didn't know the exact address. "You need to send an ambulance in a hurry—EMT," Jim implored him, his tone now more urgent. "He's still alive. He's moving." Jim was hoping to hear the sound of an ambulance siren at any moment. Tallahassee Memorial Hospital was less than a mile and a half away, at the intersection of Betton Road and Centerville Road.

For some reason, though, the dispatcher didn't seem to share his sense of urgency, trudging through a list of additional questions at a glacial pace. "Okay," the male voice asked, "What's going on with him?"

"I don't know," Jim responded. "The driver's-side window was all bashed in. He's inside, the car is running, and he's got blood all over his head. He's not responding to me." He then noticed the house number centered on the bricks just above the garage door—2116—and shared it with the dispatcher.

"What's your name sir?"

Jim spelled out his last name and, after not hearing another word for about 20 seconds, repeated, "I think you need to hurry."

"Yeah, I'm going to get them on the way to you. I just want to ask you a few questions, okay?"

"Go ahead, but send them as you're asking," Jim pleaded, his impatience escalating.

"They're already on the way," the dispatcher reassured him, though Jim still didn't see or hear any evidence confirming that. "Are you with him now?"

"I'm standing just outside the garage door," Jim answered. When asked about the victim's age, he told the dispatcher, "He looks like maybe 35 or 40. It could be our neighbor. I can't tell. It's the blood—it could be the man who owns the house." Due to the copious amount of blood covering Dan's head, he wasn't certain.

The dispatcher asked if the name of their street was "Trescott Drayton" or "Trescott Drive." "Trescott *Drive*," Jim answered, flustered over the man's confusion. A few seconds later, he overheard the dispatcher telling someone, "I'm changing the location. This is Trescott Drive, not Trescott Drayton." More precious time slipping away, Jim lamented, with his neighbor's life literally hanging in the balance.

Forgetting where he was on his list of questions, the dispatcher then asked—a second time—for the "age of the patient," with Jim, bewildered, repeating his answer.

"And is he awake?"

Jim stated that Dan was "moving his head around, but he's not responding." He told the dispatcher he couldn't tell if Dan was conscious, but assumed he was breathing since his head was moving.

"Did you ever hear him talk or anything?" the man asked, as if the answer weren't obvious from Jim's prior responses.

"No," Jim replied curtly.

"You said he's sitting in the car, right?"

"Correct. In the driver's seat. The car is running."

"Where exactly is he—in the driver's seat?" the dispatcher asked. "Do you know?"

"In the driver's seat," Jim reiterated in an exasperated tone, beginning to wonder if the man had any training whatsoever before being placed such a crucial role. More than five minutes had already elapsed since the emergency call began, and still no sign of an ambulance on the way. He overheard the man telling someone, "The police needs to go."

"Could you direct the emergency crews to him, sir?" the dispatcher asked.

"Sure, sure," Jim replied quickly, eager to help.

"All right. I'm sending the paramedics to help you now," the man told Jim, much to his relief. "Just stay on the line. I'll tell you exactly what to do next."

After what seemed like an eternity, the dispatcher finally said, "If it's safe for you to do so, see if he is conscious and breathing or moving at all. Okay?"

"It's not safe for me to do," Jim replied. "I don't want to put my hands in here."

"Okay. Well help is on the way." The man then asked about the other vehicle Jim saw driving away.

"It looked sort of like it was light-colored, white or silver," the former schoolteacher said. "I want to say it was a Prius, but it could have been a different car but a small car about that size. And it hurried— it left the scene rapidly, which seemed to be unusual."

Jim noticed Sharon walking toward him from their driveway. She told him that she was leaving for her doctor's appointment. "I'm going to be over here waiting for the EMT, honey," he told his wife. "Go ahead. But just tell the kids to hold on inside. They're okay. Just tell them I'm out here."

The 911 dispatcher repeated that help was on the way. Jim told him he'd be standing in the street, ready to direct the emergency vehicles to Dan. But nine minutes into the call— which under the circumstances seemed more like 90—Jim still didn't see or hear any evidence indicating help was actually on the way.

"So he won't respond to you at all?" the dispatcher asked—another question Jim had already answered. He inquired whether it appeared as if the vehicle had crashed into the garage. Jim assured him that wasn't the case.

After another lengthy pause, Jim asked where the emergency vehicles were being sent from—as there was still no sign of them. The dispatcher replied that he wasn't sure and would check. Nearly two minutes of dead silence ensued. "We've got several people on the way," he finally said. "It looks like one person's coming from Maclay Road."

Jim's frustration boiled over. Maclay Road was easily a ten-minute drive away. He asked why someone wasn't coming from the hospital, just down the road, and reiterated the urgency of the situation, telling the dispatcher that Dan's head was "all bloody and he is not responding."

"So you're saying his head is bloody now?"

"Yes. *It's been bloody,*" Jim answered, thoroughly exasperated, as he'd already referred to Dan's bloody head several times. "The window is shattered," he repeated. "I don't know if he was trying to shoot himself. I don't know what the situation is." He was now standing beside the driver's-side door once again. "He's still moving around, so he's alive."

Yet another two minutes elapsed before the dispatcher said another word. Meanwhile, Dan Markel was no closer to receiving the emergency medical attention he desperately needed.

"It looks like I should have an officer coming up the roadway," the dispatcher finally said, breaking the silence.

"Okay, well, *we need EMT,*" Jim insisted, nearing his wits' end that the man on the other end of the line still didn't appreciate the desperate and deteriorating situation.

"The officer's going to be there first. EMT is not going to come until we figure out what's going on. But they're on the way as well. Okay?"

"It better be if this guy's been shot," Jim replied, as he finally noticed a car approaching him.

At 11:17 a.m., a plain-clothes investigator stepped out of an unmarked vehicle as Jim ended his frustrating call with the 911 dispatcher. He directed the man to Dan's garage. Within seconds, he overheard the investigator on his phone stating the obvious: "We need an EMT." Precisely what Jim—to no avail—had been trying to get across for a solid 15 minutes while his neighbor sat in his car, unconscious, struggling to remain alive.

Finally, Jim heard the welcome sound of an ambulance siren, faint at first, but becoming very loud in just an instant. Additional first responders were racing down Trescott Drive minutes later.

Standing at the edge of his driveway, Jim watched as emergency personnel extracted Dan from his car and placed him onto a gurney. His head was bandaged from the middle of his face to the back of his neck. He was wearing a red T-shirt and black gym shorts. Paramedics gently placed the gurney into the back of the ambulance, which then sped off toward Betton Road at 11:28 a.m., just as the light-colored car had some 30 minutes before. Dan Markel's next-door neighbor hoped and prayed it wasn't too late.

•••

TRESCOTT DRIVE WAS ALSO home to Jeremy and Tracey Cohen, who lived across the street, about 15 houses further from Betton Road than Dan's. It was actually Dan and Wendi who'd told them about the "For Sale" sign being placed in the front yard of 2275 Trescott five years earlier.

The young couples had first become friends after meeting at a Christmas party in 2007. Which was just a little ironic, considering all four were Jewish. Indeed, prior to Dan and Wendi's separation, Jeremy and Tracey had been frequent guests at their home for Shabbat dinners. Dan would go to great lengths to assemble a different eclectic mix of friends and acquaintances for each Friday's meal, many of whom weren't even Jewish.

Their friendship only grew after the Cohen and Markel children came along—the Cohens' girls Molly and Paige becoming fast friends with Ben and Lincoln, even attending the same preschool. The two families would gather at neighborhood parks, hang out at the pool, and take day trips together. Before Dan and Wendi's separation, Tracey and Wendi would meet fairly regularly for lunch to break up the monotony of their workdays.

Shortly after the Cohens had moved to Tally in 2004, Tracey began working for her mother's printing business, Target Copy. Ten years later, she was now at the helm as its president, the enterprise having expanded significantly under her leadership. She was at her office the afternoon of July 18, 2014 when an ominous text message from her sister appeared on her cellphone.

There had been a shooting on Trescott Drive, the text said, which naturally concerned Tracey. She instinctively reached out to Dan, texting to ask him what he knew about the incident and trying to confirm he was all right. But he didn't respond. She freed herself from work as soon as she could and headed home, finally reaching Trescott at about 4:00 p.m. When she pulled up alongside Dan's house, she saw a police cruiser in his driveway.

Tracey rolled down her car window. "What happened?" she asked the officer. He told her the occupant of the home had been injured but wouldn't reveal additional information. As she headed further down the street, to her own home, she dialed Tallahassee Memorial Hospital. "Has a Dan Markel been admitted as a patient?" she asked, hoping HIPAA regulations wouldn't prevent her from finding out. The hospital confirmed that Dan had been admitted and was in intensive care, but wouldn't divulge any additional details.

The Cohens received only bits and pieces of information throughout the late afternoon and early evening—including that Dan had been shot. Late that night, a friend who taught at the law school told Jeremy that a limited number of visitors would be allowed to see Dan in the hospital and that he could come for a visit. He arrived at about 10:30 p.m., having no idea what to expect—still unaware his good friend had been shot in the head at point-blank range.

Upon entering Dan's room in the ICU, Jeremy found his friend hooked up to an assortment of wires and tubes, machines chirping and beeping all around him. Dan was all alone. A mechanical ventilator was breathing for him. The law professor's head was covered in white gauze, though one of his eyes, swollen shut, was exposed.

The image confronting Jeremy was jarring, almost surreal. Dan was either in a coma or unconscious—he wasn't sure which. Though he was shaken by the frightening spectacle, Jeremy felt certain his neighbor would pull through. He knew Dan would fight with every fiber of his being to make sure he'd be there to see his boys—the center of his universe—grow up.

Jeremy made small talk, reminiscing about the many good times they'd shared together as friends and families. Even though he knew Dan couldn't hear a single word he was saying, he felt talking to him was the right thing to do. He sat in a chair next to the hospital bed for more than an hour, holding his composure together as best he could, his soliloquy unabated.

Just before midnight, Jeremy rose to leave, telling his unresponsive friend, "We're going to do everything we can to figure out who did this to you—and to get justice." As he approached the door, he told Dan he'd return the following day for another visit.

But about an hour later, the life of 41-year-old Daniel Eric Markel came to an abrupt, premature end.

2.

"Who Would Do This?"

THE DOORBELL TO WENDI ADELSON'S two-story, four-bedroom house rang at 8:20 a.m. that same Friday morning. The attractive rental property on Aqua Ridge Way—some five miles northeast of Betton Hills—had been her home since she'd abruptly pulled the plug on her six-year marriage nearly two years before. The 35-year-old divorcée and clinical law professor was home alone feverishly working on an article she was hoping to complete before the new school year began.

Wendi had been productive without the kids, as it was Dan's week with them according to the marital settlement agreement they'd hammered out the prior July. The boys rotated between their parents' homes every Friday afternoon, but spent Wednesday overnights with the opposite parent to ensure they had quality time with both each week.

The mother of two opened the door and politely greeted the Best Buy repairman standing on the front porch—a member of the electronics chain's "Geek Squad"—who was there to determine if her large-screen TV could be fixed. Though it was nearly brand new, one of the boys had thrown a toy at it and cracked the screen. Much to her dismay, the repairman ultimately confirmed the crack wasn't covered by the warranty and that her most economical option was to replace the TV altogether. By 9:15 a.m., he was gone.

Wendi had planned to get some housework done that morning before heading out to meet a couple of girlfriends, both psychiatrists, for lunch at 1:00 p.m. That evening, she'd be donning an elegant cocktail dress for a stock-the-bar engagement party for another set of friends.

Running far behind schedule, however, she gave up on taking a much-needed shower, pulled her long, artificially colored dirty-blonde hair into a scraggly bun, and rushed out the door in the same navy blue T-shirt and light blue shorts she'd been wearing all morning. It was already nearly 12:30 p.m. and she had errands to run before lunch. She backed her burgundy Honda Odyssey minivan down the driveway and was soon heading south on Centerville Road on her way to the liquor store to purchase bourbon for the evening party.

As was her custom, Wendi turned right onto her old street—Trescott Drive—which served as a convenient shortcut to Thomasville Road, Tally's busiest north-south artery. While chatting on the phone with an old friend who was living in England, she was startled to see a police car turned sideways behind yellow crime-scene tape that stretched across the entire road—about a mile from where she'd turned onto Trescott. The police barricade had been erected just a few houses up the street from her old home.

Wendi had no time to investigate. She told her friend she suspected a tree had fallen into the road—knocking down some power lines—which occurred several times while she and her ex-husband lived on Trescott. Her effort to use the shortcut aborted, she made a three-point turn and retraced her route back to Centerville Road.

She arrived at ABC Fine Wine & Spirits on Thomasville Road just before 12:45 p.m. Wendi admitted to the salesclerk—thoroughly embarrassed—that she'd never purchased bourbon before and didn't know how to find it. She told him she was looking for a bottle of Bulleit—pronounced "bullet." As he directed her to the whiskey section, the clerk marveled at how blue her eyes appeared. Wendi grinned. Her color-enhancing contact lenses had made a favorable impression yet again.

By the time she pulled into the Market Square shopping center, where her friends Jeannine Silberman and Ritu Ghai were patiently waiting at a popular restaurant named Mozaik, she was a good ten minutes late. Apologizing for her tardiness, Wendi took her seat at the table, a bit frazzled by the day's events. She settled down quickly, though, enjoying some girl time, good food, and gossip. She shared with Silberman and Ghai the latest in her ongoing and escalating legal battle with her ex.

At about 2:30 p.m., just after the three women paid for their meals, a burly man with short-cropped, gray hair approached their table. His large frame was outfitted in a black golf shirt tucked neatly into a pair of khaki pants. "Is there a Wendi Adelson here?" he asked. The three women stared back at him quizzically, wondering who he was and why he was there.

"I'm Wendi Adelson," Wendi tentatively responded.

"I'm Investigator Craig Isom with the Tallahassee Police Department," the man said, flashing his credentials, his words enunciated with a distinct southern drawl. "So sorry to interrupt your lunch, but I'm going to need you to come with me to the police station. There was an incident this morning we need to discuss with you."

Slowly rising from her seat, with an incredulous expression, Wendi clutched her purse, said good-bye, and walked toward the law enforcement officer, leaving her psychiatrist friends— stunned by the sudden turn of events—behind.

•••

WENDI SAT ALONE in a small, barren interrogation room at the Tallahassee Police Department (TPD), her sunglasses perched atop her head between her unkempt hair bun and her forehead. She was hunched over, virtually motionless—deep in thought—elbows pressed into her thighs, the palms of her hands cradling her cheeks. The clock on the wall registered 2:45 p.m.

Though Wendi didn't know it at the time, a tiny camera

in the corner of the room was recording even her slightest movement.

The eerie silence was broken by the sound of the door lurching open. Investigator Isom entered, taking a seat diagonally across from Wendi at the short side of the rectangular, wooden table. She told him she'd received a voicemail from her real estate agent indicating there had been a shooting on Trescott Drive. "Yeah, that's what this is about," Isom interrupted, finally revealing what he refused to discuss during their ten-minute drive from the restaurant. "I'm sorry you had to hear it that way." He asked Wendi to play the message so he could hear it.

A woman's voice came over her iPhone saying, "I feel like an idiot doing this, but I just heard that there was a shooting over on Trescott and I promise I'm not trying to be dramatic or even nosy—I don't know. Just checking on you my friend. I hope all is well, I hope your sweet boys are well, and if there's anything you need, let me know. It just ran a chill down my spine when I heard that there was something going on on Trescott." When the voicemail ended, Isom asked Wendi for her identification. She reached into her purse and pulled out her driver's license.

"All right," the investigator said, glancing at the small plastic card. "So you never took the last name of Markel?" he asked, mispronouncing her ex-husband's last name, placing the emphasis on the first syllable rather than the second.

"No," Wendi answered. As Isom jotted down notes, she stared at him with a pained, uncomfortable expression, her mouth agape. It wasn't yet clear where their conversation was heading.

The investigator looked up from his notepad and got straight to the point. "There was a shooting at your home, or your ex-husband's home, at 2116 Trescott, okay? Your husband—your ex-husband, excuse me, Daniel, all right—has been taken to the hospital. He's not going to survive."

"Oh my God!" Wendi shrieked, beginning to sob in an instant, burying her head in her hands. "I have a message from him this morning," she somehow got out through her tears, in a piercing, high-pitched tone. "What happened?"

"Well, before we get into everything, I have to establish where you were, and who you were with, and so forth."

"Okay," Wendi whimpered, nodding her head up and down.

"And then once we've established all that," Isom continued, "I can give you more details."

"Okay," she said, her voice still well above its normal pitch.

"Do you understand why I wanted you to come here before we discussed this?"

"*Oh my God!*" Wendi repeated, the upper half of her body now folded over its lower half—her head once again buried in her hands. She was in full-blown shock, wailing from deep within her diaphragm for more than half a minute, her body rocking back and forth catatonically. "I'm sorry," she apologized, finally catching her breath long enough to speak.

"That's okay. You have nothing to be sorry about," the investigator said, though he had no way of knowing—at that early juncture of the interview—whether that was in fact true.

"I just don't understand," Wendi was able to force through her sobs. "How did this happen?" She tried to get more words to the surface, but her blubbering prevented them from escaping.

"Let me get over this hump, okay," Isom interjected, hoping to calm her down. "Can we do that first?" Wendi nodded, almost imperceptibly. "Can you tell me what time you left your house this morning?"

"Yeah, I was there. I didn't leave this morning. I didn't leave until noon," she said, calming down quickly, her voice returning to its normal pitch. "Oh my God!" Wendi shrieked again, remembering, "I tried to drive up Trescott, and I saw that it was blocked."

"Uh, it was blocked at some point," Isom confirmed. He asked her who'd been at her home that morning. Reaching for the first of what would become an impressive collection of tissues over the next five hours, Wendi told him her TV was broken and a repairman was there to see if it could be fixed. She recounted her trip to the liquor store and how the salesclerk had commented on her striking blue eyes, confessing to Isom that her contact lenses enhanced their color—making them appear almost turquoise—a secret she usually didn't reveal except to her closest friends.

"Do you know anyone who would have a beef against your ex-husband?" Isom asked bluntly.

Wendi told him that Dan "always meant well, but he would sometimes rub people the wrong way. But I don't know who would do something *like this*."

Isom asked if Dan owed money to anyone. Wendi disclosed that her ex owed money to her, her right hand touching her chest for emphasis. She paused. "But not—not me," she said with a half-smirk, trying to convey that she wouldn't have shot him over that. The waterworks resumed. "Oh my God! My poor kids," she sobbed, the reality now sinking in that they'd grow up without a dad. The emotion gripping her was palpable. Gut-wrenching.

Though Isom didn't ask her whether Dan was suicidal, Wendi volunteered that he never would have taken his own life. "He was a very positive person," she declared, for the first time referring to her ex in the past tense. "We've been separated for two years, so I don't know like, you know, if he had something going on I wouldn't know about."

"I know a lot of people didn't love him, but not anyone who would, like, hate him. Everybody that knew him knows he means well," she said. "He didn't do anything except work and take care of his kids. He wasn't involved in anything bad. I can't believe this is happening," she wailed, the shock and horror still setting in.

"He wouldn't do this to himself," Wendi repeated. "He has a girlfriend now." She shared with Isom that Dan's new companion, Amy Adler, also was a law professor who taught at NYU Law. She'd just met Amy for the first time the morning of June 30, she recounted, when she stopped by 2116 Trescott to retrieve the boys for a two-week trip to South Florida to celebrate her father's 70th birthday. "I think she was here for one more day," Wendi recalled, "and then she and Danny went up to New York because I was going to be gone so long." Amy was recently divorced herself, she noted, and had a son. "They seem very happy," Wendi added, now employing the present tense. "I think that's a really good thing in his life ... She met the boys and I met her and she told me how great— she loved the boys."

Wendi's remarks about Amy piqued Isom's curiosity. He asked how long Amy and Dan had been dating. Though she wasn't sure, Wendi said, "It seemed kind of serious if she met the kids." She told the investigator Dan had been attending conferences in New York for three-and-a-half years, "so my guess is that they might have known each other for a long time but have been dating I don't know how long."

Isom asked whether Dan's relationship with Amy had something to do with their divorce—if he'd been having an "extramarital affair." Wendi quickly dismissed any such notion, assuring him that wasn't the case and that Dan had been referring to Amy as his "girlfriend" only since the prior December. A new thought then popped into Wendi's head. Maybe Amy's ex-husband wasn't very happy she was dating Dan, she speculated. Maybe he would have wanted to harm Dan.

Less than 20 minutes into the questioning, she broke down again, crying hysterically. "I'm trying," she told Isom through her tears, her breathing labored, chest heaving. "I just can't believe this is happening."

"You're doing fine," he reassured her. "I know it's all a shock and it's coming to you all at once, okay?"

"I don't know who would do this," Wendi squealed. She wanted to be helpful, but couldn't come up with anything that made much sense.

"Well, it appears from what we've seen so far that someone intentionally hurt Daniel, okay, intentionally," Isom repeated.

"But you don't know who it is?" Wendi asked, struggling again for her words. The burly investigator told her he didn't.

She then had a terrifying thought, her emotions intensifying. "What if they come after the boys?"

Isom told her that didn't seem to be a concern. But she wasn't convinced. She began cradling herself, her hands grasping her opposite shoulders. "I don't know if I can take care of them like this."

Isom quickly changed the subject, asking about her and Dan's extended family members. Wendi told him that her family lived in Coral Springs, a city of approximately 125,000 some 40 miles northwest of Miami. "I have two brothers, but I'm very close to one of them who is in Fort Lauderdale," she said, indicating she'd spoken with him that morning. When her thoughts turned to Dan's parents, Ruth and Phil Markel, Wendi broke down again. "His family's in Canada. *Do they know?* Did you tell them?" she asked in a high-pitched shriek. Isom told her they hadn't yet been notified.

"Oh my God!" she screeched. "His parents are going to be *devastated*." She buried her head in her hands again, bawling uncontrollably.

"Daniel's been shot," Isom reiterated sternly, trying to get Wendi to focus. "And we have to find out why, and who did this. Can you help with that?"

"I'll try," Wendi replied meekly, her voice muffled through her blubbering.

Before continuing their discussion, Isom told her that he wanted to take her cellphone so its contents could be downloaded. "Do you have a problem with that?"

"No," Wendi answered, shaking her head side to side.

She then had another thought, telling the investigator she had many friends who knew "Danny didn't treat me very well. And I'm so scared that maybe someone did this not because they hate Danny, but because they thought this was good somehow."

Intrigued, Isom asked, "Oh, are you saying one of your friends might have done something like this?"

In a piercing, high-pitched tone, Wendi responded, "Who would do this?" She gesticulated with outstretched hands, palms facing upward.

"Would *you* ever ask someone to do something like this?"

"Not in a million years," she responded, emphatically dismissing the notion that she was somehow involved.

"Do you think someone would do this for your benefit without asking you?"

Though it was Wendi herself who first raised that very possibility, she responded with a firm "No." But she immediately volunteered information belying that confidence. "I mean, my brother, the one—his name is Charlie—the one I'm really close to, he makes a lot of jokes in bad taste and it was a joke he made. He bought the TV for me this morning, that got broken, and then I was talking to him about whether it made sense to pay to fix it, or whether I should get a new one and it was always his joke that like— he knew Danny treated me badly and it was always like his joke, he said, 'I looked into hiring a hitman and it was cheaper to get you this TV, so instead I got you this TV.' I mean, he would *never*—"

Wendi paused to gather her thoughts. "He's my big brother, and he's been taking care of me since I was little, but he would *never*—" She trailed off again. She told Isom that when the repairman asked her how much she'd paid for the TV, she told him she didn't know because her brother had gotten it for her as a "divorce present," telling her at the time "it was cheaper than a hitman ... Such a horrible thing to say," she whimpered. "I'm so sorry."

"But even my family," she quickly added, "who felt like I had been mistreated, would never do something like this. *Never*." The waterworks were unleashed—again.

Investigator Isom then raised a new topic, asking whether Dan had been abusive toward her since their divorce. "Of him towards me? No, no. He's litigious," Wendi said. "And we have an ongoing case." She shared how Dan had failed to pay what he owed under the marital settlement agreement and that her attorney had filed a motion to force him to pay. "He filed a counter-motion for sanctions against my attorney because he thought that she did something wrong, which she didn't." Her attorney had to withdraw from the case, she explained, so she could be a witness at an upcoming hearing.

For some reason, Wendi steered the conversation back to her family, acknowledging that her parents were "very angry" at Dan. "But even when they're around my kids they would never say a bad word about my kids' father. They're really, really careful about that. They dislike him, but they know he's the father of my kids. They would *never*. They would never do that. I don't know who would be angry enough with him to do something like this."

Isom wanted to know more about her brother Charlie. "Tell me what kind of car he has."

"He has like five cars," she said. "I think one of them is an unmarked police car."

"Oh really?" Isom asked, his interest in Charlie escalating.

"He's a bit of a character," Wendi revealed, telling Isom she wasn't sure what he was driving at the moment. But it wouldn't be hard to find him, she noted. "He's a periodontist, and he has this practice where he works from early in the morning 'til late at night" with offices all over South Florida. She told Isom that Charlie had a girlfriend, but didn't provide her name—one of the few leads the experienced investigator failed to chase down.

Seemingly out of nowhere, Wendi's sobbing resumed. "Oh my God! I can't believe this is happening!" she exclaimed. Her legal training finally kicked in. "Do I need to be read my Miranda rights or something if you're going to look at my phone?"

Isom assured her that wasn't necessary, but said he would read her her rights if that was her preference. "I have no reason, at this point, to suspect you in this incident, okay?"

"I couldn't tell from the way you were talking to me in the car if I was a suspect," Wendi said sheepishly, like a young child seeking reaffirmation from a parent. At that moment, she realized that the subject of their conversation wasn't actually dead—at least not yet. "Is he still at the hospital?" she asked. Isom told her he was.

"And he's alone?"

"Yes," Isom confirmed.

"And nobody knows he's there?" Wendi followed up, increasingly emotional, wiping tears from her eyes.

"Well, *you* know now." Isom said he was going to take her phone and would have a victim advocate meet with her, who would obtain contact information for Dan's parents.

The mention of Dan's parents rocked Wendi once more. "Oh my God!" she blurted out, once again clutching her head in her hands. She told Isom that Dan also had a sister with whom he was really close, repeating that his family lived in Canada. *"They're going to think I did it."*

"Now, let's don't jump to conclusions on that," the investigator said reassuringly.

"Oh my God! Oh my God! I can't believe this is happening," Wendi repeated as Isom stepped out to gather a consent form to authorize a search of her phone.

•••

FOR THE FIRST TIME in 30 minutes, Wendi was all alone in the spartan room. "Oh my God!" she muttered to herself, wailing uncontrollably. When Isom returned, the cause of her despair became apparent. "Our last interaction wasn't nice," she told him. Wendi explained that she wanted to get the boys early that afternoon, before it was technically time for them to transition to her custody. Dan had resisted, telling her he wanted to take them to the pool. It was actually her brother Charlie, she said, who'd convinced her that Dan wanting to take the kids swimming wasn't worth getting upset over.

Wendi also told Isom that she and Dan were in the process of deciding where Ben would attend kindergarten that fall—they needed to make a decision by Monday. They were supposed to discuss the subject by phone after Dan finished his workout class at his gym that morning, which he told her in a voicemail—while she was with the repairman—would be over sometime between 10:15 a.m. and 10:30 a.m. When she didn't hear from him, she called and left a message letting him know they really needed to talk.

Isom showed her the consent form to allow the TPD to search her phone, reading it aloud verbatim, including her right to consult with an attorney before signing it. Barely glancing at the document, Wendi scribbled her signature and handed it back. "Okay. Can I have your phone now?" the investigator asked.

"Yes," she agreed, handing it to him. "Stupid question, but are you going to give it back?" Isom assured her they would and that the process wouldn't take very long. "I feel like I need to tell my family what's going on," she said, realizing she'd need her phone to do that.

The moment the door closed, Wendi broke down again. She gathered herself and soon was deep in thought, eventually asking out loud, "What is going on?" She assumed the "thinker" position, hands on her chin, inhaling and exhaling heavily and rapidly.

Isom reentered the room. Wendi asked if she could use the restroom and the two stepped out together, only to return once the investigator realized her hands first needed to be swabbed. Resuming their seats, Wendi told him she'd just "hold it." "I'm assuming I'm a suspect," she surmised from being denied permission to use the bathroom.

"No, you're not a suspect," Isom reiterated. "I don't consider you a suspect. I asked you to come up here. You came up here voluntarily. I've not read you Miranda. You're not under arrest. You are the closest thing to family I have to Daniel right now, okay?"

"I'm so sad," Wendi replied tearfully. For the third time, she stated there was no way Dan had done anything to harm himself, explaining he had "all kinds of plans" in New York and wasn't even sure he'd be back in time for his Wednesday overnight with their kids. "I can see him being really sad when we first got divorced," she said. "But now, he's got Amy and he loves those boys and things are really good for him. There's *no way* he did this to himself."

"I believe you," Isom told her, curious as to why Wendi kept repeating that sentiment when he'd never even raised that possibility—and actually told her someone else had intentionally shot her ex.

Wendi told him the notion that someone else had attacked Dan "really scares me, because that means there's someone out there that's willing to do this to him and I'm scared for the kids." Something else then dawned on her, which released her tears yet again: "I don't know how I'm going to tell them."

As he tried to reassure her, Isom referred to Dan by his formal name, "Daniel"—what he'd been calling him the entire 45 minutes they'd been talking. Seemingly annoyed, Wendi told him that her ex-husband "goes by Danny. No one calls him Daniel." She explained it felt "really impersonal" hearing him referred to as "Daniel."

Isom asked when she last saw him. Wendi told him she didn't recall any in-person interactions since getting the kids from Dan's house on Monday, June 30, for her trip to South Florida. She returned home on Friday, July 11, she said, noting her parents came back with her. Though Dan picked the kids up from her house late that afternoon, she wasn't there, having left her parents in charge of exchange.

Isom redirected the conversation back to Amy Adler. With mild embarrassment, Wendi confessed to having conducted some internet research on Dan's new love. Pulling another tissue from the box, she told the investigator Amy was 50 years old—nine years older than her ex-husband—and had a 14-year-old son. "She doesn't look 50," she said with an envious snicker. "She's very beautiful. Not that you can't be beautiful at 50, but she looks really young. She's very pretty and accomplished."

Wendi again asked for permission to use the bathroom, her need now more urgent. This time, Isom was able to enlist a forensic specialist, Joanne Maltese, to enter the room and swab her hands. Noticing the "GSR" acronym on the outside of Maltese's kit, Wendi asked what the initials stood for. "Gunshot residue," Isom answered—blurring the question of whether the divorced mother of two was or wasn't being considered a suspect.

As she swabbed Wendi's fingers, Maltese asked if she'd washed her hands since noon. "I wish I could tell you I have," Wendi responded, "but I haven't. I'm filthy." At Isom's direction, the female officer had Wendi stand against the wall for some pictures. She posed uncomfortably as the camera flashed.

The resulting images failed to capture the beautiful woman Wendi Adelson was under more normal circumstances—they weren't even driver's license worthy. Her hair was a mess, matted down from her lack of bathing and mad dash out the door that afternoon. Her eyes were bloodshot and puffy, nose red as a beet, cheeks flushed, and lips swollen—from nearly an hour of on-and-off crying spells—the shock and horror of the day's events etched noticeably into her sullen expression. The penetrating, wide-eyed stare of a black-and-white owl on her T-shirt—as if the creature were also posing for the camera— made the photo session all the more bizarre.

Finally, pictures taken, Wendi was led to the restroom for her long-overdue biology break.

3.

Circle of Suspects

WHEN SHE RETURNED to the interrogation room, Wendi recalled that she actually had seen Dan that Wednesday evening, July 16, though they didn't come face to face. She'd retrieved the kids from preschool for her midweek overnight, she told Isom, and driven to Whole Foods for dinner. But when she pulled into the parking lot, she noticed Dan through the store window, working on his laptop. She realized that if she'd gone inside, the boys would see him and they'd end up all together.

"It was my one day with the kids," she reasoned, "and I wanted time by myself with them." They went to BurgerFi instead, the boys none the wiser she'd seen their father through the window.

The police investigator returned to his primary focus area: "I'm looking for some reason that someone would want to hurt him."

"Not just hurt him," Wendi corrected him. "I could see one of my friends wanting to *shake* him," she said, gesturing with outstretched hands. "But with a gun? No, no," she whimpered despondently, tears streaming down once more. She found Dan "hard to be around," she acknowledged. "But so did a lot of people. They all knew he meant well. He was a decent, good human being. He wouldn't hurt anybody. I don't know who would want to hurt him like this. I really don't."

Isom asked whether her divorce had anything to do with infidelity—"no extramarital affairs or anything like that?"

When Wendi answered in the negative, he asked if her ex "was belligerent to you?"

"He never hurt me physically," she answered, "but he was emotionally abusive. And I didn't tell most people that, so all most people know is it just didn't work out and the kids are young and this is just better this way. So other than my family, who saw the way he treated me, most people were—well, I think his family was very surprised. He told everyone around the community that I was mentally ill—because only a crazy person would leave him."

"The circumstances, plain and simple," she continued, "were it just wasn't a really a healthy marriage and I thought it would be better for the boys if they didn't grow up thinking that's the way you treat a woman. But he wasn't—he didn't hit me. He didn't hit them. He didn't have a drug problem, you know. He didn't gamble. He didn't cheat on me. I didn't cheat on him." She speculated a second time about Amy Adler's ex-husband, sharing that Dan was "very, very public" on Facebook, wondering whether Amy's ex was trolling her and became jealous after seeing pictures of his ex with Dan.

Isom had Wendi provide additional details about Dan's family and biography. His mother and father and immediate family lived in Toronto, she said, with aunts, uncles, and cousins in Montreal. He came to the United States for college at 18 and never left, ultimately graduating from Harvard Law School. At the time they met and then got engaged, she was in law school at the University of Miami, near her family. When he landed a position on the Florida State faculty, she still had a year left to obtain her law degree—so she finished up at Florida State so they could be together.

That discussion led Wendi to the reason she believed Dan's family would consider her a suspect. After they separated, she told Isom, "I wanted to move to South Florida and I filed a petition to relocate in the court and the court said 'no.'" She explained that although the court system can't prevent a divorced parent from moving, "you just can't leave with your kids." She was therefore forced to remain in Tallahassee due to Dan's faculty position at Florida State. For some reason, though, she neglected to mention that she too was on the same faculty.

•••

AT 4:00 P.M., A VICTIM ADVOCATE named Sara LaTorre entered the room and took a seat to Wendi's right, turning her chair to face her more directly, close enough to touch her. Investigator Isom left the two women alone.

Wendi's demeanor brightened almost immediately, seemingly relieved to be talking to a woman. "I have that skirt," she said with a grin, glancing at LaTorre's long, black-and-white striped garment. She even felt LaTorre resembled her, giggling when she told her, "In a way it's like looking at my sister"—even though Wendi didn't actually have one.

"You have very pretty blue eyes," the victim advocate reciprocated, prompting Wendi to remark—with evident embarrassment—"I must look awesome right now." In view of her current circumstances, she found the young woman's soft, warm disposition reassuring and comforting.

"I'm sure you do this all the time—it's your job—but like I cannot believe this is happening," Wendi said despondently. Choking back her emotions, she confided in LaTorre that she was "so worried about my kids. I don't know how I'm going to tell them what happened. They're so little. They *love* their dad." She tugged another tissue from the box, burying her face in it. She was "very scared," she said, fearful that whoever had harmed Dan would next come after her and the boys. She asked if she could get some protection that evening "to make sure that nobody comes after us."

Despite everything going on with the divorce, Wendi told LaTorre, the kids had been doing remarkably well. "They're really like happy, well-adjusted kids. There are so many people in their life that love them." Her train of thought diverged.

"And I get why I would be a suspect, but the idea that— we were divorced, but I would— the idea that I would ever do anything it's like … I understand why they need to check, but, I don't know who would though, I don't know who would do this. I can see why they would think it would be me."

The victim advocate asked Wendi who she could rely on for support. "I'd really like my family to come," Wendi replied. "I'm just so upset right now, I'm worried about parenting effectively, so if my parents were here, they could help me. They're really close with the kids."

Jotting down notes, LaTorre asked for her mother and father's names. "My parents are Donna and Harvey Adelson," Wendi answered. She told LaTorre they were "sort of in the process of retiring" and worked together. "They're super happy and in love, 40 plus years in. So they like live in Coral Springs for part of the week and Miami for part of the week." Her brother Charlie had gotten a place for them in Miami, she explained, "so sometimes on the weekends they all hang out together."

LaTorre had Wendi focus on who could retrieve the kids from preschool—which prompted tears yet again. Wendi told her the boys referred to Dan as "Abba," the Hebrew word for father. He was supposed to pick them up and take them swimming, she said, before bringing them to her home for their weekly exchange. Clearly Dan wouldn't be there to get them— and there certainly wouldn't be any swimming. "I don't know if I could drive a car right now," Wendi confessed, the mound of crumpled tissues piled before her a fitting metaphor of her emotional state.

"I just feel like I'm in a *Twilight Zone*," she added. "And I keep picturing my kids like at a funeral, having to say goodbye to their dad, and I just—I can't believe I have to do this to them."

She gave LaTorre permission to call a couple of her friends to see who could help take care of the boys. The victim advocate stepped out to make the calls. A few minutes later, Sergeant Joanna Baldwin entered the room, intent on making arrangements for Wendi's kids. She also told Wendi her minivan was outside and asked for permission for the TPD to search it.

"Absolutely, you can look—you can search the car," Wendi replied. Isom came back in with a form authorizing the search, which she signed with only a passing glance. Pulling the car keys from her purse, Wendi asked—perplexed—how they were able to get the minivan to the police station without the key. "Tow truck," Isom responded with a chuckle, taking hold of the keys and marching out the door.

"I feel like I'm in the middle of a nightmare," Wendi muttered. She reflected again on Dan. "We were divorced—it wasn't good," she told LaTorre, sniffling. "But like, this is never something you would ever want to happen. I just—I understand why I'm a suspect. I guess I'm not a suspect. I just understand why you would think that I would do this, but—"

Her focus shifted again to Ben and Lincoln. "I'm just worried about the kids. And I'm so sorry for his family. And for his children. Who are now going to grow up without a father." She buried her head in her left hand, sobbing. "And I have no idea who would do this, and I feel like they're out there, and if they're capable of this, like what's to keep them from going after the kids. Like, if they hate Danny, then why wouldn't they hate his children?"

Wendi pondered again how she'd tell the boys, sharing with LaTorre that only the prior day they had their first conversation about God. Ben had said to her, "Mommy, I bet Abba knows a lot more about God than you." She told the victim advocate the boys had a concept of superheroes dying and seeing dead animals in the road. "And they even quasi understand."

LaTorre interrupted her with an apparent revelation. "I'm not sure what Investigator Isom kind of told you. You know he's still alive?"

"No, I didn't know that," Wendi replied—completely caught off guard nearly two hours into the interview. She began choking up. "Is he possibly going to make it?" she asked, her voice crackling with emotion.

"I don't know the answer to that. I know—"

Interrupting, Wendi told LaTorre that Isom "made it sound like he was gone. So does that mean he might be okay?" The victim advocate backtracked, telling her she didn't want to give her "false hope."

"I'm sorry," Wendi said, calming down quickly. "I just thought he was gone and now I don't know how to tell—it's sort of a game changer." She asked LaTorre if there was any way to find out, "because if he might be okay, like, I want to bring the kids to him." Dwelling on it a bit more, she added, "Like, if he's not going to make it and he can see the kids one more time, then he should see them. So is there—like are we getting updates from the hospital?" LaTorre assured her they were.

"So when it happened," Wendi asked, "did someone call the police because they heard a gunshot or something? Like how did they know? Like did he call the police?" LaTorre told her she didn't know but that Investigator Isom could possibly answer her questions when he returned. If Dan was still alive, Wendi insisted, "I want the boys to be with him … Does he look scary?" LaTorre told her she didn't know.

Wendi quickly reconsidered. "I think that would be more traumatizing for the kids to see something horrible. I don't want them to—" LaTorre interrupted, agreeing it wouldn't be a good idea for such young children to see something like that.

"Like, I want them to have," Wendi added, "if it's going to have to be memories, I want them to be good. Because their last memory would have been him taking them to school this morning." She buried her head in her hand, bawling once more.

Minutes later, Isom was back in the room, apologizing for his absence, explaining "I'm trying to be in a bunch of places at once."

"My grandmother once said, 'You can't have your *tuchus* in two places at once,'" Wendi deadpanned, injecting a touch of levity into the emotionally charged atmosphere. Yet in the same breath, she told Isom, "I'm losing my mind over here."

She asked him if Dan was still alive.

"Clinically, he's not going to live," Isom answered bluntly, telling her his brain had been damaged beyond repair.

"Someone shot him *in the head*?" Wendi asked, a painful grimace washing over her face. Isom deftly sidestepped her question, telling her, "There's too much damage to recover from, okay? That's why we need to get ahold of his parents."

"Is he still alive?" Wendi pressed him. "Should I bring the kids to see him?"

"*No, no, no,*" the investigator responded firmly. "He has severe facial injuries. I'm sorry and I know this is tough, but I would not want my children to see—" Wendi nodded in agreement, pulling more tissues from the box. Isom told her they'd soon need to make decisions about organ donation, which prompted even more tears.

Wendi reiterated that she understood why she'd be considered the "primary suspect." But Isom again assured her that wasn't the case. "I think you're a straightforward person. And I think at this point if you had anything to do with this, you would have already told me." But he then asked her an odd question. "If you found out that this was someone that you personally know, would that change your mind about what should happen to that person?"

"If somebody tried to kill my ex-husband," she replied, "they should be prosecuted to the full extent of the law."

"Regardless of who it is?"

Wendi quickly backtracked, telling Isom, "It would be different if I thought it were my brother, but I don't think it was my family. Anyone outside my immediate family, that's a tough one."

Zeroing in on her brother—who Wendi herself kept bringing up—the investigator asked, "Would you think that this guy Charlie would even be capable of doing something like this?

"No, no," she answered resolutely, shaking her head side to side.

"He's just talk?"

"He's a joker," Wendi said with a half-smile. But Isom wasn't entirely convinced.

•••

AT 5:10 P.M., WENDI'S FRIEND, Jane McPherson, entered the room. Sergeant Baldwin had called her at Wendi's suggestion, hoping she could pick up Ben and Lincoln from preschool. By the time she arrived, however, another of Wendi's friends, Lynn Grossman—with whom the kids were more familiar—had been summoned to undertake that task. McPherson was nevertheless comforting to have around, a friend who would soon receive her Ph.D. in social work.

Upon seeing her familiar face, Wendi stood up and collapsed into her embrace, tears flowing freely once again. Feeling her friend's ice-cold bare arms, McPherson asked if there was a blanket or something to keep her warm. LaTorre scurried out of the room, soon returning with a black fleece jacket she draped over Wendi's back and arms.

Though she'd heard about a shooting on Trescott, McPherson had no idea Dan was in the hospital, with no hope of survival. When Wendi shared the news, she didn't fully believe her. It took Craig Isom's confirmation for the reality to soak in—leading to McPherson's own tears. She tried to console Wendi, hugging her tightly and rubbing her back.

Wendi asked her friend why she thought she'd been summoned to the police station. "My thought was that Danny had probably assaulted you," McPherson replied. "But this scenario—which is now not seeming real to me—that was not what I thought of."

Isom stepped out of the room. The three women sat around the table, Wendi flanked by LaTorre to her right and McPherson—sitting on the floor—to her left.

"I am losing my shit," Wendi announced bluntly. "Jane, who would have done this?"

"Is Jeff this much of a lunatic?" McPherson asked, referring to her colleague and Wendi's most recent romantic flame, Jeff

Lacasse, a professor of social work at Florida State.

"I didn't even think of Jeff," Wendi answered, suddenly taken aback. "I hope to God not."

Now LaTorre's interest was piqued. "Are you currently seeing him?" she asked. "Or is this something you kind of let taper off maybe?"

Wendi told her that she and McPherson had taken a walk together earlier that week to help her sort out her feelings about Lacasse. "I took a one-week break from communication with Jeff to figure out what to do." They'd been dating around ten months, Wendi revealed. "He was my boyfriend and involved with the kids, I mean, yeah. And we had kind of a fight recently and he's been trying to get back together and I didn't know if I wanted to."

McPherson noted that the divorce between Wendi and Dan had been very stressful "and Jeff has been stressed out by the stressfulness of your divorce, you know?" She shared with the victim advocate that Lacasse had been in the military and was jealous—without specifying of whom.

LaTorre shifted gears, asking what Dan's students thought of him—an angle Isom hadn't yet explored. "I think there are some that really like his method," Wendi answered, "and there are a lot that don't like him at all."

"So you'd say he's more disliked?"

"Feared," Wendi responded. "He's a very abrasive guy," McPherson chimed in. Wendi told the victim advocate that Dan was "difficult in like an ivory tower kind of way" and "fairly elitist." "The students felt like put down by him a lot... But again, we're not talking about hateful and awful. We're talking about like, difficult."

"He has colleagues that really don't like him," McPherson added. But she also pointed out, "He's important in the Jewish community and he is loved" among Tallahassee's Jews. "It would be hard to overestimate how involved he has been in the Jewish community."

"And that was kind of one of the reasons we got divorced is I just—like I'm Reform," Wendi explained. "I'm kind of culturally Jewish. Like we just had really different religious perspectives." She took a deep breath, then laughed. "I'm in the middle of a fucking nightmare."

LaTorre stepped out to find Isom so Wendi could tell him about Lacasse. The moment the door closed, Wendi looked McPherson dead in the eye. "Jane, you believe I didn't do this, right?"

"I assume you didn't do this," her friend whispered back reassuringly. The two women focused on Dan, lying all alone in the ICU. "Shouldn't someone who loves him be there?" McPherson asked.

"Yes, yes," Wendi replied, as if a light bulb had suddenly illuminated. "Should I go? Someone needs to go there. He's by himself." She told her friend that Dan's family hadn't been notified yet. McPherson suggested that his rabbi be contacted. "Yeah, that's a really good idea," Wendi agreed. When Sergeant Baldwin returned to tell her that Lynn Grossman was on the way to the boys' preschool, Wendi gave her the names of two rabbis to call. Not another word was spoken about her being the one to be at her ex-husband's bedside.

Isom reentered the room, politely informing McPherson that it was time for her to leave. Before she departed, the doctoral student told Isom what she knew about Jeff Lacasse and why he might be a person of interest. She cradled Wendi's head in her arms, kissed the top of her head, and walked out the door—40 minutes likely to be seared in her memory forever.

•••

ISOM RETURNED WENDI'S IPHONE and they sat together going through some of her calls. "I didn't call any weird sex hotlines or anything this morning," she quipped. "That's okay," the investigator shot back with a wry smile. "We've seen that before."

News of the shooting had ricocheted all across town. Wendi scrolled through several texts and voicemails she'd received while her phone was with the investigators. Of some relevance, her divorce attorney had called, telling her they really needed to talk because a new judge had been assigned to her case. Apparently, he was in the minority who hadn't yet heard the news.

Isom asked Wendi to fill him in on Jeff Lacasse. She apologized for not mentioning him earlier. "I just didn't think to tell you about him," she said. "We've been dating since the end of October. Jane actually set us up, which is why Jane thought of him first." She elaborated on the fight she and Lacasse had at the end of June. "And it was weird and then I went away for two weeks and just got back and we'd been— I asked him to just no contact for a week just so I could kind of figure out whether I wanted to be with him or not."

They attended a yoga class together that Monday evening, she recounted, after which he asked if they could see each other the next day. Instead of telling him "no," Wendi emailed him after getting home. "I really just need a week of silence to get some clarity on where we are," she wrote, ending the message, "I'm going to take your silence as acceptance." As requested, Lacasse didn't respond.

Wendi told the investigator it was only that February when "he started being more like my boyfriend. He started spending time with the kids and they really adore him." But he never spent the night when the boys were with her. Rather, he'd "join us for dinner and play with the kids and then go home. And things actually were great and I was very happy."

That changed dramatically on Saturday, June 28, she said, just before her two weeks in Miami. She and Lacasse were on a short trip to Gainesville, where he was teaching a class at the University of Florida. "We went out to dinner, we came home, and he just like was convinced that I had been cheating on him for months." She told him that wasn't true. That episode "just made me really uncomfortable. And after that happened, I wasn't sure that I wanted to be with him anymore."

His suspicion now heightened, Isom asked for a description of Lacasse's vehicle and home. Wendi described his car as silver-colored with two doors, "very old and very run down." She thought it was a Nissan, but wasn't sure. He lived alone in a basement apartment off Park Street. "I've actually only been over there once," she explained, "because he was kind of embarrassed."

The investigator drilled down further on her boyfriend's jealous behavior. Wendi told him Lacasse had gone through her phone at some point that spring and found a call between her and a man she'd been dating the prior fall—coincidentally, another Dan, Daniel Sack. But Lacasse didn't share anything about his snooping at the time. When he finally confronted her while they were in Gainesville, Wendi told him that she hadn't seen Sack more than as a friend since February and was very upset he'd been rummaging through her phone.

Wendi told Isom she cried the entire drive back home that Sunday. She and Lacasse parted company under a dark cloud. A couple of hours later, her parents arrived so they could caravan to Miami together. She confessed—somewhat embarrassed—that her parents were so overprotective, they preferred accompanying her on the seven-hour drive and were willing to drive twice that distance to ensure that she and their grandchildren made the trip to Miami safely. Her dad, she noted, was actually standing beside her on the front porch of 2116 Trescott that Monday morning when she retrieved the boys from Dan and met Amy. Who she found "perfectly lovely."

"Is Jeff a violent person?" Isom asked bluntly, now apparently focused on him as a potential suspect. Wendi answered in the negative.

"Not at all?"

"*No,*" she insisted. She told Isom she didn't believe Lacasse owned a gun, but noted he'd been in the military, ultimately stationed at Elgin Air Force Base in the western Panhandle. Before long, the investigator was out the door to find a photo of Lacasse he could append to his notes.

As she scrolled through her phone making idle chit-chat with LaTorre, almost under her breath, Wendi muttered, "I can't help but feel like this is all my fault."

"Why do you feel that way?" the victim advocate asked.

"Why would somebody do this, right? Like if I had still been married to him, there wouldn't be anyone that was angry, right? … This can't be a random act of violence. This has to be on purpose. Someone did this for a reason."

•••

CRAIG ISOM RETURNED. He and Wendi began reconstructing the timeline of her activities that morning, including each of her telephone calls—which included the Best Buy repairman, her mother and brother, and a handful of friends. She then had an idea: "If you took my computer, you could probably find records of like what time I saved the document. And I'd be happy to sign a waiver so you can look at my computer." For some reason, though, the investigator didn't jump at the opportunity, focused instead on documenting Wendi's phone calls. "Call your folks," he abruptly instructed her.

"I really don't want to make that call," Wendi resisted— delaying the inevitable—explaining that although she wanted her parents to be with her, "I don't want to tell them what happened and what's going on because they're very emotional." While she hemmed and hawed, Isom stepped out again and Baldwin reappeared.

The sergeant reported to Wendi what was going on with her boys and that another victim advocate had made contact with Dan's father, who was in Aspen, Colorado. "I'm sure he's devastated," Wendi said softly, with a pained expression. Baldwin told her she'd also been in touch with the ICU, where they were actively working on donating her ex-husband's organs.

When the police sergeant left, Wendi turned to LaTorre, expressing concern over how she'd tell her parents. "They're very angry with him," she acknowledged. "This is a very, pardon my language, fucked-up situation." It was another five minutes before she summoned the courage. "Okay, here goes," she finally said, more to herself than to LaTorre. "This is the worst day of my life." She sighed deeply as she dialed her mother's number. It was 7:03 p.m.

"Hi Mom. How's it going?" Wendi said once the call connected, her voice calm, surprisingly unemotional.

"Good," her mother replied, proceeding to make small talk with her only daughter.

"Mom, I need you to sit down. I am fine. The boys are fine."

"Can I put you on speaker?" Donna asked, wanting her husband to be able to hear the conversation. Wendi told her that was fine. "Okay, what's the matter?"

"Danny has been shot," Wendi blurted out.

"*What? What?*" Donna exclaimed.

"And I don't think he's going to make it." She told her mom she was at the police station "and I am trying to help them figure out who may have done this," providing her a brief synopsis of the situation. "I really need you to come here and be with me." She told her parents that she preferred for them to fly to Tally rather than drive, reassuring them the boys were fine. "But they don't know anything yet."

"Where did this happen?" Donna asked, her tone one of bewilderment.

"In his house."

"When you said he may not make it, where is he? Is he in the hospital?"

"He's in the ICU in the hospital," Wendi told her, beginning to tear up.

"Okay. We're going to get there as soon as we can, all right?"

"But be careful, okay?"

"We'll be careful," Donna promised. "I'll call you later. I love you."

"Love you, too," Wendi replied. "Bye."

"My mom handled that pretty well," Wendi said to LaTorre, relieved she wasn't more emotional. She also was relieved for a second reason. "Well, my parents sounded really surprised, so that's at least a relief," she said softly—almost in a monotone—looking down at her phone as she spoke. "I was trying to think of who would be angry enough to do something to him. My parents would be angry, but they're not capable of *this*." She took a deep breath. "Thank God," she sighed. "I really couldn't handle that right now."

Though she didn't say it out loud, her vague reference to "that" was the possibility that her parents had arranged for her ex-husband's cold-blooded execution.

•••

ISOM AND BALDWIN stepped back into the room to discuss logistics. Isom told Wendi that Baldwin would drive her home in her minivan and that he'd follow behind. He wanted to take her computer, he said—accepting her invitation after all. "Sure," Wendi replied. "I don't imagine I'll be getting much work done." She laughed. "I mean, obviously, this is more important, so if you need my computer you can have my computer and I just won't work for a little while, that's all."

Isom spent his final 15 minutes with Wendi focused on Jeff Lacasse. By then, the mother of two had fully regained her composure, engaging in casual banter with the investigator, smiling and giggling, as if she were catching up with an old friend. He left the room to make final arrangements to transport Wendi home, leaving her alone with LaTorre one final time. Wendi told the victim advocate that during the ride to the police station all those hours ago, she was already wondering "if I could be framed for something. Like, if I didn't do something, but I'm still going to end up in jail."

"I can't imagine who would do this," she said for the umpteenth time, telling LaTorre she now understood why Lacasse was "a good suspect." She wasn't trying to be protective of him initially, she explained, noting, "I even thought of my own family." Wendi again expressed relief over her mother's reaction to hearing the news. "It's like my parents have more reason to dislike Danny than almost anyone else," she said. "He hurt their daughter. But listening to my mom just like cry and be horrified on the phone and be like—" She trailed off.

"I feel like a fierce mama cat right now," Wendi declared. "I just want to get to my boys." And then it hit her all over again. "What do you tell your children when their father was murdered?" She became weepy, dreading the conversation she knew was inevitable, grabbing one final tissue from the nearly empty box to blow her nose.

She also thought of Dan's parents, telling LaTorre she didn't have a good relationship with them. "They're pretty difficult people, but these are their grandkids, you know. So I want to make sure they can have a relationship with them."

Investigator Isom and Sergeant Baldwin walked through the door. "Time to go," he said. It was nearly 8:00 p.m. The end of a day that was sure to change many lives forever.

● ● ●

CONGREGATION SHOMREI TORAH serves as Tallahassee's Conservative, lay-led Jewish synagogue. Dan Markel had been a member since beginning his stint at Florida State in August 2005—before he and Wendi were even married—and had served on its board of directors. He was in attendance nearly every Saturday morning, the Sabbath, where he'd often recite psalms in Hebrew and lead the congregation in a prayer for the State of Israel. He considered worshiping at the temple a source of comfort and solace and had formed abundant friendships within the congregation.

His hastily planned memorial service began at noon that Sunday afternoon, less than 36 hours after he was officially pronounced dead. Over 100 people whose lives Dan had touched filled the sanctuary: his colleagues from the law faculty, current and former students, friends and neighbors from Betton Hills and throughout the region, and the Jewish community writ large. Dan's parents Ruth and Phil and sister Shelly were seated in the front row, having flown in late Saturday afternoon. Wendi and her parents were near the back with Ben and Lincoln—her dad stepping outside with them several times as their attention wandered.

The atmosphere was extremely somber, the shock of Dan's violent slaying adding a palpable and unsettling edge to the afternoon's proceedings. The question of who had committed such a despicable act loomed large, as did speculation that someone in attendance might have been involved. Theories abounded. Many in the crowd already suspected Dan's ex-wife, eyeing her from a distance for even the slightest hint that might expose a guilty conscience.

One by one, Dan's friends, including Jeremy Cohen, took to the stage to share their fond remembrances of his generosity, thoughtfulness, and extraordinary intellect. His sister Shelly added poignant memories from their childhood, struggling mightily to hold her composure.

Ruth Markel hadn't planned to speak, but found herself on stage as the service neared its end. She invited Wendi to come forward and join her along with her grandchildren. Her ex-daughter-in-law reluctantly obliged—not quite sure what to expect—holding three-year-old Lincoln in her arms, but leaving Ben behind with her parents.

"Danny is no longer here to tell you boys this," Ruth said in her Canadian accent, "but I want to make sure you know what was in his heart. He loved you to infinity. And he wanted you to have roots," by which she meant a life grounded in Judaism.

When the service ended, one of the first people to offer Ruth her condolences was Donna Adelson—exuding what appeared to be warmth and empathy—tears streaming down her face. "I'm so sorry," she said, one grandmother to another. "I promise you they will always have those roots."

Donna also introduced herself to Craig Isom, who'd shepherded Dan's parents and sister to the synagogue and attended the service along with another TPD investigator. "I'm Danny's former mother-in-law, Wendi's mom," Donna told him, extending her hand. "This is such a horrible tragedy." Isom told her that he fully concurred. She waved her husband over and introduced him.

"Look, I know you won't be in town very long," Isom told them, trying to be discrete. "While you're here, I really need to meet with you and get a statement. I understand Danny's parents will be with the boys this evening at Wendi's house. Why don't you come downtown and meet with me at the police station so we can get that out of the way?" Harvey told him they wouldn't be able to, explaining they'd be very busy that evening, with Wendi and the boys.

"Any other time is fine," Isom told them, handing Harvey his business card. "Give me a call so we can meet before you head back home."

"Sure," the 70-year-old grandfather responded. "No problem."

Meanwhile, as attendees walked through the sanctuary's rear doors, they found Wendi seated in a chair—alone—in the middle of the lobby. A receiving line of sorts formed at the far edges of the room, one mourner after another walking up to her, embracing her, and expressing sympathy. Those who didn't know any better would have assumed she was the grieving widow—and she certainly looked the part, her tears and raw emotion on full display. She appeared completely broken. Crestfallen.

When a group of her former friends who'd sided with Dan during the divorce proceedings huddled around her, Wendi insisted that she wanted to leave the past in the past. "I'm a single mom to these boys now," she said tearfully. "They don't have a father figure in their lives anymore, so they really need the love and support of all of you." She urged them to come together for Ben and Lincoln's sake.

Yet the very next day, they were all gone—Donna, Harvey, Wendi, and the boys—on the road to South Florida. Except for very brief return visits, Wendi was gone for good. Neither she nor any member of her family would speak with law enforcement again—not a single word.

The life of Dan Markel had been brutally extinguished. Execution style in broad daylight. If the mystery surrounding his murder was to be solved, it would have to be without the input or assistance of anyone bearing the last name of Adelson.

4.

Jilted Boyfriend

WHILE THE ADELSON CLAN was on the road to Coral Springs—caravan style in Donna and Harvey's Lexus and Wendi's minivan—Professor Jeffrey Lacasse found himself seated across from Investigator Corey Hale at the police station. He was wearing a tattered gray Florida State T-shirt and jeans, fidgeting in his seat, chewing gum furiously. His nervous energy was jarring—his speech so jittery, and head nods and gestures so hyperactive, it appeared as if he'd downed six or seven cups of coffee, or cans of Red Bull, just before arriving for his 90-minute interview. Many of his answers were punctuated by gratuitous profanity more befitting a mob boss than a college professor.

But what struck Hale more than anything was Lacasse's uncanny resemblance to Dan Markel—thin, wiry frame, rugged face, glasses, and light beard. At 42, he was a year older than Dan, seven years older than Wendi. Unlike Wendi's ex-husband, however, Lacasse told Hale he wasn't Jewish, though he considered himself an "honorary Jew" because his circle of friends was heavily Jewish.

Just minutes into the interview, he asked the police investigator if he could talk with him "off the record" because there were "a couple of theoretical things that I don't want to be quoted on." Hale told him they could possibly do that later, and then began drilling down on Lacasse's biography and his relationship with Wendi.

The professor indicated that he was at Florida State working on his Ph.D. in social work from 2000 to 2008, taught in Arizona for five years, and then came back to Tally to join the faculty in the fall of 2013, which is when he met Wendi. He was living in a "shitty" apartment he rented for $500 a month, hoping to save up enough money to buy a house.

Lacasse said he and Wendi had begun dating in September and dated throughout the fall, though their relationship wasn't serious back then. He was fully aware she was dating other men besides him. After Christmas break, however, they talked and decided to date "more seriously. By March 1, we're a couple, we're boyfriend and girlfriend." He told Hale that around Valentine's Day he "hit her with the romance and all that and we clicked together." No one had been with Wendi more over the preceding six months than he had, Lacasse boasted, telling the investigator he slept over at her place nearly every night the boys weren't with her.

They began fighting in May and June, he recounted. Hale wanted to know the source of the friction, but the professor was reluctant to answer, aware Wendi might learn what he said. "See, I'm in an awkward situation because there's a 1% chance Wendi and I get back together, you know what I mean? We're estranged at the moment."

He told Hale the primary source of their problems was Daniel Sack, another Florida State professor. Wendi had told Lacasse that she'd stopped seeing Sack romantically in the fall, but continued to see him as a platonic friend—merely grabbing coffee with him and going for walks. "But I did not believe Wendi. I have a pretty decent bullshit detector. It just didn't sound right, you know?" He asked Wendi whether she was in love with Sack or if he was just her "fuck buddy." She wouldn't answer—offended both by his question and distrust.

A week after that confrontation, Lacasse inadvertently ran into the pair having coffee at All Saints Café. "And I started to walk up to the table. And I was annoyed, but I was prepared to shake the guy's hand and be the better man, say, 'How you doing?'" Even though he knew Sack was moving to Massachusetts the following day, "I didn't like what I saw. She's giggling too much. She's twirling her hair. He's leaned in close. I was like, 'Oh, I see what this is.'"

But he didn't actually confront them because he realized his temper was flaring and didn't want to cause a scene. "I thought, 'I do not need to get arrested at All Saint's Café.' So I just went to the bathroom and she ran to the bathroom and was sobbing in the bathroom. It's her worst nightmare." For his part, Lacasse explained, "I lost all trust at that point." He told Hale he was 99% sure Wendi had been seeing him and Sack simultaneously.

By June, Sack had already moved up north and "Wendi became the best girlfriend all of a sudden. It was really interesting. All of a sudden, I had this new girlfriend, like she's all attentive and everything." But that only heightened Lacasse's suspicions. "I got pissed off and I did some snooping. I looked through her calendar." He told Hale he found entry after entry for Daniel Sack. "They're going on dates in public and stuff. They went zip-lining. Tallahassee Museum. So I didn't tell her I did that" at the time, unsure of how to address the issue.

"Have you met Wendi?" Lacasse asked abruptly, diverging momentarily from his lengthy monologue.

"Not personally," Hale responded.

Lacasse described her as somewhat of a mythical goddess: "Once you date this girl, you'll do anything for her. I'm not the only man that's been under her thumb in that way. I mean, she really has this *charisma* and *sexuality* and so, you know, you'd throw yourself in front of a bus for this girl." He told the investigator Wendi was able to put men under her spell—including him.

Returning to his soliloquy, Lacasse shared that he and Wendi had a major blowout while the two were together in Gainesville, where he was teaching a short class. He "laid into her" about what he found on her calendar, telling her he knew what was going on between her and Sack behind his back. "This is bullshit," he told her. Wendi "went to complete pieces," he told Hale. "She's very fragile emotionally. She just lost her shit. So we had the most awkward drive ever from Gainesville to Tallahassee the next day." Lacasse said he knew Wendi would crumble once he confronted her because she had "too much shame, too much guilt."

Something else that irked him was all the time Wendi had been spending in South Florida, resulting in them being together only two weekends from March until May. He informed Hale she had full-time childcare there with her parents. "They love those kids. They're all into it. Mom's an ex-kindergarten teacher. They get off on it." For some reason though, Wendi almost never invited him to South Florida and would barely call him while there, claiming she was too busy with the kids. "And that never made sense, especially eight, nine, ten, 11 o'clock at night."

While in South Florida in early July, after their big blowup, Wendi was "completely miserable," Lacasse revealed. "She gets depressed and anxious and she's got her baggage, but I never—even though we didn't have much contact—I never heard her as bad as she was this trip to South Florida. I mean, this blew up her world." He told the investigator how much Wendi hated Tallahassee. "She does not want to be here and I was the only thing that was kind of her anchor here and, *boom*, so this puts her in an odd position."

Lacasse acknowledged that their relationship was likely damaged beyond repair. "But I was in love with this girl, man, so it's hard. I mean, I've been with the kids, like a co-parent basically. It was really rough." He mentioned the "no contact" email Wendi had sent him shortly after returning to Tally, suggesting to Hale she'd likely told her therapist that he was an "abusive male" just like her ex-husband. Shortly after sending that email, he recounted, "She posts these pictures on Facebook with her boobs hanging out. People are telling me she's messing with you on the internet." He told the investigator Wendi had a "big mouth and tells me when men worship her."

Investigator Hale abruptly changed the subject, asking Lacasse about his own interactions with Dan Markel. The professor was able to recall the exact date they'd met—January 12, 2014—six months, almost to the day, before Dan was gunned down. He told Hale that he and Wendi were going to a comedy show that evening and that he arrived at her home a little early; Dan, on the other hand, was running late for the custody exchange, so their meeting became unavoidable. It was "pretty awkward," he said, noting that Dan insulted him multiple times during their ten-minute conversation.

Lacasse told the investigator that Wendi was so afraid of Dan, she "would almost have a panic attack" in front of him. It made him wonder "if he used to beat her ass" because her reaction to being in Dan's presence "seemed out of proportion for a guy who's just kind of a general dickhead." She'd even get heart palpitations. Lacasse took credit for "keeping her shit together for nine months," telling Hale, "She really can't do life very well. It's kind of sad and she gets by being really attractive and all this kind of stuff, but day-to-day life, she needs some— she's dependent. She needs a lot of help."

One of his key roles as Wendi's boyfriend, he noted, was to "run interference" and be a buffer between her and Dan when they both attended the kids' events. Lacasse estimated he'd been in close proximity to Dan some 20 hours during the boys' soccer practices, swim lessons, and the like. "We were friendly to each other," he said. "He was condescending, but nice."

Hale wanted to know about Lacasse's whereabouts at the time of the shooting, still unsure of his potential involvement. The professor told him he'd been on a trip to Tennessee to visit a close friend. He'd stopped 20 miles south of Atlanta on Thursday evening, staying at "a really crappy Days Inn," and arrived in Tennessee that Friday afternoon. He was on his way back that morning, Lacasse said, when Hale called to request an interview. He made the trip in his ten-year-old, metallic gray Nissan Sentra, using his credit card several times along the way.

•••

LACASSE EVENTUALLY REDIRECTED their conversation to the subject he initially wanted to discuss "off the record," telling Hale he was concerned about his own safety. "Because it's just speculation, but Danny Markel just got fucking killed and I don't want to be next. I'm sorry if that sounds paranoid, but I do have some ideas." He said he very much wanted to help "find whoever did this. This is terrible. I didn't like Danny, but no one deserves this, you know?" His central theory zeroed in on Wendi's family, who "desperately wants her back in South Florida." Having heard a little bit about Charlie Adelson from Craig Isom following his marathon session with Wendi, Hale was eager to learn what the good professor knew about him.

"Her brother is an unusual guy, not much empathy," Lacasse opined. "He's a dentist and he's very wealthy, but he kind of hangs out with people from both sides of the tracks. And, you know, he goes boating and to South Beach with his rich buddies and he also goes to his gym with some other kinds of characters kind of thing, so—"

"Some less savory individuals?" Hale interrupted.

"I think so. He's got a buddy who was Special Forces."

Hale abruptly pivoted, focusing again on Lacasse himself, asking if he'd ever been to Dan's home on Trescott Drive.

"Drove past it a hundred times," Lacasse acknowledged, "but never stopped."

"And you never had any kind of physical contact with Danny?"

"No. I'm surprised you guys didn't call me earlier, though, 'cause I probably said a hundred times in public that I'd like to kick his ass because he kept really making Wendi suffer— things like that." Lacasse chuckled. "But no, I would never. I'm a professor. *I'm a pussy.* I'm not going to do anything like that. No. No."

Hale asked if he'd be willing to supply a DNA sample.

Lacasse assured him that wouldn't be a problem. He

suggested they examine his credit card transactions to confirm his alibi, telling Hale, "I'm not involved, it's obvious, so I'll do whatever you want."

At that point, Craig Isom entered the room and asked what had prompted the professor's trip to Tennessee. The trip had been pre-planned, Lacasse said, "and I was upset 'cause it's not good getting an email from your girlfriend who you love telling you don't contact me for a week. It was like, 'Oh, I'm fucked. This is not good,' you know? So Thursday night, I just took off driving."

He told Isom that while Wendi was in South Florida for two weeks, he barely heard from her. "She came back. We tried to reconnect." They had dates on Monday and Tuesday, "and the second date she was done, it seemed like, but that's when I got that email right after that date. It's really sad."

"You cared about her a lot?" Isom asked.

"Oh, yeah," Lacasse confirmed. "I'm in love with that girl. I mean, I don't think there's anyone that spent more time with Wendi in the last nine months than me." He asked the investigators whether they'd started looking through the divorce pleadings, telling them Dan's filings were "almost insane" — even attempting to get Wendi disbarred. "He calls her names. It's the rantings of a lunatic, basically. Every time she got one of these, she would melt down for like two weeks."

Dan, he said, had been "manipulating the legal system to keep her in stress and it was punishing her."

Lacasse reiterated that "Wendi didn't want to be in Tallahassee. She wanted to live in South Florida ... This is going to sound totally narcissistic, but if we were doing well, she's like, 'Yeah, I'll stay here in Tallahassee *for you*,' because Markel's got this custody agreement." And then "we broke up and this happens. It's kind of strange."

"Okay, I see what you're saying," Isom said, starting to follow the professor's logic.

"Just the timing's weird to me."

• • •

A BIT LATER IN THE INTERVIEW, Lacasse told Hale that he and his colleagues needed to investigate Charlie. "He's very angry about Danny," Lacasse said. "And if you met— I know he's down there. You can't get him in front of you, but you're, you know, an experienced investigator. If you got in front of this guy, he'd set off your radar." He told Hale he used to do juvenile justice and forensic psychiatry and that Charlie "set off my radar a little bit. He's a weird guy, strange guy. He's a conduct disorder kid and *he hates Danny.*"

Lacasse had something else to say, telling Hale he needed to express it in vague terms so as not to be quoted. But the investigator pressed him for specifics. Reluctantly, Lacasse finally revealed what he'd wanted to share off the record from the start: "Wendi had reported to me that Charlie considered all the options possible to take care of this problem, put it that way." She'd asked Lacasse if she could tell him something "confidentially," and then blurted out, "'I think Charlie kind of looked into some options, like literally saw how and why and how you would do this.'"

Though Charlie was "a very successful dentist," Lacasse explained, "he reeks of anti-social behavior," noting that he hung out with his Special Forces friend—a former Navy Seal—"all the time." Someone who'd been in Afghanistan for five years.

"What did she say to you specifically," Hale pressed him, "I mean, when you say 'all options?'"

"I can't remember exactly, but it had something to do with the amount of money it would cost to have someone killed." Lacasse told Hale he'd met Charlie only once, when he and Wendi stayed at her brother's house in Fort Lauderdale in mid-March—the one time she invited him to South Florida. While having a beer in his hot tub, Lacasse said, Charlie was bragging about how he was able to move money around to avoid paying taxes. "I don't know exactly what, but he's not doing it on the up and up with his finances. It was pretty clear. He's pretty open about that."

"Please don't write this down," he begged Hale. "He's so

inappropriate. We're sitting in the hot tub and he starts talking about sex acts with his girlfriend that he did to punish her for bad behavior—in front of his sister. I'm like, this is the— I didn't know what to do. I just met him." The entire experience left him with a disturbing feeling that Charlie's "social radar is way off in the sense of right and wrong."

Lacasse told Hale he didn't know whether Charlie was deranged enough to have contracted for Dan's slaying, "but if you're looking at somebody, *don't miss him*. And I could also see him doing this without ever telling Wendi he did do it," noting how "fiercely protective" he was of her. "I could see Wendi being innocent, puzzled that Charlie did it."

Chillingly, Lacasse revealed that Wendi's brother was the very first person who came to mind when he heard the news of Dan's murder. Charlie, he added, was a millionaire with "a lot of resources," had no qualms about having three girlfriends at the same time, was "arrogant and narcissistic ... I think he would set off your alarm bells. Doesn't mean he did it, but he's aggressive, he's argumentative, so focused on himself completely." He told Hale, "I hope to God it wasn't Charlie, honestly, but that's what popped into my head."

Charlie wasn't the only one Lacasse wanted law enforcement to be aware of. There was an unhealthy—almost creepy—family dynamic as well. "The family is so unhealthily enmeshed," he said, "so completely enmeshed that Wendi is not really an adult." Her parents still considered her a baby— "they infantilized her." They'd actually drive all the way to Tally—some seven hours—if Wendi wanted to return home because they didn't trust their grown daughter to drive to South Florida by herself. Rather, they would caravan together for another seven hours all the way back to Coral Springs.

In Lacasse's view, Charlie was "impulsive, angry, fiercely protective over Wendi, and I've heard him say, *'I'd like to kill that motherfucker.'*" And if not his buddy in the Special Forces, he speculated, Charlie could have hired "some seedy guys down in the Cuban neighborhood or something like that."

● ● ●

FROM THE VERY BEGINNING, Lacasse told the investigators, Wendi never wanted to be in Tallahassee. After Dan was offered the job at Florida State, they planned to remain only a year. Dan then had a position on the faculty at the University of Miami. But "he was an asshole so he lost it. They said, 'No. Go back to FSU and stay there.' So they're stuck here." Wendi had told Lacasse that Dan had been so abrasive while in Miami, his colleagues there didn't want to put up with him anymore. "He had to work pretty hard to lose that job, actually," Lacasse said derisively.

But Dan rebounded and wound up doing well at Florida State. Wendi, on the other hand, "gets a shitty job that she doesn't really like. Doesn't like the area. She's doing her best to make it work, but she hates it." In contrast, "she loves Miami, just loves it. When we were down there, she just lights up. It's a whole different thing."

Lacasse provided some additional details about Wendi's marriage, telling the investigators that every friend she had begged her not to marry Dan, telling her, "he's the biggest asshole we've ever met," but that she "got caught up in the Harvard Law and elitism and all this kind of stuff and she was in a bad place. Made a bad decision." He explained that "it was a bad marriage from day one, I mean, pretty much, according to her at least. By the second year it was awful."

And it got worse once the kids arrived, Lacasse added, because Dan was an absent father, coming home at 9:00 p.m. every night, becoming bored with the kids in minutes. Meanwhile, Wendi "did everything, kind of like a house slave."

Dan also wasn't well liked in the community, the professor noted, telling Isom and Hale the newspaper stories "about what a great guy he was" missed the mark completely. Only one person he knew and respected thought that. "Everyone else says that guy's a son of a bitch" who had a way of talking down to people. An unapologetic snob. "He's one of those

Harvard guys," Lacasse said with disdain. "He thought his shit didn't stink."

Isom asked what he knew about Donna and Harvey Adelson. Lacasse said he found them to be "strange people," but didn't believe they'd have been involved in the murder. "I mean, nine months of dating her, they probably said 20 words." Yet when he learned about the murder, "I thought of Charlie within a couple of moments." Wendi's brother lived his life differently from most people, he explained: "Goes to South America, sees prostitutes … He does his own thing." And had "no empathy for other people."

"Kind of a deceitful person to start with?" Isom asked.

"Sure," Lacasse agreed. "The whole family really."

•••

TWO DAYS LATER, the good professor was back at the police station, telling Corey Hale that, with additional time to reflect, "I'm starting to see things a little more clearly." He began a soliloquy that lasted nearly 25 minutes, Hale sneaking in only a handful of questions the few times Lacasse paused to breathe.

Before getting to his new revelations, he told Hale he'd thought of two additional people they might want to investigate. The first was another law professor, in his sixties, who'd been calling Wendi a "goddess and he would send her inappropriate texts" and who also disliked Dan. Lacasse said he didn't know the professor's name, but noted he had "really bad teeth." The second was a student of Wendi's who'd sent her inappropriate emails and "actually kissed her on the mouth during a student-teacher meeting in her office."

Yet neither of those individuals was what caused him to race back to the police station. It wasn't any new revelations about Charlie either. Rather, it was Wendi herself Lacasse wanted to talk about. He was now seeing her in a whole new light. "I still love Wendi," he acknowledged. "I was under her spell. If she called me tomorrow, I'd probably go back to her. But there's a lot of stuff that, as I look back—it was really strange."

The more he dwelled on Wendi's psyche—including in sessions with his own therapist—the more he realized "she's a sociopath, and I didn't tell you guys that before ... Wendi has this public persona and she's a very good actress and she's very charismatic and all this kind of stuff and she knows a lot of people." Behind that facade, however, was a person who had "no sense of guilt, no empathy, hypersensitivity to criticism." In his view, she was "a total, pathological liar. And I feel bad saying all this because I still love her."

Lacasse told Hale he had somewhat of an epiphany looking back through Danny's legal pleadings in the divorce case—because Wendi's ex-husband was identifying the very same flaws. "He's constantly talking about her systematic pattern of deception, how she lies all the time. And she told me once, 'I have a really hard time telling the truth when it's inconvenient or unpleasant. I lie all the time.' I mean, she said that to me."

Another reason his feelings about Wendi were wavering, Lacasse explained, was because everyone was now saying "what a nice guy Markel is." Yet Wendi had led him to believe Dan was Satan himself, how he was a "psychopathic, stalking, emotionally abusive, controlling jerk." He never doubted her during the time they were a romantic couple. But now he was, for the first time realizing the picture Wendi had consistently painted of her ex was wildly distorted. "What I've heard from everyone else is he's an arrogant dick as far as an academic ... But he's a good man, that's what I've heard people saying. He was a good father." But he was "really upset with Wendi. I'm starting to understand why."

Though he was pretty certain Wendi "didn't pull the trigger or anything like that," he was starting to feel "creeped out"—now that he was out from under her "spell." Could she have been an accessory? he wondered. "It makes a lot of sense to me at a certain point ... When you see behind the curtain, she's a total train wreck. My psychologist would say, 'Man, she just meets the checklist of the narcissistic sociopath,' you know, going down the list."

"I'm pretty heartbroken over all this," he added, "but if

you want information, I have some things to say." He went back over the big blowup he and Wendi had over Daniel Sack and how she was then in South Florida for nearly two weeks. During that time, he said, they were texting one another "about trying to get back together and desperate to see each other." Wendi had written, "'Sucks that we're separated in this bad situation.' I can show you the texts. 'I can't imagine my life without you. God, I fucking miss you.'" He told Hale those were exact quotes.

When she got back to town initially, Wendi was syrupy sweet, Lacasse recounted. But when he showed up at their yoga class that Tuesday evening, "something was completely different. She was gone." They walked to her car following class and he could tell, "she's done." But then, out of the blue, she asked if he was going to be in town over the weekend. "Now if she's done, why does she give a shit if I'm here Friday? She asked me directly, 'Are you going to be here Friday?'" Those were the last words Wendi said to him. "I just thought you should know that. It might mean nothing, but it was kind of strange to me."

Lacasse showed Hale the Facebook picture of Wendi he'd mentioned when he'd come to the police station two days earlier—in a purple dress, flanked by her boys, with "her boobs hanging out." His friends were telling him how narcissistic that picture was because the kids didn't look good—only Wendi did. She posted that picture Thursday evening, he noted, intimating that she wanted to look good since she knew she was "going to be all over the media" the next day.

Lacasse also found it troubling that Wendi hadn't reached out to him a single time since the murder. They'd been co-parenting the boys for six months, he said. "We talked about Danny for hundreds of hours. No one knows that case better than—as far as her friends—than me. It's really, really odd."

Her lack of contact, he suggested, made Wendi look guilty. "Maybe she's just a cold-blooded, damaged, needy woman that decided she was done with me. Maybe. But if there's any interest in her at all, there's a lot of sociopathic stuff here, it seems like. The ease with which she lies is really disturbing."

"So that's all I had to say," Lacasse said, his long-winded rant finally nearing an end. "I just thought you would want to know that." He told Hale he never would have made such statements a month earlier. But after uncovering Wendi's "web of deceit" in their own relationship, he really wasn't sure "what she's capable of. It's really, really strange. That's what I was worried about."

Lacasse ended the interview in a bout of self-loathing over how Wendi had manipulated him. While she was juggling two boyfriends, he lamented, "I'm at home with the kids every night while she's off screwing him during the day. She let me mop her kitchen floors for her. I mean, this woman had me doing things you wouldn't believe." He told the investigator, "I would have stepped in front of a truck for this woman. And I'm a mature 42-year-old guy who's dated a lot of women. I just got caught into the spell."

With that final comment, Professor Jeffrey Lacasse stood up, shook Investigator Hale's hand, and left the police station a second time. Just two days earlier, he'd been so convinced Charlie was behind Dan's murder, he was deathly afraid of sharing those thoughts. On this occasion, however, he didn't mention Wendi's brother a single time.

5.

Daniel Eric Markel

IN THE EARLY 1960s, Montreal was by far the largest city in all of Canada, its 1.1 million inhabitants nearly twice the population of the nation's second-largest city, Toronto. The French-speaking metropolis served as a haven for European Jews, particularly following the rise of Adolf Hitler and Nazi Germany. It also was the birthplace of Phil Markel and Ruth Isakson, each of whom was raised by European immigrants. The two met at a summer camp in 1963 while both were on break from college; they were married in 1966. Shelly arrived in September 1969, and her baby brother, Danny, in October 1972. Dan Markel went big right from the start, a ten-pound bundle of joy the day he sucked in his first breaths of air.

Ruth's father had died of a sudden heart attack when she was only nine. Her mother Helen's younger brother, Lazar Lapidus, quickly emerged as her father figure. Uncle Lazar had been hidden by a Catholic family in Lithuania for two years during the Holocaust. The woman he ended up marrying in 1967, Rachel, had actually survived a Nazi concentration camp. Shelly and Danny formed very close attachments not only with their "Bubbie" Helen, but also with their Great Uncle Lazar and Great Aunt Rachel.

Bubbie Helen had quite the repertoire of Yiddish aphorisms. When her grandson Danny would chase her around her home with a broom or handheld appliance, she'd bellow, "*Putch in tuchus geht arein in kopf*," a threat—never actually carried out—that a smack in the rear-end was coming if the offending behavior didn't cease. She'd counsel her grandchildren, "*Zei a mensch*," meaning that no matter what occupation or career they ultimately selected, it was far more important that each become a decent and thoughtful human being, full of integrity—a *mensch*. Her grandkids would grow up with their Bubbie's exhortation burned into their psyches.

Though Ruth and Phil had each been raised in traditional kosher homes, they chose not to foist such strict dietary protocols on their own children. Shabbat dinners on Friday evenings were important, but could be overridden by other interests or travel. They didn't often attend Saturday morning services at synagogue, or "shul," choosing to spend most of their weekends at their country cottage in the small town of Saint-Sauveur—nestled in Quebec's Laurentian Mountains—about an hour north of Montreal. They did, however, scrupulously observe Judaism's most sacred High Holy Days—Rosh Hashanah and Yom Kippur—attending a Conservative synagogue and fasting to atone for their sins. They split each year's Passover seders between Ruth's family and Phil's, the celebrations becoming ever larger as the extended family grew.

Though Jewish customs and rituals weren't a central facet of family life in the Markel household, the paramount importance of Israel as a nation was. Ruth and Phil were strong believers in Israel's centrality in Jewish history and culture and tried to inculcate that value in their children. They had aunts and uncles in the Jewish homeland whose six grandchildren—cousins to Shelly and Danny relatively close in age—became beloved members of their extended family. Each summer, the Markels would spend several weeks in Israel, a place Danny would come to cherish more than any other on earth.

•••

RUTH AND PHIL often compared their rambunctious son to

Dennis the Menace because of his rich blond hair, bright blue eyes, infectious energy, and intense curiosity. When he was just 18 months old, an interior house painter wrapped up one evening with Danny's room only partially wallpapered. When Ruth put her toddler to bed that night, his crib was in the opposite corner from where the painter had begun his work.

The following morning, however, she found the crib pushed up against the wallpaper, with a good bit of it peeled off the wall. When the painter saw the mess, he deadpanned, "This is not a boy for wallpaper." But he also told Ruth not to worry, noting that his own son was the exact same way as a toddler—and was currently in medical school.

Phil had Danny on skis when he was just two. Going up the mountain on the ski lift, he'd sit between his dad's legs, hugging the T-bar with every ounce of his strength. Coming down the mountain, he again stationed himself between Phil's legs—holding on tightly—screaming jubilantly "faster Daddy, faster" as they made their way to the bottom of the slope.

Eventually, winter weekends at the family's cottage included Danny skiing on his own. Though he learned how to bring himself to a stop, he noticed a hole in the fence at the bottom of the trail. Before his folks could stop him, Danny was beyond the resort's perimeter, skiing right through the fence and down the hill of an adjacent property. Ruth and Phil finally rescued him, admonishing their son for venturing past the fence. They were forced to pull the plug on his skiing for two years despite his obvious talent and enjoyment.

Danny attended a local nursery school run by a synagogue. One morning when he was four, his teacher panicked upon noticing that he'd disappeared from the classroom. She was about to call the police when she finally found Danny—some 20 minutes later—in deep discussion with the rabbi, clear across the other side of the building. It was actually the rabbi who received the tongue lashing on that occasion.

What did each of these incidents have in common? They were rooted in Danny's intense curiosity and refusal to accept boundaries and limitations others had prescribed. If he was interested in something, he wanted to explore whatever it was until his mind was fully satisfied. That same curiosity would motivate and inspire Dan Markel his entire 41 years on earth.

•••

BY THE MID-1970s, Montreal was changing rapidly. A political party rose to power—the Parti Québécois—whose platform centered on establishing the "sovereignty" of the province of Quebec. Legislation was enacted formally declaring French as its official language. Those events led to a mass exodus of English-speaking "Anglophones" concerned about their and their children's future. Though their extended family members remained in Montreal, in 1978, the Markels resettled in Toronto, in the province of Ontario. Shelly was eight and Danny was five. By then, Ruth was a management consultant and Phil an importer. They purchased a suburban home and enrolled the kids in an Orthodox Hebrew day school.

As a young boy, Danny had already become a voracious reader—of comic books, devouring as many as he could get his hands on. He also had a goofy side, even tacking a clown poster on the wall of his room, earning him the nickname "Bozo"—derived from the red-headed TV clown. As he got older, he shortened Bozo to "Bo." And gradually traded in his comic books for more serious works of literature. With their parents' business ventures taking off and requiring more devotion than a five-day workweek could provide, Danny and Shelly were often deposited at the local library on Saturdays, with a babysitter to watch over them. It was there that Danny's love of reading truly blossomed. Whenever Ruth and Phil were out and about with the kids, his head was always buried in a book—or two.

And it was those babysitters who exposed Danny to another developing interest—members of the opposite sex who weren't his sister. By the time he was nine, he was regularly seeking Shelly's advice and counsel on how best to woo their teenage sitters. The brother and sister spent considerable time together as youngsters, Danny fully respecting Shelly's authority and leadership. In addition to teaching her little brother about love and romance, she helped him learn the basics of more mundane tasks such as blowing his nose and tying his shoelaces.

During his childhood, Danny participated in a wide variety of activities, both in the mountains and in their local community, including tennis, baseball, ice hockey, skating, and skiing. He could dance up a storm—busting moves like Michael Jackson—the dance floor a place he felt entirely comfortable and enjoyed thoroughly all his life. He also enjoyed performing on stage, landing the lead role in several youth plays. His zest for life was so powerful, he was rarely inhibited or embarrassed—fearless in pushing the envelope, taking risks, and trying new things.

For a kid, Danny possessed tenacious determination, refusing to give up even in the face of significant adversity. When he was 11, he landed a job at a local bakery, working after school and on the weekends. One of his key functions was to tie a red string around the white pastry boxes as customers' orders were being filled. But he couldn't get the hang of making the proper bow, leading the proprietor to tell him they'd have to let him go if he couldn't master the skill. That same evening, Danny took home several dozen boxes and practiced for hours until he became a whiz at bow-tying. He kept his job.

Danny especially loved board games, which were a staple of family weekends at the cottage and vacations. His favorite was Trivial Pursuit, a game in which he nearly always decimated his opponents, children and adults alike. How did he become so good? By committing to memory each and every question and answer on the playing cards—2,400 in all—often while taking care of business in the restroom, his own unique way of multitasking.

It was in Hebrew school that Danny's most significant transformation occurred. Prior to the school day, students were permitted to participate in a religious service. Those who attended were treated to bagels when the service ended. Ruth and Phil often joked with their son that if what he really wanted was the bagels, they'd have been more than happy to serve them at home. Yet something about the religious service—and sense of belonging and connectedness it fostered—resonated with Danny. So much so that when his parents couldn't get him to school early enough to catch the service, he'd take the city bus—at the ripe old age of eight.

Hebrew school is also where Danny met Marnie, a cute blonde who sat directly behind him in the second grade. At the parents' night meeting that fall, their teacher pulled Ruth and Phil aside to inform them, "I see only Danny's back all day long," explaining that their son seemed far more interested in talking to Marnie than the lesson she was trying to impart. His romance with Marnie would continue into their teenage years.

Danny was so enthralled by what he was learning at Hebrew school, he began entertaining the prospect of becoming a rabbi himself. As he was training for his *bar mitzvah*, he asked his rabbi what benefits he could expect if he pursued such a career path. To which the rabbi replied, "Well Danny, I sometimes get baseball tickets, I have the best seat in the house, and I always have a parking place." Despite that enticing assortment of perks, not long after his *bar mitzvah*, Danny decided that a more practical goal was to become president of a shul, which would allow him to have both a deep connection to a Jewish congregation, but also a successful career.

As a teenager, Danny became curious about financial markets and began investing in American stocks, following their ups and downs in the newspaper. He also started reading about Ivy League colleges in America, in magazines such as *The New Yorker*. By age 13, he was telling his parents that he had no desire to remain in Canada after completing high school. America and the Ivy League—Harvard hopefully— were beckoning him.

•••

THE MARKEL FAMILY MOVED again in 1986—just before Danny's 14th birthday. By then, Ruth had published a book,

Room at the Top: A Woman's Guide to Moving Up in Business. She was sought after as a speaker and management consultant, frequently bringing her to downtown Toronto, some 90 minutes from the family's suburban home. Her commute was brutal, causing her to miss out on quality family time. She and Phil decided to relocate closer to downtown. Once their move was finalized, Danny was enrolled in the Forest Hill Collegiate Institute, a public high school.

One of Ruth's friends, a guidance counselor, helped Danny chart out a road map of everything he needed to do and accomplish to be seriously considered by Ivy League colleges like Harvard. Of course he needed stellar grades, which weren't the slightest problem, as he was able to coast through his coursework barely applying any effort at all. His uncanny ability to retain and recall material from dense reading assignments made exams a breeze. He also had a unique knack for writing. By the ninth grade, he could bang out a polished 20-page paper virtually overnight.

The guidance counselor also advised Danny to become active—and a leader—in student organizations. He joined the debate team, exhibiting an ability to argue and debate far more advanced than his peers. He started a club for environmental conservation and took it upon himself to resurrect the long-defunct student newspaper—becoming its editor and business manager, signing up local businesses to run ads and writing and editing most of its content.

When he was 16, Danny spent the entire summer in Israel, completely on his own. Not only did he get to spend quality time with his cousins, he forged rich friendships that would last his entire life. The following summer he was at Tufts University, just outside of Boston, in a pre-college program, his first extended stay in the United States. His final summer before college he was overseas yet again, in a program on finance at the University of Cambridge, cultivating still more friendships in England.

Toward the end of his time at Tufts, Danny received shocking news that rocked his entire world. His former girlfriend, Marnie—with whom he was still very close—had been on the beach in Tel Aviv with a tour group when the 17-year-old put her towel down in the exact spot a Hamas operative had just planted a pipe bomb. The bomb exploded, inflicting disfiguring and fatal injuries. Marnie's brutal murder at the hands of a Palestinian terrorist would mark a critical turning point for Danny—crystalizing for him how precious and fleeting life is.

At her memorial service in Toronto, Danny summoned the courage to eulogize the young woman he described as "sensitive, beautiful, intelligent, lively, caring." He spoke of being scared and vulnerable. Until that day, he'd seen himself as a shaper of his own destiny, a bright-eyed teenager "about to conquer the world. But Marnie's death forces us to confront all our repressed fears and hidden anxieties."

Danny asked the age-old question: Why do bad things happen to good people? The deep-thinking teenager questioned aloud his "faith in a just moral order." He shared with mourners that he found solace "in the same values to which Jews have always clung: the importance of establishing close families and strong friendships, of celebrating our culture" and "passing on our heritage." As he stepped away from the podium, Danny wiped tears from his eyes. He would carry the wound of Marnie's senseless murder for the rest of his days.

•••

THE SADNESS OF HIS ex-girlfriend's tragic death was eventually replaced by Danny's euphoria over learning that he'd been accepted for admission at Harvard. In September 1991, the 18-year-old Canadian arrived in Cambridge, Massachusetts brimming with anticipation and excitement. He fell in love with Harvard every bit as much as he'd fallen in love with Israel. The Ivy League school was a perfect match for the highly intelligent young man with boundless energy and intellectual curiosity. He quickly formed richly diverse social circles—at his dorm, in his classes, and within student organizations.

Danny's style of friendship was truly unique. He wasn't the least bit shy or intimidated about meeting new people. And once he decided someone was a friend, they were stuck with him. He'd appear out of the blue at a friend's room or apartment—one of his many trademarks that would continue to his dying day—plop down on a beanbag chair or on the floor and start debating whatever ideas were floating through his brain. And he had lots of them.

Though his ideas generally skewed pretty liberal, Danny particularly enjoyed discussing them with classmates who were more conservative. He could argue a point from virtually every angle, in depth and breadth that sometimes exceeded his friends' interest or stamina. But he also was an exceptionally good listener—even when he disagreed vehemently—eager to help his friends hone their positions into more coherent arguments.

Danny was unusually affectionate and sweet, often greeting friends with a hug and always a warm smile. He proceeded through college life wearing his heart on his sleeve, his optimism, energy, and joyful spirit infectious. Though he could be blunt, rarely filtering his thoughts before they escaped his lips—another trademark—his friends came to appreciate that whatever guidance he was offering was borne of genuine affection and concern. He desperately wanted them to succeed and find joy—in their family relationships, love life, or career aspirations—and took great pride when they did.

The transplanted Canadian also loved introducing people he thought should know one another—something he considered to be his obligation as a *mensch*—ultimately earning him a new nickname: the Great Connector. If one of his friends had recently traveled to an interesting place, he might introduce him or her to another friend who'd spent time there as well. Friends who shared similar interests in cuisine, music, art, or theater, Danny believed, needed to know one another and be provided the opportunity to become friends. It was the very least he could do to connect them.

Early in his freshman year, he became good friends with a Jewish classmate named Adam who lived two floors below him in their dorm. Adam was from New York, another one of Danny's favorite places. They talked endlessly about Adam's life growing up in the Big Apple. During the spring semester, Danny met another Jewish freshman named Steve, also from New York, and decided that Adam and Steve needed to meet.

Not only did Adam and Steve become friends, together with Danny, they became an inseparable threesome, with Danny providing his *mensch*y guidance to the pair on what classes to take, which girls to chase, and what careers to pursue. During their senior year, the three shared a suite until graduating and heading off in separate directions. But what none of them realized during their time at Harvard was that the attraction between Adam and Steve was destined to become permanent. The two ultimately married in 2006, Danny beaming with pride and joy on their wedding day—and taking full credit for their union.

•••

AT HARVARD, DANNY attached himself to a campus institution catering to Jewish students like him—the Hillel House, run by a group of well-respected rabbis. He enjoyed its lectures, Shabbat dinners, and formal services, expanding his social network with friends he made at those events. He relished intense philosophical discussions with the rabbis— who became both mentors and friends—time he affectionately labeled "roaming with the rabbis."

As for his academics, Danny found the coursework at Harvard intensely interesting, the professors supremely talented, and the intellectual environment intoxicating. In virtually every class, he'd take a seat near the front of the lecture hall, his hand the most frequent to spring up with a question, to amplify a point, or debate the professor. What other students—typically with derision—referred to as a "gunner." Yet that label didn't bother or deter him in the slightest, to Danny more a badge of honor than a source of embarrassment.

Two activities he immersed himself in from the outset were carryovers from his high school days: the debate team and student newspaper. It was at *The Crimson* where he was most in his element, due to his love of writing, enormous vocabulary, and unique knack for the written word. *The Crimson* billed itself as the oldest continuously published daily college newspaper in the United States—having begun in 1873—with students such as Franklin Delano Roosevelt and John F. Kennedy among the paper's glitzy list of alumni. To appear more adult-like and professional to his readers, Danny condensed his first name, publishing pieces under the byline "Dan E. Markel." He published his first column toward the end of his freshman year—"Sex at Harvard: Getting to Yes"—conveying his thesis in his first few words: "Sex. Everybody wants it, but nobody at Harvard knows how to get it."

As a junior, Dan penned a weekly column and also was responsible for editing columns written by underclassmen. He would sit side-by-side with *The Crimson* writer whose piece he was editing, reviewing the text on a computer monitor. They'd go through the piece paragraph by paragraph, Dan testing every assumption and focusing on grammatical structure and style. The process often lasted for hours. Some student writers—those with a thick skin—felt rewarded by the spit and polish Dan helped them apply to their writing. Many others, however, preferred having their work edited by anyone other than Dan Markel—editors with a less active red pen—even though they learned far less in the process.

By his senior year, Dan had become associate editorial chair. He and other editors would jointly prepare "staff editorials" representing the opinion of *The Crimson* writ large. Some 40 to 50 of the senior-level staff would gather each Sunday evening in high-back leather chairs in a massive conference room— known as the Sanctum—where they'd discuss editorials planned for the week ahead.

The group would debate the language of each editorial and work together to sharpen their arguments. The debates could become intense—even heated and rancorous—occasionally lasting until after midnight. For young adults barely old enough to imbibe legally, what happened in the Sanctum was pretty heady stuff. To Dan, the weekly intellectual jousts were more potent than any drug being sold in the back alleys of Harvard Square. The sessions served as an excellent training ground for his eventual career in academia.

Dan's final column was published just days before he graduated *magna cum laude* with a BA in Government. In the piece, he derided the shift of Harvard graduates' aspirations from deeply meaningful religious and academic pursuits to the world of entertainment. "Today, the most coveted job in Harvard's spring recruiting," he wrote, "is at Walt Disney Company, or second best, the NBA. For us, piety emanates not from Jerusalem, the Vatican, Mecca, Kyoto or Bañares. It's Los Angeles."

Pulling no punches, he labeled members of his graduating class "mosquitoes to the lights of Las Vegas and Hollywood" sucking from the "sugary bosom of pop culture manufactured by sweaty-toothed media moguls in Los Angeles." He implored his fellow graduates to aspire to more idealistic endeavors "with a relentless ferocity and a blazing fury." Precisely the path he intended for himself.

• • •

OVER THE FOLLOWING two years, Dan barely stepped foot on the North American continent. Thanks to his relentless networking among rabbis and Jewish professors, he earned a prized fellowship through the Dorot Foundation to study at Hebrew University in Jerusalem, a ten-month program anchored in both academic and experiential learning. During his time in Israel, he studied political philosophy, traveled extensively, and served as a legislative aide to the Deputy Speaker of the Israeli parliament, the Knesset—pretty impressive for a 23-year-old Canadian.

Two grievous events occurred during Dan's Israeli fellowship that seared into his psyche as deeply as Marnie's death years before. The first was the assassination of Prime Minister Yitzhak Rabin by an extremist who shot him from close range with a Baretta semi-automatic handgun. The second hit even closer to home. Dan was a passenger on a bus when suicide bombers detonated explosive devices on the two buses just ahead of his. Though he escaped unharmed, he witnessed the explosions—and the gruesome human carnage—with his own two eyes. Which shook him nearly to his core.

Dan's year in the Holy Land was mostly positive, however. He was able to spend quality time with each of his cousins—now adults like him—rekindle friendships from earlier trips, and make new friends both in Israel and throughout the Middle East. He also experienced the most serious romantic relationship of his young life.

Back in Canada, his sister Shelly was on the verge of cementing the most serious relationship of hers, to her fiancé Ian Freedman—both brand-new lawyers. Dan was delighted to play the role of best man at their August 1996 wedding. His toast to the bride and groom was as well written—and witty—as any column he'd ever assembled for *The Crimson*. With great joy and exuberance, he hoisted his sister and new brother-in-law high in the air—each seated in a chair as is Jewish custom—during the playing of the Hava Nagila.

Just a few weeks later, Dan was back across the Atlantic for a second stint at the University of Cambridge, this time in its master's program in philosophy. Thanks again to his networking, he'd landed *three* scholarships to defray his expenses. As much as he loved his classes at Harvard, there was something about his deep dive into philosophy that resonated deeply with Dan, who was fascinated by the principles fleshed out by the likes of Hobbes, Locke, Kant, and Mill. He excelled in his studies, graduating with high honors in political thought and intellectual history.

Dan's arrival at Cambridge coincided with the school's

decision to employ a full-time rabbi for Jewish students. The position was filled by a brand-new Orthodox rabbi from Scotland, Shaul Robinson—just 29 years of age—who felt somewhat out of his depth serving as the sole rabbi for the entire university. Dan became his staunchest cheerleader, encouraging the young rabbi, affirming his strengths, and telling him often what a great job he was doing. His positive and upbeat words proved vital to Rabbi Robinson finding his footing, helping form a loving friendship that would last the remainder of Dan's life.

•••

IN SEPTEMBER 1997, Dan found himself on very familiar ground—Harvard Yard—this time as a first-year law student, or 1L. Though he believed that law school was a natural progression from his undergraduate and master's studies, he wasn't yet certain whether he wanted to be a lawyer, philosopher, academic, or business leader. By immersing himself in legal studies at the very highest level, he felt certain he'd find his true calling.

Dan was as much a gunner at Harvard Law as he'd been as an undergraduate—yet with a confidence level exponentially greater than when he arrived as a freshman. He wasn't the slightest bit intimidated by law professors who'd been teaching at Harvard for decades, often making points during class discussion they hadn't even considered. He wasn't timid about expressing unusual or unpopular opinions, thoroughly enjoying the back-and-forth with professors and fellow students, as if the interchanges were a highly satisfying recreational activity.

Not only did he make dozens of new friends during law school, Dan immersed himself in a brand-new Jewish institution, the Chabad at Harvard, founded by a young rabbi named Hirschy Zarchi, who would become another close and lifelong friend. The Chabad focused heavily on the intellectual and cultural aspects of Judaism—which was right up Dan's alley, whose love of being Jewish centered on cultural identity, heritage, and community, rather than doctrinal beliefs or religious rituals. He'd begin his Friday evenings at the Hillel for formal services and then race over to the Chabad for Shabbat dinners, where he'd spend hours chatting, laughing, and enjoying fellowship with his ever-growing circle of Jewish friends.

•••

DURING THE SUMMER between his 1L and 2L years, Dan returned home, working as a research assistant to a professor of international law at the University of Toronto, pouring himself into a project related to amnesty in post-apartheid South Africa. He converted his summer research into a scholarly 57-page article that was published in the *University of Toronto Law Journal*. In the lengthy piece, Dan skillfully applied principles of "retributive justice"—a punishment theory premised on the moral imperative to punish criminal wrongdoing (an "eye for an eye")—to the question of amnesty for those who violated the human rights of Black South Africans during the apartheid era.

As he labored over the article, Dan began contemplating becoming a law professor himself. By then, he was already honing his craft as a teaching fellow, instructing Harvard undergraduates in philosophy of law, political theory, and moral reasoning. He'd also been selected to be an editor of the *Harvard Law Review*—widely recognized as the most elite legal journal in America—and was also feverishly working on *two* more articles.

One appeared as a "note" in the *Harvard Law Review*, which regularly published pieces from students within its ranks. That success, though notable, wasn't necessarily a sign of Dan's scholarly potential. But getting his other piece placed in the highly regarded *Vanderbilt Law Review* most certainly was. Dan's 86-page tome—"Are Shaming Punishments Beautifully Retributive?"—marked the beginning of his obsession with criminal punishments designed to embarrass and humiliate, rather than incarcerate. Which he decried as being far outside the realm of retributive justice.

In his first of 343 footnotes, Dan thanked 26 individuals for their assistance, a veritable "who's who" of the upper echelons of the legal academy, including a sizeable chunk of Harvard's law faculty. The list was nearly as impressive as the article's placement. By the time he graduated Harvard Law in May 2001—with honors and debt free—Dan Markel was likely the only aspiring law professor in the country to have had three articles accepted for publication before walking across the graduation stage. With an impressive cadre of mentors eager to assist him in joining their ranks. He was well on his way.

Even before earning the distinction of Juris Doctor, Dan had added yet another important title to his name—uncle. His sister Shelly had given birth to a baby girl in August 2000, to whom Dan instantly became "Uncle Bo." Looking into her squinty eyes and feeling her tiny little fingers wrapped around one of his made the rest of the world—and all the ideas percolating in his very busy brain—melt away. Being in his niece's midst stirred something in Dan he'd never felt before—a paternal instinct. Deep in his gut, he knew that being a father to children of his own would be the highest privilege—and greatest joy— he'd ever experience.

•••

LAW SCHOOL GRADUATES hoping to become law professors often follow their legal education by clerking for federal judges—a select few for the Supreme Court of the United States, or SCOTUS. Although Dan never became a SCOTUS clerk, he followed his Harvard graduation with a clerkship at the U.S. Court of Appeals for the Ninth Circuit, which handles appeals from federal trial courts in several western states, Alaska, and Hawaii. The court's roster consists of nearly 30 active judges—all lifetime appointees of the President—who assemble in panels of three to hear appellate arguments, primarily in San Francisco, Pasadena, and Seattle.

Judge Michael Daly Hawkins was an appointee of President Bill Clinton. His entire staff consisted of two administrative assistants, an experienced "career" law clerk, and a pair of law clerks fresh out of law school. Dan had beaten out hundreds of other highly qualified candidates for one of the latter, one-year positions. The six individuals who worked in Judge Hawkins' "chambers"—a fancy name for a judge's office suite—were like an intimate family.

His chambers were located in the Sandra Day O'Connor U.S. Courthouse in Phoenix, completed less than a year before Dan's arrival. From a distance, the gargantuan, 550,000 square-foot structure looks like a sleek, ultra-modern glass castle. Its signature design feature is its cavernous public atrium, rising a full six stories in height, making the aesthetic appeal of the building's interior even more striking than its exterior.

When a new clerk first reports for duty to a federal appellate judge, the job can seem intimidating, if not overwhelming. After all, the clerk is usually straight out of law school, in his or her mid-twenties, reporting to a boss just one professional rung below a Supreme Court justice, assisting in decision-making that can have life-and-death impacts on real human beings.

A clerk's primary goal in the first month or two is typically not to screw anything up too badly. And to avoid the ire of his or her judge through tardiness, irresponsibility, or careless mistakes.

Yet when Dan Markel arrived for his first day of work at the O'Connor Courthouse in September 2001, the 28-year-old newly minted attorney wasn't the least bit in awe of the glass castle that had become his workplace, the presidential appointee who was now his boss, or the nature of the work itself. From the very beginning, he felt right at home plopping down in a chair in the judge's office—unannounced of course—to engage the jurist in esoteric and theoretical discussions, just as he had with his friends at Harvard. He didn't hesitate to tell Judge Hawkins when he believed that he—the judge—was mistaken. Or to argue with the judge over how he—the law clerk—believed an appeal should be decided. On occasion, Judge Hawkins would have to remind him, ever so gently and with great tact, "Dan, please remember. I'm the judge."

Although Dan had never lived anywhere near Phoenix, he took it upon himself to learn everything he could about its best restaurants, fascinating museums, nearby hiking trails, and interesting places off the beaten track—all at a time the internet was still in its infancy. He immersed himself in the local community and its Jewish population, hosting Passover seders for the judge's family and his Christian co-clerks. When Dan traveled with the judge to San Francisco or Pasadena, he was the one typically making the dinner reservations, his choices usually spot on. He had an uncanny ability to feel completely at home wherever he was, extremely comfortable in his own skin.

From his earliest days as a clerk, Dan made no secret of his ambition to become a criminal law professor. He told his co-clerks he was working on what he hoped would become a groundbreaking article on the role of mercy and compassion in criminal punishment. He emitted an intensity level his co-clerks—and clerks for other Ninth Circuit judges—sometimes found off-putting, on occasion turning dinner conversations into marathon policy debates or legal arguments.

Dan could become so entranced by his own thoughts, his co-clerks sometimes feared he'd be hit by a car while walking from their hotel to the courthouse. In his defense, the aspiring professor was simply trying to squeeze as much out of each day as possible, working on his law review article, drafting elaborate, one-of-a-kind opinions for Judge Hawkins, taking time to exercise at the gym, and discovering more great restaurants and hiking trails. If he happened to bring a draft of his article to a spring training baseball outing to fiddle with between innings, why was that anyone else's concern but his?

One evening while Dan and his male co-clerk were walking back to their hotel following dinner in downtown San Francisco, a black stretch limousine pulled up alongside them and came to a stop. In a scene straight of Hollywood, a black-tinted window at the rear of the vehicle rolled down, revealing a half dozen or so somewhat inebriated, very attractive blondes and brunettes who informed the pair they were in the midst of a bachelorette party. "Come have some fun with us!" the women seductively beseeched them. The two young lawyers looked at each other, then back to the scantily clad women, unsure of what to do next. But then, Dan's expression suddenly became serious. "I have to get back to the hotel to work on my article," he told his co-clerk. "You go."

Which his co-clerk happily did—jumping into the back seat of the limo as if he were diving into the deep end of a pool on a scorching-hot day—as Dan continued walking back to the hotel. He wasn't about to let a night of unrestrained debauchery distract him from the important thinking and writing he'd planned for the evening. Though his co-clerk may have been wearing a much bigger smile the next morning—still pinching himself following a night he'd never forget—Dan Markel didn't have the slightest regret over how he'd chosen to spend his.

•••

THOUGH MANY LAWYERS harbor ambitions of becoming a law professor, the cold hard reality is that the shiny brass ring of legal academia is an impossible reach for all but a few. For starters, there are only about 200 accredited law schools in the country. In a typical year, those schools as a whole hire approximately 150 entry-level, "tenure-track" professors. Nearly 75% of those jobs are doled out to graduates of Harvard, Yale, and other top-ten institutions, meaning that graduates from lower-ranked schools—even pretty good ones—are left to compete for precious few spots.

Because the laws of supply and demand are so out of kilter, even bottom-tier law schools can attract graduates of Harvard and Yale to their faculties. Exceptionally well-qualified candidates end up empty-handed each and every year. With so few positions available and such a competitive environment, anyone seriously considering teaching law as a profession must be willing to relocate clear across the country—to places like Missoula, Montana, Carbondale, Illinois, or Tallahassee, Florida. Only the very top candidates can be selective enough to cross such locales off their list.

What separates the most attractive applicants from the rest of the pack? Experience as law review editors and as clerks for federal appellate judges—especially SCOTUS clerks. Employment at prestigious law firms or the U.S. Department of Justice is another good feather in a candidate's cap—just two to five years of actual practice typically the sweet spot. Aspiring professors who have already published an article or two in prestigious law reviews generally stand out from the crowd.

By the summer of 2003, Dan Markel checked each and every one of those boxes. Following his clerkship with Judge Hawkins, he'd moved to Washington, D.C. to become an associate attorney with Kellogg Huber, a well-respected litigation boutique chock full of Harvard Law grads just like him. He was the junior-most lawyer on several white-collar criminal cases and handled appeals in federal courts like the Ninth Circuit. All while earning a handsome, six-figure salary. Though he hadn't been a SCOTUS clerk, Dan was one of the more attractive candidates in the 2003 teaching market.

The recruiting process begins in earnest each August. Would-be professors complete a one-page resume of sorts on the website of the Association of American Law Schools (AALS). Those resumes are then compiled into a Faculty Appointments Register (FAR), which is provided to each law school's appointments committee. In years when the economy is strong and hiring robust, the FAR can contain as many as one thousand resumes. Appointments committee members pore over the FAR to segregate the wheat from the chaff, and to find the occasional diamond in the rough. And then call candidates to set up interviews.

The next step of the process is the one that years later

continues to send shivers down the spines of even those applicants who succeed—but especially those who fail. The Meat Market, which few call by its official name—the AALS Faculty Recruitment Conference—is a two-day event at the Marriott Wardman Park in Washington, D.C. that typically falls on either side of November 1. It is there that appointments committee representatives gather in hotel suites to meet with the slate of candidates they've decided to interview.

Dozens of interviews occur simultaneously throughout the sprawling, 1,152-room, two-building hotel complex, every 30 minutes like clockwork. Candidates literally crawl over one another in the lobby, elevators, and as they race through corridors to make their next interview—a hazing ritual nearly as brutal as those perpetrated by college fraternities. For those lucky enough to land 15 or more interviews, getting from one room to the next on time is challenging enough— remembering which school is which, and the names of the committee members, all the more daunting. The process is a diabolical mixture of chaos, terror, and endurance. Enough to fill to capacity both the hotel bar and nearby watering holes by dinner time.

By September 2003, Dan's phone at Kellogg Huber was ringing off the hook with law schools eager to schedule interviews—attracted by his stellar resume and scholarly potential. He had more than two dozen lined up—including with Florida State—more than just about any other candidate in attendance. Which made the odds of him not landing a quality teaching position very low. His only remorse heading into the meeting—conveniently taking place a short Metro ride from his apartment—was that his alma mater Harvard had passed on putting him on its schedule.

When the first day of the conference arrived, Dan's confidence level was off the charts, especially compared to the candidates against whom he was competing. Which is precisely why he struck out—failing to land a single offer. He'd entered each hotel suite trying to show off his scholarly acumen—coming across as arrogant and intimidating—not the type of colleague the professors interviewing him could envision in a nearby faculty office. His abysmal failure was a crushing blow, as Dan had arrived at the hotel certain he'd have a flurry of offers from which to choose—the thought of being completely shut out not even remotely on his radar.

As he retreated into a depressive funk, he couldn't escape the painful reality that the same faculty members who were so enamored of Dan Markel on paper were far less attracted to him as he sat in their midst—a harsh rejection of his personality. But he was undeterred, vowing to try again the following year. Hopefully having learned from his mistakes.

•••

NOT LONG AFTER his Meat Market debacle, Dan received news that perked him up considerably. The article on which he'd been laboring tirelessly since his clerkship, "Against Mercy," had been accepted by the *Minnesota Law Review* and was slated for publication in June 2004. "Perfect timing for the next Meat Market," he thought. Though he'd been knocked down hard, he was back on his feet, his confidence growing once again. Something else providing an extra spring in the young lawyer's step was the recent birth of his nephew in Toronto. Shelly and his brother-in-law Ian had graced their three-year-old daughter with a baby brother—and a second grandchild for Ruth and Phil.

His sister's growing family got Dan thinking about children of his own. Since his early twenties, he'd been involved in one monogamous relationship after another, a few even lasting a year or longer. Though they were each satisfying, for one reason or another, they'd fizzled out. With his busy law practice, the 31-year-old bachelor found it easier to meet members of the opposite sex online, posting his profile on JDate, the Jewish version of Match.com. Yet the women he'd connected with through the dating website hadn't been his cup of tea—or worthy of serious consideration to audition for the role of future mother to his children.

One day in July 2004—with a perfectly brewed cup of cappuccino in hand—Dan logged into JDate, ready to give dating another whirl. Though he had no reason to suspect it at the time, his entire world was about to change.

6.

Wendi Jill Adelson

HARVEY JEROME ADELSON and Donna Sue Jacobs exchanged wedding vows on June 3, 1971, a month shy of his 27th birthday, not long after her 21st. The groom had recently completed a dental residency in Brooklyn, the bride her bachelor's in education at Queens College. They were New Yorkers through and through, raised in working-class Jewish families. Once their honeymoon concluded, they embarked upon their new careers, Harvey as a licensed dentist and Donna as a kindergarten teacher. They were determined to do better in life than their own parents.

Before they became too entrenched in their jobs, however, the newlyweds realized the Big Apple wouldn't be an ideal place to raise children. They migrated south to North Miami Beach in 1972, ready to start a family of their own. Less than a year later, while Donna was pregnant, they resettled in Coral Springs—a small city of about 10,000 just west of Pompano Beach—lured there by its excellent public schools. Rob was born in July 1973, Charlie in October 1976, and Wendi, the baby, in April 1979. By the time Wendi graduated from high school, the population of Coral Springs would swell tenfold.

Though they were now living in the Deep South, Harvey and Donna—with their thick New "Yawk" accents—blended in seamlessly, Broward County home to nearly as many transplanted Yankees as native Floridians. Like many Jews of their vintage, they considered themselves Reform, rather than Conservative, rarely attending shul. When they did show up for services, it was more to keep up appearances than to actually pay tribute to God. Neither Shabbat dinners nor other Jewish customs or rituals were part of their everyday lives. For the Adelsons, being Jewish was an important cultural identity, rather than a religion or set of core beliefs.

Not long after Charlie's arrival, Harvey hung out his shingle in Tamarac, just south of Coral Springs. He would quickly grow the office into a thriving dental practice, the Adelson Institute, helping the family afford an upscale home in a quiet cul de sac less than three miles away. They moved into their spacious new digs just before Donna learned she was pregnant with Wendi. The sprawling, five-bedroom, 4,000-square-foot residence, nestled behind a handful of towering palms, marked quite the improvement from the cramped quarters Harvey and Donna had called home growing up in New York City.

The house sat on a half-acre lot, which included a built-in swimming pool just beyond the kitchen's patio doors. As the Adelson Institute flourished, Harvey had a clay tennis court installed alongside the pool, which served as the venue for many competitive matches among family members. Each of the kids would become excellent tennis players. Harvey eventually traded in the family's wood-paneled Chevy station wagon for a sporty, high-end Mercedes—the first of what would become a fleet of luxury vehicles, all of them black. Though he and Donna had arrived in South Florida with little more than their New York moxie, they were quite proud to show off the upper middle-class lifestyle they'd earned through grit and hard work.

Each of the parents had clearly defined roles within the family. Whereas Harvey was the economic provider, Donna—the matriarch—ran the Adelson household like a well-oiled machine. Harvey's comfort zone was on the passive end of the continuum, sometimes remaining on the periphery to avoid conflict. Donna's personality was more domineering, five of her words to every one of her husband's. Yet she could also be very warm and engaging, her bond with each of her children bone deep. She was fiercely protective of them—a quintessential mama bear. Anyone daring enough to utter an unkind word about one of her offspring, deserved or not, was certain to suffer her wrath.

Upon Rob's birth, Donna gave up her career as a schoolteacher, never returning to the field of education. Yet each of her kids received the benefit of her training and experience, learning their ABCs and 123s as they spoke their very first words. The doting mother ensured they received intellectual stimulation each and every day. By the time they began elementary school, Rob, Charlie, and Wendi were well ahead of their peers. The importance of academics was stressed relentlessly throughout their childhoods, straight As not merely a goal, but an expectation.

From an early age, Wendi played the role of family comedian, her wry and witty sense of humor on full display at the dinner table and larger family gatherings. She learned how to employ humor to adroitly defuse tense or uncomfortable situations, her jokes and witticisms providing well-timed comic relief. She relished making friends and family members smile and laugh, as if she were on stage performing a standup routine. It didn't hurt that the brunette youngster was stunningly attractive—with a megawatt smile—coupled with a magnetic personality that attracted friends in droves.

Wendi picked up her comedic timing from her Grandma Lorraine, the most important role model in her life. Donna's mom, a constant presence in all three kids' lives, would liberally sprinkle witty Yiddish aphorisms into everyday conversation. She and Wendi, the only girl in the litter, formed an incredibly close bond. Even after Lorraine's death in 1999—when Wendi was 20—the admiring granddaughter would often approach difficult situations asking herself, "What would Grandma do?"

Though they were six years apart, Wendi was extremely close with her brother Rob. He was a stellar student, modeling behavior his baby sister desperately wanted to emulate, if not surpass. But by August 1991, when Wendi was just 12, Rob was gone, off to Tulane University in New Orleans. Wendi was a wreck for weeks—shedding tears like Niagara Falls—Donna left to pick up the pieces and help her baby girl transition to life without her big brother. Rob would eventually graduate from Tulane *summa cum laude* and Phi Beta Kappa and then head off to medical school.

Meanwhile, apart from making As in all of her classes—which came effortlessly—Wendi developed an active social conscience, becoming a philanthropist of sorts when she was just 13. She recognized that she was far more fortunate than many kids in her community, with two loving parents who cared about her education and a happy, wholesome home to return to after school. There were underprivileged kids all around her, she realized, who didn't receive the same head start she had, with only nominal parental support to motivate them. She decided she could make a difference.

At the end of the eighth grade, Wendi founded a nonprofit she named Starting Blocks. With the $200 she'd saved in her piggy bank, she purchased stationery and stamps, writing letters to local toy companies and bookstores soliciting donations. "Access to educational materials and a healthy learning environment is a right, not a privilege," she wrote, her call to action. With her mom's help, she recruited a board of directors that included members of the state legislature and other local power brokers. Her pitch was wildly successful. Toy companies, including the local Toys R Us, donated books, art supplies, and instructional videos that Wendi would bag up and deliver to underfunded daycare facilities—as if she were Santa Claus descending down the chimney on Christmas Eve.

Wendi wasn't satisfied merely dropping off the books and supplies. The teenager spent quality time at the daycare centers, helping Black and Brown children experience the joy of learning. She committed at least seven hours a week to Starting Blocks during all four years of high school, ultimately collecting more than $16,000 worth of supplies and distributing them to nearly 2,000 underprivileged children. All while accumulating a 5.34 GPA, doing some professional modeling, and becoming an accomplished pianist.

Not only did Wendi serve as valedictorian of the 1997 graduating class at J.P. Taravella High—one of two public high schools in Coral Springs—she snagged a fistful of awards and scholarships. One was the prestigious Silver Knight Award presented by the *Miami Herald*, bestowed on a select few Miami-Dade and Broward County seniors for selfless community service, academic prowess, and overall achievement. The awards were presented at an evening gala replete with glitz and glamour rivaling the Academy Awards, attended by more than 2,000 students, family, and friends.

As Wendi waltzed across the stage in her elegant ivory gown to receive her eight-inch statue—her bright smile on full display—Donna and Harvey applauded vigorously, bursting with pride.

It was of little surprise that her high school classmates voted Wendi "most likely to succeed." But what was a surprise was what Donna Adelson considered her daughter's greatest achievement as she crossed the graduation stage to accept her diploma. As Wendi told her friends—without the slightest reluctance or embarrassment—what filled her mom with pride the most was that she completed high school while still maintaining her virginity.

•••

IN AUGUST 1997, Harvey and Donna drove their baby girl some 1,500 miles up the East Coast to her new home at Brandeis University in Waltham, Massachusetts, just a few miles west of Boston. Named for the first Jewish Supreme Court Justice, Louis Brandeis, the highly regarded liberal arts college—just 3,000 students in all—was a haven for Jews, who at the time comprised a majority of its student population. Students arrived on campus from all across the country and around the world. Because so many of them kept kosher, the main dining hall included a separate serving line fully adhering to kosher requirements, in which meat and dairy were served on alternating days—and pork and shellfish never at all.

As she began her freshman year, Wendi felt certain she'd be following in her big brother Rob's footsteps, destined for medical school and a career as a pediatrician—dedicating her life to the welfare of children. She excelled academically from the start. Her dedication to community service continued unabated, working with a local Big Siblings program to quadruple the number of at-risk youth who had "big brothers" or "big sisters."

By her sophomore year, Wendi had become proficient in Spanish and was searching for an opportunity to combine her language skills with a desire to work with underprivileged kids. Which is what landed her in Argentina the summer before her junior year, with a fellowship to defray her expenses. While her classmates were being wined and dined at cushy summer jobs in New York, Chicago, and L.A., Wendi was in Buenos Aires helping families search for loved ones who'd vanished during Argentina's so-called "Dirty War" of the 1970s. She spent the summer interviewing family members—entirely in Spanish—helping map out which relatives had disappeared and what might have happened to them.

She also had the good fortune of meeting a Gandhi-like figure named Adolfo Pérez Esquivel, a well-known Argentinian human rights activist, champion of nonviolence, and artist, who'd been awarded the Nobel Peace Prize the year after Mother Teresa. He became Wendi's trusted and cherished mentor. Twice a week, the two would drive two hours each way to a peace and justice service camp for abused and neglected children, helping teach campers about computers and offering life lessons. Wendi also tagged along with Esquivel when he traveled the countryside to give talks on non-violence. His influence on the 20-year-old college student was profound, helping convince her that she wanted to become a foot soldier for social change—just like him.

Their relationship led to another epiphany: that knowledge

of the law would be crucial to her ability to effect change. Thus, by her junior year, Wendi was no longer focused on attending medical school, her sights now set on law school instead. She changed her major to peace-and-conflict studies and began organizing events for the Brandeis International Center for Ethics, helping bring human rights activists just like her mentor to the Waltham campus.

It was about that time that the entire Adelson family had a frightening health scare. Harvey, who by then was 55, had been having headaches for months, which were increasingly interfering with his ability to work. When he was finally persuaded to undergo tests, an MRI revealed the existence of a healthy-sized brain tumor. Initially, his doctors didn't know whether the mass was cancerous and couldn't predict whether any damage would result from its removal. It was a scary time for the entire family. As fate would have it, the tumor turned out to be benign, Harvey's brain surgery a complete success— much to the relief of his wife and children.

During her junior year, Wendi applied for a Harry S. Truman Scholarship, an accolade nearly as prestigious as a Rhodes Scholarship. Among the criteria for the award are demonstrated leadership potential, academic excellence, service on campus and in the community, and a commitment to a career in public service. Competition for the scholarship— and the $30,000 it funds toward a recipient's graduate studies— is fierce, with only a single student from each state typically selected.

Adding to her already lengthy list of accomplishments, Wendi was the lone Floridian awarded a Truman Scholarship in 2000—and only the second Brandeis student in school history to earn one. She went right to work proving the wisdom of her benefactors' decision, thrusting herself into public service once again that summer—this time interning with the Children's Defense Fund in Washington, D.C. In her "spare time," she volunteered as a conflict resolution teacher at a girls' juvenile detention center.

Upon her return to the Boston suburbs for her senior

year, Wendi put her hat in the ring for a "junior fellowship" with the Carnegie Endowment for International Peace — and was selected as Brandeis University's sole nominee. The nonpartisan international affairs think tank — started by philanthropist Andrew Carnegie in 1910 — is headquartered in the nation's capital in a building prominently situated alongside foreign embassies. Satellite offices are located in Moscow, Beirut, Beijing, Brussels, and New Delhi. Carnegie's mission is to advance peace and international cooperation through development of policy ideas and is widely regarded as one of the world's most influential think tanks.

Junior fellows, typically recent college graduates, are assigned to work as research assistants to Carnegie's senior scholars during their one-year fellowship. Former fellows include a United States Senator, an ambassador to the United Nations, and George Stephanopoulos to name just a few. Continuing her amazing streak, Wendi was one of ten nominees Carnegie selected from among hundreds of universities nationwide. Her most notable achievement yet.

Shortly after graduating from Brandeis in May 2001 — *magna cum laude* and Phi Beta Kappa — Wendi returned to Washington, D.C. to begin her fellowship, where she worked closely with a senior scholar on immigration issues. While there, she garnered yet another scholarship — funded by the Bill and Melinda Gates Foundation — this one providing for a full ride for the master's in philosophy program at the University of Cambridge. When her year with the Carnegie Endowment concluded, she flew off to England to begin her graduate studies, where she focused on international relations, including the thorny immigration issues facing the U.K.

For Wendi, her Carnegie fellowship and graduate studies in England were life-altering experiences. She felt an unmistakable calling to help those striving to become Americans work their way through the Byzantine maze of the U.S. immigration system. Though she already had five years of college and graduate school under her belt, the former high school valedictorian was destined for three more — law school.

•••

GROWING UP IN CORAL SPRINGS, one of the few guilty pleasures Wendi allowed herself to indulge in was watching TV game shows. Donna had actually been a contestant on *Wheel of Fortune* and was a game show junkie herself. From as early as she could remember, Wendi would hunker down with her mom in front of the TV to catch any number of shows, trying to answer the questions faster, and with greater accuracy, than the actual contestants. When the opportunity arose during high school to participate in *Encyclopedia Britannica's Battle of the Brains*, Wendi jumped at it, proudly representing Taravella High in the nerdy competition.

One of the hottest game shows during the early 2000s was *The Weakest Link*, which originated in England and later swept through world TV markets like a tsunami. On the show, contestants answer trivia questions similar to those featured in Trivial Pursuit; dollar values escalate with each correct answer. Rather than having contestants buzz in when they know an answer, the host—a master of putdowns dressed in black—poses questions directly to each on a rotating basis. The more consecutive questions the group answers correctly, the more money can be "banked." During the show's primetime version, the final pot could exceed $100,000.

What makes the game show unique—and most entertaining for viewers—is that contestants vote each other off following every round, the contestant cast aside dubbed that round's "weakest link." When only two contestants remain, they compete against one another in the final round by answering three questions. Whoever answers the most correctly is crowned the "strongest link" and takes home the entire pot.

On a lark, as she neared the end of her fellowship with the Carnegie Endowment, Wendi entered a contestant search for *The Weakest Link* in Washington, D.C. A few days later, she received a call informing her that she'd earned a spot on the syndicated, daytime version of the show—with significantly less money at stake—and needed to board a plane to L.A. to film her episode.

During contestant introductions on the colorful set, Wendi explained that she was working for the Carnegie Endowment, a global think tank, prompting the host to ask, "Wendi, have you always wanted to work for a think tank? Is that what you want to do with your life?"

"No, it definitely isn't," Wendi replied.

"What have you always wanted to do?" the host followed up.

"When I was little, I wanted to be a giraffe," Wendi giggled, flashing her infectious smile, evoking laughter from the studio audience. She told the host that she'd also been a contortionist in the circus.

Not only did the camera and studio audience fall in love with the Brandeis grad, so did her fellow competitors, who refused to vote her off. Wendi's delightfully irreverent personality was on full display throughout the 30-minute episode, which aired nationwide in December 2002. She claimed victory by correctly identifying the number of articles—13—in the Articles of Confederation adopted by the new American government in 1777. Though she only pocketed $2,000, that money came in handy, funding a getaway to Kosovo and Macedonia as Wendi was wrapping up her graduate studies in England the following spring.

•••

AS A TEENAGER, Charlie Adelson was so scrawny, classmates nicknamed him Screech, after the lanky, stick-figured character on the TV sitcom *Saved by the Bell*. Though he didn't possess nearly the same academic interest or acumen as his siblings, he did wield considerable athletic talent, becoming a phenom on the tennis courts at Taravella High and throughout South Florida.

Charlie attended college much closer to home than his siblings—at the University of Central Florida (UCF) in Orlando. Though he didn't graduate *magna cum laude* or Phi Beta

Kappa, he did finish in the top 15% of his class, even named to the President's Honor Roll for achieving straight As two consecutive semesters. Which was no small feat considering he majored in micro and molecular biology.

The most notable change that occurred while Charlie was away at college was to his physical appearance. By the time he graduated in 1999, the 22-year-old had added some 50 pounds of pure muscle through a gym regimen that often had him pumping iron hours per day. His body now ripped, he attracted members of the opposite sex in droves, his sexual appetite growing nearly as rapidly as his physique. Charlie's tough-guy image was further enhanced by his penchant for guns. He'd ultimately own an impressive collection, keeping one beneath the driver's seat of his car and another by his bedside.

His goal all along was to become a dentist and work alongside his father at the Adelson Institute. Serendipitously, while Charlie was in college, Nova Southeastern University (NSU) in Fort Lauderdale—just 15 miles from Coral Springs— opened the first new dental school in the United States in nearly 25 years. His dental education at NSU was apparently a rough ride, however, as rumors abounded that Charlie was being passed through his courses at Harvey's urging, rather than by successfully completing the required work.

Whether or not the rumors were true, the Florida Board of Dentistry granted Charlie a dental license in July 2003 and he began working with his dad. By then, his mom had also become a fixture at the Adelson Institute. Though she was given the title "patient coordinator," in reality, Donna had her hands in just about every facet of the practice—the lone exception being patients' mouths.

After a three-year surgical residency, Charlie became a specialist in periodontics—extractions, implants, and bone grafts. The renamed Adelson Institute for Esthetics and Implant Dentistry was now able to earn income from those additional services beyond general dentistry. And because oral surgeries are high-dollar procedures, both Charlie and the practice were able to make gobs of money. In 2012, Harvey happily cashed in his chips, his periodontist son becoming owner of the practice—and his boss.

Raking in huge sums of cash only fueled Charlie's desire to make even more. He formed a referral network with dozens of dentists throughout South Florida, who invited him to perform extractions and implants at their offices. Because of his extensive travel, it wasn't unusual for the UCF grad to put in 16-hour days—large chunks of them in his car. To make that experience more pleasurable, Charlie began acquiring luxury vehicles, both hand-me-downs from his dad as well as flashy sports cars purchased from dealers. His favorites? A Mercedes CL550 and a Ferrari, the latter with the word MAESTRO emblazoned across its vanity plate—a far more fitting moniker for the adult iteration of Charlie Adelson than Screech.

By his mid-30s, Charlie decided to flex his entrepreneurial muscle even further, purchasing apartment complexes and a New York-style Jewish deli. Despite his grueling work schedule, he remained fanatical about adhering to his gym regimen. But he also relied on anabolic steroids to ensure his chiseled frame didn't droop as he aged. Photos of his shirtless body routinely found their way onto Instagram.

Between his appearance, bank account, and top-of-the line vehicles, the Maestro had little difficulty attracting women, gliding through life as a playboy bachelor. Though he had his share of girlfriends, that didn't stop Charlie from simultaneously playing the field—finding little virtue in monogamy or fidelity. He didn't have the slightest inclination to ever settle down, the prospect of having a family of his own as far-fetched as skiing down a snow-covered mountain in South Florida.

He even joked with his mom, "If you want to set me up with a Victoria Secret model that's 37 with two kids, you already know what I'd tell you. Thank you, but no thank you." Sans the kids, Charlie Adelson had no reservations about having a voluptuous blonde, brunette, or redhead on his arm—or in his bedroom.

• • •

ROB ADELSON'S LIFE'S JOURNEY couldn't have contrasted more sharply with his kid brother's. He was focused, disciplined, and driven, honest almost to a fault. At a tennis tournament the entire family attended when he was a teenager, Rob realized that he'd been handed too much change after ordering a snack and told his parents he was going back to return the extra money. They were mortified, pressuring him to explain why he'd do that if someone else—not he—had made the mistake. Undeterred, Rob returned the money, fully aware he was doing the right thing. From that day forward, his parents and brother would needle him incessantly about the incident, bestowing on him what they considered a fitting— and derogatory—nickname: "Honest Abe."

Not only did Honest Abe graduate in the top 10% of his medical school class at the University of South Florida, he was selected by his classmates to deliver the student address at their commencement ceremony. He then set off for Parkland Hospital in Dallas for a residency in otorhinolaryngology— ear, nose, and throat medicine—where he fell in love with an attractive emergency medicine resident from Chicago named Haritha Challapalli. Which should have been joyful news to his entire family. But wasn't.

When Rob informed Donna and Harvey he was dating an Indian woman—who was Hindu, not Jewish—his parents didn't even attempt to feign happiness, disapproving of their relationship from its inception. Though they may not have been observant Jews themselves, they couldn't stomach the thought of one of their children being romantically involved with a gentile—a *shicksa*. Rob suffered through his mother's angry tirades on the telephone, neither she nor Harvey yielding an inch as his relationship with the Indian-American continued.

About nine months into their romance, however, Rob finally broke down, telling Haritha that his parents were making him choose between them and her. Faced with that Hobson's choice, he begrudgingly chose his mom and dad, pulling the plug on the most amazing relationship of his entire life.

The breakup was incredibly painful, Rob regretting his decision almost immediately. He asked Haritha to take him back—and she did. But that only drew Donna and Harvey's ire all over again. They escalated their pressure, telling their firstborn he'd be disowned forever if he didn't end the relationship for good. The pattern of Rob and Haritha breaking up and then reuniting repeated itself several times, Donna and Harvey's poisonous interference never allowing the relationship to truly take flight.

Worn down, defeated, and heartbroken, Rob eventually surrendered to his parents' demands—breaking up with Haritha once and for all. Before long, he was engaged to a nice Jewish girl from Dallas named Debbie. His folks were elated they'd not only won the battle over the Indian-American *shicksa*, but that their son was now poised to supply them with white-skinned, Jewish grandchildren.

Yet within a few days of saying "I do," Rob was telling himself—and his new bride—"I can't." He realized he'd deluded himself into believing he could ever love any woman other than Haritha and that his marriage to Debbie was nothing but a sham intended to please his folks. Their union was annulled in just a few months. The entire series of events was the most gut-wrenching, tumultuous period of Rob's entire life.

Somehow, though, the aspiring ENT doctor was able to pivot from all the carnage and resume his romance with Haritha as if there had only been a minor bump in the road—this time, demanding that his parents accept their relationship. The newly reunited lovebirds were reciting their own wedding vows a mere ten months after Rob's failed union with Debbie formally ended.

The wedding at Chicago's Palmer House Hilton was bifurcated between traditional Hindu and Jewish ceremonies. During the Hindu portion, everyone—including Donna, Charlie, and Wendi—donned traditional Indian attire.

Following a wardrobe change, the festivities continued under a Jewish *chuppah*, concluding with Rob crushing a glass under his right foot to congratulatory shouts of *mazal tov*. During the joyous dancing that followed, Haritha's family members participated exuberantly in the Hava Nagila, hoisting the bride and groom high in the air. It was quite a night for everyone, helping heal some of the wounds borne of Donna and Harvey's relentless meddling.

Though Rob and Haritha briefly relocated to Miami for his fellowship in plastic and reconstructive surgery, they ultimately decided to settle some 1,400 miles from his childhood home — in Albany, New York — where the successful physicians would raise two mixed-race, gentile children. And live a very happy life together.

•••

THOUGH SHE'D LIVED FAR AWAY from home for six years, much to her parents' delight, Wendi decided to return to South Florida for law school, earning a full-tuition scholarship from the University of Miami (UM) over and above her $30,000 Truman Scholarship.

By the end of her first semester, however, Wendi was feeling somewhat lost. That is, until she discovered the law school's Center for Ethics and Public Service, a clinical program providing legal assistance to disadvantaged members of the local community. The very type of work she'd been doing since her teenage years. By her second semester, Wendi was interning at the Center, assisting 2Ls and 3Ls as they represented clients with a wide range of medical and legal issues. She translated for Spanish-speaking clients, helped navigate the public health system for recent immigrants afflicted with HIV, and even helped secure asylum for an Iraqi imam.

To no one's surprise, Wendi excelled academically, helping her secure an internship with a federal trial judge in Miami, Judge Patricia Seitz, the summer between her 1L and 2L years. Without the demands of classes and homework, she was able to spend most weekends in Coral Springs, sleeping in the same bed she had as a teenager. At her mom's urging, Wendi signed up for JDate, Donna insistent that the time had come for her 25-year-old daughter to identify her "Mr. Right." The search became as much a mission for Donna as for Wendi.

One Saturday afternoon that July, Wendi was scrolling through eligible bachelors on the dating website while seated at her computer, her mom standing behind her, peering over her shoulder with interest and enthusiasm. Of the dozens of men from South Florida who popped up on the screen close to Wendi's age, not a single one met all of her—or her mom's—exacting criteria. Since Wendi planned to begin her career as an immigration lawyer in Washington, D.C., she expanded her search to include men in her age range residing in or near the nation's capital, clicking through one underwhelming profile after another.

When Wendi was about ready to give up, Donna suddenly shouted, "Stop!" pointing to a profile on the screen. Staring back at the mother-daughter tandem was an image of a handsome, 31-year-old Harvard-educated lawyer—a bespectacled Canadian with an engaging smile. His profile satisfied all of their criteria—and then some. "Wendi!" her mom squealed with excitement. "I think we've found your Mr. Right."

7.

Till Death Do Us Part

SIPPING FROM HIS CUP OF CAPPUCCINO, Dan navigated to his JDate inbox hoping someone new and interesting had knocked on his electronic door. Sure enough, a woman named Wendi had left a message, indicating she liked his profile. Which naturally made him curious about hers.

Three things instantly jumped off the screen as he glimpsed Wendi Adelson's face for the very first time. First, she was drop-dead gorgeous, with penetrating, turquoise-blue eyes and a killer smile. Second, she was young—barely 25—more than six years his junior. Third, and perhaps most significant, she lived in Miami, over a thousand miles away. They wouldn't be getting together for a cup of java anytime soon. Then again, there was that drop-dead gorgeous part. Certainly worth further exploration.

As they got to know each other online, Dan and Wendi marveled over how much they had in common. Though they'd grown up a whopping 2,350 miles apart—in different countries no less—they'd attended colleges within ten miles of one another, both graduating *magna cum laude* from elite Boston-area schools. Wendi was actually at Brandeis the very same years Dan had his second stint at Harvard. Her decision to attend the Jewish-centered university held significant appeal for Dan, signaling to him that Judaism was ingrained in her identity, just like in his.

Their paths following college were virtually identical as well, each having participated in transformative one-year fellowships—Dan at Hebrew University and Wendi at the Carnegie Endowment. And they had both pursued master's studies at the University of Cambridge and then law school. Wendi had even lived in D.C. during her fellowship, just before Dan arrived to begin working at Kellogg Huber. And she was now mirroring Dan's judicial clerkship through her internship with Judge Seitz. At least on paper, the two appeared tailor-made for each other.

They arranged to meet in September, while Wendi was in Washington interviewing for a summer clerkship. Though their first date didn't quite live up to either's lofty expectations, before long, the lawyer from Toronto and law student from Coral Springs were in the midst of an exhilarating, long-distance romance. Dan felt a magnetic, physical attraction to his new girlfriend. But fell in love with Wendi more because of her intellect, wit, and zany sense of humor. He thoroughly admired her passion to help the less fortunate and to commit her life to public service. And concluded rather quickly that Wendi was most worthy of an audition to be the future mother of his children.

Similarly, Wendi felt an unmistakable, physical connection with her new boyfriend. He too had a zany, playful side she enjoyed, coming up with quirky nicknames for virtually everyone and everything. Dan would spice up a friend's birthday by referring to it as a "bam bizzle." Because he was so impressed with Wendi's ability to speak Spanish, she became his *Osita*, or baby bear.

Wendi concluded early on, from his vast network of friends, that Dan had a big, caring heart. He also was far more worldly than any man she'd ever dated; between the two, they'd already set foot on four continents and traveled to nearly 20 countries.

And then there was Dan's utter brilliance. Wendi couldn't help but admire how passionate he was about abstract ideas and how deeply he'd thought them through. Dan checked every box on her "can I envision him as my children's father?" list.

They initially agreed to split their weekends between Miami and D.C.—to share equally in the cost and burden of their long-distance relationship. Over time, though, Wendi ended up in Washington far more often than Dan traveled to The Magic City. Which was just fine with Wendi, as it gave her a chance to reconnect with friends she'd made in the nation's capital. At her request, her boyfriend evened out the imbalance in expenses through donations to her favorite charities in Argentina.

Since beginning his job with Kellogg Huber, Dan had lived alone in a one-bedroom bachelor pad in Dupont Circle, a ten-minute walk to his office. Able to control all food being stocked and consumed at his apartment, he decided to keep a kosher home, which had been on his bucket list for years. Thus, during her weekends with Dan in D.C., Wendi also kept kosher—and participated in Shabbat dinners—with different friends joining them each week. On occasion, they even attended shul together. Though incorporating Jewish customs into her life was an adjustment, it was one Wendi was perfectly willing to make for her new guy.

Dan's first visit to Coral Springs was a smashing success. He greeted Donna and Harvey with outstretched arms and affectionate embraces, as if they were close friends he hadn't seen in years. Wendi's folks found Dan a perfect match for their daughter—Jewish, handsome, wildly successful at a relatively young age, and highly ambitious. Everything Donna had hoped for when she pointed him out to Wendi on JDate. For her part, Wendi made a similar impression on Dan's family in Toronto, who found her beautiful, warm, and engaging—and from good Jewish stock to boot.

During their time in Canada, Wendi was able to glimpse a preview of what her boyfriend might be like as a father—thoroughly impressed with what she observed. Dan couldn't get enough of his niece and nephew, his eyes lighting up as he played with them on the floor. Wendi was struck by his range—writing scholarly articles one day, playing peek-a-boo with a one-year-old the next. She was pretty well convinced that Dan Markel was the complete package.

•••

DURING THEIR EARLY DAYS communicating online, Dan filled Wendi in on his quest to become a law professor, explaining the intricacies of the recruitment process and confessing that he'd bombed miserably in 2003. But he was ready to give it another whirl, he told her, when the Meat Market returned to D.C. that November. He shared with Wendi the list of more than 20 schools with whom he'd be interviewing, virtually the entire U.S. geography in play. Which held the prospect of bringing them closer together—or pushing them even further apart.

Dan's Meat Market 2.0 turned into an eerily familiar, harried adventure through the elevators and corridors of the Marriott Wardman Park. Yet with a very different outcome. This time around, when he entered the different law schools' hotel suites, the professors seated around him were bowled over by his energy, hunger, and intellectual bandwidth. He was engaging—almost charming—showing off his ability to connect as a human as much as his brilliance. With only modest adjustments in his approach, the aspiring professor had come across as passionate and ambitious—equally as impressive in person as on paper.

Which led to numerous invitations for on-campus, callback interviews. Topping that list was UC Berkeley—the nation's tenth ranked law school according to *U.S. News & World Report*—a dream job Dan believed was a perfect match for his skill set and ambition. Further down on his list of callbacks was Florida State—number 67 in that year's rankings—a school and faculty Dan considered mediocre at best. Not exactly where he hoped his teaching career would begin.

•••

NOT ONLY WERE DAN'S career aspirations taking a promising turn, his love affair with his *Osita* couldn't have been going much better. The more he and Wendi were together, the more they craved additional time together—which made it a high priority to remove the "long-distance" modifier from their romance. With Wendi still a 2L at UM Law—determined to become an immigration lawyer—she and Dan began discussing the concept of her completing her legal education wherever he landed a teaching job. That way, they could finally be together and get a sense of whether their relationship could withstand life under a single roof, seven days a week.

To Dan's deep disappointment, UC Berkeley didn't extend him an offer. As it turned out, his most attractive offer came from Florida State, whose faculty saw tremendous potential in the two-time Harvard grad. If Dan wanted to avoid another year's wait and a Meat Market 3.0, a move to Tallahassee was his most logical step forward. He swallowed his pride, yet again, and accepted Florida State's invitation for a site visit, so he and Wendi could explore Tally's cultural scene, synagogues, schools, and check out housing options.

At the time, neither knew much about the Sunshine State's capital city. What they learned during their visit gave them both pause. Tally was nothing like Boston, Phoenix, D.C., or Miami—places they'd lived as adults. Unlike each of those bustling cities and cultural meccas, Tally was quite small, with a miniscule Jewish population—just over 4,000 Jews among its 150,000 residents. Its cultural scene and public school system were marginal at best. Worse still, the Florida State campus was surrounded by dilapidated, crime-ridden neighborhoods that were most unsafe after dark.

And though it was geographically situated in Florida, Tally had far more in common with Georgia and Alabama—both a short drive away—than with South Florida. Locals they met spoke with a distinct southern drawl, and ever so slowly. For Wendi, the continuity of remaining in her home state held precious little appeal knowing she'd be seven hours from her family in an unfamiliar place where she didn't know a soul.

She wasn't at all convinced Florida State was a good fit for Dan—or Tally a place she had any interest in living.

Yet Dan felt certain he'd succeed in climbing the academic ladder in short order, with Florida State likely a launching pad for the rest of his career, one he hoped would lead him all the way back to Harvard. Or at the very least, a city more like New York or D.C. He convinced Wendi that—if in fact they were embarking on a life together—Tally would merely be a brief stepping stone in their path. Thus, for the sake of his career, Wendi reluctantly agreed to move to a place she knew from the outset she'd want to escape as quickly as humanly possible.

•••

DAN FOUND IT UTTERLY AMAZING that his well-traveled, Brandeis-educated girlfriend had never been to the Jewish Holy Land. He raved to her incessantly about his prior travels there, as excited talking about Israel as the topic of criminal punishment. With their relationship now taking a serious turn, he insisted that Wendi join him on their first overseas adventure together so he could show her the sights and introduce her to his extended family and friends in Israel. They jetted off in May 2005, just after Wendi completed her second year of law school—together for ten solid days—visiting with as many of Dan's cousins and friends they could squeeze into their crowded schedule.

Though he'd shared with Wendi their extensive itinerary long before their departure, Dan deliberately left out a surprise he'd been planning for weeks. On their fourth full day in Israel, he told her they were embarking on a hike—without offering details about where they were heading. They ended up in the Golan Heights, in a tiny Israeli settlement nestled against the banks of the Jordan River named Had Nes. When they reached the exact spot Dan considered their destination, he instructed Wendi to turn around. When she did, a breathtaking, panoramic vista of the turquoise-blue Sea of Galilee came into full view.

Before she could even get her bearings, Dan dropped

to a knee, whipping out a sparkling, two-karat diamond engagement ring. The ring had been worn by his Great Aunt Rachel to her dying day in 2003. His Great Uncle Lazar was thrilled Dan wanted to slip it onto Wendi's finger when he popped the question. Flashing a radiant smile, Wendi exuberantly shouted, "Yes! I will marry you." Less than eight months after their first date, Dan Markel and Wendi Adelson were engaged.

"Wow, did I win the lottery of life," Dan wrote his friends to share the news, which spread like wildfire all across the world. The couple's friends and family members were elated. But upon their return to the United States, everything quickly fell apart.

Wendi was spending the summer in D.C.—clerking for a big law firm—in order to be with Dan as much as possible before moving to Tally to begin their new life together. One evening, she introduced him to a law student friend. The discussion between the two men eventually meandered to the subject of affirmative action. For some reason, the soon-to-be professor began posing hypotheticals as if he were actually teaching a law school class, trying to point out the flaws in her friend's position. Wendi looked on helplessly—mortified—as her fiancé ripped her friend's analysis to shreds, seemingly unable to control himself.

Though she'd occasionally witnessed Dan making social blunders, Wendi had never seen him behave so rudely. She felt humiliated and embarrassed—apologizing to her friend profusely for Dan's behavior. Wendi was furious, suddenly doubting whether she could love a man capable of treating someone the way Dan had treated her friend. And who could be so oblivious to how that would make her feel. She told Dan she needed a few days apart and shared with friends that she was seriously considering nixing the wedding.

But just as Dan didn't give up on his teaching aspirations despite his initial setback, he refused to accept the demise of his relationship with his *Osita*. He spent the remainder of the summer trying to make amends for what he'd done. Slowly but surely, his charm offensive wore her down. Wendi finally forgave him. Their plans to start a life together in Tallahassee were back on track. As was the wedding.

•••

BY AUGUST 2005, Dan was teaching bright-eyed 1Ls in a cavernous lecture hall while Wendi sat amongst 2Ls and 3Ls in classes taught by his Florida State colleagues. Though she felt isolated at times, she did her level best to put on a happy face, taking spin classes at a nearby gym, making new friends, interning for a justice on the Florida Supreme Court, and immersing herself in the local community.

To help make her feel more at home, Dan came up with goofy nicknames for their adopted hometown—the 'Hassee, Funky T-Town, and Sweet Sassy Tallahassee—which he liberally tossed into everyday conversation. He put out feelers at more prestigious law schools in more cosmopolitan—and Jewish-oriented—cities, expressing interest in a lateral move. He approached UM in Miami about a possible move there, even though its law school wasn't more highly regarded than Florida State's. At that point in his life, Dan would have done just about anything to make his *Osita* happy, including moving to South Florida to teach at another mediocre law school, so Wendi could be near her family.

Meanwhile, back in Coral Springs, Donna was working feverishly, meticulously planning her daughter's wedding. At Dan's request, he and his bride would be reciting their vows beneath the *chuppah* at a Conservative synagogue in nearby Boca Raton. Wendi tapped eight of her high school and college friends to serve as bridesmaids. As for groomsmen, Dan found himself in quite the quandary, fearing he'd need to ask 80 of his friends to play the role so as not to offend any. But since that wasn't very practical, he filled out the ensemble with relatives instead.

Though Donna was planning the wedding, Dan had one request he considered of paramount importance—that the menu be strictly kosher. Many of his friends and family members who'd be attending kept kosher, including his rabbi friends Shaul Robinson and Hirschy Zarchi. Not only would they be unable to eat unless the entire menu was kosher, Dan believed the solemnity of the occasion required that all in attendance follow the sacred Jewish custom.

Wendi's folks, however, were dead set against a kosher wedding. Not a single member of their family kept kosher. They considered their future son-in-law's request selfish. For several weeks, the simmering issue remained unresolved. Until Donna finally relented, telling Dan that his happiness was more important than the food their guests would be served. Which was music to his ears.

•••

LONG BEFORE THERE was Facebook, there was Friendster. Like its behemoth, publicly traded successor, Friendster allowed friends and family members disconnected by geography to remain connected in cyberspace. Not surprisingly, Dan was an early adopter and frequent user, the cutting-edge social media platform helping him keep current on the lives of dozens of friends and relatives scattered across the globe. He and Wendi would often sit together scrolling through his feed, allowing her to put the names of his friends together with their faces.

In September 2005, the couple was at a hotel near Central Park attending the wedding of one of Dan's college friends. While he was at the bar fetching drinks, Wendi recognized a face she felt certain she'd seen on Dan's Friendster page. She walked up to the man, Zach Shrier, and introduced herself, telling him she was pretty sure he'd been friends with her fiancé at Harvard. When Dan returned with their beverages, Shrier was regaling Wendi in one "Dan story" after another, with her laughing hysterically over her soon-to-be husband's college exploits.

As the three talked further, it became painfully obvious that Shrier was at the wedding alone—a handsome, successful

Jewish guy who'd flown all the way from L.A. to attend a New York wedding stag. Though he was in the market for a good catch, Shrier told them, he just hadn't found the right girl yet. "I know exactly who to fix you up with," Dan told him as he scrolled through his mental rolodex. "Just leave everything to me."

Earlier that summer, before he and his fiancée moved to Tally, Wendi had introduced Dan to a friend of hers named Abigail Krauser, a Jewish woman who'd just graduated from Yale Law School and had moved to D.C. for a judicial clerkship. She and Dan hit it off instantly, with Dan insisting that she join him and Wendi for Shabbat dinners at his Dupont Circle apartment. He found Krauser highly intelligent and extremely attractive—a perfect match for Zach Shrier.

Though most people may have viewed the 2,669 miles between Los Angeles and Washington an impediment to a possible romance, Dan considered himself living proof that long-distance relationships had a bad rap. He spent the next several weeks badgering Shrier relentlessly until he finally agreed—if only to get his friend off his case—to board a plane, fly across the continent, and take Krauser out on a date. Just over 18 months later, Dan and Wendi were in attendance as the pair became husband and wife. One of two marriages the Great Connector would ultimately take credit for.

•••

DAN AND WENDI'S OWN WEDDING day finally arrived on February 26, 2006. The bride was ravishing in her strapless, ivory gown, the groom dashing in his ebony tux. Shelly—five months pregnant with her third child—looked on with pride as her brother and almost sister-in-law paced through their steps during the brief rehearsal before nearly 200 guests began arriving at the synagogue.

Per Dan's request, the ceremony was being officiated by Rabbi Robinson, his old Cambridge friend, who months earlier had become the senior rabbi of an Orthodox shul in New

York. When Robinson walked into the synagogue's kitchen that afternoon to check in with the kosher supervisor, he was startled not to find one. The catering staff informed him that a last-minute change in the menu had been requested by the bride's family, and that the food being served wouldn't be kosher after all.

Rabbi Robinson was horrified and dismayed, now in a quandary about what to do. Though he wasn't going to leave Dan in a lurch without an officiant, he also couldn't be around non-kosher food. He decided to keep what he learned close to the vest until after the ceremony, wanting Dan to experience a feeling of pure joy—not anger or betrayal—while standing beneath the *chuppah* with his beautiful bride.

But just before the ceremony began, the caterers wheeled out a food display that included chopped liver and cheese, which Dan spied in his peripheral vision. "What's going on?" he asked, bewildered—the blood beginning to drain from his face—instantly recognizing that the combination of foods on display was anything but kosher.

"Don't worry about it Dan," Rabbi Robinson reassured him. "It's a mistake." He did his level best to calm the groom down as the guests took their seats. Still confused and rattled, Dan forced a smile and powered through the service as best he could. The proceedings ended in traditional Jewish fashion, with joyous shouts of *mazel tov!* as a glass shattered beneath the crushing force of his right foot.

As the large crowd dispersed to the ballroom for the reception, Rabbi Robinson pulled Dan aside into a separate room to talk, letting him know he wouldn't be staying for dinner. "The food's not kosher, is it?" Dan asked, now realizing the chopped liver and cheese weren't a mistake after all. He apologized profusely to his dear friend, devastated that he'd flown in from New York under false pretenses. And now wouldn't be there for dinner and dancing.

"Don't give it a second thought," the rabbi replied. "You enjoy this special night." Dan called a taxi to take him to a kosher restaurant and returned to the festivities, shaken and disoriented by the unexpected turn of events. He went from table to table telling friends and family members who kept kosher not to eat the food—apologizing for the unfortunate mishap. He was furious that as her very first act as his mother-in-law, Donna had deceived and humiliated him over something she clearly knew he considered so important. Seemingly without concern over the rift her action would assuredly cause between him and Wendi—and the two sets of families—from the inception of their marriage.

Though he tried his best to smile and enjoy himself as he took to the dance floor with his new bride—and was hoisted into the air during the Hava Nagila—what Dan hoped would be the most perfect day of his entire life fell considerably short of that mark.

•••

WHEN THE NEWLYWEDS RETURNED to Tally following their sun-drenched honeymoon in the Bahamas, they were greeted with surprising news that quickly put the wedding fiasco in their rearview mirror. Dan received a lateral job offer to teach criminal law at Washington University in St. Louis. Not only was the Gateway City a much better place to live than Funky T-Town, the law school at "WashU" was ranked in the top 20 in the nation—a considerable upgrade from Florida State—with a faculty Dan considered far superior and befitting of his scholarly potential.

In late March 2006, the law school's faculty laid out the academic red carpet for Dan and his new bride—wining and dining them like royalty—eager for the first-year professor to accept their offer. Dan was thrilled at the prospect of a quick leap up the academic ladder, Wendi equally delighted over her impending escape from Tallahassee. But neither actually happened.

After they returned from St. Louis, WashU's dean asked Dan for a list of requirements—compensation and otherwise—that would lure him away from Florida State. His message was that

WashU stood ready to do whatever was necessary to attract top talent to its ranks. Which Dan interpreted as an engraved invitation to shoot for the moon, leading him to request a salary similar to what young professors at Harvard and Yale were earning. He also asked for a healthy travel budget, so he could fly around the country giving talks on his latest articles, and a large research budget to hire law students to assist with his scholarly endeavors. Dan also insisted that the law school provide good employment for Wendi—since they were a "package deal"—preferably in the area of immigration law.

His laundry list of requests, however, apparently went too far, rankling both the dean and other WashU faculty members, who until then had been gung ho about Dan becoming their colleague. The dean curtly replied to Dan's email, "I'm so sorry that we will not be able to make you and Wendi happy here"—and rescinded the offer. Blindsided by the sudden turn of events, Dan reached out to let him know that his email was simply a wish list, and that he was quite willing to negotiate—pleading for another chance. But it was too late, the damage to his standing with the WashU faculty from his apparent overreach irreparable. The Gateway City wasn't in his or Wendi's future after all.

Whether it was destiny or merely dumb luck, shortly after his offer to join WashU's faculty went up in smoke, UM Law in Miami offered Dan a "visiting" position for the fall 2006 semester. The law school's dean informed Dan that he was being given a "look-see" opportunity—a semester-long job interview—that could result in a permanent, tenure-track position. The only people more thrilled by this unexpected development than the newlyweds were Donna and Harvey Adelson, whose baby girl was coming back home.

What made UM's offer so attractive was that it *was* a package deal, with Wendi—by then a UM Law graduate studying for the Florida bar exam—landing an academic-year position as a staff attorney and instructor at the Center for Ethics and Public Service, where she'd done tons of work as a student intern. At the Center's Children & Youth Law Clinic, she'd be handling her own cases and supervising students representing abused and neglected children in immigrant visa proceedings. That the law school was offering his wife employment beyond one semester signaled to Dan that the faculty was already predisposed to offer him a permanent slot. On the heels his WashU wipeout, that was certainly welcome news.

During his first couple of months in Miami, Dan quickly befriended several established professors who were already prodigious scholars as well as young, hungry professors—like himself—who were actively pursuing that goal. In Dan, they saw a brilliant scholar with boundless potential who could help bring prestige and acclaim to UM Law. Those scholarly inclined professors became Dan's most ardent supporters as the vote on his promotion neared.

But not everyone was on the Dan Markel bandwagon. A few of the female professors—critical race and gender scholars—disagreed with Dan's views about criminal justice. Another group who'd be weighing in on his promotion were UM's clinical professors, who, rather than teaching in a classroom setting, oversaw students providing legal services to actual clients.

Unlike at many law schools, UM's "clinicians" had equal standing with traditional faculty members, including the right to vote on faculty appointments. They became a significant obstacle to Dan's promotion. Why? Because despite finding Wendi perfectly likable as a person, they concluded she wasn't a particularly good lawyer, leaving them to correct her frequent mistakes. They had no desire for Wendi to continue on in her role, and knew that voting against her husband would achieve their objective.

The faculty debate on Dan's promotion was heated, at times acrimonious. Though his supporters exceeded his detractors when the meeting began, the tide turned against Dan when one of his female colleagues accused the two-time Harvard grad of being a misogynist. Her accusation, as it turned out, was based solely on the fact that Dan wouldn't look her in the eye when they spoke at an informal meeting, instead focusing his gaze on a male colleague. Despite that slender reed, the mere label "misogynist" scared off a few of Dan's more tepid supporters, who reluctantly switched sides. Their shift was just enough to tip the balance against him and scuttle his opportunity to land a permanent slot.

Because neither Dan nor Wendi were permitted to attend the faculty meeting that decided his fate, they never learned the actual reasons their colleagues expressed in arguing against his promotion. What they were told was that the decision resulted solely from UM Law's interest in increasing the diversity on its faculty and that, as a white male—albeit a Canadian one—Dan's promotion wouldn't help achieve that objective.

When Dan received the news, he was shocked. Flabbergasted. Heading into the vote, he felt reasonably certain his promotion was a foregone conclusion. Though he didn't consider UM Law a particularly good landing spot, he was quite willing to make a go of it in Miami for the sake of his *Osita* and her family. He dreaded telling his new bride they'd be returning to the 'Hassee after all. Worse still, Donna and Harvey had already latched onto the belief that their grandchildren would be born and raised within an hour's drive from their front doorstep. He felt certain their disappointment would be intense.

Dan licked his proverbial wounds—yet again—and returned to Florida State for the spring semester. The dean was so happy to have him back, he gave Dan a raise, hoping it would quell his penchant to seek greener pastures. To ease the blow to Wendi and her family, Dan encouraged his wife to remain in Miami to complete her academic-year appointment. Which is precisely what she did, pushing the newlyweds into yet another long-distance relationship.

•••

CONFRONTED WITH THE REALITY that Florida State would likely be more than a brief stepping stone in his career, Dan and Wendi purchased a home in one of Tally's oldest neighborhoods, Betton Hills. When their realtor showed them

2116 Trescott Drive, the young couple fell in love with its open floor plan—the kitchen, dining room, and living room all blending together seamlessly without walls or columns. The spacious master bedroom suite was downstairs. There were two more bedrooms upstairs, one of which they envisioned as a future nursery, the other as a guest bedroom for when either's family came to visit. Another attractive feature was the home's two-car garage.

Once a child or two came along, they'd have two parks within walking distance, Winthrop Park to their south and McCord Park—with hiking trails and a fish-filled pond—to their north. Their new home was just a ten-minute drive from the law school, which was directly across the street from Wendi's new office at the Center for Advancement of Human Rights (CAHR), where Dan had secured her full-time employment. Wendi's official position was program director for the Center's Human Rights and Immigration Law Project, where she advocated on behalf of abused and battered immigrants and victims of human trafficking and supervised law students engaged in the nonprofit's mission.

Wendi reluctantly agreed that their new home could be kept strictly kosher, with separate dishes in different cabinets for meat and for dairy. She also acceded to Dan's wish to host weekly Shabbat dinners, though decided against regularly attending shul with him. Dan placed himself in charge of grocery shopping to ensure that kosher rules were strictly adhered to and assembled an invitation list of friends and acquaintances who would join them for dinner on Fridays—Jews and gentiles alike. Other frequent visitors included Donna and Harvey—sometimes together with Charlie—and Ruth and Phil for the High Holy Days.

Despite all that life had thrown their way during their short time together, Dan and Wendi were as deeply in love as the moment she accepted his proposal. They referred to each other mostly by pet names—Lady Bear or *Osita* for her and Danny Bear for him—a flirtatious vibe enveloping them wherever they went. They had no inhibitions about displaying their affection in public, Dan playfully kissing every square inch of his wife's face whenever seized by the moment, doting on his *Osita* as if she were his prized possession. For her part, Wendi seemed to enjoy being the focus of her husband's amorous attention. If they made friends uncomfortable by their frequent, over-the-top PDAs, they didn't seem to have the slightest concern.

By Wendi's thirtieth birthday—which her husband punctuated with a surprise party that included her parents and brothers—she was nearly six months pregnant. Just a couple of weeks later, however, Dan's excitement over his wife's milestone, and the impending arrival of their firstborn, was dampened by his Bubbie Helen's passing. She was 95. He returned to Montreal for the funeral and to sit *shiva*—the customary Jewish mourning ritual—penning a beautiful eulogy, telling those gathered that his grandmother's life had been "marked by its incessant buoyancy of spirit," and that his Bubbie had been a "ray of bright, shining light."

• • •

BENJAMIN AMICHAI MARKEL arrived late in the evening on July 29, 2009. In a Facebook post to his friends and relatives across the planet, Dan—beaming with pride—described the newborn as his and Wendi's "little and delicious 7 lb 5 oz baby boy," posting a picture "of the little guy, dreaming of whitefish salad and other smoked delicacies to come." The day was by far the happiest of the 36-year-old law professor's life, the love he felt as he gazed into his son's tiny face and squinty eyes beyond measure.

Donna was the first extended family member to hold Benjamin, the grandchild she'd been pining for since learning of Wendi's engagement. Not only were she, Harvey, and Charlie in town for his birth, they'd pretty much taken up residence at 2116 Trescott Drive. Though Harvey and Charlie returned to Coral Springs to keep the Adelson Institute running, Donna hunkered down in the 'Hassee for the long haul, remaining with her daughter and son-in-law for six weeks to provide an extra set of hands to help with the baby.

As is Jewish custom, eight days after Benjamin's birth, both sets of grandparents, aunts, uncles, and close friends joined the proud parents for his *brit milah*, or *bris*—a religious ceremony celebrating the circumcision of a newborn Jewish boy. Dan explained to his guests how he and Wendi had selected their son's name. Benjamin's English name was intended to honor both his and Wendi's paternal grandmothers, as well as Phil's Uncle Benjamin, whose grandchildren Shlomi, Zvika, and Elad were Dan's treasured cousins in Jerusalem.

Benjamin's Hebrew name, Lev—meaning "heart"—was chosen to honor Wendi's Grandma Lorraine. His middle name in both English and Hebrew, Amichai—meaning "my people lives"—was selected as a tribute to Dan's Bubbie Helen, celebrating her "unwavering commitment" to the Jewish people and Jewish tradition. The proud father told those assembled they were also welcome to call Benjamin "Cubby," extending his bear theme to a brand new generation. As well as Bam-Bam, in homage to the Flintstones.

Wendi and Dan barely had time to find their groove as parents when they learned Lady Bear was pregnant yet again, Bam-Bam a mere six months old at the time. Lincoln Jonah Markel arrived on October 13, 2010—four days after Dan's 38th birthday—forming a matched set of cubbies at 2116 Trescott Drive. Which was, once again, invaded by the Adelson clan, whose matriarch hunkered down for another extended stay.

•••

OVER TIME, THE THRILL Dan experienced over the birth of his sons morphed into an intense love he felt each time he was in their presence—the boys becoming the epicenter of his universe, eclipsing his love affair with his *Osita* and his career. The proud father simply couldn't get enough of his little Ben-Ben and Linc—cuddling with them, giving them baths, pushing them through the neighborhood in their stroller, reading them books, singing them songs and Hebrew hymns, playing with them on the floor, and gazing at them as they slept blissfully in their cribs. He kissed their faces, arms, and hands incessantly, unable to contain his adoration, his syrupy sweet, loving connection with them always on display in social gatherings and photos posted on Facebook.

When Dan was with his boys, the larger world around him faded into the background—the serious legal scholar transformed into a silly and playful dad, his focus and attention on them alone. It was impossible for him to talk with friends and colleagues without regaling them over his kids' latest exploits and accomplishments—crawling, first words, new discoveries—always at the ready with pics and videos on his Blackberry. His pride in Ben and Lincoln was off the charts—eyes lighting up every time he spoke of, or even thought about, his delicious cubbies.

Dan enjoyed taking the boys to the two neighborhood parks—carrying one or the other on his shoulders as they explored—pushing them in the swings, watching them descend the slides, and teaching them about birds, fish, and nature. When they began attending preschool, he'd make regular appearances to read stories at circle time. He proudly displayed their "artwork" in his third-floor office at the law school, which he found just as impressive and masterful as 18th century paintings adorning the walls of the Louvre.

As his boys learned to talk, there was one word Dan enjoyed hearing them enunciate more than any other—Abba. Hearing Ben or Lincoln refer to him as Abba made his heart melt with joy and pride.

What began as a simple message in his JDate inbox had led inexorably to Dan fulfilling what he considered the most important role he'd ever play—fatherhood. Watching his boys mature and develop, and being there for every milestone and joyous occasion they'd celebrate, was precisely how he intended to spend the rest of his life.

8.

Ivory Tower

UNLIKE MOST JOBS, law professors have neither a supervisor nor a defined job description. Beyond their time in the classroom—typically only a handful of hours each week—how law professors structure their day is almost entirely up to them. Newly appointed "assistant" professors spend significant time preparing lesson plans and lecture notes for their classes. They also focus heavily on research and writing to publish articles in their area of interest—at least three substantial articles typically required to obtain tenure. Additionally, assistant professors are assigned to faculty committees and expected to perform some type of service within the broader academy or profession. Collectively, those tasks establish the bare minimum.

Not surprisingly, Dan Markel didn't set his sights on the bare minimum. He'd already published *four* law review articles—with a fifth slated for publication—and was actively engaged in his new academic role months before arriving in Tallahassee. Together with an equally ambitious lawyer friend named Ethan Leib, who was about to begin his own stint as an assistant professor at UC Hastings in California, Dan founded a cutting-edge blog devoted to legal academia and scholarship. At a time when blogging on the internet was still in its infancy.

"Aloha! Welcome to PrawfsBlawg!" Dan began his April 5, 2005 post, introducing himself as a "blogger-ab-initio" about to embark on his teaching career. "This blawg," he informed readers, "will mostly be by law people, and mostly quite junior, including some who might not even be prawfs yet." Three days later, the blogosphere pioneer toasted PrawfsBlawg's successful launch: "Thousands of visitors!! Come hang around, drink scotch and bubble tea with us."

Dan, Leib, and a handful of their colleagues across the country would gradually grow PrawfsBlawg into a thriving, burgeoning community of like-minded young professors, ultimately garnering more than 250,000 page views per month. The idea was that fledgling members of the legal academy were "in it together," reaching for higher rungs on the academic ladder as a collective enterprise—rather than in monastic seclusion—able to benefit from each other's wisdom and experiences. Though Dan posted more frequently than anyone else, a handful of junior professors became permanent contributors. Invitations to guest blog provided an invaluable platform for young faculty members languishing in obscurity to introduce themselves to the ever-widening Prawfs readership and forge professional connections.

PrawfsBlawg wasn't all serious business, doubling at times as Dan's personal diary—replete with his whimsical posts about his and Wendi's engagement, their wedding, Ben-Ben's arrival and *bris*, and marking his "56th month of wedded bliss." It also was where he ruminated about the goings-on in Funky T-Town, proper attire for teaching law students, even his introduction to Baby Ruth candy bars.

Dan used the blog to solicit contributions for Haiti following a devastating earthquake and for ALS research during his colleague Steve Gey's brave battle with the dreaded disease. He'd post his "shitty first drafts" of new articles, soliciting feedback to help hone his arguments—and encouraged other Prawfs to do likewise. He also used PrawfsBlawg to trumpet the accomplishments of Florida State faculty members and up-and-coming scholars from coast to coast.

Live gatherings of Prawfs became a staple at large academic conferences, the community of ambitious legal scholars as much about social connection as academic ambition. Dan would set up shop in the hotel lobby, greeting fellow Prawfs as they checked in much like a Walmart greeter—with his trademark bear hug and warm smile—meeting spouses and children and catching up on the latest faculty gossip. He organized Prawfs dinners and happy hours that would often last until the early morning. If he discovered junior professors who seemed out of place or too introverted to network, Dan would introduce himself and insist they join him and his fellow Prawfs at a restaurant or bar—helping the timid professors meet everyone he knew—the Great Connector in action as always.

Long after the conferences had concluded, Dan would reconnect with the junior professors he'd met, soliciting their draft articles so he could help sharpen their analysis. His offers weren't merely empty gestures. Dan would spend hours in the evening reading drafts and exchanging emails with his newfound colleagues, investing in them as if their careers were inextricably intertwined with his own. He'd return their drafts teeming with insightful comments and helpful suggestions, all designed to make their arguments more logical and persuasive. His thoughtfulness, generosity with his time, and eagerness to help earned Dan a loyal cadre of disciples, the Canadian-born professor becoming a Pied Piperesque mentor to emerging scholars all across America.

Dan felt a particularly special kinship with Prawfs colleagues who were observant Jews. At conferences, they'd join together for intimate Shabbat dinners in Dan's hotel room, often with Wendi and the kids. At a conference at the luxurious Ritz Carlton in Palm Beach, Florida, a Jewish colleague came up to Dan in the corridor in full-on panic because the hotel didn't serve kosher food. Within ten minutes, Dan had organized a road trip, he and five Jewish colleagues in a desperate search until they located a rinky-dink kosher deli in a West Palm Beach strip mall. They barreled inside, plopped down at a table, and enjoyed their kosher sandwiches as if they were sumptuous delicacies being served at a five-star restaurant.

Perhaps Dan's greatest gift of all was his tremendous capacity for friendship, his circle of friends—both academic and non-academic—not just amazingly wide, but exceptionally deep as well. His joyful spirit, energy, and infatuation with ideas was infectious. Even as he came into his own as a scholar, his mischievous streak, wit, and zest for life was always on display. He'd call friends in distant places at all hours of the day to catch up and make sure they were well. There was no such thing as a "quick call" with Dan, never the first to end conversations, seemingly unaware that not everyone was able to manufacture time the way he could. He'd invite friends for long walks to shoot the breeze and catch up. It wasn't unusual for him to send a blizzard of emails after midnight with his latest news. And he never forgot a birthday, his bam bizzle greetings as reliable as a Timex watch.

When Dan traveled, he'd show up unannounced at the doorstep of friends who had no idea he was coming to town, often inviting himself over for Shabbat dinners. Even when his blindsided friends indicated they were too busy for a visit, Dan would hang around just the same, not wanting the moment to slip by. In his world, there was always time for friendship, and he gave of his time prodigiously, particularly if a friend was stressed or in a bad way. He wasn't shy about demonstrating his warmth and affection or telling his friends he loved them, viewing them more as brothers and sisters. If Dan's goal as an adult was to make his late Bubbie Helen proud by being a perfect *mensch*, he was achieving that objective with flying colors.

• • •

APART FROM BEN AND LINCOLN, there was nothing Dan found more enthralling than thinking through his ideas and expressing them in writing, a craft he honed like a finely tuned instrument. Yet the process of transforming those ideas into polished articles was tedious, hard work. Dan would save his drafts like versions of a computer program, his first always version 1.0, his tenth 2.0, and so on. By his own admission in a PrawfsBlawg post, his first 50 or so drafts were "typically drenched with shame and marinated in self-disgust." It wasn't uncommon for his articles to reach version 10.0 or higher—meaning 100 or more drafts—before he considered them worthy of serious scholarly attention.

In addition to posting his "shitty first drafts" on PrawfsBlawg, Dan would send more mature versions to numerous faculty friends—Prawfs and non-Prawfs alike—seeking their input and suggestions. His emails would always end with an affectionate, over-the-top closing, "Love and kisses" and "xoxo" the most common. If he didn't hear back after a week or so, he'd send an email reminder, bluntly explaining that he expected a response. And if a reply still wasn't forthcoming, he'd email again—and again and again—badgering his colleagues until they finally offered their written feedback, if only to get him off their backs.

Though some found Dan's relentless hounding annoying and overbearing, his friends were well aware of his eagerness to return the favor with their drafts. Dan relished the opportunity to improve his colleagues' written work, a task he took on more often, and with greater thoroughness, than just about any member of the academy.

His incessant back-and-forth with other professors over their respective writing led to an epiphany, that a live forum was needed for emerging scholars—particularly those looking to lateral their way to more elite schools—at which they could critique one another's drafts and work collectively to improve them. Which is how Prawfsfest! was born. The in-person PrawfsBlawg spinoff, spearheaded exclusively by Dan, was a twice-per-year, two-day workshop that took place at host law schools, restricted to about a dozen Prawfs at each, with specialties running the gamut from constitutional law to tax law. The group would discuss each participant's draft article for about an hour, the professors working their way around the table until each had provided input. Though the cast of characters—and legal topics—would change from one "P-fest" to the next, Dan was the one constant.

What transpired during these intimate gatherings is

what Dan referred to as his "cocaine"—a potent cocktail of intellectual stimulation and pure, unadulterated joy he'd experience while the group worked in common purpose to improve each other's analysis and exposition. Each day would conclude with dinner at a swanky restaurant—paid for by the host school—where the libations flowed freely. The social connections forged through the workshops were nearly as important as the scholarly mission bringing the professors together.

Dan established several rules for Prawfsfest! he expected participants to follow. The first was that each needed to thoroughly read the ten or so drafts up for discussion before arriving at the host school. Another was that authors weren't permitted to say a word about their own drafts—as the primary goal was for them to absorb their colleagues' feedback, not regurgitate their arguments or defend their reasoning. A third rule was that Dan would provide his feedback last, as it was always extensive, and as P-fest's founder, he felt entitled to have the last word.

The final and most important rule was one Dan labeled with sexual terminology: "no foreplay." By which he meant that comments weren't to be watered down with prefatory statements such as "this isn't my area of expertise" or "this may seem trivial." And also, that idle praise for the author's arguments, analysis, or writing style—which Dan considered an utter waste of time—was strictly prohibited. After all, the goal wasn't to make love to the authors, but rather, to help them improve what they had to say.

Dan also co-organized an annual event intended solely for criminal law professors, the CrimProf Shadow Conference, which occurred each summer alongside the national meeting of the Law & Society Association. The three-day conferences were chock-full of panel discussions, typically with ten to 15 separate panels of four to five professors, which nearly always included Dan himself. Very few of the panelists were from elite law schools and nearly all were ambitious young professors eager to climb the academic ranks. The shadow conference became a "must" for any young criminal law professor hoping to make a scholarly splash.

•••

THE MAJORITY OF DAN'S scholarly writing focused on how and why retributive justice should be applied to the punishment of convicted criminals. In a groundbreaking article entitled "State, Be Not Proud: A Retributivist Defense of the Commutation of Death Row and the Abolition of the Death Penalty"—published just after he arrived at Florida State— Dan fleshed out the essence of his thinking, what he labeled the Confrontational Conception of Retribution, or CCR. His CCR construct was comprised of a three-legged stool: moral accountability for unlawful actions, equal liberty under the law, and democratic self-defense.

Punishment for criminal wrongdoing, Dan wrote, "is one of the ways society makes clear that one cannot disclaim responsibility for the reasonably foreseeable consequences of one's actions, one of the core notions underlying retributive thought." His equal liberty concept was rooted in the broader social compact in that, "by his act, the criminal implicitly says, 'I have greater liberty than you, my fellow citizen.'" By punishing his criminal conduct, the state communicates the norm that no individual's right to liberty is greater than any other's. The principle of democratic self-defense explains why the state is the entity that decides how to punish—"because it, and it alone, has the capacity for legitimacy among all actors in society."

Prior to "State, Be Not Proud," the prevailing consensus among legal scholars was that retributive justice supported, and for some, required, imposing the most severe punishment— the death penalty—for the most severe crimes. Dan utilized his CCR construct to stand retributivists' acceptance of capital punishment on its head, promoting instead "the retributivist case *against* the death penalty." Empirical studies, he pointed out, had exposed high error rates in death-penalty cases, meaning that the ultimate punishment had frequently been imposed on wholly innocent defendants—a result utterly at odds with retributivist principles.

If the state "gets it wrong" with other forms of punishment, Dan noted, it can "make plain its contrition" for a wrongful conviction. "When the guillotine drops," however, "this opportunity is forfeited." "A posture of modesty," he argued, "should thus be implicit in all retributive punishments because quite simply, we may be wrong for reasons we cannot or will not discern until much later." Inherent in Dan's CCR was "a commitment to respecting the dignity of every person, a dignity we affirm by punishing offenders for the consequences of their freely chosen and autonomous actions." The death penalty "degrades dignity," he asserted, by "unnecessarily extinguish[ing] human life in the presence of viable alternatives." Dan concluded the piece by advocating for blanket commutation for every individual on death row and "abolition of the death penalty itself."

One of the ancillary topics Dan took on in "State, Be Not Proud" is the role of victim impact statements, articulating his strong opposition to victims playing a direct role in the sentencing process. "In the context of the death penalty," he cautioned, "the fear of victim influence on sentencing looms even more menacingly." Permitting victim impact evidence, he contended, "undercuts the retributivist commitment to fair and equal application of criminal sanctions."

Why? Because the moral reprehensibility of the crime at issue, and hence the appropriate punishment, shouldn't "hinge on whether the jury finds the victim or his allies persuasive or sympathetic" or on the victim's positive characteristics. Dan believed strongly that those attributes are "morally immaterial" to whether the death penalty—or any particular punishment—should be imposed.

Another area on which his scholarship focused is the interaction between family status and criminal law. In a pair of articles he coauthored with Ethan Leib and a Wake Forest professor named Jennifer Collins, Dan critically reexamined long-standing "family ties benefits" in the criminal law—such as the spousal privilege preventing the state from unearthing information from one spouse against another. On the flip side, he and his coauthors questioned several "family ties burdens," such as the criminalization of conduct based solely on family relationships. Their central thesis was that the criminal justice system shouldn't give special treatment—positive or negative—based on one's family ties. In April 2009, Oxford University Press published a synthesized version of the articles in book form, entitled *Privilege or Punish: Criminal Justice and the Challenge of Family Ties*, which Dan dedicated to Wendi, "my everything, my world without end."

The most controversial argument presented in *Privilege or Punish* was that incest, so long as it is consensual, shouldn't be punishable under the criminal law. Dan and his coauthors asserted that criminal prosecution isn't necessary to prevent such conduct because "most of these relationships will be deterred by social stigma." Their opinions diverged, however, on applying this rationale to minors, with Dan alone arguing in favor of decriminalizing consensual sexual acts among relatives who'd reached the age of consent. He suggested that "it should be immaterial from the state's perspective" whether such activity occurs between brothers, first cousins, or friends.

In addition to *Privilege or Punish,* by 2010, Dan had published 18 law review articles, many in elite law journals including at Harvard, Yale, Cornell, UC Berkeley, Northwestern, and the Universities of Pennsylvania, Virginia, and Texas. Just five years into his academic career, he'd emerged as nothing short of a rock star, quoted in articles appearing in the *New York Times, San Francisco Chronicle, Slate Magazine,* and *The Economist* and being interviewed by the likes of CNN, BBC Russia, NPR, and CBS Radio. And as rock stars are wont to do upon the release of a new album, Dan would take his newly published articles on the road—sans tour bus and roadies—traveling to law schools throughout the nation to give lunchtime presentations and meet with faculty members and students. His tours even went worldwide, including stops in Vancouver, Toronto, and

Israel.

•••

LAW PROFESSORS TYPICALLY employ the Socratic method to impart their wisdom in the classroom, rather than the lecture style that predominates in undergraduate education. Students are called on randomly—drafted without their consent—and are asked a series of questions about the assigned reading. "Mr. Jones," the questioning might begin, snapping the unfortunate soul in the back row to attention in an instant. "Why did the court consider the gun the fruit of the poisonous tree?"

The initial question is nearly always followed by progressively more difficult ones even seasoned attorneys would struggle to answer. The professor will often toss hypotheticals into the questions designed to flesh out how malleable legal principles are to different factual scenarios, the student on the hot seat merely a prop to illustrate the law in action. For brand new law students, being on the receiving end of a professor's rapid-fire interrogation can seem intimidating, even fear-inducing. That was especially true when the intense gaze of Professor Dan Markel was locked on a 1L who wasn't thoroughly prepared.

Dan desperately wanted his students to succeed, but expected their complete buy-in in their own education. Which left him bitterly disappointed when they showed up late or unprepared, or when he detected them surfing the internet on their laptops or texting instead of focusing on him. On occasion he'd lock the classroom doors the moment class began; when he didn't, he'd berate students who sauntered into the classroom a few minutes late, instructing those who arrived even later to leave. Because he was such a stickler for punctuality, it wasn't uncommon to see students racing through the hallways to make it to his class on time.

Dan's brilliance was always on full display in his back-and-forth with students over questions of criminal law or procedure, which some of them appreciated, but others found condescending and belittling. He developed a reputation of being intense and aggressive in his use of the Socratic method. A hardass. He would often push students beyond their comfort zone, trying to get them to think outside the box. Brighter students would rise to the occasion. Weaker students, however, would wither under the pressure.

But with each passing year, Dan would modulate his approach to make classes more fun and less intimidating. He'd get students on their feet for stretch breaks and randomly incorporate photos of Ben—and later Lincoln—into his PowerPoint slides. "Before we get started," he'd sometimes begin class, "I've got to tell you what Baby Ben-Ben did this morning."

For students who took the time to get to know Dan outside the classroom, they were astonished to learn how personable and affectionate he was. He'd ask them about their families, what they did for fun, and about their career aspirations. If he learned of students who landed summer jobs in places he'd previously lived—such as Boston or Washington, D.C.—he'd provide them a list of things to see and do, restaurants at which to eat, and reach out to his friends who lived there to take his students under their wings.

He became particularly close with the handful of students who served as his research assistants each year—whom he encouraged to call him "Danny"—often steering judicial clerkship opportunities their way and writing glowing recommendation letters on their behalf to judges and prospective employers. He performed the same function for his top students, even years after they'd graduated, often emailing them into the early morning hours to dispense helpful career advice. He formed a close bond with the students who served as senior editors of the *Florida State Law Review*, acting as the publication's informal advisor and helping weed through thousands of submissions to identify the most promising scholarly work.

When he taught upper-level seminars on sentencing or punitive damages, Dan always ended the semester with an intimate dinner at his Betton Hills home. Students got to see an entirely different side of the hardass professor who, as 1Ls, had them quaking in their shoes. The home they encountered was one in which children ruled the roost, Ben and Lincoln's artwork strung across the living room, toys strewn about everywhere, picture frames revealing Dan as a doting and playful dad positioned prominently on the bookshelves. As they enjoyed their meal, students couldn't help but sense the unabashed pride Dan felt for his boys. The homey experience helped them see their demanding professor in a whole new light.

•••

THOUGH DAN SERVED ON SEVERAL faculty committees, the one he found most rewarding was the appointments committee, which led him back to Washington, D.C. for the annual Meat Market—the tables now turned—with entry-level faculty candidates trying to impress *him* with *their* potential. He formed strong opinions about which aspiring professors to pursue and voiced them passionately, as eager to argue and debate their strengths and weaknesses as his ideas on retributive justice.

Though he was generally successful persuading committee members to gravitate toward his preferred choices, on occasion they failed to garner the committee's approval. Dan didn't accept those defeats well, often badgering the committee chair in a vain attempt to force a revote. He cared deeply about improving the quality of the faculty, hoping to land as many promising young teachers and scholars as possible.

The prestige of Florida State's law school was clearly on the rise—due in no small part to Dan's surging prominence as a punishment theory scholar—reaching number 52 in the *U.S. News & World Report* rankings in 2009. Which was when another lateral offer was dangled in front of him, this time from the University of Houston. Though accepting the offer would arguably have been a slight step down the academic ladder—

as Houston Law stood at number 59 in that year's rankings—its dean offered Dan a 50% salary increase, from $120,000 to $180,000. In addition to an immediate grant of tenure. In late April 2009, Dan and his very pregnant wife hopped on an airplane to get a better sense of what living in the nation's fourth largest city might be like.

Nearly four years into his stint at Florida State, however, Dan was no longer itching to leave Tally for something better. Not hardly. The sleepy town that seemed so alien to him when he and Wendi arrived in 2005 had grown on Dan considerably. He'd formed numerous close friendships and felt fully invested in the local community—especially its Jewish population—Funky T-Town as much a "home" to him as Boston or D.C. had ever been. Dan felt a deep sense of belonging he wasn't sure he could replicate anywhere else.

Though the University of Houston's offer was tempting, Dan ultimately decided to leverage it to improve his compensation package at Florida State, whose dean, Don Weidner, couldn't bear the prospect of losing his most prolific scholar. Though Dean Weidner couldn't offer him immediate tenure—which because of rigid university requirements would have to wait another year—he told Dan that if he rejected the University of Houston's offer, he'd bestow on him an endowed professorship named for Sandy D'Alemberte, a former dean of the law school, longtime president of the entire university, and the 1991-92 president of the American Bar Association.

Dan gladly accepted the D'Alemberte professorship, becoming the only faculty member in the law school's history to be awarded an endowed position prior to achieving tenure. It was quite the feather in his cap. In addition, his salary was immediately bumped to $167,000 with Dean Weidner promising to increase it to $180,000 within a year. Considering the low cost of living in Tally, he and Wendi were going to be far better off financially than if he'd accepted Houston Law's offer. And just like that, Dan went from one of the lower-paid members of Florida State's faculty to one of its highest.

"Can you ever say no to this guy?" more senior, tenured

professors groused to the dean when they learned about Dan's new compensation package, which leapfrogged their own. Though he knew his preferential treatment of Dan would draw the ire of some members of his faculty—who already found Dan arrogant and self-absorbed—Dean Weidner considered their disenchantment well worth the tradeoff of locking down his superstar for the foreseeable future. And if Dan needed anything else to help make him even more comfortable or productive—a larger travel budget, a standup desk for his ailing back—the dean was more than happy to oblige. Thanks in no small measure to Dan's ascending prominence, Florida State rose to number 45 in the *U.S. News* rankings in March 2014.

Despite the petty jealously and ruffled feathers of a few of his fellow professors, Dan became close friends with many of his colleagues, who admired his boundless energy, creativity, and everything he was doing to promote Florida State and enhance its reputation. The example he was setting was rubbing off on the law school's youngest professors, who viewed Dan almost as an idol. He'd pop into their offices regularly and take them to lunch to shoot the bull and find out what they were working on. He'd provide thoughtful comments on their latest drafts, just as he did for Prawfs colleagues. And he helped them with article placements, championed their accomplishments, and introduced them to friends and acquaintances across the academy.

During the summers, Dan would grab his colleagues from their offices and escort them to an empty classroom for weekly "writer's retreats," putting the group on a one-hour timer—with no WiFi or devices permitted—where they were expected to pound away on their laptops and make progress on their drafts. For at least that one hour, he and his posse had no excuse for procrastination, the peer pressure of the group setting offering a helpful antidote to writer's block.

Dan's care and concern for his Florida State colleagues wasn't just about their academic success. For his unmarried colleagues, he was always on the prowl for a romantic match, constantly trying to fix them up with attractive members of the opposite (or same) sex. And on the other end of the match-making continuum, Dan downed more than a few glasses of bourbon while lending an empathetic ear to fellow professors whose own marriages were withering and dying.

•••

WENDI'S CAREER WAS ON an entirely different trajectory than her husband's. Even though she worked just a few steps from the law school and supervised a few of its students, her position as a public interest attorney and adjunct professor with the CAHR wasn't technically under the law school's umbrella. Her meager $35,000 salary was funded by a grant from the Florida Bar Foundation, a statewide legal aid program, that had to be renewed annually—creating significant risk to her job security. The dilapidated staircase at the front entrance of the converted home housing the CAHR and her shoebox-sized office—the building's water heater just a few inches from her desk—couldn't have contrasted more with the ivory tower setting across the street in which Dan and his colleagues were comfortably ensconced.

Despite her less-than-optimal working environment, Wendi poured herself into her job, ably representing immigrant women and children fleeing domestic abuse, persecuted migrants seeking asylum, and victims of human trafficking. Her clients' heart-wrenching stories fueled Wendi's passion to seek and obtain justice, providing them assistance far beyond her duties as a lawyer. She drove immigrant clients to appointments with doctors and therapists, often serving as their Spanish translator, and helped them jump through the myriad legal hoops required to remain in the United States. Hearing her clients refer to her as *Abogada Wendi* filled her with immense pride and satisfaction.

When the University of Houston offered Dan a tenured position in April 2009, Wendi was part of his package deal, a job as director of the law school's immigration clinic all but guaranteed. Though she considered the clinical position her dream job, with her firstborn's arrival expected a month before her likely starting date, the timing just wasn't right. As enticing as the prospect was of directing one of the premier immigration clinics in the country, Wendi couldn't fathom being 1,150 miles from her family with a newborn in tow. For the moment at least, she was content remaining in Tally, advocating on behalf of the immigrant women and children for whom she was playing such a vital role.

•••

LIKE DAN, WENDI LABORED tirelessly over her scholarly articles—without the assistance of a single research assistant—her writing focusing on the intersection between immigration law and child advocacy. Unlike Dan's placement in elite law reviews, however, her articles were published by the likes of *The University of St. Thomas Law Journal* and *Journal of Transnational Law & Policy.*

In "Child Prostitute or Victim of Trafficking?" she argued that child prostitutes shouldn't be punished as criminals because they are victims—not perpetrators—of criminal activity. In "The Case of the Eroding Special Immigrant Juvenile Status," Wendi lamented how the Department of Homeland Security's policies were "chipping away" at the path to citizenship for abused, abandoned, and neglected immigrant children. Just as he did for his colleagues, Dan toiled over Wendi's drafts, providing thorough feedback, helping sharpen her arguments and polish her writing. He was the first person to whom Wendi expressed appreciation in her initial footnote in each article.

While drafting those pieces, Wendi felt an intense calling to tell her clients' stories in a different way—one accessible to ordinary people rather than high-browed academics. As she'd later write, she wanted "to give voice to a population that often has none" and educate everyday folks "how criminals and traffickers exploit human vulnerabilities; what the experience of being trafficked is actually like; and the struggle to piece together broken lives when (and if) it ends." The result, two years in the making, was a 276-page work of fiction entitled *This is Our Story*. Its cover featured Wendi's partially obscured face—and penetrating turquoise-blue left eye—an image captured and Photoshopped by her dad. For nearly two years, Wendi reached out to agents and publishers hoping to find a suitable landing place for her debut novel. A huge pile of rejections later, she ended up self-publishing on Amazon.

This is Our Story's 46 chapters alternate the first-person narratives of Lily Walker Stone, a corporate attorney turned public interest lawyer, and her clients Rosa Hernandez and Mila Gulej. When the story begins, Rosa, a 14-year-old living in poverty in Argentina, is visited by an impeccably dressed Miami businesswoman, Señora Cuenca, who selects her and a friend named Ana to live in her Miami home and learn the restaurant business in America.

But once Rosa and Ana arrive in Miami, it becomes clear that Señora Cuenca is actually a diabolical monster, holding the two girls captive and forcing them to perform slave labor to pay off their "debt" for the supposed cost of bringing them to the States. The woman's deviant son sexually abuses and impregnates Ana, who dies several months into her pregnancy. Señora Cuenca becomes more and more violent toward Rosa with each passing month—eventually breaking her arm when she finds her in the shower with Mr. Cuenca, believing the naked encounter had been orchestrated by Rosa rather than her husband.

Mila, a 17-year-old working in a Slovakian restaurant alongside her mom, is lured to America by an ad that convinces her she's coming to New York, where she believes she'll be discovered and become a famous actress. Instead, she ends up gutting chickens at a Chinese restaurant in Atlanta owned by two Hispanic brothers, Chico and Jose, who work Mila to the bone to pay off her "debt." When she falls in love with Chico, he invites her to live with him and his brother. Though Chico is good to her at first, he later allows Jose to rape her. Chico also forces Mila to become a nude dancer at a strip club—where she performs sexual favors for patrons—to make extra money. The story concludes when Rosa and Mila finally escape and find their way to *Abogada Lily* who, with the assistance of a local sheriff, helps bring their tormentors to justice.

Throughout the book, Wendi's wry sense of humor is on full display, providing well-timed comic relief to the migrant women's depressing, heartbreaking narratives. In her afterword, Wendi reveals that Rosa and Mila "are composite characters embodying many of the stories I have heard while practicing immigration law." Her hope was that writing their stories would prevent other girls and women from suffering their fate. "I wouldn't be half the attorney, or person, that I am today without having met people like 'Rosa' and 'Mila,'" she explained, expressing gratitude to her clients "for the invaluable lessons they have taught me by opening my eyes to courage and resilience."

Just as her husband would do upon the publication of his articles on criminal punishment, Wendi took to the road to promote *This is Our Story* and give speeches on the evils of human trafficking, appearing at numerous events throughout the Sunshine State. Articles about the book appeared in legal magazines. Wendi was even interviewed on the local TV news. Harvey and Donna beamed with pride as their baby girl spoke before gatherings in Miami and Fort Lauderdale, events Dan attended as well. He proudly trumpeted *This is Our Story* and his wife's speaking engagements on PrawfsBlawg.

Wendi also founded her own legal blog, the Human Trafficking Law Blog. "Hello and welcome," her inaugural February 2011 post began. "The purpose of this blog is to create a space to update and advance the legal discourse on human trafficking as well as discuss various aspects of the prevention and prosecution of the crime, as well as treatment for its victims. We hope you'll come visit us often." She used the blog to promote *This is Our Story* and her upcoming appearances. Though it garnered only a tiny fraction of the page views PrawfsBlawg enjoyed, Wendi was quite proud of her foray into the blogosphere and the attention it was bringing to the plight of human trafficking victims.

•••

JUST AS HER CAREER was finally taking off, Wendi's position at the CAHR was eliminated when the funding for her job dried up. Dan quickly sprang into action, lobbying Dean Weidner to create a position for his wife on Florida State's clinical faculty. Though the dean knew he'd take more flak from senior faculty members by granting Dan's request, he happily obliged — anything to ensure that his criminal theory superstar didn't revive his interest in a better gig.

Thanks to her husband's efforts, in August 2011, Wendi became a "visiting" clinical professor, directing the brand new Medical-Legal Partnership, an expansion of the law school's Public Interest Law Center and its clinical faculty. She happily moved into a real office — sans water heater — at the academic palace she'd been ogling from across the street for years. Not only that, she finally had a salary worthy of her law degree — $85,000 — though again with little job security because her contract had to be renewed each August in the dean's discretion.

Each semester, Wendi supervised ten 2Ls and 3Ls who represented homeless, indigent, and undocumented patients at the Neighborhood Medical Center, a free community health clinic. Wendi and her students helped clients file and prosecute disability claims and represented them at immigration proceedings in Orlando. She taught her students in a classroom setting six hours each week. Wendi spearheaded an "alternative" spring break in Southwest Florida, where her law students worked together with medical students to provide legal assistance to migrant farmworkers and their families. She also traveled the country giving presentations about her unique clinic — in places such as New Orleans, San Francisco, and Los Angeles.

In December 2012, Wendi received a promotion of sorts, the word "visiting" dropping from her title, making her a permanent member of the law faculty, at least in name. In August 2013, her salary increased to $100,000. By all accounts, she was well liked by students and her fellow clinical faculty members and was doing excellent work.

The following spring, the administration on Florida State's main campus selected *This is Our Story* as assigned summer reading for all 7,000 incoming students as part of its One Book, One Campus initiative. Wendi, its author, was selected to serve as the keynote speaker at the New Student Convocation— where the entire Class of 2018 would be in attendance—the crowning achievement of her budding academic career. Donna and Harvey couldn't have been any prouder.

On August 24, 2014, a large swath of Florida State's faculty took their positions on stage at the basketball arena, a sea of vibrant colors in their academic regalia. The assembly's pomp and circumstance rivaled a formal graduation ceremony. Thousands of freshmen brimming with anticipation and excitement packed the audience. Each of them, presumably, had read Wendi's novel, learning the valuable lessons she'd imparted about the horrors of human trafficking.

But when it came time for the keynote address, a former colleague of Wendi's from the Center for Advancement of Human Rights approached the podium in her stead. Five weeks following Dan Markel's savage execution, neither Professor Wendi J. Adelson nor her proud parents were anywhere to be found.

9.

Pearl Harbor
Monday, September 10, 2012

A DOZEN OR SO criminal law professors were seated at a sizable conference room table at NYU Law School in Greenwich Village. Most in attendance that afternoon lived in New York, though a few, like Dan, had flown in for the occasion. When Dan and a colleague at Brooklyn Law started the NYC Criminal Law Theory Colloquium in January 2011—a Prawfsfest!-like workshop intended solely for criminal theorists—the email list of invitees numbered barely 20.

That list, which Dan curated singlehandedly, had grown to more than 200, and included law professors from as far away as Israel, England, Canada, and California. Those able to attend assembled in New York at least every other month, working collectively to transform each other's unfinished drafts into polished articles on criminal law theory. Their workshopping sessions—Dan's "cocaine"—would last for hours, focusing intensely on just two papers each afternoon. His own piece was slated for discussion the following day.

As the professors were going around the room offering insights and critiques on one of his colleague's drafts, Dan noticed his iPhone vibrating. Glancing down, he saw Wendi's name appear on the screen. During the three days he'd been in New York, she hadn't answered his calls or responded to his voicemails or texts. Something was definitely amiss, but Dan had no idea why she was so upset. He excused himself and stepped out into the hallway to take the call.

"Hello," he said tentatively.

"I'm leaving and taking the boys with me," Wendi said, her voice firm and resolute.

"*What*?" Dan exclaimed.

"I'm filing for divorce," his wife of six-and-a-half years declared, her words landing like a boxer's thunderous blow to the head.

"Please don't do that," Dan pleaded, steadying himself as he tried to absorb the shock. "Let me come home first and we'll talk. I'll be on the first flight back. Please don't do anything rash until I get there." The next thing he heard was the clicking sound terminating their connection.

He was blindsided—frozen in the hallway panic-stricken—struggling to process Wendi's words. When he finally reentered the conference room, Dan's colleagues couldn't help but notice the blood had completely drained from his face. It was obvious he was shaken. He gathered his laptop and papers, politely excusing himself, explaining that a "personal matter" had arisen back home. He wouldn't be there on Tuesday to workshop his paper after all.

•••

OVER A THOUSAND MILES AWAY at their home on Trescott Drive, everything was proceeding flawlessly, like a meticulously designed military operation. Donna and Harvey Adelson had been there throughout the weekend, helping supervise and execute a plan they and Wendi had hatched together early that summer. Professional movers were loading furniture into the truck while Wendi's friends helped her pack up the last of her clothes, accessories, jewelry, and the kids' clothing and toys.

Barely three and not even two, Ben and Lincoln weren't nearly old enough to appreciate the flurry of activity surrounding them—or what it would mean for the rest of their lives. They'd already begun adjusting to their new home on Aqua Ridge Way, where—unbeknownst to their dad—they'd been living since Friday.

Nervously fidgeting in his seat during his two-and-a-half-hour flight back to Tally that evening, Dan racked his brain for what he'd done, what might have precipitated this sudden turn of events, Wendi's harsh words still reverberating in his head. Yes, she'd been expressing that she was unhappy, telling him he was disengaged from her, not doing his part around the house, traveling way too much, and focusing on his career to the exclusion of almost everything else. But as far as he was concerned, things were still mostly good—certainly no reason to bail on the marriage and tear the family apart.

When Dan pulled into his garage, the gravity of the situation became immediately apparent. The shelving sections ringing its walls had disappeared—everything resting upon them gone as well. His bicycle, designer luggage, tennis racquet, and kids' toys were missing too.

Dan entered the house through the garage-side door and flipped on the lights. He took two steps in and stopped dead in his tracks. What he observed hardly resembled the home he'd left behind before heading to New York. Precisely half of the living room furniture was gone, glaring empty spaces where chairs and couches once sat. Though the dining room table was still there, half the chairs were missing. Dishes and silverware had vanished from the kitchen cabinets, as had most of the food from the pantry and refrigerator.

Dan walked upstairs to assess the damage there. What he found on the second floor was even more distressing. The guest bedroom had been ransacked—nothing left at all. The boys' room was laid bare as well—all except a crib mattress haphazardly tossed onto the floor. Ben's bed and Lincoln's crib were gone, as was the changing table, toys, stuffed animals, and most of the clothing in their closet. But what was most disturbing were the walls, which, prior to Dan's trip, had been covered with colorful letters to help his boys learn the alphabet. All 26 letters were now gone—ugly splotches of torn, white plaster defacing the bright blue walls where they'd been affixed.

With a golf-ball-sized lump filling his throat, Dan descended the staircase and marched toward the master bedroom, fully expecting it to be pillaged as well. To his surprise though, the bed he'd shared with Wendi until he left for New York was still in place, as was much of the furniture. He was comforted knowing he'd at least have a place to sleep. But as he approached the bed, and gazed downward, that relief vanished instantly.

Centered perfectly atop the neatly arranged comforter was a legal document—a ten-page divorce petition—bearing a court stamp indicating it had been filed at 4:00 p.m. that afternoon, just after Wendi had called him in New York. Dan reached for it, his heart now thumping furiously in his chest.

The pleading recited that the "marriage between the parties is irretrievably broken." Wendi was asking the court to adopt "a parenting plan that provides Wife with the majority of timesharing." She was seeking child support, alimony, and an equitable distribution of their property. And because of the imbalance in their incomes, she asked that her husband be required to pay her attorney's fees. As he studied the petition more closely, Dan noticed that Wendi had actually signed it on September 5—before he'd even left for New York. Her lawyer had completed one of the required forms on August 23.

Though the divorce petition had been conspicuously placed to ensure he'd see it, Wendi hadn't left a note or forwarding address. Dan didn't have the slightest idea where she—or the boys—might be. His calls and texts were met with stone-cold silence. His wife was asking the court to take the kids away from him, he thought, and had already achieved that objective on her own. He was shocked, angry, and deathly afraid all at once.

In tears—reeling from the day's events—Dan called his mom for the third time since hearing Wendi's ugly words that afternoon, filling her in on the besieged war zone masquerading as his home. Ruth and Phil were already scheduled to arrive later that week for Rosh Hashanah, the Jewish New Year. What was to be a festive holiday celebration would instead turn into a desperate mission to locate his sweet, innocent cubbies.

•••

CLUES THAT THIS DAY was fast approaching had been swirling all around the tenured law professor for nearly two years. The love and respect Wendi once felt for him had been withering in inverse proportion to Dan's meteoric rise in the legal academy. It wasn't just that he was basking in the attention of being a renowned and sought-after criminal-law scholar. The bigger problem, in Wendi's view, was that he was consistently dismissive of her own work and aspirations.

Had he bothered to crack open *This is Our Story* to celebrate his wife's most significant achievement, let alone review a draft in progress—which to her annoyance he hadn't—he couldn't have escaped notice of the nakedly autobiographical narrative she'd woven in its pages. In the book, Wendi's protagonist, Lily Walker Stone—an immigration and human trafficking attorney just like her—follows her husband, Josh Stone, to a strange, "Godforsaken place" in the Florida Panhandle she feels she doesn't belong, Hiawassee Springs—or, as Lily nicknames it, "the 'wassee." What prompts the young couple to move there? Josh landing a professorship at a fictional *North* Florida State University.

Had he perused the book's pages, Dan surely would have recognized the uncanny resemblance between himself and Josh. As well as scenes Wendi had lifted whole-cloth from actual moments in their lives together. More importantly, he would have glimpsed a preview of where his own marriage was heading, as the fictional one between Lily and Josh—who, like Dan, never wore his wedding ring—begins disintegrating, ultimately ending in divorce. And Wendi didn't merely leave it to her readers' intuition to appreciate how closely Lily's journey resembled her own, sharing in the afterword, "I, selfishly, wanted you to know a bit about my story, which has much—but not all—in common with Attorney Lily."

Dan was too absorbed in his career—and what he considered important scholarship—to credit Wendi's creative writing as being worthy of serious recognition. After all, he'd never before wasted his valuable time reading novels. Why should it matter that his own wife had toiled for two years to write one? He was utterly oblivious to the deeply personal feelings she'd spilled onto the pages of *This is Our Story*—and how they served as an ominous harbinger of his own marriage's demise.

Wendi first told him she wanted a divorce in early 2011, when Lincoln was just an infant. Dan's knee-jerk reaction at the time was to tell her she was welcome to leave, but that he'd be the one to keep the house—and the kids—and would leave her penniless. Somehow, they ended up in counseling with a local psychologist. But their sessions had trailed off rather quickly. In Wendi's view, the counseling hadn't even scratched the surface of their problems. She confided in friends that she'd fallen in love "with the wrong man," that she simply didn't like Dan anymore and felt diminished and devalued by him, explaining that he didn't treat her as an equal.

The same facility with words that made Dan Markel a prolific and revered legal scholar transformed what should have been innocuous husband-wife quarrels into verbal fisticuffs that cut straight to the bone. "Danny used to tell me that everyone thought that I was such a nice and such a good person," Wendi would later reflect, but in the same breath would tell her "he was the only one who knew the truth about what a bad person I was. He was convinced I had deluded everyone but him."

Unlike Dan, who relished a good argument and was often too transparent for his own good, Wendi's approach was to avoid confrontation at all costs. She retreated and withdrew, often employing the silent treatment as her weapon of choice. And that annoyed Dan all the more, as not knowing what was on her mind—and why she was upset—would torment him far more than biting or sarcastic words. The clash of their personalities could be toxic at times.

Also tearing at the fabric of their relationship was how each approached life as a Jew. To Dan, being Jewish was his very essence—his soul—and he was determined to instill that same identity and sense of "roots" in Ben and Lincoln. Despite their young age, he took them to shul every Saturday morning, making excuses for Wendi's absence. It also was of paramount importance to him that their diet consist exclusively of kosher foods.

Wendi's view of Judaism was altogether different, having grown up in a family where being Jewish was merely a component of her cultural heritage, not something that defined who she was. Her four years at a Jewish-centered college hadn't cultivated any stronger affinity to Judaism than had existed during her childhood. Before meeting Dan, Wendi had never kept kosher or regularly attended synagogue. As Dan's wife, she made clear she had no intention of becoming more observant just to please him, though she ultimately—albeit reluctantly—acceded to his request that their Trescott Drive home be kept kosher.

But she resented being pressured into capitulating to Dan's preferences, especially regarding how much Judaism would be part of the boys' lives. Every chance she got, she rebelled against Dan's "rules," taking Ben and Lincoln out for non-kosher meals—her husband none the wiser—Asian food among her favorites. Not wanting the leftovers to go to waste, she'd have them packed up to take to a friend, knowing she couldn't bring pork or shellfish into their kosher home. She wouldn't breathe a word to Dan about how his cubbies had salivated over their special treats.

Something else that had been fraying the fabric of their relationship was Dan's seeming inability to pick up on social cues, body language, and nuance—not just with his wife, but with others in his orbit as well. He ruffled feathers frequently without the slightest awareness—or concern—over how friends and acquaintances perceived his words and actions. For a man whose intellectual prowess set him apart from virtually all other creatures on the planet, his insensitivity could at times be rather stunning.

Dan's massive reservoir of confidence often made him appear abrasive, arrogant, and condescending, especially to complete strangers. Which made first impressions especially challenging, his Meat Market 1.0 catastrophe a prime example. Virtually everyone who knew Dan well had seen these weaknesses manifest in various ways. He could be rude or annoying without realizing it. He sometimes took esoteric arguments with others far beyond their comfort zone—as he had with Wendi's law student friend, nearly ending their engagement—or made comments never intended to be insulting or demeaning, but which were perceived in precisely that manner.

Dan's friends, Florida State colleagues, and Prawfs buddies were accepting of these foibles—recognizing they were far outweighed by Dan's other attributes, most especially his warmth, desire to connect people together, and genuine interest in their welfare. Some even found his social quirks charming and endearing. And early on in their relationship, Wendi was of a similar mind. Yet unlike his friends and professional acquaintances, Dan's wife had to endure these shortcomings on a near-daily basis.

Initially reluctant to confront her husband with her concerns, Wendi became more transparent about her feelings as time marched on. To his credit, Dan didn't take her criticisms personally, even coming to rely on his wife to give him a nudge, or a look, whenever he was stepping out of line. But that hardly solved the problem, only accentuating in Wendi's mind the embarrassment she felt over Dan's social peccadillos. Added to the mix of the other problems infecting their marriage, it simply made Wendi want out all the more.

•••

LINCOLN'S IMPENDING BIRTH couldn't have been timed more perfectly. Having received tenure in the spring of 2010—while Wendi was pregnant—Dan was in the ideal position to request a leave from his teaching responsibilities. Dean Weidner happily obliged, allowing his prodigious young professor to take off the entire 2011 calendar year, an enormous perk reserved for only the most accomplished professors in the nation. Once he completed grading exams in December 2010—with Lincoln only two months old—Dan had 13 months of empty space on his calendar to recharge his batteries, decompress, reconnect with his *Osita*, and enjoy his two cubbies.

Yet just like their religious beliefs, Dan and Wendi held very different notions about what it meant to be on leave. He viewed an entire year without teaching responsibilities as a golden opportunity to double down on his scholarly endeavors and to *increase* his travel schedule—becoming a "Scholar in Residence" at NYU's law school, spending nearly a week each month in the Big Apple, residing in housing furnished by NYU. Not to mention trips to Arizona, Boston, Virginia, Connecticut, San Francisco, South Carolina, Iowa, and Washington, D.C. to attend academic conferences and present his latest articles. As well as two-week pleasure trip to Israel. His extensive travel schedule left Wendi fully responsible for the kids far more than she cared to be—just as she was beginning her new role as a clinical law professor.

Though Dan, his *Osita*, and the boys also ventured off on some family trips, it was Wendi who was often saddled with the driving, the omnipresent clacking of her husband's laptop keys an apt metaphor of their decaying relationship. Dan would literally tell her not to speak with him during their long drives because he needed to focus on his writing. And when he wasn't traveling or doing his own writing or blogging, he was reviewing and commenting on countless drafts from Prawfs and Florida State colleagues.

When Dan was gone for extended periods, Wendi stayed with her parents in Coral Springs or had her mom come to Tally to help with the boys. Donna had a front-row seat as her daughter became more and more frustrated, hopeless, and depressed. This was hardly what the fiercely protective mother had envisioned in her mind's eye when she peered over Wendi's shoulder seven years earlier and pointed to Mr. Right on the computer monitor. In her considered judgment, the passage of time had established with crystal clarity that Dan Markel was actually Mr. Wrong.

In August 2012, Wendi and Dan joined their good friends Tracey and Jeremy Cohen and Courtney and Darrin McMahon on a beach trip to St. George Island in the Gulf of Mexico, about a 90-minute drive from Tally. As they were unloading their respective vehicles in the parking lot, Wendi pulled the other women aside, swearing them to secrecy. She told them she'd finalized her plans to leave Dan and would be doing so when he next left town. Her husband of six years was standing just a few feet away, making silly faces while placing the boys in their double-wide stroller. He didn't have the slightest inkling what the women were discussing, oblivious to the reality that his marriage was weeks away from ending.

•••

DAN FINALLY MADE CONTACT with Wendi on September 11—the day after he returned from New York—persuading her that he'd file kidnapping charges unless she let him see the kids immediately. She relented. They met for ice cream so he could see for himself that the boys were still in town and were fine. Wendi had their mutual friends Allen and Lynn Grossman accompany her, hoping their presence would tamp down her husband's anger.

Merely getting to see and hug his cubbies lowered Dan's temperature considerably. And when his parents arrived for the Jewish holidays, Wendi even allowed the kids to spend a few days at their home on Trescott Drive. The immediate crisis was averted.

Yet those small victories were short-lived. With each passing day, Dan would make additional discoveries that—in his eyes at least—amplified the magnitude of his wife's betrayal. On her way out the door, he learned, she'd taken the boys' passports, which would prevent them from traveling with him to Toronto to visit his parents and sister's family. Their safety deposit box at the bank had been emptied of its contents, mostly jewelry. Among the valuable items stored there—and of immense sentimental value to Dan—was the two-karat diamond engagement ring his Great Uncle Lazar had given his Great Aunt Rachel. The very same one he'd slipped on Wendi's finger in Israel when he proposed. His wife had helped herself to more than $300,000 in their Charles Schwab investment account—exactly half the balance—and the entirety of a second Schwab account, valued at approximately $50,000, which had been a gift from her parents.

Dan also learned that Wendi had been planning her sneak attack for months. In Florida, a parent isn't permitted to obtain a divorce until completing a parenting course sanctioned by the State. Dan discovered his wife had taken and completed hers *in July*.

But what infuriated him more than anything was her refusal to let him know where she and the kids were staying. Not knowing where his boys were putting their heads down to sleep each night produced more anguish than he could tolerate. Every chance he had, he'd tell his family and friends how inhuman it was for Wendi not to let him know. The only place he knew he could see Ben and Lincoln without Wendi's interference was at their preschool, where he found himself every school day for breakfast, circle time, or lunch. Yet seeing them for just an hour only made the desperate father crave his children that much more.

By late September, he couldn't take it anymore. Dan barged into Wendi's office at the law school and angrily demanded that she provide an address and telephone number to her new home. He threatened to press federal kidnapping charges if she refused. Startled and afraid, she finally relented. Which, for the moment at least, prevented the powder keg from exploding.

•••

ON OCTOBER 9, 2012, Dan Markel turned 40. His birthday gathering at 2116 Trescott Drive was small and very subdued—nary a hint of bam bizzle. To his friends, the atmosphere seemed more like a funeral than a celebration. Dan was extremely morose—tears flowing freely—a captive audience there to hear his sorrows. He truly was in mourning, devastated over the loss of his marriage and destruction of his family, spilling his guts to anyone who would listen about Wendi's surprise attack, labeling the stunt his "Pearl Harbor" moment.

For his dear friends across the country and around the globe, Dan tapped out a lengthy email that evening, informing them that "the boys and I are celebrating under, well, different circumstances. To my profound chagrin, the bear family is reconfiguring. Wendi moved out of the house while I was on a short business trip to NYC." He shared the gory details of the ransacked home to which he returned, explaining his wife "just determined things weren't working for her, notwithstanding my (from my perspective) heroic efforts to make her as happy as possible."

Dan's email wasn't all doom and gloom, however. "The good news: We've been sharing the boys equally and acting on civil though pretty much silent terms (indeed, I'm trying to be as warm as possible …) And I've lost almost 10 pesky pounds."

His promotion process at Florida State had gone well, he noted, and he was trying his best to adapt "to this bizarre new world" and to "raise our boys in the global village of love and friendship that you've helped create over the years." Though he sometimes woke up in a cranky mood, "by the time I take a walk in our beautiful neighborhood and have a friend or family member to talk to, I feel better and ready to take on the day."

Ever the teacher, Dan ended his email with an important life lesson he'd sadly discovered too late: "Everything wonderful is also and already fragile. Love mightily while you can."

•••

AS ANGRY AS DAN WAS at Wendi, he also wanted her back. Desperately. He sent her a barrage of lengthy emails, laying bare his raw emotion. He outlined the changes he was willing to make—committed to making—to improve their marriage. He had stunning floral arrangements delivered to her office and, on one occasion, even dropped to a knee, begging her to take him back. As he told his friends in his birthday email, "My basic plan is I'm trying to be as *menschy* as possible to her, following the advice of a wise friend who said, act so that your boys will always be proud of you."

Yet days would pass without a response to his emails. When Wendi would finally write back, her words were cryptic and unresponsive. Dan was hoping for any signal, however small, that she was open to giving him another chance. But his wife was careful not to convey any.

Nonetheless, she agreed to bring the boys to a Halloween party being thrown by a mutual friend, which would give Dan a chance to spend quality time with them before heading to Canada, without them, the next day. He arrived at the party full of hope and excitement—still clinging to the increasingly remote possibility that Wendi would give him another chance. He waited. And waited some more, his impatience mounting steadily with each passing minute. Finally, Wendi texted to let him know that neither she nor the boys would be coming. Dan was crushed, unable to shake the sensation that his blood was beginning to boil.

Yet he wasn't the only one feeling that way. Earlier that day, Wendi actually had every intention of attending the party with Ben and Lincoln. That is, until she learned from a friend that Dan had been spreading rumors about her. Ugly rumors. Apparently, he'd been telling his friends as well as his colleagues at the law school—her colleagues too—that his wife was mentally ill. And also, that she'd stolen significant sums of money from him. Hearing about those rumors hours before the Halloween party squelched any desire she had to "play nice."

And in Dan's eyes, her pulling the rug out from under

him—on Halloween of all days—was the last straw. She clearly wasn't going to give their marriage another try and didn't have the slightest reluctance using the kids as pawns to cause him pain. Battle lines now drawn, the war was about to begin.

10.

Relocation

ACCORDING TO THE OLD ADAGE coined by Abraham Lincoln, "a man who represents himself has a fool for a client," the sixteenth President's clever witticism conveying the folly of appearing in court without a lawyer. It isn't often, however, that a lawyer finds himself embroiled in his own litigation. Preeminent legal scholar that he was, Dan Markel was tempted to ignore Lincoln's sage wisdom, supremely confident he could outsmart Wendi's lawyer, Shannon Novey, who fell far short of his Harvard pedigree and had been a divorce attorney for only five years.

But since he knew nothing at all about family law—and deciding to err on the side of caution—Dan retained a local divorce attorney, Thomas Duggar, a Florida State grad one of his colleagues highly recommended. Duggar had all of eight years under his belt since passing the bar exam. More than enough, Dan concluded, already hunkered down with every family law resource he could find, fully intending to do virtually all of the work himself, Lincoln's admonition notwithstanding.

With Duggar's input and his comprehensive knowledge of all things Adelson, Dan felt certain it was only a matter of time before Wendi began pushing to move to South Florida—with their toddlers—what divorce attorneys refer to as "relocation." He was well aware that, since their separation, Donna had been spending more time in Tally helping Wendi with the boys than at her own home in South Florida. He had little doubt his mother-in-law considered that arrangement untenable—having to choose between her husband, beloved son, and the family dental practice on the one hand, and her daughter and grandsons on the other.

The newly separated father harbored no illusion he'd be battling just one Adelson. The quest to move the children to South Florida would surely become Donna and Harvey's mission every bit as much—if not more so—than their own daughter's. They and Wendi's brother Charlie would undoubtedly be pumping as much money into the legal proceedings as necessary to ensure daily access to their grandchildren and nephews. If that resulted in Dan's bond with his sons being irreparably damaged, he was quite certain his in-laws would consider that a bonus, rather than a life-altering injury to Ben and Lincoln.

Not only did he conduct extensive research to obtain a solid command of Florida law on relocation, Dan absorbed reams of social science literature analyzing the problems in the growth and development of young children that can result from a divorcing parent relocating them to a brand new community. There was no way on earth he was going to allow the Adelson family to move his little guys seven hours away from him. He'd be more than ready to fight—and win—that battle.

The first sign that something was afoot occurred only five weeks into the litigation, when Wendi retained a new lawyer named Kristin Adamson. With 24 years' experience in family law and holding every designation and certification imaginable, Adamson was one of North Florida's most experienced and sought-after divorce lawyers—a significant upgrade from Shannon Novey. Dan heard through the grapevine that his mother-in-law had been the driving force behind Wendi swapping horses so early in the process, jettisoning Novey because she wouldn't pursue relocation. With Adamson now at the helm, a petition to relocate was surely imminent.

By late November, as part of Team Adelson's strategy to effect the relocation, Wendi had secured a job offer from Grossman Roth, P.A., a reputable personal injury firm with two offices in South Florida. One of its senior partners, Gary Cohen, had been very close with Donna and Harvey since Wendi was in diapers. He was more than happy to facilitate her employment in South Florida—as a medical malpractice attorney—to help his good friends gain increased access to their grandkids.

Adamson filed Wendi's petition to relocate in January 2013, with an email confirming her Grossman Roth job offer—at an annual salary of $115,000—attached. The petition stated that Wendi would begin living at her childhood home in Coral Springs on May 1, when her new job in Boca Raton was set to begin. According to the petition, the move would provide a "better quality of life for the children by increasing their access to close family and providing more stability and consistency." Adamson noted the close bond Ben and Lincoln had with their grandparents, who "have visited every 3-4 weeks since the birth of the children." In contrast, their father, she wrote, "travels a great deal, approximately 45-55 days away from the family each year."

There were professional reasons for Wendi's move as well, her lawyer asserted. Unlike Dan's tenured status at the law school, her clinical position was "tenuous," her husband frequently intimating that Wendi's employment on the faculty was "solely dependent upon his discretion." Dan had also created a "hostile work environment" for her "by telling the administration and their joint work colleagues that the Wife has stolen from him and that she has mental health issues." Furthermore, Dan was "constantly dropping into Wife's office unannounced, uninvited and undesired," which ceased only after a stern warning from Adamson.

The petition contended that Dan himself had no intention of remaining in Tally, revealing that he'd been trying to climb the academic ladder ever since arriving at Florida State in 2005. With teaching responsibilities only twice a week, Adamson wrote, Dan could easily commute back and forth to South Florida, able to reside free of charge with two sets of relatives who lived in the area—including his Great Uncle Lazar. Dan also had several health-related issues, the petition stated, that made him "unable to care for the children on his own," including Crohn's Disease, persistent episodes of vertigo, and back problems that had required surgery in December 2012.

For five solid weeks, Dan poured his energy into his response to Wendi's relocation petition as if he were writing a groundbreaking article for the *Harvard Law Review*. Family court judges might not have been accustomed to reviewing scholarly writing, but that is precisely what the judge deciding Wendi's petition would receive from this tenured professor—23 pages replete with dense footnotes, citations to social science research, and a healthy dose of vitriol. Though the document contained his attorney's signature, Thomas Duggar's contributions didn't extend much further than that.

Dan's second footnote—containing 11 lines of text in tiny font—was a play-by-play recitation of the events of September 10, 2012: "Wife was gone, the boys were gone, the house was half plundered, the Schwab accounts had been raided, and divorce papers were left on the bed. Most importantly, there was no indication of where the Wife and children were." Dan would return to this Pearl Harbor theme in virtually every document he filed in court, believing his wife's misconduct sufficiently egregious to tilt the entire playing field in his direction.

He belittled Wendi's economic rationale for her proposed move, contending it was asserted in bad faith. Not only had she never worked for a private law firm, the law school had just promoted her to the position of clinical professor, at a salary of $100,000 a year. Factoring in the difference in the cost of living between Tally and South Florida, she'd actually have less earning power at her supposed new job. Further, considering the hour-long commute between Coral Springs and Boca Raton and more grueling work schedule, Dan argued that Wendi would end up with far less time with the boys, evidence of her "inability to prioritize the children's well-being."

He labeled as "specious" her contention that Ben and Lincoln would have "more stability and consistency in South Florida," noting they'd lived their entire lives in Tally, had deep connections with some 50 families, and were "enmeshed in a loving community." According to their preschool director, they were "flourishing." The only inconsistency and instability in their lives, Dan contended, "has been introduced by the Wife's abandonment of the Husband and her move to a new and unfamiliar home."

He pushed back against Wendi's argument that he was chomping at the bit to climb the academic ladder. Though that had been true earlier in his career, Dan acknowledged, he was now a "chaired, tenured, and (beginning August 2013) full professor," quite content with his role on the Florida State faculty. "More urgently," he wrote, "with a separation thrust upon him by surprise and deception, one that he neither wanted nor expected, the Husband has no desire to further disrupt the lives of his beloved children, with whom he is actively engaged in parenting."

Dan excoriated Wendi for using the children "as pawns," asserting that, due to her "penchant for deception," she couldn't be trusted to adhere to her commitments on timesharing if she and the kids moved to South Florida. As examples, he pointed to her failure to permit the boys to Skype with him on numerous occasions and how she kept them away from him at Halloween. He also complained that, since their separation, she'd "done nothing to facilitate the children's connection to the Jewish community," introduced them to a non-kosher diet, and wouldn't permit him to take them to synagogue during *her* weekends. And if the court was going to consider health issues, Wendi had some of her own it needed to be aware of, Dan pointed out, "both physical and mental."

Between "the broken promises, communication withdrawal, and deceitful behavior," Dan wrote, "Wife really cannot be trusted to consider the children's best interests or the Husband's reasonable parenting interests." He contended that she had "unclean hands" — a legal phrase meaning unethical behavior — due to her "numerous false statements ... lack of integrity, and other instances of bad faith." At bottom, he said in closing, her petition to relocate was "frivolous."

•••

WHETHER DAN REALIZED IT or not, those stinging words didn't merely sit idly in the court's electronic filing system. Kristin Adamson dutifully emailed his pleading to her client, Wendi, who in turn forwarded it to the people paying Adamson's bills: Donna and Harvey Adelson.

Dan's in-laws weren't just angry as they read through his scathing attacks on their daughter. They were furious. Enraged. Had Dan been in their midst, there's no telling what they'd have done to him with their own bare hands. They were determined to win this battle at all costs, and were willing to stoop far lower than their miserable son-of-a-bitch son-in-law — who was merely fighting with words.

Donna poured herself into her email to Wendi just as fervently as Dan had into his legal filing, lamenting that his "23-page rant" left little doubt he had "made his divorce a full time job to attempt to get what he's always gotten. His way."

She told Wendi, "The most important part of your divorce is relocation. I sincerely hope your attorney understands that this is your NON NEGOTIABLE." Donna wanted to make sure Adamson fully appreciated the sacrifices she and Harvey had been making, traveling to Tally incessantly and for extended periods to care for the boys "to get them through a transitional time with people who love them." The significant time away from home had resulted in decreased profits in their dental practice and a loss of patients. That also was unfair to Charlie, "a wonderful uncle to Benjamin and Lincoln," who'd purchased the practice from his father the prior July.

If Wendi and the kids were able to relocate to South Florida, Donna wrote, "they will have an incredibly warm and loving family as an integral part of their lives." She wanted the judge to understand that the boys would be living with their amazing grandparents, in their own well-furnished bedrooms, with the "huge bonus" of spending their days with a retired elementary school teacher.

Also at stake for Wendi, her mother added, was a much higher paying and more flexible job, reminding her of the extensive travel associated with her existing position at Florida State. "Those trips need to be coordinated with a very angry man who will not be cooperative with you in this regard," she predicted, but who expected her to drop everything for his monthly travel to New York, "his regular NYU crap."

Though Donna had no legal training to speak of, she outlined a blueprint of what she wanted Adamson to include in her legal filings: A "hot temper and verbal abuse is what you need to emphasize that you suffered under his 'reign.' Narcissistic personality disorder causes major problems in a marriage. Especially when one believes that because he attended Harvard undergrad and Harvard Law, he's clearly better and smarter than anyone else ... including you." Only an "idiot like him" would think that, she snarled.

Donna wanted the judge "to get the message that this guy is a big bully," instructing Wendi to gather up some of Dan's emails to prove the point. So "sweet, caring, and concerned," she noted sarcastically, he decided to spend two weeks in Israel toward the end of Wendi's pregnancy with Ben. She also thought the judge should know that her son-in-law was a "religious zealot" who was "indoctrinating" the kids into Judaism, and who had taken them to synagogue as infants to "absorb the music and the prayers."

Donna urged her daughter to play dirty to force Dan into submission. "What's going to happen in June when he wants to go to three different conferences? DON'T LET HIM GO. If you do, you're enabling and facilitating you're [sic] stay in Tallahassee." She even suggested a "bribe" to entice him to allow the relocation—airfare for trips to visit the boys in South Florida—"a last ditch effort if all else fails."

Wendi's mother groused that "this bastard has not paid

one cent to your bridge gap alimony. Why??? Why only two months of a child support payment over an 8 month time frame? Loving, caring father that he is." She ended her five-page email only because she was "too angry to write any more."

Three days after pounding out her lengthy diatribe, Donna informed Wendi she was on anti-anxiety medications, with episodes of hysterical crying interfering with her daily life. Just thinking about her worthless son-in-law and the way he was treating her precious daughter was more than she could bear.

•••

ON MONDAY, JUNE 3, 2013, Wendi found herself in Thomas Duggar's law office, seated at a conference room table, sandwiched between Adamson and a court reporter. Dan and his attorney sat directly across the table. She was a nervous wreck.

Though her law professor husband had been able to ghostwrite all of his pleadings, Florida law required that Duggar, as his attorney, ask all questions posed to Wendi during her deposition. And as much as Donna would have jumped at the chance to answer each and every question he posed, Wendi's mom wasn't permitted to attend, not even to provide her daughter moral support.

Over the course of nearly three hours, Duggar asked Wendi every question he could think of—and those Dan scribbled onto yellow Post-it notes—that might bear on the subject of relocation. In her answers, Wendi didn't hesitate to take jabs at her soon-to-be ex-husband. "The boys tell me that he hurts them when he buckles them into the car," she testified. "He made a bad decision with a babysitter that my son, Ben, told me hit him and then continued to employ her." Their eldest also was afraid of swimming, she said, "because Danny was forceful with him in the water and made him swim when he didn't want to." Wendi told Duggar her husband shouldn't be granted equal parenting time because she had a better relationship with the boys, "a closer bond."

Asked when she first decided that she wanted to relocate to South Florida, Wendi answered, "I've wanted to relocate for the *past six years.*" The only reason she hadn't included a request to relocate in her initial divorce petition, she acknowledged, was because Shannon Novey had told her "it wasn't possible."

Turning to the subject of Pearl Harbor, Duggar asked about the items Wendi grabbed on her way out the door. She explained that she needed the boys' passports because Dan wasn't an American citizen and couldn't travel with them internationally without her written permission. Which was true, as Dan had only gotten as far as securing his green card, never having made it a priority to complete the citizenship process. As for his late Great Aunt Rachel's diamond engagement ring, Wendi claimed it was a gift from Dan's Great Uncle Lazar and therefore hers to keep—even though she never wore it. She nevertheless agreed to surrender the ring if Dan's 96-year-old great uncle personally asked for its return.

Without any restrictions limiting Duggar's interrogation, Wendi was forced to admit she'd been seeing a psychiatrist and was on medication for depression. The statements Dan had made about her mental health—which had so infuriated her and led to the Halloween imbroglio—actually did have some basis in fact.

Dan's lawyer asked Wendi to explain why she hadn't been facilitating Skype sessions between Ben and Lincoln and their father. She claimed it was impossible to make her children—all of two and three years of age—sit still, noting it was "very hard to keep their attention span, keep them engaged." Instead of interactions between father and sons, the video chats ended up devolving into calls with just her. "And Danny was often using it to ask questions about who we were meeting with and where we were going and what was going on. And so I found it to be intrusive."

"If the court denies the relocation," Duggar asked, "is it still your intent to take the job and go to South Florida?"

"I wouldn't go without my kids," Wendi answered.

"If you wouldn't go without yours, why would you ask him to go without his?"

"Because we never planned on staying here," she replied. "At some point soon, Danny will want to leave Tallahassee."

•••

DAN SNUCK IN ONE additional court filing on the eve of the relocation hearing, once again laced with biting adjectives and adverbs. "The Wife's pleadings are vague," he wrote, "filled with rank and obvious falsehoods, the legal analysis is fundamentally inept." He blamed Donna and Harvey for driving the litigation, suggesting their meddling had prevented him and Wendi from having a cooperative co-parenting relationship. He asked the judge to award him costs, as otherwise, "Wife and her affluent parents, who are bank-rolling Wife's litigation so that they can enjoy closer access to the grandchildren, will persist in vexatious and groundless litigation."

The hearing was held on June 18, 2013, with Circuit Judge Barbara Hobbs presiding. The African-American jurist had been on the bench less than half a year, first elected two months after Wendi filed her divorce petition. Dan and Duggar were seated at one counsel table, Wendi and Adamson the other. The lawyers and their clients were prepared for a contentious, daylong hearing, their witnesses—including Donna Adelson—seated just outside the courtroom, ready to come forward to testify when summoned.

Adamson called Wendi as her first witness. The Coral Springs native testified for three solid hours, outlining the many reasons why she wanted to move to South Florida with the boys. When her direct examination concluded, rather than having Duggar commence his cross, Judge Hobbs asked Wendi to step down from the witness stand and instructed the lawyers to approach the bench for a sidebar. Dan and Wendi looked on anxiously as the judge and their lawyers whispered to one another for several minutes.

Judge Hobbs told Adamson she was unimpressed with Wendi's case for relocation. After reading the court filings and listening to Wendi's testimony, she couldn't find any basis to uproot the children and move them clear across the state. The desire to be with extended family members, the judge added, should never trump the rights and needs of two loving parents. She told Adamson she couldn't stop her from putting on additional evidence, but believed doing so would be a waste of everyone's time and energy.

With that, the lawyers retreated to share with their clients what they'd just heard. After huddling with Wendi at their counsel table, Adamson begrudgingly agreed there'd be no further evidence. The judge summarily denied Wendi's petition and ordered the parties to participate in mediation prior to their three-day trial, which was set to begin July 31.

Judge Hobbs's words were an utterly satisfying vindication for Dan—music to his and Duggar's ears. They were also a complete repudiation of everything Team Adelson had been fighting for—at great expense—for five months. A truly devastating blow. Dan called his mom before even leaving the courthouse, filling her in on the judge's decision. He was elated. He'd been on pins and needles for months. Finally, he could breathe a huge sigh of relief.

Outside the courthouse, Wendi got behind the wheel of her minivan, her mother seated beside her in the passenger seat—seething over what had just transpired. Theirs would be a very different conversation.

•••

DESPITE JUDGE HOBBS'S RULING, Donna Adelson wasn't about to concede defeat. With a week to gather her thoughts, she emailed Wendi, telling her, "Just like it says on your necklace, 'Never, never, never give up.'" It was time for "action," she insisted, "time to take control of your life" and not let Dan believe he'd won anything "by having you remain in Tallahassee, eight hours away from the only family you have, and lose out on what will be a job that will afford you and your children advantages they will never otherwise be able to enjoy." She told Wendi they'd "show this f----- what will make him absolutely miserable."

Looking ahead to the July 31 trial, Donna told her daughter a lot was riding on "how well you can perform/act" prior to then and that she, Harvey, and Charlie were counting on her. "You can be a good actress when you want to. I've seen you in action. You need to put on the performance of your life! Jibbers"—her derogatory nickname for Dan—"hasn't beaten the Adelson family yet."

Donna outlined a five-step "PLAN OF ACTION" to bring her son-in-law to his knees, centered on convincing him that Wendi would be raising Ben and Lincoln in the *Catholic* faith. The first step was for Wendi to take a photo of the boys standing at the front door of a Tallahassee church, making it her Facebook profile picture, "so everyone will see this." Donna predicted, "Within minutes, Jibbers should either see this, or will be getting calls from his friends/acquaintances about this. Hmmm. How happy do you think he will be?"

Step two involved a private tutor, preferably a "teenage Catholic church member," to come to Wendi's home and "teach the young men about Jesus," someone who could serve as a "babysitter assistant" while she prepared dinner. Donna offered to arrange for such a tutor if Wendi didn't have time.

Third, Wendi would let "Jibbers know that your children WILL be baptized in the Catholic church." Donna informed Wendi that she'd "already checked this out and a baptism can be arranged within 2 weeks. We can send out evites to Jibbers, his parents, sister and anyone else you want to invite." The fourth step was to enroll the boys in Christian camps for the summer, for which Donna offered to pay. Fifth, Wendi was to register the kids for toddler classes at church. "I've looked into this," her mom wrote, "and even if they don't go, we can show Jibbers that they are enrolled for the fall semester." She implored her daughter: "TAKE CONTROL FROM HIM! GET TO HIM PSYCHOLOGICALLY! HE'S GOING TO WANT

YOU TO STOP THIS!"

The primary goal of her plan was to make Dan "angry. We want him ticked off so he realizes that he could lose control over his kids." Donna expressed particular concern over Dan's "religious influence over these children" and how they might soon refuse to eat in her daughter's non-kosher home. "And, if they see you don't want to attend their shul functions, you will be the outsider. As they get older and more involved under Jibber's [sic] religious influence, they will be able to request which parent they want to live with. Don't allow Jibbers to have this power and control over them."

She reiterated how much she, Harvey, and Charlie had altered their lives to support Wendi during the divorce process. "Charlie has accepted the loss in office business income for us to do this because he loves you and wants only the best possible future for you. It's time for you to show us that you can put on the performance of your life." Donna closed her three-page email, "With our love and only the best intentions, Mom & Dad."

But to her grave disappointment, her daughter rebuffed her plan of action—each and every step. Wendi told her that even the slightest actions aimed at altering the boys' religious upbringing would make her look far worse in the judge's eyes, and could backfire badly at the upcoming trial. That wasn't just her view, she said, but also Kristin Adamson's.

Already furious with Wendi's attorney for what she perceived as a lackluster performance leading up to and during the relocation hearing, Donna lashed out at Adamson, telling Wendi in an email that she and Harvey had been wasting $600 an hour on her services for ten solid months: "All she cared about was if the father hasn't been pulling out their toenails, you should give up any financial betterment for you and your children and raise them in a place that you agreed to go to because Jibbers only had FSU as a job offer. Of course, as a graduate of FSU Law School and a native of Tallahassee, she sees nothing wrong with living there. Obviously, as a native of South Florida, you know better."

Donna also sought to entice Wendi with the luxurious perks she'd enjoy in Coral Springs: "I don't know how much of the 'big picture' you're seeing honey… Aside from living in a far better city with family … you can have someone cleaning your home, a nanny to help with your children, a lifestyle in which you and your boys can travel. This is a once in a lifetime opportunity to really turn your life around and make a positive difference in the lives of your children."

She told Wendi she disagreed with the suggestion that Judge Hobbs would hold it against her for introducing the children to Christianity. "She goes to church," Donna pointed out. "There were multiple donations from her church pastors & ministers on her financial contributions website. She's a Southern Black lady. How do you know it won't be music to her ears to hear this?" Yet Donna also lashed out against the judge: "It's clear since Judge Hobbs [sic] last ruling that she could care less about anything you had to say in your behalf."

She was particularly irate about the prospect of Dan having "sole control of the boys [sic] religious lives. Why let him? Why not stand up to this fucker! Why not fight!" She urged Wendi to reconsider her decision about the acting performance she'd proposed. "We're all willing to help you accomplish this. And that's all it is, Wendi, an *act*. An act of defiance that will put a scare into this jackass. It will infuriate him. It won't infuriate a judge that you found Jesus."

"Jibbers has tried to aggravate and screw you since day one of this divorce," Donna groused, from "vicious emails" to "bad mouthing you to the faculty at the school you will be working at; everything he does is done with malicious intent." What she was asking of Wendi, she said, would only be necessary for a few days. "You know him. You know which buttons to push!"

Donna tried to frighten Wendi over the prospect that, left unchecked, Dan would transform her boys into "two little Orthodox young men." He was "brainwashing" them with his extremism, she said. "He's already got them thinking that people who eat shrimp are bad. Hot dogs are disgusting.

Lobster is gross. Wait. Ben's not even four years-old. Wait till he's 8." That was all part of Dan's "organized plan." Their entire lives would be "shul, shul, shul," she predicted. Every Saturday morning, Sunday, and holiday. "That will be their life."

Donna revealed that she and Harvey planned to retain yet another lawyer to make a financial offer to Dan, to persuade him to allow the relocation after all. The amount? One million dollars, split three ways between Donna and Harvey, Charlie, and Wendi herself. Invested properly, Dan would have $4 million in 15-18 years. "Certainly nothing he'd ever save in 10 lifetimes!" Donna noted. Before making that offer, she asked Wendi "to show us that you're doing your part in this too. We're a team. We can't do this without your help."

Donna also pushed back against something Wendi had said when they spoke—that divorce isn't about winning and losing—telling her daughter: "Well, it is about winning and losing. We're trying to get a 'WIN!' You deserve it! You deserve so much more than a life without family, teaching in Tallahassee." She suggested to Wendi that her Grandma Lorraine, were she still alive, would "tell you to fight with every bone in your body. Fight for yourself, your boys, and for the best possible life you can have."

Yet despite her mother's strident pleas, Wendi wouldn't budge. She didn't take Ben and Lincoln to church, plan a baptism, or hire a Christian tutor. No financial offer was extended to Dan. The upcoming mediation would therefore be Donna's final chance to wrest control of her grandchildren from the person she loathed more than anyone else on earth.

• • •

MEDIATIONS ARE CONDUCTED for one singular purpose: to keep cases out of the courtroom by encouraging parties involved in litigation to settle. In a family law mediation, the husband and wife begin and end in separate conference rooms, to avoid having to see one another and stir up painful memories. What either says to the mediator remains confidential, and can't be used in further court proceedings. The hope is that, with the cone of confidentiality protecting the entire proceeding, the litigants can speak their minds freely, leading to a full and frank discussion and, hopefully, a settlement.

Dan and Wendi had already been through one round of mediation on May 9, prior to the relocation hearing. It had been a complete and utter bust. They selected a new mediator for their July 17 mediation, the stakes considerably higher with a full-blown trial scheduled to begin in two weeks. Yet after eight grueling hours shuttling back and forth between the two rooms, the mediator couldn't get the warring spouses to budge—Dan insisting on a 50/50 split in their time with the boys and Wendi holding firm at 65/35 in her favor. It appeared certain the case was heading to trial.

But at literally the eleventh hour, late in the afternoon of July 30, they somehow managed to reach a compromise. Dan agreed for Wendi to be the primary custodian during the school year for three years, his visitation limited to six out of every 14 nights. Summers were to be divided 50/50, as were school years commencing in 2016. Though Dan pressed hard for the children to be with him for all Jewish holidays, he ultimately relented, agreeing to alternate Rosh Hashanah, Yom Kippur, and Passover with Wendi every other year.

The marital settlement agreement (MSA) Dan and Wendi signed—which bore Donna's signature as a witness—contained several financial terms as well: Dan was to pay $841 per month in child support and be responsible for 65% of the boys' preschool, extracurricular activities, and summer camps. Wendi agreed to forego alimony. The home on Trescott Drive would become Dan's in exchange for him paying Wendi $120,000 within 60 days. He also agreed to pay $10,000 in Wendi's attorney's fees, directly to Kristin Adamson.

Thus, on July 31, rather than slugging these issues out before Judge Hobbs, the attorneys presented the MSA for filing. The judge, delighted the spouses and parents were able to avoid trial, signed the final judgment dissolving their marriage. Seven-and-a-half years after exchanging their vows under the *chuppah*, Dan Markel and Wendi Adelson were husband and wife no longer.

That evening, Dan sent a jubilant email to his closest friends—subject line "feeling better"—in which he shared the "serendipitous news." He noted that although he'd been "wailing about the injustice of this settlement process and outcome," in the end, he actually wound up with 24 weeks of parenting time each year, very close to 50/50. He dropped a link to a satirical *New Yorker* cartoon he was reminded of by his lengthy battle with the Adelsons. At the center of the drawing was a medieval warrior mounted on an armored horse—sword raised triumphantly—the animal's hind legs perched atop a heaping pile of human carnage, plumes of smoke rising up across the horizon. The caption beneath the image was most apropos: "Let the healing begin."

•••

IN EARLY DECEMBER 2013, Dan traveled to Los Angeles for Prawfsfest! 11 at Pepperdine University—where he workshopped his new article on sentencing. While in town, he had dinner with his good friends Zach and Abigail Shrier and their three kids. He was very upbeat—beaming—as he filled the Shriers in on his blossoming relationship with NYU law professor Amy Adler. It was abundantly clear to them that their good friend was falling in love.

Dan also was euphoric over winning the court battle on relocation, gloating to the Shriers how he'd easily deflected Donna and Harvey's best shot and defeated them resoundingly. He told them he was now less concerned about the Adelsons, convinced he had the upper hand—whatever legal maneuvers they might attempt in the future—extremely proud of himself for mastering the legal chess board more ably than Wendi's entire team.

The three adults sat together at the Shriers' breakfast table as

Dan thumbed through picture after picture of Ben and Lincoln on his iPhone, playing the entirety of a video he'd taken of the boys singing a Hannukah song at their preschool days earlier. His friends could feel his love and pride for the boys oozing through his pores.

But Dan's victory lap about his legal triumph left them somewhat unsettled. The Shriers had met Donna and Harvey and had heard plenty of Dan's stories about them since Pearl Harbor. They had a sixth sense that getting under Wendi's parents' skin and riling them up could have serious consequences. Yet for some reason, as well as Dan himself knew them, he seemed utterly oblivious to any such possibility.

11.

Gloves Off

THE INK HAD BARELY DRIED on the marital settlement agreement before the newly divorced couple was back in court. Though the MSA obligated Dan to pay Wendi $120,000 and her lawyer $10,000, he refused to comply with those provisions, paying his ex-wife only $54,725.38 instead. When she asked him where the rest of the money was, Dan told her that he had compelling reasons not to pay the remainder, but wouldn't specify what they were. Her hand forced, Wendi—at her mother's urging—had Adamson file a motion to enforce Dan's payment obligations, or be held in contempt of court. A hearing was scheduled for February 17, 2014.

Three days before the hearing, with a new attorney named Scott Snavely on board, Dan filed his own "counter-motion" to enforce the MSA and to sanction Wendi for her alleged misconduct. His Valentine's Day filing was even more caustic—and the attacks on Wendi more personal—than anything Dan had filed during their relocation battle. He accused his ex-wife of filing "false and misleading" financial disclosures—and outright fraud and perjury—in failing to disclose over $240,000 in assets on her financial affidavit and by refusing to surrender his great aunt's diamond ring despite his 96-year-old great uncle's written request for its return.

Not only did Wendi's "avalanche of misconduct" excuse

Dan from paying what he owed under the MSA, he argued, it required the judge to send "a strong message" that "dishonesty and malfeasance will not be tolerated by this Court by lawyers, regardless of whether they are advocates or clients." He noted that Wendi wasn't merely a lawyer, but rather a clinical law professor "instructing the next generation of lawyers how to comport themselves." A strong remedy was necessary, he asserted, "to sanction and censure this misconduct."

Wendi wasn't a "helpless character in this drama," Dan's motion continued. "She is a 34-year-old public interest lawyer, the winner of numerous national fellowships and prizes, who simply helped herself to over $600,000 in cash, liquid equities and other assets upon separation." Her "wealthy parents" had "placed her in a financial cocoon and, upon belief, by paying her legal fees, they allowed and encouraged her to take the most aggressive and unsubstantiated legal postures possible." Dan again assailed her "frivolous" relocation petition, contending that her written filings "contained no legal support" and included "many factual falsehoods." He told the judge Wendi's "demonstrably false testimony" at the relocation hearing would have been exposed had she been subjected to cross-examination.

Dan also asked Judge Hobbs to punish Wendi for the manner in which she exited the marriage, "pillaging" the home and helping herself to whatever she wanted, never producing an inventory of what she took. Leaving him with no way to determine "the scores of books, CDs, art, and pictures she took," including "sentimental children's photos or music or other things the couple shared. Again, a court acting in equity should not countenance this kind of Visigoth-like sacking of the marital home absent special (and here, inapplicable) conditions of domestic violence."

Though his repeated and exquisitely detailed descriptions of Wendi's Pearl Harbor-style surprise attack made clear Dan was still reeling from that humiliation—just as bitter some 17 months later—what wasn't clear was why the MSA didn't foreclose each and every one of these arguments. After all, he'd knowingly and willingly resolved all financial and property issues in a settlement agreement that contained no specific provisions about his great aunt's ring or any other item he was now contending Wendi had "plundered."

Dan's attempt to explain why these arguments were still viable fell flat: "The MSA is admittedly underdeveloped with respect to what remedy is warranted regarding other undisclosed or undervalued assets," he conceded. "But it does not mean that the MSA or this Court in its equitable power cannot award any remedy." Dan stated that he'd settled the financial issues at the eleventh hour simply to avoid putting "his children (or even Ms. Adelson) through the ordeal of a trial." In contrast, his ex-wife refused his request to resolve the parenting issues separately from the financial issues, "showing that she wanted to tie the children's time-sharing to a property outcome, which basically means that she put them up for ransom."

• • •

TO BOLSTER HIS POSITION, Dan had Snavely send out a notice for Wendi's deposition to be taken—a second time—to address the issues raised in his counter-motion. Adamson responded by seeking court protection, contending that Dan was merely attempting to harass Wendi and shouldn't be allowed to depose her again. The attorneys agreed to postpone the upcoming hearing so the judge could first decide whether Wendi's deposition would be allowed to proceed.

On February 17, 2014, for the second time in eight months, the once blissfully happy husband and wife found themselves at their respective counsel tables ready to do battle, Donna Adelson seated in the gallery as a keenly interested observer. Adamson filled Judge Hobbs in on how the parties had gotten to this point so soon after resolving the entirety of their disputes, arguing that Dan had contrived a bogus excuse to avoid paying what he owed under the MSA. She asked the judge to enter an order precluding Wendi's deposition, as no legitimate purpose would be served by forcing her to answer questions, under oath, a second time.

Though Judge Hobbs lectured Dan for failing to pay what he owed under the MSA — threatening to hold him in contempt and throw him in jail if his refusal persisted — she agreed he had the right to take Wendi's deposition again. The judge told the lawyers to make sure the deposition was scheduled in time for the hearing on both parties' motions to enforce the MSA, which was pushed back to May 15.

Once again, Donna left the courthouse fuming, beside herself at the injustice being perpetrated on her daughter — by Dan, his lawyer, and especially the judge. In her email to Wendi the following day, she complained, "It just seems ridiculous for him to be able to depo you but for you and Kristin not to give him the same crap he's pulling on you. It's time to give it to him!" Adamson, she declared, "MUST depo Elvis," her new nickname for the ex-son-in-law she despised more and more with each passing day. "[L]et's aggravate him the way he's trying to aggravate you."

Donna again questioned Adamson's performance: "It seems like you're always on the defensive but I don't see her doing anything offensive." She suggested that Wendi's lawyer "request that Elvis be court ordered for psychological testing" and be prohibited from taking the boys out of the country. Donna also wanted Adamson to seek help from the dean of the law school or perhaps the provost of the entire university, insisting, "Something has to be done with this asshole!"

Though it may not have lived up to Donna's expectations, Adamson did fight back, filing a motion to strike Dan's counter-motion as a "sham pleading." In her four-page motion, Wendi's lawyer argued: "The Former Husband appears to believe that the best defense to his case is an offense. Under no family law case law, statute, or rule is it recognized that one good breach deserves another." Dan's counter-motion, she argued, was "filled with scandalous allegations regarding Former Wife and her attorney which are irrelevant and immaterial." His court filings "only prove that he is a disgruntled former husband who cannot move past this dissolution and continues to dredge up his emotions regarding this divorce rather than address his noncompliance with the Martial Settlement Agreement."

• • •

IF WENDI, HER MOM, or Adamson had the slightest expectation their motion to strike would result in Dan's surrender, they were sadly mistaken. On March 26, 2014, he filed yet another counter-motion, this one cutting straight to the core of Wendi's role as Ben and Lincoln's mom and Donna's as their grandmother.

He accused his ex of "brazenly" ignoring the MSA's parenting provisions, refusing to allow him reasonable Skype and telephone access to the kids while they were in her custody. During the first five months following entry of the MSA, he pointed out, "the Former Wife missed well over 18 required telephone calls, with no remedy to correct this pattern of intransigence." Worse still, over the Christmas holidays, "she did not facilitate any contact on 12 of the 19 days she had with them." She often had the children speak with him "in a noisy environment" and routinely failed to return dropped calls. Wendi had even "ignored his plea to speak to the children to wish them good night while he was out of town" because his call came in slightly after 7:00 p.m.

Dan also complained that instead of allowing him to watch the boys while she attended cocktail parties, guest lectures, and leadership requirements—what family law attorneys refer to as the "right of first refusal"—Wendi left the boys with her mother. "By violating the MSA in this way," he declared, "Ms. Adelson deprives Mr. Markel of any physical access to the children, in contravention of the MSA's co-parenting clause."

He accused Wendi of "inhibitory parental gatekeeping," borrowing the phrase from social science literature on the role of fathers in child development. He cited Wendi's refusal to allow Ben and Lincoln to be with him during *her* custodial time when the boys—all of three and four—invited him to join them for a snack at McDonald's or to play with them after soccer practice. Dan complained that Wendi hadn't allowed him to spend any time at all with the kids during *her* weekends since their September 2012 separation, "not even for a few moments," even though he granted her "unfettered access to the children during his weekends." Even more egregious, she often pulled them out of preschool before or after her weekends, resulting in "four or five day stretches where the children are deprived of unhampered contact with and free access to their father."

Dan also raised the issue of "one-on-one time" he believed Ben and Lincoln should have with each parent. Although this concept had been endorsed by the family therapist and preschool director, it wasn't included in the MSA's parenting provisions. Nonetheless, Dan believed Wendi's refusal to permit such one-on-one interactions required judicial intervention. He also expressed concern that his ex-wife was making unilateral decisions about the children—pointing to her signing them up for soccer without consulting him. He noted that Ben would be transitioning to kindergarten in the fall, but that Wendi was refusing to discuss options with him. She also was refusing to communicate with him about other "important parenting issues," such as "potty-training or the children's diet."

Finally, there was a matter of urgent importance regarding his mother-in-law. On three separate occasions the prior November, Dan wrote, the boys told him, "Abba, Grandma says you're stupid." Asked why she'd say such a thing, "the children replied jointly that it is because 'she says you are trying to take her Sunshines away from her.'" During a phone call in December—while Wendi and the kids were in Coral Springs—Lincoln told him, "Abba, Grandma says she hates you." Dan expressed dire concern "that continued exposure to such negativity forms the foundation for parental alienation," exacerbated by the fact that Wendi would often leave the boys "unsupervised with her parents in violation of his court-ordered right of first refusal."

Among his *ten* requests for relief, Dan asked the judge

to prohibit Wendi from allowing her mother "to have unsupervised time with the children" and to erect additional safeguards to prevent Ben and Lincoln "from being subjected to disparaging comments about their father." He requested that each parent be permitted to spend time with the boys during the *other's* custodial time—"at least 45 minutes of (shared or solo) contact time with both children." He also wanted provisional decision-making authority on matters related to the boys' health, education, and welfare "until Ms. Adelson no longer evidences the intransigence and inability to communicate that has required this Counter-Motion." Finally, he asked Judge Hobbs to hold Wendi in contempt and to impose sanctions for her willful failure to comply with the MSA's parenting provisions.

Dan's new motion raised the stakes considerably—especially in the eyes of Donna Adelson. Wendi's mom was livid—apoplectic—over his personal attacks and what she considered to be false accusations. But at the same time, she also was very worried. Despite her very best efforts and expenditure of untold sums of money, her despicable, wretched ex-son-in-law was winning at every turn. He seemed to have Judge Hobbs in his back pocket, as she kept on ruling in his favor. Wendi, Ben, and Lincoln were already stuck in Tally for who knows how long. If Jibbers won this new motion, what would it mean for her relationship with her precious grandkids?

And Dan wasn't done either. Two weeks later, in his response to Wendi's motion to strike, he told the judge the motion was itself "a textbook example of the type of sham pleading she refers to in her motion," which required the imposition of sanctions against both Wendi and her counsel. His response was littered with corrosive, biting adjectives, labeling Wendi's motion "facially absurd," "silly," "preposterous," "spurious," "scandalous," and replete with "syntactical hiccups." Contrary to the assertions in Wendi's motion, he argued, "the scandal is not that the former husband alleges these claims; the scandal is that Ms. Adelson perpetrated these actions and has thus far enjoyed immunity from consequence and censure."

•••

THE LITIGATION HAD BEEN TAKING a serious emotional toll on Wendi, who began seeing a therapist to help her cope with stressors coming from two different sides. On one side, she was having to process and deal with Dan's incessant legal pleadings—growing more incendiary seemingly by the week—which was stress-inducing enough. On the other was the persistent push from her family members, urging her to fight back even harder, and expressing disappointment when she wouldn't. That tug-of-war on her psyche made everyday life enormously challenging. It wasn't in her nature to "fight back." She simply wanted the conflict to end—the sooner the better.

Returning an email from an old Brandeis friend late in the evening of April 29, Wendi shared her frustrations: "My parents and Charlie have been very supportive, but they are so angry at Danny that I don't involve them in most of the details." Therapy was helping "a bit," she said, and she loved her "blissful parenthood times." But it was particularly hard on days she didn't have the kids. And then there was the never-ending litigation. She told her friend she'd "just have to ride this one out," hopeful that "things get a lot easier after May 15th, which is soon, thank goodness."

•••

DAN UPPED THE ANTE yet again on May 5 with a new, 13-page memo, chock-full of legal citations and dense footnotes—another law review article in all but name. He contended that under basic contract law principles, he was well within his rights not to pay the remaining balance owed to Wendi and her lawyer, due to his ex-wife's willful failure to disclose assets and surrender the items she was required to return, most significantly, his great aunt's diamond ring. And further, that Wendi and her lawyer were subject to sanctions based on their misconduct and unclean hands.

Wendi and Adamson had taken a "simple divorce," Dan asserted, "and made it complicated, nefarious, and expensive. Unless this conduct is sanctioned, the former wife will continue to enjoy impunity and her attorney, and indeed, the local bar at large, will be emboldened to advise future clients that there are no adverse consequences for ignoring discovery, flouting judicial orders, filing frivolous motions, concealing assets, and falsely testifying under oath." He asked the judge to award him the $40,000 in legal expenses he'd "incurred based on Ms. Adelson and Ms. Adamson's vexatious and bad faith misconduct."

Dan also contended that Adamson could no longer represent Wendi due to a "clear conflict of interest." He told the judge he'd been trying to settle matters with his ex-wife, but the $10,000 he'd yet to pay Adamson was interfering with his ability to do so, suggesting "her attorney's pecuniary interest is now clearly at odds with that of her client."

Finally, he asked Judge Hobbs to grant him decision-making authority over the children, pointing to Wendi's continued refusal to speak with him about where Ben would attend kindergarten. He noted that the director of Creative Preschool, where the boys attended, had urged him and Wendi to keep Ben enrolled there for one more year due to his late birthday and emotional development. Though Dan wanted to follow her recommendation, Wendi hadn't yet disclosed her preference.

Two days later, on May 7, Adamson filed a motion asking Judge Hobbs to allow her to withdraw from representing Wendi, telling her that Dan's contentions that she'd engaged in misconduct required her to be a witness at the upcoming hearing. Under Florida's ethical rules, she wrote, she couldn't be a witness and Wendi's lawyer at the same time. Adamson also moved to continue the hearing until her client could secure new counsel. Wendi's and Dan's depositions—each scheduled for the following day—were therefore postponed. Wendi then retained an attorney named Jimmy Judkins, now her third divorce lawyer in less than two years.

Small city that Tally is, Judkins' paralegal just happened to be Scott Snavely's wife. Though that didn't present a formal conflict of interest, Snavely informed his client that he wasn't willing to have his own marriage jeopardized by Dan's continuing battles with Wendi. He too withdrew and helped Dan find his own third lawyer. And on July 1, a new judge replaced Judge Hobbs on the file. The entire case was in limbo, with no resolution in sight.

•••

DAN MARKEL WAS AT A significant crossroads in his life. On the one hand, he was involved in a thoroughly fulfilling romantic relationship unlike any he'd ever experienced. Not only was Amy Adler beautiful, witty, and charming, she also was a whip-smart law professor who savored intellectual pursuits every bit as much as he did. Her short visit to Tally in late June left little doubt she was wonderful with the boys and might someday make a great stepmom.

On the other hand, however, the fighting and litigation with Wendi had been sucking him into a deep, dark abyss. The nasty brawl had escalated significantly over the last several months—soon to reach a boiling point once the upcoming hearing could be rescheduled. Dan found himself obsessing over the smallest legal nuances—with gaining the upper hand so critically important. He sometimes was more focused on the legal battle than on his career or even his precious cubbies.

Family law attorneys often employ a metaphor to assist their clients in better understanding this conundrum, analogizing their situation to driving on the highway. The road to their destination—and safe passage—is through the front windshield. The more they focus there, the better off they will be. Unfortunately, divorce has an uncanny way of distracting one's focus to the rear-view mirror, where the carnage of a now-destroyed relationship can be viewed in high-definition.

Over and over again, Dan found himself gazing at that rear-view mirror, hopelessly mired in the havoc he believed

Wendi had wreaked by abruptly terminating their marriage and pillaging their home and financial accounts. Nearly two years had passed. Yet the wounds at times seemed as fresh and deep as on that fateful day. He was struggling mightily to train his eyes on the front windshield—and all the good he knew was waiting for him if he could just find his way there.

A significant source of his frustration was that he fervently believed he and Wendi could have had a successful, post-divorce co-parenting relationship, which would have improved their lives as much as their children's. Dan had a friend and colleague who taught criminal law at the University of Tennessee, Neil Cohen, who'd been divorced since his kids were very young. Yet Cohen and his ex-wife remained very close friends in the years that followed, even taking vacations together with their children—and eventually their new spouses as well. To Dan, the Cohens' relationship was a shining example of how great post-divorce life could be for the entire family.

In his view, it was counterproductive for him and Wendi to be charting completely separate lives—not when they had a common objective of successfully raising their boys. No matter what the divorce lawyers might have been telling them, he believed it was perfectly natural for him and the boys to spend time together during Wendi's custodial time and for her to spend time with them during his. The blurrier those lines, Dan believed, the better they could work together to solve problems for the benefit of their children.

His anxiety, frustration, and ultimately hostility toward Wendi was borne largely of her refusal to embrace the Cohen model as her polar star. Like most divorced parents, however, Wendi expected her time with the kids to be exactly that—*her* time. She viewed Dan's ideal of co-parenting like the Cohens wholly unrealistic in view of the deep wounds left behind from their failed marriage. The last thing in the world she wanted was to be in Dan's presence a second longer than was absolutely necessary. She felt fully justified refusing any and all of Dan's requests to blur the lines between her custodial time and his.

• • •

WHILE WENDI WAS WITH her family in Miami for her father's 70th birthday in early July, Dan was in New York enjoying a solid week with his girlfriend Amy. While there, he popped by the apartment of his good friend and coauthor Ethan Leib, who'd moved to the Big Apple in 2011 after accepting a position at Fordham University's law school.

As they chatted in his living room, Leib was thrilled to see how happy Dan was in his relationship with Amy. But he was gravely concerned over his friend's preoccupation with the divorce proceedings. Dan recounted all of Wendi's misdeeds: her false disclosures on her financial affidavit, her failure to return his great aunt's ring, how she wasn't letting him speak to the boys—or see them—during her custodial days. He told Leib that Wendi and her lawyer's misconduct was so extreme, he was seriously contemplating filing complaints against each to have them disbarred.

Leib had heard enough, concluding his good friend needed a dose of tough love—a wake-up call. "You've got to stop fighting about all of this crap—it's driving you crazy," he said, exasperated. "Is a fucking ring really that important? Is the world going to explode if you don't speak with your kids for a day? Look at all the good stuff going on in your life! You need to let go of all of this negativity. Your work is suffering. You're going to ruin your life if you keep fighting about a stupid piece of jewelry and all this other garbage. It's time to get yourself out of the muck!"

For just that moment, Dan didn't try to get a word in edgewise. He actually listened to Leib's entire sermon. And from his friend's facial expression, Leib could see his words were actually penetrating Dan's frontal cortex. Dan told him he was right. The litigation was driving him crazy. It was preventing him from being truly happy. He agreed he had many positive things going on in his life—so much to be thankful for. The moment seemed to be a true epiphany. Dan gave Leib a huge hug on the way out the door. "Thanks," he told him. "I really needed that."

•••

DESPITE ETHAN LEIB'S loving intervention, upon his return to the 'Hassee the following week, Dan was thrown right back into the muck. On July 16, he received a voicemail from someone at the School of Arts and Sciences (SAS), a charter school for students from kindergarten through the eighth grade. The message indicated that Ben's application in the lottery had been accepted and that SAS was holding a spot for him in its kindergarten class.

Though winning the lottery is ordinarily a cause for celebration, Dan didn't see it quite that way. He had no idea his eldest child had been entered in the charter school's drawing. Not only had Wendi rebuffed him every time he tried to discuss with her where Ben would attend kindergarten, she'd apparently gone behind his back and entered him in SAS's lottery. Yet another brazen act of deception and another violation of the MSA's parenting provisions.

Dan was beside himself. The same negativity he'd vowed to Leib—and to himself—to put behind him came surging back in an instant. He needed to vent. Instead of calling Leib—who he felt certain wouldn't provide a warm and receptive audience—he dialed another law professor friend, Jack Chin, who was teaching at UC Davis in California.

Chin barely got a word in edgewise, Dan going on a 90-minute rant about Wendi: the ring she refused to return, her improper financial disclosures and false testimony, her failure to follow the parenting plan's requirements on Skyping, and how he was considering having her and her lawyer disbarred. And now this new transgression, enrolling Ben in a charter school without his knowledge, let alone approval. Dan told Chin he wasn't going to let Wendi get away with it and shared details of his plan to "control her bad behavior" through further legal proceedings.

He dropped by SAS's campus, demanding to speak with someone in the administration. Dan explained that he was Benjamin Markel's father and that Wendi had no right to enter their son in the lottery—or agree to his admission—without his approval. Thoroughly diplomatic, the assistant principal assured Dan they wouldn't enroll Ben at SAS without his consent. Yet he also tried to sell Dan on the school, extolling the many virtues of its academic and extracurricular programs.

As the administrator talked up the school's attributes, Dan's anger subsided. SAS actually did have an excellent reputation and a lot to offer. He was intrigued. If Wendi had just talked with him about the school in a civilized manner, he may well have agreed it was the best place for Ben. He told the assistant principal he'd think about it some more and discuss the option with his ex-wife.

•••

JULY 18, 2014, BEGAN as an ordinary summer morning at 2116 Trescott Drive. Dan woke the boys up, fed them breakfast, and helped them get ready for their day. They were strapped into their car seats in his black Honda Accord promptly at 8:30 a.m. He backed out of the garage, down the driveway, and began their familiar drive to Creative Preschool, singing fun songs along the way. When he dropped them off at 8:50 a.m., Dan embraced them tightly, reminding Ben and Lincoln he'd be back early to take them swimming. "Love you guys," he said with a big smile as he watched them walk toward their classrooms.

On his way to the gym, Dan reached out to Wendi, hoping to speak with her about SAS, an option he was now willing to consider despite her deception. His call rolled to voicemail. He indicated in his message that he was taking an exercise class and expected to be done between 10:15 a.m. and 10:30 a.m. They could talk after that. He pulled into the parking lot at Premier Health & Fitness at 9:12 a.m. and hustled to his class.

When the class ended, Dan headed straight to his car, cooling off in the driver's seat while scrolling through his texts on his iPhone. One of the messages was from a music teacher at SAS named Stewart Schlazer, who said he was reaching out to provide information about the school. "Please call anytime," the text read. "I'd love to answer your questions." Dan backed out of his spot, exiting the parking lot at 10:38 a.m.

Ten minutes later, while driving southbound on Thomasville Road, he connected with Schlazer, clutching his cellphone in his left hand while listening through its speaker. Dan told the music teacher about Wendi's surreptitious lottery application, letting the complete stranger know that he and his ex-wife didn't see eye-to-eye on very much. Dan explained that he'd received somewhat of a sales pitch from the assistant principal and was looking for a different perspective. Finally given the chance to speak, the teacher began outlining the attributes he believed SAS could offer Dan's soon-to-be kindergartner.

From his end of the conversation, Schlazer eventually heard the ambient road noise dissipate, as if Dan had arrived home. "Hold on a second," Dan said. "There's a person in my driveway that's unfamiliar to me."

"Sure, no problem," the music teacher replied. He waited for Dan to come back on the line. Suddenly, he heard a loud noise—as if a person was grunting—and then some muffled voices he couldn't make out with any clarity.

"Mr. Markel?" he said loudly, mispronouncing Dan's surname. "Mr. Markel?" The only thing Schlazer could make out from his end of the connection was the sound of ultra-deep, heaving breaths—as if Dan's mouth were pressed up against the phone and he was gasping for air. He feared Dan was having a heart attack.

"Are you all right? Is everything okay?" Schlazer shouted. "Can I help you?" No response. He hung up and tried calling back, but the new call rolled straight to voicemail.

He texted Dan, asking, "Are you okay?" But there was no reply.

Unbeknownst to Schlazer, at that very moment, Dan's

next-door neighbor Jim Geiger was standing beside his vehicle, peering through the shattered driver-side window at a horrifying sight. He too was on the phone—calling the 911 emergency dispatch center with an urgent plea for help.

PART TWO
Police Work

12.

Breadcrumbs

TALLAHASSEE POLICE SERGEANT David Sims was the first officer to arrive at 2116 Trescott Drive—flagged down by Jim Geiger, who was standing in the street frantically waving his arms. When Sims entered the garage, he found Dan's black Honda Accord still running, but locked, with Dan slumped over in the driver's seat, breathing rapidly and gasping for air. His left hand was still clutching a light-blue iPhone.

Dan's face and shirt were drenched in blood. Piles of jagged glass shards littered the driver's seat and floorboard. As Sims reached through the shattered window to unlock the doors, he noticed half of Dan's black, plastic-framed eyeglasses—broken off at the bridge and missing its lens—on his lap. The lens was later discovered on the driver's seat.

The sergeant carefully entered the vehicle through the passenger side. He noticed a white towel on the front passenger seat with a deep-red splotch of blood covering its corner. As Sims reached over to pull the keys out of the ignition, he spotted the other half of Dan's glasses, as well as a second lens, lying amid the broken glass on the driver's-side floorboard. Dan's overstuffed, worn leather wallet, containing $68 in cash and nearly 20 credit cards, was located in the glove compartment; his Dell laptop computer was found in a black computer bag in the backseat.

After additional law enforcement personnel arrived and Dan was whisked away to the hospital, the officers used his keys to enter the home through the garage-side door. They searched the entire house thoroughly, finding no evidence of a break-in or anything else that appeared suspicious. The officers then secured the scene, stretching yellow crime-scene tape across Trescott Drive about five houses in either direction of Dan's property, as well as around its perimeter.

Meanwhile, at the hospital, Joanne Maltese, the same forensic specialist who would later swab and photograph Wendi Adelson at the police station, was documenting Dan's injuries. There were two distinct bullet wounds to his face. The first was just above the tear duct of his left eye, by the bridge of his nose. The second was on his left cheek, below the opposite corner of his left eye, where a nurse had removed a piece of glass embedded in his flesh. Maltese also photographed a narrow band of black gunpowder residue across Dan's left forearm.

During the autopsy the next morning, the medical examiner, Dr. Anthony Clark, removed two .38-caliber bullets from Dan's head, referred to in his report as "lead missiles." He concluded both had been fired from a distance of 18 to 24 inches from Dan's face.

The bullet that penetrated Dan's left cheek was lodged in the soft tissue just below his left ear canal. The medical examiner felt certain Dan was still conscious after being struck by that first bullet and surmised that he reflexively raised his left arm when the bullet and glass fragment struck his face. That explained the gunshot residue on his left forearm, likely deposited when the gun fired a second time. In Dr. Clark's opinion, the wounds from that first gunshot, though serious, weren't fatal.

The second bullet—which blasted through Dan's face just above his left tear duct—had burrowed through his brain and was found in the back of his skull. Dr. Clark concluded that the second bullet initially struck the bridge of Dan's glasses, flattening its tip milliseconds before penetrating his face. The deformed nature of the projectile increased the damage it was inflicting as it plowed through the law professor's brain, causing massive hemorrhaging. It was that hemorrhaging, Dr. Clark determined, that ultimately ended Dan's life.

•••

JIM GEIGER REPORTED seeing what he thought was a light-colored Prius speeding away from Dan's driveway moments after hearing what investigators now knew were two gunshots. They were convinced that finding the getaway vehicle would lead them directly to Dan's killer. A team of investigators dedicated weeks of research and analysis to that endeavor.

Their first significant breakthrough occurred at Premier Health & Fitness, Dan's gym, which provided security camera surveillance footage from both inside and outside the building that had been recorded the morning of the murder. Not only did investigators isolate video of Dan walking through the gym's front doors at 9:13 a.m., and leaving at 10:34 a.m., they hit a forensic home run with footage from the parking lot.

The parking lot cameras captured Dan's black Accord entering the lot and pulling into a parking space at 9:12 a.m. Moments later, a greenish-silver Prius rolled into the parking lot, driving around in a circle as if it was on a stakeout. The Prius moved to two different parking places during the 81 minutes Dan was inside, though nobody appeared to exit the vehicle. Because it had dark, tinted windows, the footage didn't give investigators any indication of who was inside.

After Dan completed his workout and reemerged through the gym's front doors, the outdoor cameras captured his car leaving the parking lot at 10:38 a.m. Trailing directly behind him was none other than the greenish-silver Prius. Jim Geiger's observation from his living room window had been dead on the money.

The gym's surveillance footage took investigators only so far, however, because the image of the Prius was too blurry to make out its license plate. They needed a sharper picture to move the investigation forward. The investigative team collected additional security-camera footage from businesses along Thomasville Road, between Premier Fitness and Betton Hills. The same Prius appeared in footage from a Circle K convenience store and a Sunoco gas station. But again, no images were sharp enough to provide any additional details.

Footage from a Centennial Bank branch on Thomasville Road, closer to Betton Hills, did provide an additional glimpse. The bank's outdoor security camera captured Dan's Accord traveling westbound on Betton Road just after 8:30 a.m. —with the Prius following directly behind. That would have been just after Dan had left home to drive his boys to Creative Preschool, where investigators learned he was dropping them off at 8:50 a.m. Thanks to this new footage, they now knew Dan's assailant had been stalking him like prey for two-and-a-half hours.

On July 23, the TPD released a still image of the Prius — which was published by the local newspaper, the *Tallahassee Democrat*, and shown on TV news broadcasts. Investigators were hoping someone might recognize the vehicle and provide additional details. But no one came forward. Even though they'd connected several important dots, their investigation was seemingly stuck in neutral.

That is until one of the investigators, Greg Wilder, had a brilliant idea. City buses. Tallahassee StarMetro buses also used surveillance cameras, not only to film activity inside the bus, but also surrounding it. Wilder ultimately had in his hands footage from two buses that operated along Thomasville Road between 10:30 a.m. and 11:00 a.m. the morning Dan was shot: Bus 505, which ran southbound during that time frame, and Bus 707, which ran northbound.

At 10:44 a.m., a camera at the front of Bus 505 captured both Dan's Accord and the Prius heading south on Thomasville Road — between Premier Fitness and Betton Hills. At 10:47 a.m., the bus pulled up directly behind the Prius — which had stopped at a traffic signal — with Dan's vehicle now out of view. Though the white Florida license plate on the rear of the

Prius was visible, the video footage didn't provide sufficient clarity to decipher any letters or numbers.

The instant the traffic light turned green, the Prius sped away, presumably to catch up with its prey. Though Bus 505 momentarily lost track of the hybrid, at 10:51 a.m., while waiting in a right turn lane at the intersection of Thomasville Road and Betton Road, a camera mounted on its left side captured the Prius turning left onto Betton Road in the direction of Trescott Drive. Dan was shot in his garage less than four minutes later.

Footage captured by Bus 707 proved even more vital. At 10:55 a.m., while stopped at a traffic signal in the right lane at the intersection of Thomasville Road and Armistead Road, its rear security camera captured the Prius—now headed north following the shooting—rapidly shifting from the right lane to the left. The Prius also had to stop for the red light and, in an incredible stroke of good fortune, pulled up directly beside Bus 707.

It was at that point in the video that Wilder and his fellow investigators made a critical discovery. Even though the Prius had dark, tinted windows, the security camera mounted on the bus's left side captured animated movement from the hybrid's passenger seat. Reducing the video's speed, it became apparent that a person wearing a white shirt was sitting in that seat. Though investigators couldn't make out the race, age, or even gender of that person, this revelation left little doubt that at least *two people* had been involved in Dan's murder—the driver and the passenger.

With all of this video footage now at their disposal, coupled with information provided by Toyota corporate representatives, the investigators were able to reach several important conclusions: First, Toyota had manufactured the Prius model at issue between 2006 and 2009. Second, the paint color—which could appear as either green or silver depending on the sunlight—was most unique, one Toyota labeled "silver pine mica." Third, the suspect vehicle was missing a front tow-hook cover, which should have been attached to the bumper below the driver's-side headlight. Fourth, an aftermarket black casing surrounded the passenger-side mirror.

Fifth, and most importantly, was the discovery of a small, white object affixed to the interior side of the front windshield any Florida driver would have recognized instantly: a SunPass transponder used to pay tolls electronically on Florida's ubiquitous tollways.

With all of that information in hand, police investigators felt confident they were on the right track and had narrowed the universe of potential suspects considerably. After all, how many Florida residents could possibly have owned a 2006 to 2009 silver-pine-mica Prius? The Florida Department of Transportation (FDOT) would soon provide that answer.

•••

IN THE DAYS FOLLOWING the murder, another crew of investigators was dispatched to canvass the Betton Hills neighborhood, knocking on doors, asking Dan's neighbors for any information that might allow them to place additional pieces into the slowly evolving puzzle image. Though none of his immediate neighbors reported anything particularly noteworthy, a resident of the nearby Ashford Club Apartments provided significant new details.

She told investigators that around mid-morning on Thursday, July 17, a "bluish-silver" Prius-like car parked in the southeast corner of the complex's parking lot. Two men, she said, exited the vehicle and walked down a path that paralleled a large storm drainage ditch. On the opposite side of the ditch was a chain-link fence marking the rear boundary of Dan Markel's property.

The resident told investigators the car's driver was a tall man with a runner's build and fair complexion who was wearing a light-colored baseball cap. The passenger, she said, was a shorter man with a dark complexion—possibly Hispanic or Italian—who had a stocky build and short dark hair. Though they disappeared from her view, the two men reemerged about ten minutes later. She noticed that the shorter man was holding a black object in his hand and was soaking wet, apparently from having fallen into the ditch. She also observed that the taller man's pants were wet up to his knees.

This information aligned nearly perfectly with the revelation generated by Star Metro Bus 707. If the Ashford Club resident's reporting was correct, the occupants of the Prius that pulled up beside Bus 707 just after the shooting were two men, one light-skinned and the other dark-skinned. Both had been in Tally the day before the murder, casing the eventual crime scene. But who were they? And why did they want Dan Markel dead?

• • •

INVESTIGATORS WITH THE TPD worked quickly to eliminate potential suspects. Jeff Lacasse's credit card statements revealed a transaction at a K-Mart store in Sweetwater, Tennessee at 1:14 p.m. on July 18, some two hours after the shooting. To confirm Lacasse's alibi, an investigator obtained surveillance footage directly from the K-Mart. Sure enough, the video showed the lanky professor hundreds of miles from Tallahassee. To the extent Lacasse was ever considered a suspect, he was crossed off the list.

Investigators considered the possibility that a disgruntled student or colleague could have murdered Dan, who had a reputation of being somewhat prickly at times. They reached out to the Florida State University Police and obtained license plate information for every student who'd taken his spring semester class. Not a single one was the registered owner of a 2006 to 2009 Prius. Their search of Dan's law school office, review of more than 15,000 emails from his work account, and interviews with his colleagues convinced them that no student or faculty member harbored any significant grudge against the Canadian-born professor.

They also developed a theory that whoever killed Dan could have accessed his home address from the county appraiser's website. Investigators requested all computer IP addresses that retrieved information from the website on Dan's Trescott

Drive residence in the month prior to the homicide. As it turned out, there was only one matching IP address, belonging to a woman named Elizabeth Boyette. Coincidence or not, Boyette was employed as an administrator at the law school. She was promptly brought downtown for questioning.

Boyette told investigators she and her husband had recently moved to a new home. In the process, the investigators confirmed, the law school administrator had conducted more than 30 searches on the county appraiser's website, not just the one involving Dan's address. Boyette was quickly eliminated as a potential suspect.

Another lead investigators explored stemmed from Dan's prolific blogging. They learned of a fellow blogger, "Atheist ATL Lawyer," who had his own blog on which he'd made many disparaging comments about Dan and others—leaving little doubt that he held strong, antisemitic views. Atheist ATL Lawyer, they learned, was the handle of a 40-year-old Georgia man named Cyrus Malekabadi, who still lived with his mother. FBI agents were dispatched to speak with him. Not surprisingly, the man told the agents he was home working on his computer at the time of the murder. But that alibi was corroborated and Malekabadi was crossed off the list as well.

Investigators also focused on Dan's ongoing work in a federal criminal case in New Jersey against an ultra-orthodox Brooklyn rabbi named Mendel Epstein. The Orthodox rabbi advocated on behalf of Jewish wives whose husbands refused to grant them a *get*—a document formalizing a Jewish divorce. With funds provided by the wives and their families, Epstein would hire Mafia-like tough guys to kidnap the recalcitrant husbands and coerce them into signing the *gets*—through violent means, including electric cattle prods, stun guns, screwdrivers, and by placing plastic bags over their heads. These tactics earned Epstein a fitting moniker: "The Prodfather." His catchphrase, supposedly, was "a divorce or a funeral."

An FBI sting operation in late 2013 resulted in the arrest of Epstein, his chief lieutenant, Rabbi Martin Wolmark, and several others who'd assisted in the diabolical scheme. Though

Wolmark had his own defense lawyer, he brought Dan on as an outside consultant. Investigators working the Markel murder case hypothesized that Epstein could have viewed Dan as a threat, particularly if he suspected the law professor might advise Wolmark to flip and testify against the more senior rabbi. But when TPD investigators spoke with the FBI agents involved in the Prodfather case, they were assured that Dan wouldn't have been targeted by Epstein or any of his henchmen—who apparently drew the line at torture, and had little appetite for murder.

•••

CRAIG ISOM HAD BEEN an investigator with the TPD since 1989, when his now gray hair was still jet black and his frame wasn't carrying nearly as many pounds. For the last five years, he'd served as a violent crimes investigator in the Criminal Investigations Division. From its inception, he was assigned as the lead investigator on the Markel case.

Though he'd been involved in plenty of homicide cases during his 25 years with the TPD, Isom had been lead investigator on only a handful. In view of the circumstances, he was fairly certain this would be his highest-profile investigation yet. The glare from the media spotlight was sure to be amplified by Dan's status as a prominent law professor, as well as the potential involvement of a wealthy family from South Florida. Every avenue he explored and every decision he made, Isom realized, would be subjected to intense scrutiny from inside and outside the TPD.

While his junior investigators were scouring the crime scene, canvassing Betton Hills, and reviewing surveillance video, Isom was focused like a laser on answering one crucial question he hoped would lead directly to Dan's killer—motive. That's why he spent more than five hours questioning Wendi Adelson, figuring she probably knew Dan better than anyone else. It's also why he spent the first few weeks following Dan's death speaking with a wide circle of his friends.

After the Sunday memorial service at Congregation Shomrei Torah ended, Isom was approached by a woman named Tamara Demko. She told the investigator she and Dan had gone to Harvard Law School together and that she'd been good friends with him ever since, especially since moving to Tally herself in 2007. Despite the divorce, she told Isom she also was still friendly with Wendi, even guest lecturing for her on occasion, as recently as June. Isom invited Demko to meet with him at the police station later that afternoon.

Demko told him that the divorce between Dan and Wendi was the nastiest she'd ever seen, with the two fighting bitterly over Wendi's attempted relocation to South Florida. She told Isom that Dan had won that battle, forcing Wendi to remain in Tally against her will. She also mentioned that Dan had recently discovered his ex-wife had hidden assets from him when they negotiated their divorce settlement and that he was about to drop a "legal bomb" on her, seeking sanctions for her deceit. Demko believed that Wendi's parents had been overly involved in the divorce and were pushing their daughter to get everything she could from Dan because he "owed her" for their failed marriage.

The most intriguing morsel she shared was her interaction with Harvey and Donna Adelson at Wendi's house the prior day, where Demko had gone to pay her respects. Even though she'd met Wendi's folks several times, something about them seemed off, she said. Harvey in particular appeared uncomfortable, seemingly unable to look her in the eye. Demko indicated that she also was very suspicious of Charlie, who she believed hated Dan and was very protective of his sister. "I wouldn't put it past her father or her brother to do something like this," Demko speculated, but expressed hope that Wendi herself hadn't been involved.

•••

ONE OF DAN'S CLOSE FRIENDS who spoke at the memorial service was Alex Greenberg. As Isom listened to Greenberg's heartfelt remembrances, he had an inkling that Alex and his wife Mya might be a good source of information about the last few months of Dan's life. The lead investigator invited the couple to the police station to chat. They swung by that Wednesday evening, speaking with Isom and one of his colleagues, Michael Hubbard, for about 45 minutes.

Although the Greenbergs were members at Congregation Shomrei Torah—and had gotten to know Dan primarily through Tally's Jewish community—they actually lived and worked in Cairo, Georgia, about 30 minutes north. Mya worked as a dentist and Alex as a veterinarian. Though they'd been friends with both Dan and Wendi before their separation, they were firmly entrenched in the "Team Danny" camp after the couple split.

The Greenbergs explained to Isom and Hubbard that Dan felt lost after Wendi left and, over time, attached himself to them and their three kids as if they were family. The professor came to their home for Shabbat dinners every other Friday when Ben and Lincoln were in his custody and often stayed for the weekend, he and the boys sleeping together in the guest bedroom. Dan also stayed with them during holidays if he had nowhere else to be.

Mya noted that the public face of Wendi and Dan's marriage was almost "too perfect." As an example, she cited Dan's Facebook post on their fifth anniversary, in which he referred to his "60th month of wedded bliss." But it became clear to her and her husband that there was trouble behind closed doors, the two ultimately learning that Dan and Wendi were in marital counseling. Many of their problems, the Greenbergs revealed, stemmed from their vastly differing beliefs about Jewish customs and practices, especially the importance of keeping kosher.

Their troubles escalated once they separated, Alex and Mya said. Alex told the investigators that Dan had shared with him how "unreasonable, vindictive, and mean" Wendi was behaving. He was particularly annoyed she wouldn't facilitate his Skyping with the boys on a daily basis, even though their agreement provided for it. He also was upset about his great aunt's ring she refused to return. Wendi would do things deliberately designed to get under Dan's skin, they recounted, like having Ben and Lincoln eat bacon during the few times she did allow them to Skype with their dad.

The Greenbergs told the officers that Amy Adler had been a true blessing in Dan's life, noting she'd been to Tally twice and that Dan saw her regularly in New York. Amy first came to town around Valentine's Day, when the couple stayed in the Greenbergs' home. Alex and Mya sensed some "tension" during Amy's two-day visit in late June, but stated that things got much better when Dan was with her in New York in early July. The Tuesday before the murder, he'd phoned Alex to tell him that he and Amy had a "breakthrough" in their relationship, which she was finally willing to make public.

Isom was curious about Amy's ex-husband, recalling Wendi's speculation that he might have been upset with Dan over his current role in Amy's life. Alex dismissed any such concern, noting that Amy's ex was a New York sportswriter named Lenn Robbins and that he and Amy were actually on good terms. In fact, Dan and Amy had a running joke about how she had a "bad marriage, but a good divorce" whereas Dan had a "good marriage, but a horrible divorce." Alex told the investigators that Robbins was well aware of Dan's relationship with Amy and had even offered use of his apartment when Dan needed it—partly because Amy wasn't yet comfortable with her new boyfriend staying at her home while she had custody of her nine-year-old son.

Dan had talked with the Greenbergs extensively about his escalating divorce proceedings with Wendi, including about a motion they believed he was going to file the day before his death. That motion, Dan had told his friends, focused on his ex-wife's "perjury" in her financial disclosures, and would possibly lead to Wendi being disbarred and big problems for her lawyer. Dan had explained to Alex that one of the reasons his own lawyer had decided to withdraw from representing him was because he felt badly about going after another lawyer.

One of the more titillating subjects the Greenbergs touched on was Dan's sexual trysts with a trio of women just before he and Amy began dating. Alex told the investigators Dan wasn't bashful about sharing intimate details with him. All three women hailed from other parts of the country and were law professors just like him. They'd meet at academic conferences and "hook up," Alex said, noting Dan had told him that while attending a conference in New Orleans, he'd been intimate with two of the three, though not simultaneously.

One of these women, named Nancy, was actually married — to a lawyer — though they supposedly had an "open marriage." Mya had warned Dan not to be involved with her, telling him he was "nuts" for hooking up with a married woman. Alex told the investigators that Dan eventually concluded that Nancy was "crazy." He'd arranged to rendezvous with her at the beach, not far from Tally. Nancy even made Dan get tested for STDs before arriving, which only enhanced his anticipation, believing there would be plenty of festivities between them at the beach. But once the two were together, Mya recounted, "She kind of freaked out on him" and told him not to touch her. The weekend turned out to be an unmitigated disaster — no festivities at all.

Toward the end of the interview, Alex echoed something Demko had told Isom — that Wendi's family seemed very defensive and standoffish following the murder. He speculated that was likely because "everyone's first thought is going to be Wendi or her family." "I would not be surprised if that's how this all turns out," the veterinarian said in a deadly serious tone. "I'll lay it out there." Alex shared his belief that Wendi's folks had been "mean" to Dan, adding, in his thick, southern drawl, "You hate to think somebody would actually ever do — You know, I'm assuming someone was probably hired to kill him. You hate to think that … but somebody did, you know, so — It just makes more sense to me than anything."

Chiming in, Mya noted how strange Harvey's behavior seemed at the memorial service, setting off her radar. "Just because he wouldn't look at me and didn't speak with me." She paused to collect her thoughts. "It's either her family, a bad student or—

Her husband interrupted. "Or one of these crazy women."

•••

ONE CONSISTENT THEME had run through virtually every interview Isom conducted: the nasty divorce between Wendi and Dan coupled with her parents' over-involvement in the case and their hatred for their former son-in-law. Though he wasn't a lawyer by trade, the seasoned investigator felt pretty certain that the key to solving the *murder* case was to obtain a deeper understanding of the *divorce* case. Within weeks of the homicide, a copy of the entire divorce file was lying on his desk.

Isom carefully sifted through the papers both sides had filed during the 2013 relocation battle. He surmised how bitterly disappointed Wendi and her parents had likely been when Judge Hobbs ruled she couldn't move to South Florida with her boys—leaving them seven hours away from Coral Springs, their grandparents, and uncle.

He also reviewed the more recent motions in which Dan had accused Wendi and her parents of horrible things, asking that his ex-wife and her lawyer be sanctioned and that her mom be prohibited from having unsupervised contact with her grandkids. Though he'd only just met the Adelsons, the burly investigator felt pretty sure they hadn't taken kindly to the brutal attacks their daughter's ex-husband was leveling against anyone and everyone bearing their last name.

Isom made arrangements for FBI agents to drop in on Wendi's oldest brother, Rob, in Albany, New York, who told them that he wasn't close with either of his siblings. Charlie disliked Dan intensely, Rob noted, and definitely had adequate financial resources to hire a hitman. He described his younger brother as "cold" in the way he talked about people and "flashy" with money, cars, boats, and guns.

Sometime that fall, one of Isom's colleagues dropped some additional paperwork on his desk: the vicious emails Donna had written Wendi in the midst of the divorce battle, which had come straight off the laptop computer Wendi had voluntarily provided the evening of the shooting. Those emails left no doubt that Donna and Harvey had become enraged by their ex-son-in-law and were willing to consider extreme measures to fulfill their objectives. Isom pondered whether Wendi's parents were capable of hiring a hitman—perhaps one driving a silver-pine-mica Prius with tinted windows. To explore that possibility, he made sure that the subpoena issued to the FDOT sought SunPass transponder activity for any Toyota Prius driving on tollways between South Florida and Tally in the days surrounding the murder.

Investigators also discovered other interesting tidbits from Wendi's computer. She'd recently performed Google searches about Amy Adler, Amy's ex-husband, and her brother. As well as for porn sites, including websites depicting sex between teachers and students. They also learned that—at least before the divorce was finalized—she'd been listed as the primary beneficiary on Dan's life insurance policy, which, due to his death, was now set to pay out a cool $2 million.

•••

ONE OF THE MOST valuable tools employed in modern-day criminal investigations is what is commonly referred to as a "tower dump." When a cellphone transmits or receives a call or text, or connects to the internet, its signal connects with—or "pings"—a nearby cell tower, thereby creating a permanent record of the phone's proximity to the tower. These records can consist of thousands of pages of phone numbers that connect with a single tower during a given period of time—hence the term "tower dump." They are generated solely from the cellular connection, rather than the GPS technology embedded in phones, which, surprisingly enough, isn't a tool that proves very useful in solving crimes.

Sergeant Chris Corbitt, who'd been with the TPD for 20 years, had received specialized training in analyzing tower dumps. He had search warrants issued to the four phone carriers that owned cell towers in Tally: T-Mobile, AT&T, Verizon, and Sprint, ultimately receiving a CD from each. Each disk contained many thousands of pages of data. With the assistance of his computer, Corbitt was able to sift through the phone numbers of each and every cellphone that on July 18 had connected with towers near Dan's house, near Creative Preschool when he dropped off his kids, and near Premier Fitness while Dan was working out.

After many hours of tedious work, Corbitt concluded that not a single telephone number pinged cell towers at all three locations that fateful morning. Though he knew from the gym and city bus surveillance footage that the suspect Prius had been at each location, the tower dumps didn't help identify who was inside the car.

Corbitt then had another idea to leverage the tower dumps. He knew that Investigator Isom's working theory was that one or more of the Adelsons had hired whoever was in the Prius. Search warrants had been issued for the cellphone records for Wendi, Donna, Harvey, and Charlie. If Isom's theory was correct, Corbitt reasoned, whoever was in the Prius would have communicated with one or more of the Adelsons in the weeks preceding the murder. Using sophisticated software, he had the phone numbers listed in the four Adelsons' cellphone records compared to the phone numbers that connected with cell towers near the preschool, gym, and Dan's house the morning of the murder.

That strategy hit paydirt immediately. There was only one telephone number that appeared in both the tower dump records and the Adelsons' cellphone records: (786) 372-5986. On July 1, 2014, 17 days before the murder, that number had connected with Harvey Adelson's cellphone. That same number had pinged a T-Mobile tower near Premier Fitness at 9:36 a.m. and 9:58 a.m. on July 18. Who did that number belong to? A T-Mobile subscriber named Sigfredo Garcia, who'd provided the phone carrier an address in Miami Beach that just so happened to be a short drive from Donna and Harvey Adelson's front door.

Investigators pulled Garcia's photo and records from the DMV and learned that he had a fair complexion, was 32 at the time of the murder, stood 5'11", and weighed 180 pounds. Sigfredo Garcia was identified as Hitman Number One.

Corbitt had a search warrant issued for Garcia's T-Mobile records to determine whether any of his frequent contacts matched any other number from the tower dumps. Sure enough, one of Garcia's most frequently called numbers, (305) 570-8153, had pinged an AT&T cell tower near Dan's gym while he was working out the morning of the shooting, as well as a tower near Betton Hills the prior day. That particular phone number was owned by one Luis Manuel Rivera, another resident of Miami Beach.

Investigators pulled Rivera's photo and records from the DMV, which revealed that he was 31 in July 2014, was 5'4", weighed 160 pounds, and had darker skin than Garcia's. Between the two, he and Garcia were a perfect match to the description provided by the woman from the apartment complex behind Dan's home. Luis Rivera was identified as Hitman Number Two.

•••

EVEN BEFORE GARCIA AND RIVERA were identified, Craig Isom had a hunch that the hitmen had traveled to Tally all the way from South Florida. If he had to make that trip, Isom would have driven west across the southern tip of Florida on Interstate 75, or Alligator Alley, which extended from Broward County on Florida's east coast to Naples on its west. SunPass toll plazas were stationed at both locations. The subpoena issued to the FDOT specifically sought SunPass transponder activity at each plaza from July 16 to July 18, 2014.

When the records finally arrived, they confirmed Isom's hunch: only one Toyota Prius of the model type caught on surveillance video had made a round-trip through Alligator Alley between July 16 and July 18. The transponder on that particular 2008 Prius had pinged the westbound Broward County plaza at 2:18 p.m. on July 16 and the eastbound Naples plaza at 5:23 p.m. on July 18. That timing perfectly matched everything Isom and his team of investigators already knew.

They used the transponder number associated with that particular Prius to identify a small, off-the-beaten-track car rental company in North Miami—Hybrid Auto Rentals. Its owner, Daren Schwartz, was more than happy to pull up his company's July 15 rental agreement for the Prius, which, coincidentally enough, was completed in the name of Luis Rivera. The contact number Rivera supplied matched his AT&T account. Moreover, on the top left corner of the rental agreement, written beneath the word "Brother," was a second telephone number—Sigfredo Garcia's. Though the agreement indicated the Prius was to be back on July 17, Schwartz confirmed it wasn't actually returned until July 21.

As if that weren't enough evidence to complete the puzzle, Schwartz also informed investigators that GPS technology was embedded in all of his cars as a theft-protection measure, recording vehicle location every 25 hours. The GPS service provider, Spireon, supplied TPD investigators records establishing that the Prius Rivera rented had been on North Monroe Street in Tally, near 6th Avenue, at 12:26 a.m. on July 18, the morning of the shooting. That just happened to be the location of a Rodeway Inn, a motel that was less than three miles from Dan's house. Corbitt dove back into the tower dumps and confirmed that both Rivera's and Garcia's cellphones were pinging towers near the Rodeway Inn the evening of July 17 and, in Rivera's case, until 8:03 a.m. on July 18.

With just a little more digging, investigators determined that the two hitmen had stayed at the Budget Inn near Florida State's campus the prior evening, checking in at about 1:00 a.m. on July 17. Though he didn't provide the motel his correct phone number, Rivera actually registered at the front desk in his own name and indicated that his party consisted of two people. Between the rental agreement for the Prius, GPS data, and hotel registration, Isom and his team were now pretty well convinced they'd identified Dan Markel's killers. And they were about to uncover an additional piece of evidence that would increase their level of certainty to 100%.

•••

THE FINAL PIECE WASN'T inserted into the puzzle until investigators received Rivera's bank account records from JPMorgan Chase. Those records revealed that he'd withdrawn $40 from a cash machine at a branch location in Pembroke Pines—in Broward County—at 6:46 p.m. on July 18, as he and Garcia completed their long journey back from Tally. Investigators reached out to the bank to obtain its ATM surveillance footage.

The video captured by the drive-through ATM revealed the exact same Prius that Premier Fitness and city bus cameras had recorded in Tally earlier that morning—with its dark, tinted windows, missing tow-hook cover, and aftermarket mirror casing. This time, the license plate was clearly visible, matching the tag number in Rivera's rental agreement with Hybrid Auto Rentals.

And in yet another stroke of good luck, the tinted windows didn't prevent investigators from peering inside the car because Rivera lowered the driver's-side window to access the cash machine. As he reached through the open window frame to mash the ATM's buttons, the security camera captured a stunningly clear view of the stocky Rivera, who had a faint goatee, hair shaved close to his scalp, and was wearing a long-sleeved black shirt. He was kind enough to stare directly into the camera—as if he were deliberately striking a pose.

But that wasn't all the security camera revealed. There *was* someone sitting in the passenger seat—who *was* wearing a long-sleeved white shirt, the sleeves pulled up just below his elbows. Even though he wasn't withdrawing any cash, the passenger also looked directly into the camera—providing a reasonably clear view of his face. Which was a dead ringer for the DMV image of Sigfredo Garcia. All in all, the ATM surveillance footage proved to be an investigative grand slam. All arising from a measly $40 withdrawal.

There was still plenty more to investigate and learn before any arrests could be made. But by late 2015, Craig Isom had to be immensely pleased with his team's progress. He also was convinced that it was only a matter of time before they'd establish the connection between Rivera and Garcia on the one hand, and the Adelsons on the other. And before his police department and the State Attorney's Office would bring them all to justice.

13.

Tato and Tuto

THE LATIN KINGS STREET GANG traces its roots to 1954, when a young man from Chicago, Ramon Santos, formed the Imperials, a Puerto Rican progress movement established to overcome racial discrimination against Hispanics. When the Windy City's Latino community began suffering repeated violence at the hands of Greek, Irish, and Italian gangs, the Imperials merged with Puerto Rican and Mexican street gangs to form the Latin Kings. Its three founding principles were to "protect our families, protect our neighborhoods, and protect each other."

Though its origins were noble and peaceful, the Latin Kings ultimately evolved into the largest Hispanic criminal enterprise in the United States, particularly prevalent in major cities such as Chicago, New York, and Miami. Its central criminal activity has been the distribution of narcotics—primarily cocaine, heroin, and marijuana—though its members often perpetrate violent crimes as well. At the grassroots level, the rigidly hierarchical organization is divided into local "tribes," each of which has five leaders, symbolizing the five points of a king's crown. A tribe's highest-ranking officer is the "first crown," "Inca," or "*primero*." The first crown reports to regional officers, who then report to state officers, who in turn report to national officers.

Kings agree to follow the strict code of behavior prescribed by the "King Manifesto," part constitution, part bible. Members must pay dues and regularly attend meetings. Many refer to their organization as "The Nation" and their ideology as "Kingism," which often takes on the complexion of a religious cult. The Manifesto contains laws similar to those adopted by political bodies, as well as elaborate procedures for disciplinary action when those laws are "violated." Loyalty is valued above all else. Disloyalty—in the form of snitching on fellow Kings—is punishable by death. The tribe's first crown decides when and how to mete out such punishments, including orders to "KOS"—kill on sight.

Members of the Latin Kings often demonstrate their allegiance by having crown tattoos burned into their skin, some of which feature the gang's colors of black and gold and the initials LK (Latin Kings), ALK (Almighty Latin Kings), or ALKN (Almighty Latin King Nation). Another common King tattoo is a lion, the ferocious animal a fitting symbol for a gang priding itself on toughness.

Membership can be earned by proving oneself worthy through an assortment of gangbanging activities, including drug trafficking and robbery. The Latin Kings also have "legacy" members—children born into the organization by virtue of having a family member who is already a King. A new member receives a "King name." For instance, Juan Rivera was dubbed King Chino; his brother Sammy went by King Little Sammy. The two were active members in Chicago when their nephew, Luis Manuel Rivera, was born in Puerto Rico in April 1983. Luis Rivera, therefore, became a legacy member. Because his godmother had assigned the infant the nickname Tato, his King name became King Tato.

Luis was the second of six children born to Hector Rivera and Maria Cabrerra—four boys and two girls in all, including a brother with the same first name, Luis Cabrerra. When Tato was a mere toddler, the growing family—four children by then—moved to North Miami Beach, into an almost entirely Hispanic enclave on 71st Street. Most of the families in the neighborhood, like them, were dirt poor—fathers long gone, imprisoned, or dead.

Rivera became an active King at the ripe old age of ten. By then, he'd been diagnosed with schizophrenia and bipolar disorder. His first arrest occurred at age 13, when he was charged with shooting a neighborhood kid in the head with a BB gun. A string of additional charges in the ensuing months landed Rivera in the juvenile justice system. He cycled in and out of reform schools and the public school system, never advancing beyond a third-grade reading level. By middle school, he was regularly using marijuana and cocaine.

Though teachers and administrators allowed him to advance to high school at Miami Beach Senior High, Rivera rarely attended classes, more interested in using and selling drugs. While at home one day during the tenth grade, he was busted by a SWAT team, leading to his first foray into the adult criminal justice system and his immediate expulsion from school. Not that he cared too much, as he was rising rapidly in stature in the Kings' North Miami tribe, becoming *primero* of the 100-member chapter when he was just 15.

By then, King Tato had become a human canvas of tattoo art. A gigantic five-point crown was centered just above his belly button, the first and fifth points extending to his nipples and middle point reaching his sternum. The word "King" was scrawled in giant letters just above the crown, with a smaller crown dotting the "i." All four members of the Teenage Mutant Ninja Turtles—in vibrant color—were inked into his lower legs. Other animal symbols were tatted onto his shoulders. He even had a letter burned onto the outside of each finger, K-I-N-G spelled across his right hand and L-O-V-E across his left. Tato also had an affinity for extravagant jewelry, an $18,000 gold chain his first of many such purchases over the years.

As a mere teenager, Rivera had already become quite the ladies' man, a tattoo of a pair of a woman's red lips prominently displayed on his neck below his right ear. By 14, he was regularly seeing a 20-year-old woman named Leona "Annie" Diaz—who had a five-year-old son named Anthony. Rivera moved in with the two while Diaz was pregnant with their first child. They would ultimately have two daughters of their own—Karitza, born when Rivera was 17, and Kayshla, when he was 19. Why did both of their names begin with the letter K? Because they were descendants of King Tato. The gang leader had Kayshla's name inked across the back of his left hand and "Karitza" and "Anthony" above his nipples.

Rivera was determined to be a good father to all three children—taking responsibility for raising Anthony in addition to his biological daughters—living by the motto "family comes first." Though he looked after Diaz as if she were his actual wife—and referred to her as such—his fidelity toward her was notably different from his loyalty to the Latin Kings. When he went out partying with friends, it wasn't unusual for Tato to end up with whatever *chica bonita* happened to be on his arm at the end of the evening. He had confidence that his "wife" would take good care of their kids while he freely sampled the delights other Latinas had to offer.

To his credit, though, alongside his drug trafficking activities, Rivera began holding down an honest job when he was just 17. He worked as a laborer for Coastal Masonry, a commercial construction contractor often engaged to lay block for high-rise buildings. He was as punctual and dedicated an employee as any in the company's workforce. Even if he stayed out all evening partying, he'd come home, shower, and show up on time at the job site the next morning, often the first to arrive and the last to go home. Tato was ultimately certified to operate heavy machinery and became a foreman in his twenties. He even had health insurance and a 401(k) retirement account, his earnings directly deposited into his JPMorgan Chase account. He remained on Coastal Masonry's payroll for 15 years.

The short-statured, stout Puerto Rican faced his first serious criminal charges as an 18-year-old, charged with aggravated assault against a law enforcement officer as well as marijuana and cocaine trafficking. Though his life of drug running and armed robberies continued unabated after his release from jail,

Rivera managed to evade another arrest for several years. That is, until his own "wife," Diaz, swore out a warrant against him in 2008 for domestic violence—which landed him in jail for 30 days. He also was convicted on drug and weapons charges a couple of years later, though he was sentenced only to probation, rather than hard time.

In 2010, Rivera met a woman at a local gas station named Jessica Rodriguez, who'd only recently been released from prison herself—after serving five years on two separate robbery convictions. Like Tato, Rodriguez was born in Puerto Rico and raised in South Florida. She had an eight-year-old daughter named Sianna. For the next few years, Rivera lived like a gypsy, rotating freely between the homes of Rodriguez, Diaz, his mom, and his baby sister Maria—or wherever he landed after a sexy lady invited him for a night of passion. By 2013, however, he had moved full-time into Rodriguez's apartment, taking responsibility for raising Sianna in addition to Anthony and his daughters. He even added Sianna's name to the already crowded shrine on his chest.

Rodriguez was well aware her boyfriend was selling drugs and had no qualms over the extra cash being generated to help pay her bills. But because she was on probation, she insisted that those activities occur at Rivera's sister's or mother's homes. Any time she found a baggie of cocaine lying around their apartment, she'd flush it down the toilet before Tato could stop her. She wasn't about to have her probation revoked if the cops decided to search her home—five years in prison had been more than enough.

Unlike Diaz, Rodriguez didn't get along with Rivera's family members—in particular his mom. Over the years, they'd grown fond of Diaz and continued to invite her to family get-togethers, much to Rodriguez's consternation. But no matter how much Rodriguez complained, Annie Diaz remained a fixture in Tato's life, as did Anthony, Karitza, and Kayshla—even after Rodriguez gave birth to Rivera's third biological daughter on June 27, 2014.

Khaleesi, who Rodriguez nicknamed Lulu, was born with a

small hole in her heart that eventually healed without surgery. Shortly after her birth, Tato reported to the tattoo parlor to have his infant daughter's name inked just beside Sianna's. Which wasn't the only pattern he continued. Just a few months later, he'd find himself back in jail for domestic violence, this time with his new baby mama the one swearing out the warrant.

•••

LUIS RIVERA'S BEST FRIEND in elementary school was a boy named Sigfredo Garcia, whose family lived in the same Latino neighborhood. Garcia was a full year older than Tato, born in April 1982. The bond between the two grew so strong over the years, they considered themselves brothers. Garcia had his own nickname, Tuto, which as a teenager he had burned into the skin beside his left bicep in old-English lettering. He and Tato grew more inseparable with each passing year, their level of mischief increasing rapidly as teenagers.

Garcia's parents, Sigfredo Sr. and Suzzana, emigrated to the United States from Cuba before their first child was born, ultimately raising three girls and two boys, Sigfredo the youngest of the bunch. His first memory of his father was as a five-year-old, when his dad was released from prison—one of several times the elder Sigfredo was incarcerated. His mom worked multiple jobs to try to provide for the family, from sunup until late in the evening. She was a strict disciplinarian, often throwing a sandal at a misbehaving child to obtain compliance with her rules—her aim incredibly precise.

Sigfredo Sr. was very handsome, luring Latina women into his web whenever he desired—which was quite often. Even during occasions Suzanna left him responsible for the kids, lady friends in various stages of dress would often be in his— and their—midst. He admonished his kids to keep quiet about his dalliances. Sigfredo Sr. also was an avid cocaine user, and would often partake in front of the children—Tuto's first snort occurring before the age of ten, when he snuck some powder from his dad's stash. His father even taught him how to break into cars and smoked marijuana with him. But by the time Tuto was 11, Sigfredo Sr. was gone for good, having fled to Mexico to avoid prosecution for additional drug crimes. He never even said goodbye.

From a very early age, Tuto had trouble sitting still, full of energy and frequently hyperactive. The child possessed a complicated mix of bravado and timidity. He showed not even the slightest hesitation to jump off the roof of a two-story house or a bridge, but also was afraid of the dark and very anxious in social settings. On occasion, his irritability became uncontrollable.

Tuto's first arrest occurred when he was just six. He set a building on fire when he was 12. He also used marijuana and alcohol fairly regularly, often at home with his siblings while his mother was at work, precipitating a 28-day stint in a drug treatment program and reform school by the seventh grade. By the time he was 16, he was working out regularly, molding his once scrawny body into sculpted, muscular physique.

Tuto eventually found his way back to public school at Miami Beach Senior High. But he cut classes frequently, hanging out with his good friend Tato, selling drugs to support his own habit, which gradually transitioned from weed to cocaine. Instead of the Latin Kings, he joined a local Miami gang named the Latin Syndicate. By 15, he was having more frequent brushes with the law, charged with a slew of auto thefts, burglaries, possession of explosives, and an assault on a law enforcement officer.

Though he inherited his father's good looks, Garcia's social anxiety precluded any deep connections with the opposite sex until he was 16, when he fell madly in love with a neighborhood girl named Elizabeth and moved into her family's home. Elizabeth provided a steadying influence that was a marked departure from the upbringing—or lack thereof—he'd received in his own home.

But Tuto's love affair with Elizabeth, as well as his formal education, would come to a sudden halt when, at 17, he was charged as an adult for breaking into another car. Though he avoided a prison term, he spent six months in jail before being released. His stint in the slammer, however, didn't exactly deter him from a life of crime. He was convicted again as a 20-year-old for selling narcotics and amphetamines and for intimidating a witness.

When he was 21, Tuto fell in love yet again, with the most beautiful human being he'd ever laid eyes on. Katherine Diana Magbanua was another girl from the neighborhood he'd eyed from afar for years, but who was nearly three years his junior. She wasn't actually a Latina, having lived the first seven years of her life in the Philippines with her mom, dad, and two brothers. The entire Magbanua clan emigrated to the United States in 1993, leaving behind a number of relatives who were content living in the island nation. Like Garcia, Katie was the youngest child in her family. The pair started dating in 2003, just after she graduated from Miami Beach Senior High.

As an 18-year-old, the Filipina immigrant was incredibly attractive, her penetrating brown eyes, long, jet-black hair, olive skin, and beautiful smile an enticing blend capable of stopping any young man in his tracks. Unlike Tuto, she was both straightlaced and smart, shying away from drugs and alcohol—not even a parking ticket besmirching her squeaky-clean record.

The couple shared an apartment while Katie attended Miami-Dade Community College. It was quite the eye-opening experience for the attractive brunette, as her live-in boyfriend could no longer conceal his unglamorous habits. Tuto was arrested again on a misdemeanor count of marijuana possession and driving without a license. Katie eventually had enough, and kicked him out. In August 2005, she ventured off to the University of Central Florida in Orlando to complete her college education, majoring in health services administration.

Meanwhile, Tuto moved in with a friend named Mike Fernandez, who was raising his 14- and 16-year-old brothers as if he were their actual father. He and Tuto "co-parented" the boys, taking turns getting them to and from school. On occasion, they relied on the city bus system for the boys' transportation.

In December 2005, the teenaged brothers were on the No. 27 bus on their way home from school. They noticed a short, balding man staring at them with a creepy grin. The man got off when they did and began following them, ultimately telling the teenagers they could make some serious money posing nude on the internet. The stranger even offered to disguise their faces so no one could recognize them. The boys said "no" and outran the pedophile to their apartment, where they told Fernandez, then 22, and Garcia, 23, what had just happened.

The two adults hightailed it to the spot the boys said they'd last seen the creep, determined to kick his ass. They found the man right where the teenagers said he'd be—but didn't count on him being armed. Before Tuto and Fernandez laid a hand on him, the man pulled out a gun and shot them several times, striking Tuto in his lung and his liver. He and Fernandez were rushed to the hospital, where they laid unconscious, in critical condition for days. Neither was expected to survive. But miraculously, both did.

And just as miraculously, when Katie learned about the incident—and that Tuto had nearly died—she agreed to allow him to move into her Orlando apartment so she could care for him while he recovered from his injuries. Before long, not only did his gunshot wounds heal, so did the couple's romantic wounds. By the end of her junior year at UCF, Katie was pregnant with their first child. The proud parents welcomed Ethan Garcia into the world in December 2006, during Katie's senior year.

At the time, they were a blissfully happy couple, referring to themselves as "husband" and "wife," though their union was never formalized in a legal ceremony. Garcia managed to stay out of trouble during his less than 18 months in Orlando, keeping his alcohol and cocaine use to a minimum. He received training in block masonry and landed an honest construction job to help pay the bills while his "wife" attended classes and looked after Ethan.

When Katie graduated in May 2007, the family of three

moved back to South Florida, into an apartment in North Bay Village they shared with Katie's mom Cecilia, a nurse. The new parents had a built-in babysitter and were saving up money until they could afford a place of their own. In 2009, Garcia joined Rivera as a laborer at Coastal Masonry—even becoming certified to operate heavy machinery after obtaining his GED. For a while at least, he was pouring consistent income into the family coffers—through honest means no less. But that wouldn't last.

It was his own best friend who had Tuto fired—for swigging booze while at work. Operating heavy machinery was far too dangerous to have employees drinking on the job. As a foreman, Rivera had to enforce the company's rules, no matter who it was who ended up being laid off. Garcia also developed problems with his sciatic nerve, causing him to be laid up—flat on his back—for long stretches of time. During those stints, he was unable to pull his weight financially, which put increased strains on his "marriage." He grew restless, and began using alcohol and cocaine more and more.

Over time, a dynamic developed in which Katie would tear into Tuto for not doing his fair share financially or around the house—or for being irresponsible or reckless with his drinking and drug use. Ever distrustful, she'd check his phone regularly to investigate whether he was cavorting with other women. She wasn't averse to striking her "husband" in order to make a point. They'd break up for a few days, but would always try to repair the damage and move on. Their once happy "marriage" morphed into a roller-coaster ride that even their close friends described as "tumultuous."

Unlike his best friend Tato, Tuto never laid a finger on his "wife" in anger or frustration, simply taking it each time she lashed out at him over what she perceived to be his latest instance of irresponsibility or infidelity. For a tall, muscular man who had no compunction breaking the law, he was timid and obsequious when it came to Katie, who became the domineering partner in their relationship. Fittingly, when Katie had her own tattoo inked into her skin, she chose a bumble bee because, as she'd later tell a friend, "I love to fucking sting people." For better or worse, her "husband" was the person who most often felt her stinger.

Yet that didn't stop the on-again, off-again couple from conceiving a second child, Kaylee, who was born on May 30, 2012. In the afterglow of their daughter's birth, the "marriage" between Katie and Tuto seemed to have somewhat of a renaissance. In part, because Tuto loved being around his kids. He was an ever-present parent, determined to "out-father" his own dad, who'd left a void that Tuto believed had caused many of his problems as an adult. He never drank or did drugs around his children—unlike Sigfredo Sr.—saving those activities for evenings out with friends like Rivera. Which suited Katie just fine. Nothing in the world was more important to her than her kids. As much as she wanted Tuto involved in their lives, she didn't want them surrounded by drugs, alcohol, or other nefarious activities.

But her "husband's" life of crime continued unabated. In October 2012, he and an older friend jumped a 67-year-old man who was fishing at a pier, placed him in a choke-hold, and ripped open his pants pockets before violently throwing him to the ground. They robbed him of every penny he had. The elderly man reported the incident to the police a few days later and was able to identify Garcia from a photo lineup. A squadron of uniformed officers showed up at the North Bay Village apartment Tuto was sharing with Katie, her mom, and their kids. Initially, his "wife" refused to open the door for them.

When the door finally cracked open, Garcia barged out into the breezeway with clenched fists. "I'm not going to jail for some shit I didn't do," he growled defiantly. "I'm not going to jail." When he refused the officers' demand to drop to the ground with his hands behind his back, they wrestled him to the pavement, Garcia kicking and flailing wildly as they did. As they pummeled him in the back and face while securing handcuffs around his wrists, Tuto scoffed, "You guys aren't hurting me. This isn't my first rodeo."

Which, if anything, was a severe understatement. By the time the 32-year-old felon arrived at the Miami-Dade County Jail that evening, he was on pace for a record of sorts, having been incarcerated there no fewer than 25 times since his days as a juvenile offender. Though Katie helped him post bail—leading to his release the following day—she was growing increasingly impatient with his out-of-control behavior, father to her children or not.

•••

FOLLOWING HIS BRIEF VISIT to the clink, Tuto worked steadily at Coastal Masonry until he was laid off again in August 2013. His drinking and drug use were escalating, in inverse proportion to Katie's patience. So was his life of crime. At the spur of the moment, he'd happily join Rivera when his lifelong friend ventured off to rob drug dealers. Why drug dealers? Because they tend not to report when their drugs and money are stolen by other criminals.

Her "husband's" lack of earnings, drinking, drug use, and criminal mischief, however, had nothing at all to do with why Katie finally threw him out of their apartment for good. It was actually a "butt dial" from his cellphone that turned out to be her last straw. Unbeknownst to Garcia, his "wife" was listening as he bragged to friends about his sexual escapades with another woman. Katie was mortified, ashamed, and most of all, livid. As she threw his belongings out the front door that evening, she told him this time she was really "done."

Though he left willingly, Tuto was determined to win her back. No matter how difficult their relationship had become, Katherine Diana Magbanua was the only woman he'd ever truly love. Their destiny, he believed, was too intertwined to not end up together.

Katie, however, plowed forward, heading to work each morning to support herself and her kids, serving as the front-desk receptionist for SoFi Dental Care & Orthodontics in South Beach. Hard at work one fall afternoon in late 2013, she caught the eye of a traveling periodontist, who just so happened to be a handsome, muscular, and most eligible bachelor. Not to mention, dripping with money, exotic sportscars, and a waterfront home. With Sigfredo Garcia now in her rearview mirror, the Filipina immigrant's life was about to change in ways even her wildest dreams couldn't have foretold.

14.

Cellphones, Cars, Cycles, Cash, Checks, and C-Cups

FROM THE MOMENT WENDI ADELSON shared with him details surrounding her nasty divorce, Craig Isom had been convinced that the plot to kill her ex-husband had arisen from that highly contentious legal battle. Donna's venomous emails about her ex-son-in-law made that theory seem all the more plausible. As did the revelation that two Miami residents— Rivera and Garcia—had driven a rental vehicle some 500 miles to commit the heinous crime. But what continued to elude Isom and his team was the connection between Dan Markel's killers and the Adelsons. That is, until Sergeant Chris Corbitt completed his deep dive into the phone records.

Corbitt noticed that Garcia's call detail records revealed approximately 2,700 connections between his phone and the number (786) 564-1312 from May 1, 2014, to July 19, 2014—the day Tuto stopped using his T-Mobile account. With just a little more digging, Corbitt learned that the owner of that particular 786 number was one Katherine Diana Magbanua. A review of her DMV records disclosed a birthdate of December 22, 1984, a North Bay Village address, and that she stood 5'6" and weighed 122 pounds. As Sergeant Corbitt stared at the radiant smile Katie offered for her DMV picture, neither he nor anyone working on the murder case had any idea who she was. That was about to change.

A search of vital records revealed that the attractive, olive-skinned woman was the mother of a boy named Ethan and a girl named Kaylee. Investigators' eureka moment came when they read the name filled in on the children's birth certificates above the word "Father"—none other than Hitman Number One, Sigfredo Garcia. State corporation records revealed that Katie also was the vice president of a company named S. Garcia Solutions, Inc. Though there was no public record of a marriage between Katie and Garcia, she used his surname, Garcia, as her last name on her Facebook and Gmail accounts.

But the connection between Katherine Magbanua and Sigfredo Garcia—interesting though it was—wasn't the bombshell revelation that provided the rocket fuel to power the investigation to even greater heights. That rocket fuel was provided by Charlie Adelson's call detail records. What number appeared more than 900 times in his records between early May and mid-July 2014? The very same 786 number that belonged to Katie Magbanua.

Moreover, Katie's phone records revealed that she and the Maestro were both in Key West for several days in late June 2014, their phones pinging off the exact same cell towers. It didn't take a degree in rocket science to conclude that Katie and Charlie had been lovers at the exact same time her baby daddy and his lifelong best friend were planning Dan Markel's murder. That was the bombshell revelation: Katie was at the center of a love triangle between a man who wanted his ex-brother-in-law killed and a man who was in Dan Markel's driveway achieving that very objective.

Sergeant Corbitt and his team assembled a timeline of telephone calls that occurred the day of the shooting, July 18, 2014, which was most illuminating.

Katie had spoken to Garcia at 12:01 a.m. and with Charlie from 12:07 a.m. to 12:14 a.m. At 1:02 a.m., Charlie contacted his mother, and a minute later was back on the phone with Katie for another 20 minutes. After all the key players presumably had a night of slumber, the frenetic phone activity picked back up, beginning with Donna calling Wendi at 8:09 a.m. and Charlie reaching out to Wendi at 9:12 a.m. The brother and sister were on the phone from 9:19 a.m. to 9:37 a.m. Immediately after hanging up with Wendi, Charlie contacted his mom. Between 9:58 a.m. and 10:09 a.m.—in the hour before the shooting—he spoke with Katie three more times.

Meanwhile, it appeared from the lack of cell tower activity that both Rivera and Garcia had powered their phones off at about 10:00 a.m. while they awaited Dan's departure from Premier Fitness. Following the shooting, Charlie spoke with Donna from 11:22 a.m. to 11:29 a.m. and with Katie from 11:31 a.m. to 11:36 a.m. And at 12:30 p.m., minutes after apparently powering his phone back on, Garcia dialed Katie, a call that lasted 44 seconds.

A flurry of calls occurred later that day after Rivera and Garcia returned to Miami, starting up not long after Rivera's $40 ATM withdrawal in Broward County at 6:46 p.m. Katie spoke with her "husband" at 7:10 p.m. and 8:05 p.m., each call lasting a minute. She was on the phone with Charlie from 8:36 p.m. to 8:39 p.m. and three more times with Garcia between 8:40 p.m. and 9:22 p.m. Over the following hour, she spoke with Charlie twice and with Tuto once.

According to the cell tower data, just after Katie hung up with Tuto at 10:22 p.m., the two were at the same location—Rivera's apartment. Which is why there were no more calls between them that evening. Between 3:00 a.m. and 3:30 a.m., however, Katie's baby daddy tried to reach her three more times—each call rolling to her voicemail.

Corbitt also pieced together the timeline leading up to Rivera's rental of the Toyota Prius on July 15, the day before he and Garcia departed for Tally. The TPD sergeant concluded that Charlie and Katie had dinner together the prior evening and then drove to Katie's apartment. The records showed Charlie leaving shortly after 12:30 a.m. Katie then called Garcia five separate times between 12:48 a.m. and 2:00 a.m. on July 15.

Some 16 hours later, at 6:15 p.m., Rivera received the keys to the silver-pine-mica Prius from Hybrid Auto Rentals.

Within 15 minutes, Katie and Charlie were on the phone again—from 6:29 p.m. to 6:40 p.m. She and Tuto were texting and calling one another incessantly from 7:54 p.m. until 9:30 p.m.—approximately 30 separate communications in all. The "husband" and "wife" were also in touch frequently during Tato and Tuto's trip to Tally, speaking by phone three times and exchanging texts twice on July 16 and on the phone together nine times on July 17.

This dizzying array of circumstantial evidence allowed investigators to flesh out a theory as to how the murder went down: Charlie and Donna wanted Dan Markel out of the way so Wendi and her boys could join them in South Florida. They certainly had the means to hire a hitman to accomplish that objective. Conveniently, Charlie was sleeping with a woman whose kids were fathered by a convicted felon and frequent guest at the Miami-Dade County Jail. Katie, they reasoned, had been the conduit between her lover, Charlie, and Hitman Number One, Garcia. The call detail records revealing her incessant phone chatter with both—often within minutes of each other—seemed to provide solid support for that theory.

•••

FURTHER ANALYSIS OF THE phone records revealed something else of interest. The July 16-18 trip to Tally had actually been Tato and Tuto's *second* excursion to Funky T-Town. Their first had occurred June 4-5.

Corbitt was able to track Rivera's cellphone beginning at 3:13 a.m. on June 4, pinging towers in Miami, across Alligator Alley in South Florida, and then in a northerly direction all the way up the Gulf Coast until he reached Tally at 12:38 p.m. Though Garcia's cellphone didn't ping any towers, investigators knew he was right beside his lifelong pal for the entire journey. How? Because the rental agreement for the Hyundai Sonata that arrived in Tally that afternoon was filled out in his name.

Garcia had actually completed two rental agreements at Comfort Rent A Car near the Miami International Airport. The first was on June 2, for a Nissan Altima. Not long after leaving the rental company, however, he received a traffic citation. He returned the following day to exchange the Altima for the Sonata. Significantly, just like the Toyota Prius that Rivera rented in July, the Sonata that Garcia rented was equipped with a GPS tracker. On the morning of June 5, the device signaled its presence in the parking lot of a Budget Inn near the Florida State campus—the very same motel the duo stayed at when they came to Tally in July.

Where did the GPS tracker indicate the Sonata was the afternoon of June 4? In the parking lot of Betton Hills' Winthrop Park, within walking distance of Dan Markel's home. Rivera's cellphone was pinging a tower in that vicinity most of the afternoon. And at 12:34 p.m. on June 5, the records revealed Tato and Tuto on the phone with one another, with Rivera's phone, once again, revealing its presence in Betton Hills.

By 3:30 p.m. that afternoon, King Tato was on the move, his phone pinging towers in a southerly direction down the Gulf Coast, eastward across Alligator Alley, all the way back to Miami, where his phone pinged just after midnight. Though the lifelong friends didn't assassinate Dan Markel during the June trip, the tower dump and GPS data left no doubt that the tenured law professor was clearly the person they'd come to see.

Corbitt dove back into Katie's call detail records to determine whether she'd been in contact with her "husband" during his June trip to the 'Hassee. Indeed she had. The data revealed 11 phone calls and five text exchanges between the two from 9:55 a.m. on June 4 to 11:06 p.m. on June 5. The pattern of communications appeared very similar to their interactions during the July trip—and just as incriminating.

• • •

INVESTIGATORS NOW KNEW there had been a nearly six-week gap between the hitmen's two trips to Tallahassee. Given that, they decided to delve into the phone calls during that time stretch as well.

One day in particular, July 1, practically jumped off the page. It appeared that Katie and her periodontist boyfriend had been together that morning, as both of their phones were pinging towers near his waterfront home on Whale Harbor Lane in Fort Lauderdale from 10:04 a.m. until 1:20 p.m. For about five hours that afternoon, Katie was blowing up her "husband's" phone, calling him 48 different times without reaching him. They finally spoke for six minutes at 5:05 p.m. Nine minutes later, Garcia called Harvey Adelson's cellphone, a call Corbitt concluded rolled to voicemail.

Katie then tried to reach Tuto an additional 30-plus times and placed her own call to Harvey's cellphone at 7:43 p.m.— which also rolled to voicemail. She finally reached Tuto at 7:44 p.m. for a relatively short conversation. Between 8:29 p.m. and 9:57 p.m., Katie and Charlie were on the phone three different times for a total of 52 minutes. She had several more phone and text communications with both men until just after midnight. And then, at 12:43 a.m. on July 2, Charlie had his own 12-minute call with his 69-year-old father.

Surely all of this back and forth on July 1 had to mean something in view of the hitmen's aborted June trip to Tally and their "successful" July trip. But until they had someone on the inside willing to talk with them, the investigators knew they were unlikely to discover precisely what had been going on—or why Harvey Jerome Adelson was involved.

•••

A COMPREHENSIVE CRIMINAL investigation is multifaceted—tracking the criminal activity itself, attempts by those involved to cover their tracks, as well as the "fruits of the crime." Because hitmen were involved in Dan's murder, investigators naturally suspected a payoff. Though most hitmen aren't dumb enough to deposit their proceeds into legitimate bank accounts, a surprising number are careless enough to make purchases with their ill-gotten gains that can be traced through public records. To the good fortune of TPD investigators, Tuto and Tato fell into that group.

It took Garcia all of eight days to make his first acquisition: a 1984 Chevy Monte Carlo coupe. In August 2014, he also purchased a Honda Racer motorcycle and in October acquired a 2000 Nissan Maxima. For his part, in the two weeks following the murder, Rivera purchased a 2003 Suzuki motorcycle and a Toyota Camry. In December 2014, Garcia actually posted a photo on his Facebook page of himself and Rivera seated on their colorful new bikes, for the entire world—not to mention TPD investigators—to see.

Craig Isom and his team would have even a bigger field day tracking all of the benefits Katie had seemingly raked in during the months following the murder. Unlike Tato and Tuto, she *did* deposit large sums of money into the bank. During the final six months of 2014, she made $34,000 in cash deposits into her two accounts—in increments ranging from $300 to $2,000— often making multiple deposits in a single day. During the corresponding period of 2013, she'd made all of $2,800 in cash deposits.

While poring through Katie's finances, investigators made another startling discovery. In mid-September 2014—some two months after the murder—she'd apparently been placed on the payroll of the Adelson Institute, drawing a biweekly paycheck of $450.00 before taxes. She received 44 paychecks in all, totaling nearly $18,000. Investigators had actually been tracking Katie's movements during that entire time period through her cell tower pings. Not once had she pinged a tower anywhere near the Adelson Institute.

Of some significance, the funds the dental practice paid Katie weren't auto-deposited into her accounts. Rather, they were delivered in the form of handwritten checks, signed by none other than Donna Adelson. What was even more suspicious was that although the checks were for the most part dated two weeks apart, 15 of them were consecutively numbered.

It wasn't just how those checks were issued to Katie that

made it appear she was receiving them in clumps. It also was how she deposited them. On eight occasions, she deposited multiple checks on the same date. Her deposits were often weeks after the dates written on the checks: her January 7, 2015 check was deposited on February 2, her February 5 check on March 11, and her September 16 check on October 15. Which was all highly suspicious. As was the fact that 19 of the checks were issued before the payment period described in the memo line had concluded.

The biggest question raised by these paychecks was why Katie was drawing them in the first place if she wasn't actually working at the Adelson Institute. TPD investigators believed the answer was pretty obvious: to ensure that she wouldn't squeal on Charlie or Donna if ever questioned about the events surrounding Dan Markel's murder. Essentially, to buy her loyalty—and complete silence.

•••

IN THE FALL OF 2015, Katie started driving a sweet new ride—a black 2001 Lexus LS 430—which would have listed for more than $60,000 as a new car. How did she get her hands on the luxury vehicle? As a hand-me-down from Charlie Adelson's impressive fleet. A puzzling oddity considering that Katie's romantic relationship with the playboy periodontist had ended many months before, Katie having reunited with Tuto earlier that spring.

Charlie having loaned his Lexus to an ex-girlfriend was suspicious enough. But what happened on January 23, 2016, was even more incriminating, which was when Harvey signed the official title to the vehicle—which bore his name rather than Charlie's—over to Katie. The odometer section revealed 150,000 miles and the selling price was listed as $1,700. Even if paid, that sum would have been far below the car's Kelly Blue Book value. But there wasn't an iota of evidence in Katie's bank records that she'd actually withdrawn the sum of $1,700—or any similar amount—to pay for it. Rather, the Lexus appeared to be a most generous gift.

There was one additional item of interest investigators discovered as they searched through Katie's Facebook accounts. Actually, *two* to be more precise. Boobs. Close inspection of images she posted in March 2015 revealed a noticeable difference from pictures she'd posted a year earlier. Her chest had swelled considerably—which she proudly flaunted in numerous photos in low-cut tops that accentuated her cleavage. She'd obviously received breast implants. Investigators would learn that they'd been the handiwork of a Coral Gables plastic surgeon whose patients referred to him as "Dr. Boobner."

When they made this discovery, TPD investigators had nothing beyond their intuition and experience to suspect that Katie's new "endowment" had been funded by Charlie or members of his family. But if the Adelsons were willing to put her on the payroll and provide new wheels to keep Katie happy—and quiet—it seemed pretty logical that they'd also have been willing to endow her with new curves as well.

•••

SPRING WAS IN THE AIR in the Sunshine State's capital city. Trees were greening up and colorful flowers were blooming throughout the landscape. The days were getting longer and more pleasant. And the investigation into the execution of an acclaimed law professor was finally starting to heat up. Though no arrests had yet been made, by April 2016, Craig Isom and his team had every reason to believe they were making enormous progress. Plus, they even had a few tricks up their sleeves they were waiting for just the right moment to unveil.

15.

Tightening the Noose

APRIL 19, 2016 WAS A relatively comfortable day by South Beach standards—the temperature reaching only 81 degrees—a cool, gentle breeze blowing off Biscayne Bay. At about 1:45 p.m., Donna Adelson walked out the front door of her 40-story, waterfront condominium building where she and Harvey had lived for the past two years. She was on her way to the elementary school across the street to pick up her five- and six-year-old grandsons—her routine every weekday afternoon while her daughter Wendi, who lived nearby, worked in Miami as a law clerk for a federal appellate judge.

On this particular Tuesday afternoon, the 66-year-old grandmother was sporting a tank top with vibrant colors splashed across a white base, which she'd thrown on over a pair of black shorts. Her dirty-blonde hair was pulled back into a scraggly bun, her eyes protected from the mid-afternoon sun by a pair of designer shades. A black purse hanging from a long shoulder strap rested against her right hip. Donna descended the condo's towering staircase that fronted Alton Road and began walking briskly along the sidewalk toward 4th Street. Her day—indeed, her entire life—was about to be turned upside down.

Seemingly out of nowhere, a heavy-set, middle-aged, white man approached her from the opposite direction, stopping the former kindergarten teacher dead in her tracks. The bald-headed stranger had a thick, brown goatee extending from his chin, his ultra-casual attire projecting an image of someone who definitely ran in a different social circle than Harvey and Donna Adelson.

"Excuse me, Mrs. Adleson?" he called out, mispronouncing her surname, enunciating a short "A" sound rather than a long one. "How ya doin'?" he greeted her in a friendly tone. "I just want to give you this." He extended his right hand, which was clutching a piece of paper.

"Who are *you*?" Donna asked with a nervous laugh, placing her right hand on her chest for emphasis. "You're scaring me."

"No, don't be scared," the stranger said in a calm, reassuring voice, chuckling himself. "Listen, just want to let you know that we know that your family has been taking care of Katie and her friend Tuto for quite some time after your problem up north has resolved. And I want to let you know that my brother—he's incarcerated. He helped your family with this problem you guys had up north, and we want to make sure that—he's going through some rough times—and we want to make sure that you take care of what he's going through the way you're taking care of Katie and Tuto."

"I don't know what you're talking about," Donna protested—her words expressed in a slow, cautious cadence—her right hand pressed against her forehead as she stared at the barrel-chested man with a bewildered expression.

"Well, this will explain it," the man replied, sticking the piece of paper in her right hand. "Thank you." The stranger turned around and began walking down the sidewalk toward 4th Street without saying another word, Donna following close behind. When she reached the corner, she stuffed the paper in her purse without even a casual glance, then crossed the street and continued walking toward Ben and Lincoln's school.

What the Adelson family's matriarch had no way of knowing at that moment was that the man she'd just encountered was an undercover FBI agent named Oscar Jimenez. And that additional FBI agents and Miami Beach police officers stationed in a van across the street were videotaping their entire interaction—as was Jimenez through a body camera. They even had a small plane flying at a high altitude peering down at them from the sky.

The elaborate, undercover sting operation had been in the planning stages for weeks, with Special Agent Pat Sanford—a wiry, 17-year FBI veteran—in charge. Sanford, whose office was in Tally, had been working closely with Craig Isom beginning just days after Dan Markel's murder. Through the FBI, the TPD had access to resources, equipment, and personnel far beyond anything the mid-sized police department could have mustered on its own. Though he wasn't physically in South Beach on April 19, Isom was on the phone with Sanford and his team as they provided a play-by-play account of the entire event in real time.

The interaction between Donna and the undercover agent near the Icon Condominium complex was what investigators refer to as a "bump." The strategy is for an undercover agent to deliberately rattle the cage of someone suspected of a crime, causing the suspect to engage in incriminating behavior or communications. In this case, investigators were hoping for the latter. Twelve days before the bump, Isom had obtained an order allowing wiretaps to be placed on Charlie's and Katie's cellphones. All of their conversations since then had been intercepted and recorded for posterity. That would continue for the foreseeable future.

The bump with Donna was intended to "tickle the wire"— to precipitate conversations among Donna, Charlie, and Katie that might expose their connection to the hitmen's murderous activities. The sheet of paper Jimenez handed to Donna was a printout of a July 21, 2015, article from a weekly newspaper, the *Miami New Times*, marking the one-year anniversary of Dan's vicious slaying. An enlarged, color photo of the law professor's smiling face appeared just beneath the headline. Written in handwriting on the printout was Jimenez's covert telephone number, (305) 712-6570, as well as the figure $5,000.

Investigators wanted Donna and her son to believe that

someone close to Luis Rivera, perhaps a fellow Latin King member, was trying to blackmail them, the sheet of paper an implied threat that the mother and son would be reported to law enforcement—or maybe even harmed—unless they paid up. Five thousand dollars to be precise.

How did investigators know that Rivera wouldn't foil their plan? Because, as Jimenez alluded to in his brief conversation with Donna, the Latin Kings gang leader was in federal prison, having recently been sentenced on racketeering charges. That's what Jimenez was referring to when he told Donna, "My brother—he's incarcerated."

Just as Sanford and Isom hoped would happen, the moment Donna returned home to her 26th-floor condo that afternoon, she reached out to Charlie's cellphone. Because his phone was wiretapped, investigators were listening. "I got some paperwork hand-delivered to me," Donna reported in a deliberate, cautious tone—clearly worried.

"You're being sued?" Charlie asked, wondering aloud if it was the IRS.

"No," his mom answered. "That's what I thought it was, but I'm going to need to talk to you." She told Charlie she might drive up his way to fill him in.

"Does Dad know about this?" he asked.

"No, Dad's at work today," she said. "Fortunately."

"Does Wendi know that? Is [sic] it involve Wendi?"

"No, no, no. No. *No*. No. No," Donna replied emphatically, as if Charlie had touched a nerve. "Let me just talk to you later."

"Does it involve me or other people?" he persisted.

"Well," Donna began, but then paused. "Probably both of us," she finally said, her words hesitant, her voice barely above a whisper.

"What's that?" Charlie asked, apparently unable to decipher his mom's soft-spoken words.

"Probably the two of us, so— You probably have a general idea what I'm talking about," Donna added, without elaborating. "So let's— let's just find some time to talk to each other and take the boys for a ride, okay?"

"So, it's urgent you talk to me today?"

"Today or, um, tomorrow. I mean, it's important." She told her middle child she didn't know what to do.

Charlie asked who had sent the paperwork. Donna explained that it "was something that came hand to hand to me as I exited the building today."

When her son asked whether the paperwork was anonymous, Donna stressed that it wasn't.

"I just don't want to discuss it over the phone," she finally said. With Charlie off from work the next day, they decided he'd come to South Beach to discuss the situation in person. Not wanting Harvey to be aware of what was going on, Donna suggested they meet after her husband departed for work at noon. "Love you honey," she said, ending the call. "Love you. Bye," Charlie replied.

But about 20 minutes later, he called back. "Listen, whatever it is" he said, "whatever someone sent you, I wouldn't worry too much about anything." He assured his mom he'd be there the following day so they could talk and told her not to stress about it. Somewhat playfully, Donna replied, "I'll make you take me out to dinner, so make sure you bring cash with you."

"So I need to bring cash?" Charlie asked, seemingly puzzled.

"That's probably a good idea, right?" Donna inquired, seeking his guidance.

"Is someone blackmailing you?" he asked.

"Well, that's always a good possibility," she said, her word choice somewhat peculiar.

Charlie's tone suddenly became serious. He repeated his question. "You think someone's trying to blackmail you?"

"Um, maybe," Donna answered cautiously. "Could be."

"*Nooo*," Charlie responded in disbelief. "That's crazy!" He asked if she knew who'd sent the paperwork.

"I have a pretty good idea," she answered. "Yeah, it's amazing. Somebody knew exactly who I was. Called me by name." Donna told her son, "I wouldn't forget that face."

"That's crazy that someone handed you a letter like that." Charlie asked his mother whether the man was "like threatening you or anything?"

"You know, you never know how to interpret these things," Donna replied. "So, let's not worry, and let's meet tomorrow afternoon."

Charlie asked his mom if she could send him a screenshot of the paperwork, but Donna declined, telling him, "No, no, I really don't want to do that."

"So it wasn't the government or the military?" he pressed her. "It was just some random person?"

"Yeah," she confirmed.

"That's fucking crazy!" Charlie reiterated. "Is the person threatening you?" he asked a second time.

"You know, I don't think we should talk about this," Donna hesitated.

"It's the kind of thing," he interrupted, "if there's a threat, you go to the police."

"Yeah, yeah, this time," Donna replied, "I don't think that's a good idea." She didn't elaborate on why "this time" was different from any other.

"Let me see what it is, let me see what nonsense it is first," Charlie said. "It won't be the first time I've been threatened." He ended the call telling his mom, "If it's something serious, you know I'm going to recommend going to the police."

"I know, I know," Donna said. "It's what I'm tempted to do."

At 3:00 p.m., Charlie called back yet again, unable to contain his curiosity—their third conversation in less than an hour. Before his mother could get a word out, he instructed her, "Obviously, don't talk about things in the apartment or anyplace."

"Oh, obviously," Donna agreed. Yet the sound of Ben and Lincoln's voices in the background left little doubt she was speaking from inside her condo, despite her son's warning.

"Did they try and ask for money or something?" Charlie asked, attempting to better understand what the stranger wanted.

"Yeah, yeah," Donna confirmed.

Charlie reiterated his feeling that they probably needed to go to the police. "I may have to," Donna agreed, "but I'd rather talk to you first." She told him she wanted him to look at the paperwork "because I don't want your father upset."

"Don't say anything to Dad until I take a look at it," Charlie cautioned her. "Because Dad flies off the handle.

"*Absolutely*," Donna agreed emphatically. "Absolutely. That's why I suggested, after he goes to work tomorrow." She added that what the stranger wanted was "clear."

"Can I just ask you, what did they ask for?"

Oddly, Donna answered in code, telling her son, "This TV was probably about five."

"They asked you for $5,000?" Charlie asked incredulously, ignoring his mom's desire to disguise their language. "That's fucking crazy!"

She told him that the stranger had also mentioned "an ex-girlfriend," but didn't reveal that he'd referred to Katie by name.

"That's crazy," Charlie repeated. "Let me take a look at it and then I'll go from there."

A few minutes after hanging up, he called Katie, telling her that someone had approached his mom on the street, called her by name, and handed her an envelope with something in it. "I have no idea what this is in reference to," he said. "But something regarding her son, something regarding his ex-girlfriend, and the person asking my mom for some money."

"*Whaaaat?*" Katie responded, seemingly in disbelief. Charlie told her he'd initially thought his mother was saying something about the IRS or a patient suing "or something like that. So I don't even know what the fuck it's about at all."

"She should have called the cops or something," Katie said. Charlie indicated that was precisely what he advised his mom to do. "I said you got to go straight to the police."

"My mom said it involved 'your ex-girlfriend.' I don't even think she said who." Charlie told Katie that he was calling her because she was his "last girlfriend." But that wasn't actually true. In the year plus since they'd ended their romance, he'd had two additional girlfriends.

Katie asked why he was calling her if the stranger had merely mentioned an "ex-girlfriend." "You have like a thousand ex-girlfriends," she chuckled. "Well fuck," he agreed. "It could be anyone." But later in the conversation, Charlie said, "I thought when I spoke to my mom she said it involved— they mentioned your name in it. That's why I was calling you. But I'm going to feel like an idiot if they didn't." He told her that if it did have something to do with her, he would want to see her the next day.

Charlie called back about 90 minutes later. Katie told him she was scared. "Like your mom must be like freaking out and shit … Like somebody fucking framed her. Like *hello*."

Katie suggested—a second time—that his mom and dad call the cops. "What does it have to do with me?" she wondered aloud.

"I don't fucking know," Charlie responded. But then said that he was "99% sure" that his mom had said the "letter mentioned your name." He told her he'd talk to his mother in person the next day to confirm that. If it didn't mention her name, he added, he'd try to find out "which one of my other 87 exes it could be." He wanted to meet up with Katie in person to pick her brain either way, he said, "because you're like one of my best friends."

Katie asked whether she'd become involved because "I work for you?," telling Charlie she should be considered "like employee of the month" in view of what was now transpiring. To which he responded, "Just make sure you call those patients that I gave you the list from the other day."

"I did," Katie replied. "I always do." Though their words implied that Charlie's onetime flame was actually working for the Adelson Institute, their tone was tongue-in-cheek, as if they were joking. Which investigators knew full well they were—as the wiretap on Katie's phone didn't reveal her making a single call to any dental patients.

•••

AT ABOUT 1:00 P.M. the next afternoon, Charlie and Donna met at the edge of the marina behind a restaurant named Monty's, just a short walk from her condo. They sat at a circular, concrete picnic table, elbow to elbow, talking barely above a whisper. Though Pat Sanford and other FBI agents were close by to surveil their conversation—the nearest agent seated at a bench just 40 feet away with an audio recording device pointed in their direction—the isolated area in which they were sitting made it impossible to capture any useful audio without blowing an agent's cover. And by 1:30 p.m., mother and son were on the move, walking along the boardwalk back to the Icon tower.

Charlie then made the hour-long trek to Sunny Isles Beach, where Katie had just begun a job at Optimar Realty. They met in his car for about ten minutes, then walked over to a small pizza and gelato restaurant in the same strip mall named Dolce Vita, grabbing a table at the rear of the dining room. Unbeknownst to the pair, another undercover FBI agent was in a vehicle just a few feet from the Maestro's and watched as the former lovers entered the restaurant. As soon as they walked in, the agent left his vehicle and came through the restaurant's front door himself, taking a seat at the table directly across from Charlie and Katie's. A few minutes later, he was joined by another undercover agent.

Each of the agents walked into Dolce Vita clutching what appeared to be laptop bags. Rather than computers, however, what was inside the bags were sophisticated recording devices that filmed the discussion between Charlie and Katie through small holes at the edges of the bags. Though the video they recorded wasn't terribly sharp, Charlie was clearly visible seated at one side of the table in his white T-shirt and gray cargo shorts, with only Katie's skin-tight blue jeans and feet visible at the other.

Even though the undercover agents were able to station themselves within just a few feet of their subjects, the audio they captured was extremely difficult to decipher because the restaurant's kitchen was directly behind Charlie and Katie's table. Thus, rather than a clear back-and-forth conversation between the two, the audio stream the recording devices picked up was filled with loud background noise from the kitchen.

Other agents working with the audio later, however, were able to make out a few phrases. At one point, Charlie told Katie how he wanted to deal with the blackmailer: "You call him on the phone. All I want you to say is, 'I got a call from some friends who said that you reached out to them and that you mentioned my name.'" He told her to deny knowing anything, but to agree to pay the blackmail demand as "charity to help the less fortunate." Katie needed to warn the blackmailer, he instructed, "Do not contact these people again or they're going to go to the police." Paying someone off, Charlie told her, "is not an admission of guilt."

Midway through their conversation, the recording devices picked up what agents believed was Charlie saying, "If it's the police, they can't take the money, and won't even come to meet you. They fucked up. If it's this guy, maybe that's— *You better kill him*, because he's going to be a big problem. If you can't do it, I'll have someone else do it." He told Katie his mother couldn't be involved. "Problem is, if you give in and Mom meets him to pay, what happens next month when he needs help again? If it's the cops, she's guilty as hell."

On his way home from Sunny Isles Beach, Charlie reported to his mother that "everything's good. So I hung out with my friend," who he said was "going to sleep on some stuff."

"So you think she'll be okay with everything involved— that it's good for her?" Donna asked, seemingly referring to the instructions her son had just given Katie at Dolce Vita.

"Yeah, yeah," Charlie answered. "I would worry about absolutely nothing."

"Well, if your theory is correct," Donna responded, sounding less confident. "We don't know that."

Charlie assured his mom that whoever had handed her

the note wouldn't gain anything by attempting to extort their family. "They're still going to be in the same situation. Listen, it's not like you've ever threatened anybody or hurt anybody, so—"

"No, I know that," Donna concurred.

Charlie told her he found the situation "very weird" because "it's the kind of thing that can easily be traced, they can easily be caught, and they will easily have charges put against them," noting that "extorting people is like up to ten years in prison."

He felt confident, he said, that the situation was something "that can be dealt with. It's not that bad." "Without a doubt," he assured her, "everything is fine. No question in the world."

•••

INVESTIGATORS WERE WELL AWARE that the on-again, off-again relationship between Katie and Sigfredo Garcia was on again—and had been for some time. For several months, their two-story, North Miami townhouse had been under continuous surveillance through a hidden camera affixed to a telephone pole. Investigators therefore weren't the least bit surprised that the wiretap on her phone was picking up frequent communications between the two. But the couple now had things to discuss far more critical than their children.

The day after the Dolce Vita meeting, Katie pressed Garcia to find out who the blackmailer was and to call the telephone number Charlie had given her at the restaurant. Though she told Charlie she'd call the number herself, Katie was now delegating that assignment to her "husband." Initially, he was resistant. But she pushed him hard, almost bullying him: "You're fucking me over," she said. "You're going to tell me, 'I'm going to make a phone call.'"

He pushed back just as hard, telling her, "I'm not making that fucking phone call!" Katie screamed at him, prompting Tuto to say, "I just want you to have a pussy between your legs and act like you have one." As she usually did, though, Katie worked her powers of persuasion and wore him down. By the end of their conversation, her "husband" had agreed to "take care of this fucking problem … because the less you know, the better off, man."

But there was apparent confusion over the last four digits of the blackmailer's telephone number. In another call, speaking to Garcia in code, Katie indicated that she couldn't recall whether the balance she owed for their son's clothing was $60.57 or $65.70. "The amount that I gave you on the piece of paper," she added. "I don't know if it's $60.57 or $65.70."

Garcia finally clued into her encoded message. "Got it," he replied, now aware she was referencing the last four digits in the blackmailer's phone number. And that he should therefore try both.

• • •

ON APRIL 25, AGENT SANFORD and his team decided to generate some additional heat on their suspects. A letter was dropped in the mail addressed to Donna and Harvey's South Beach condo with "Adelsons" as the addressee. It was short and sweet, and unsigned: "MY PHONE IS NOT RINGING SO YOU DONT CARE ABOUT TATO AND WHAT HE DID FOR YOU. HE KNOWS HE IS FUCKED AND SOON SO WILL YOU." It was the first time the name "Tato" had been interjected into the blackmail demand.

The next day, Katie reported to Charlie that she wasn't sure she'd written the telephone number down correctly when they'd met at Dolce Vita, once again employing encoded language. "Like I, for some reason, I know you were like telling me something about for the client, but I— like, I got it mixed up with the number. And I'm calling both numbers, but nobody is picking up. So I need to figure out because— or else I could set up, you know, with the realtor to show the property." She told him she needed the number "like stat."

Charlie hung up and dialed his mom to see whether she still had the telephone number. "Someone just called me asking for it, because they—they thought they remembered it," he told her. "But evidently, they—they remembered it wrong." He was careful not to mention Katie's name. Donna reminded him that she'd given him the piece of paper and no longer had it. He was forced to drive home, find the paper, and then share the number with Katie a second time. Which she promptly supplied to her "husband"—three times—telling him the number was for "one of the listings, one of the properties."

That same day, Garcia texted Katie, telling his "wife," "What ever is going on with you and ur homie"—by whom he clearly meant Charlie—is "ur business u guys witk [sic] that shit out. Dont text me."

By the following day, April 27, the letter purportedly from the blackmailer had arrived in South Beach. As it turned out, Harvey was the one who opened it. During a phone call that afternoon, Charlie asked Donna if his dad was "still upset about everything?"

"Yeah," she confirmed. "He's not having the best day."

Charlie told her that everything was being taken care of and that the letter was incorrect because "they" actually did call the blackmailer—by which he meant Katie. Which is what Katie had reported to him.

"*Oh my!*" Donna replied, clearly relieved. "Thank goodness." Yet her relief evaporated when Charlie told her that no one had answered the call. He assured his mom that she'd "done nothing wrong. And it's because of that, you have nothing, literally nothing, to worry about. Someone's fishing and someone wants to try to make some money because they're struggling." Charlie told her not to "drive yourself to the point where you get sick because of that."

"I know, sweetheart," Donna said with a big sigh. "I do."

"The truth is, is that the number was called," her son reiterated. "They didn't even pick up." Charlie added that "she"—now interchanging pronouns—tried calling both the 305 and 786 area codes. One of them rolled to voicemail, he explained, and the other didn't pick up.

Yet as of that moment, Oscar Jimenez's undercover number hadn't actually been called a single time. What Garcia was telling Katie, what she was telling Charlie, and what he was telling his mother, was all entirely false.

•••

THE HEAT BECAME EVEN MORE intense on April 28. That morning, Jimenez called the Adelson Institute asking to speak with Donna, telling the employee who answered the phone that his name was "Sammy." He explained that he'd given Donna some paperwork. The employee took down his phone number, indicating that Donna wasn't available, but could perhaps call him back. "Just tell her it's very important," Jimenez said. "We need to find out immediately what she thinks about the paperwork. I met her last week."

Minutes later, investigators were listening in on another intercepted call between mother and son. Donna seemed very stressed out. Erika had just called from the office, she explained to Charlie, telling her that a man named Sammy had called to speak with her about "some very important papers" he'd given her last week. Erika indicated the man was upset because he hadn't heard from her. "So obviously, I'm not going to call the number," Donna said. "What's your suggestion?"

Charlie first verified that the number "Sammy" provided Erika was identical to the one he'd given Katie at Dolce Vita and then again by phone from his house. It was. He was puzzled because Katie had assured him the number had been called and that no one had picked up. "So let me do this," he said. "Let me call somebody." He tried reassuring Donna: "Mom, trust me when I tell you, I wouldn't worry at all."

Charlie attempted to reach Katie several times until she finally called back, leading to a 23-minute, profanity-laced exchange investigators were listening to in real time. Charlie explained that "a guy by the name of Sammy" had called the dental office agitated because no one had ever called him after he left his paperwork.

"No," Katie responded. "Somebody is pulling your bones and shit … That number, nobody is picking up. That is a nonworking number. It's like a Gmail number."

His disbelief and irritation mounting, Charlie demanded, "I'm just asking you to find out who the fuck it is."

"This is like a fucking bullshit game," his ex-lover replied, equally frustrated. She'd called the number herself, she insisted—which the investigators listening in knew was a lie.

Charlie threatened her. "Find out who the fuck it is, because the other phone call is going to be to the FBI ... And then, when they do catch the person, they're going to be asking him lots of questions about who Katie is ... Find out who the fuck it is. That's all I'm asking you."

"It's fucking bullshit," Katie shot back, now riled up herself, "and fucking somebody is trying to fucking pinpoint some bullshit. Like it's getting aggravating."

"All I'm saying is find out who the fuck it is and tell them to stop playing their games," Charlie demanded. "I don't know who you have to talk to but it's— it needs to be nipped in the bud."

"No, I'm going to handle this shit myself, bro," Katie snarled. "Because this is some fucking bullshit. I'm going to handle it my motherfucking self ... Call straight from my motherfucking number ... I have your *fucking*— whatever fucking shit taken care of. Okay? Because this is fucking bullshit." Katie was seething. "I'm about to go to the fucking FBI. I'm fucking getting irate with this shit already. It's either the FBI fucking, fucking playing games or fucking whatever it is because I'm fucking getting pissed ... *I'm pissed the fuck off.* Like I'm going to fucking go to the cops right now."

"Well, either you go to the cops, or we go to the cops," Charlie warned, his voice calmer and more composed than hers. "Find out who the fuck this is because this person evidently knows you and knows your family. And they know me."

"Exactly. And you don't, you don't think that fucking scares the shit out of me?" Katie retorted. "Like somebody fucking saying my name out loud or whatever?"

"Well, Katie, don't mess— someone's messing with you.

They're messing with me."

Katie repeated that she'd already called the number and that it wasn't a working number. "Shit! *Fucking A, bro!* I'm going to fucking fuck up whoever the fuck is fucking with me!" she screamed into the phone.

Charlie hung up with her and called his mom back, telling her he was ready to take matters into his own hands. "I have a strong feeling what I think it is … either some private investigator or I think it's the FBI. Or someone trying to fish around and stir the pot and see— and see how people react." Which was dead on the money.

Then, almost as if he knew the FBI might actually be listening, Charlie said, "So, it's somebody really stupid, because we don't— we don't have any information. We're— if I did, I'd go collect my reward." By which he meant the $100,000 reward the TPD had announced in July 2015 for information leading to arrests in the Dan Markel case.

Whoever was blackmailing them, Charlie continued, "thinks they're going to, like, try to solve this case, and they think because we're the family that we had something— somehow something to do with it. So they're going to go ahead and be, like, and make some demands and see how we'll react." What was even odder, he told Donna, was that "they're not bugging Wendi. Because that would be the first person I would go to."

His mother suggested that perhaps Charlie had "a friend" who could take care of the situation. "That's what I'm working on," he reported. "But I think I'm just going to— I think I'm just going to call them up and see what they want."

And to the investigators' immense satisfaction, that is precisely what the playboy periodontist did. Jimenez aka Sammy answered in Spanish. "*Hola. Diga.* Hello? *Diga*?"

"Who's this?" Charlie asked, his voice hesitant.

"*Who's this?*" Jimenez asked back, his tone forceful.

"Someone's been calling my family," Charlie said, without identifying himself. "I'm trying to figure out who this is."

"In reference to what, man?"

"Someone by the name of Sammy called."

"Yeah. That's me, man."

"All right. What's, what's going on?"

"Well, what's going on is my brother, Tato, okay. My brother Tato has not been taken care of. His family has not been taken care of. I talked to the dentist— Why are you calling me? Who are you? I gave the number to a lady."

Once again, the Maestro evaded the question, refusing to reveal his identity or his relationship with Donna. Instead, he merely told Jimenez, "I don't know Tato."

"You don't know Tato?" Jimenez asked.

"No," Charlie answered, sounding confused.

"I'm sure you know Katie and Tuto. They've been taken care of since the family problem been taken care of up north."

"I don't know who these people are," Charlie responded, though that obviously wasn't true. He didn't probe Jimenez for any explanation as to what the supposed family problem "up north" even was.

"It's not going away my friend," Jimenez threatened. "Because let me tell you something. I was in Broward with Tato, and he told me the whole story. He told me nobody was taking care of him. Nobody was taking care of his family. The family was taking care of Katie and Tuto and nothing's been taken care of with Tato. So we know," Jimenez added. "We know what's going on. And Tato needs to be taken care of. Do the right thing. The lady already has the paperwork. She knows what I'm talking about."

All Charlie could muster in response to Jimenez's long-winded speech was, "Let me, let me look into things."

"No more, *no more fucking around man!*" the undercover agent hollered into the phone. "No more fucking around. This ain't going away ... You guys need to do the right thing for Tato. That's my brother man. That's my brother, and he needs to be taken care of. His family needs to be taken care of just like Katie and Tuto have been taken care of."

"I've never met these people," Charlie lied once more. "But let me call you back. Okay?"

"*That's bullshit man!*" Jimenez shouted. "You know exactly

what I'm talking about. You know this lady. I don't know your relationship to this lady, but we know what the fuck is going on. This ain't going away."

Charlie told him he'd call him back, ending the call as quickly as he could. He immediately dialed Katie. Twice. Though she didn't pick up, she returned his call an hour later. Charlie provided a summary of his call with Sammy—for some reason now calling him "Simon"—telling her, "He didn't sound like a tough guy when he picked up the phone," noting how polite he was at first. Charlie misremembered the name of the man "Simon" said was with him at Broward, referring to him as "Tuco," explaining, "I don't even fucking know who that is." He recounted that "Simon" had said Katie's family was "being helped out, which I don't fucking know. I mean, other than the hours that I give you to go up in the office on the weekend to take care of shit."

"Right," Katie said. "Exactly."

"I do— I do kind of help you out. You fucking earn the money on the weekend when you go up."

"Simon," Charlie said, "kept referencing that, like, we're giving all this money to a fucking family, like, and referencing—there's two names. There's Tuto and Tuco or whatever, that supposedly I'm giving money to you and some other dude and your family. I don't know these people. Never met 'em. So it's real interesting."

The brother "Simon" mentioned, Charlie noted, was supposedly incarcerated. "He referenced something that, 'I was with him in Broward.'" He then asked Katie, "Is *this guy* incarcerated in Broward County? Is he from Broward?" Those questions implied that he knew something about "this guy"—whatever his nickname.

Charlie speculated that "Simon's" language—"do the right thing"—"sounds like a fucking cop that's fishing. That's an investigator, or someone, playing games." Which, of course, was correct. He told Katie he didn't like "Simon" "referencing you and your family. And who— I don't know who this dude is that you're with or if they're just making up names… We should just go to the FBI and say, you know what, let's play phone tap." Just a touch ironic, considering they were actually speaking on a wiretapped line. Katie agreed to call the number yet again to tell "Simon" to "stop this shit."

"They need to know that this— it's fucking stupid what they're doing," Charlie told her. "Nothing— I'm not paying anything." Instead, he said, "The only thing I want to do is collect my reward from the FBI if I know who it is... Dude, you know what kind of vacation I can get with that money? I need a fucking vacation."

●●●

KATIE THEN DIALED her "husband," providing him a detailed synopsis of Charlie's call with the undercover agent— referring to the periodontist by the pronoun "they" rather than by name. "And like, they're very, very close to reporting it already."

Garcia was alarmed that the blackmailer had referred to both him and Katie by name. His "wife" explained that "Simon" indicated "they're a brother of this other person that's supposedly incarcerated ... and that they know him from Broward."

"*It's getting too detailed,*" she complained. "It's somebody that knows. For sure. For sure."

Though Charlie had referred to the jailed "brother" only as "Tuco," Katie made clear she knew full well the blackmailer's reference was to Luis Rivera. When Garcia asked her "what person and what family" the blackmailer indicated needed to be helped out, she replied, "Tato and his family, because they need it."

"Whoever the fuck this is, it needs to stop," she seethed. "They obviously know somebody. They're putting my name, they're putting your name ... and they're harassing the family."

Despite Katie having assured Charlie she'd call the blackmailer herself, once more, she persuaded her "husband" to do her dirty work, providing him the telephone number yet again. Garcia told her he'd make the call from his cellphone and then "dump it," because "trying to find a fucking payphone is impossible, bro."

This time, he finally did make the call, but it connected with the undercover agent's answering machine. He didn't leave a message. As he reported to Katie, "It's some fucking Puerto Rican, Mexican shit. I don't know who the fuck. I don't know."

The answering machine message, he told her, said, "'*Di y le estoy puto*, I'm busy. Call me back. Dale.' That's what it says, I swear to God." He told her the voice sounded like a New York, Puerto Rican "nigger."

A few hours later, Katie informed Charlie that *she* had called the number but hadn't successfully reached "Simon." "Like some ghetto guy, like talking on an answering machine and said one of the names you said," she reported. "Like, I don't understand the joke."

Charlie then filled Katie in on his new strategy, which was to confront "Simon" to find out who in the Adelson family supposedly owed money to his incarcerated "brother." He turned their conversation into a diatribe about his own brother, Rob. "If it was my brother who is behind this, I'm going to fucking find out. I mean, fuck. If it was my brother, I'll turn him in and get the reward money. My brother's a piece of shit."

Charlie pivoted to the person who supposedly hadn't been paid, seeking Katie's help in figuring out who it could be. "He said it was this— that guy's 'Tuco,' or whatever's brother. He said, 'I'm his brother, who was with him up in Broward when he told me everything that had happened.'" Katie played dumb. She knew perfectly well her ex-boyfriend was talking about Luis Rivera. But never let on.

Charlie's frustration boiled over, the sting operation now burning under his skin—precisely as the investigators intended. "Like, they're still harassing my fucking family and I want it to stop," he fumed. "I mean, when you, when you meet someone face-to-face on the street, when you send them a letter, and then when you start calling their office, the next call is to the FBI." But in his very next breath, he talked himself down from that ledge, telling Katie, "I don't want to put anyone in jail who knows where I fucking live." Because "people get mad when they go to jail, and they feel like they have to get somebody back."

Katie played dumb a second time when Charlie told her "Sammy"—now recalling the undercover agent's pseudonym correctly—"was talking about you, your name, and then some other guy's name that starts with a 'T.'" Instead of telling him, "that's my 'husband' Tuto"—who Charlie did know by name—Katie told him, "I know a *million* people that starts with a 'T'" and provided the examples of Tavia and Taco. But neither Tuto nor Tato rolled off her tongue. As for Sammy, the former lovers agreed he was about to have a "fucking, big-ass problem." Katie noted, with evident pride, how she'd "fucked bitches up for no reason" and how delighted she'd be to do that to the guy that kept dropping her name.

•••

BY THE MORNING OF APRIL 29, Katie was telling her former boyfriend the situation was under complete control. Her "friend," she said—by whom she meant her "husband"—was handling it himself. She reported to Charlie that the friend had left the blackmailer a message on his answering machine, telling him, "Whoever the fuck it is, or whatever fucking playing fucking games, I'll fucking fuck you up in your motherfucking asshole. Don't mess with my fucking family. It's going to be a big, fucking problem." Katie apparently had no idea that Garcia had lied to her, yet again. He'd done nothing of the sort.

She told Charlie she wanted to help him because, "I don't like anybody disrespecting your family, scaring your family, after everything you guys have been through, you know? You've told me stuff that's happened before, so it's not like I'm oblivious to it … I've never probed you on it because that's some personal shit."

"He was livid—my friend," she added. "And I was like, 'Look, can you do me this favor because, I'm not a guy and I don't know if it's me they're talking about?' And I— and then he's like, 'That's some fucked-up shit.' And he's like, 'Don't worry. Like no matter what, like, whatever it is, like, I'm going to handle it,' point-blank." This "friend" told her he'd take "full responsibility" for handling the situation, she told Charlie. If that meant "somebody gets their ass whooped," she had no problem with that.

Despite Katie's repeated use of the word "friend" to obscure Sigfredo Garcia's identity, Charlie knew exactly who she was talking about, even expressing appreciation for Garcia's help and apologizing for not having done anything to acknowledge his birthday—which had been two days earlier. "I never got a chance to go to Hallmark," he said, trying to inject some humor, "so forgive me." They discussed whether Charlie should purchase a Go-Pro camera as a belated birthday gift.

When he and Katie had spoken on Garcia's actual birthday two days earlier, the Maestro *had* done something to recognize his special day, telling Katie he was going to leave her a gift card for a getaway to the Florida Keys. "I think mama needs a vacation with daddy," he'd suggested at the time. "So why don't you guys go on a vacation, leave the fucking kids at home, and have a cocktail? Call it a day. Wake up and just fish." He told her the gift card would be waiting for her in his garage.

When they spoke again on April 29, Katie confirmed that she still had the alarm code for his garage—it was tattooed on her ribs in Roman numerals. She asked Charlie, jokingly, if he could also gift over his Ferrari, complaining about the problems she was having with his Lexus. An Escalade, she said, would also suit her needs just fine. "We'll work something out," he assured her. "Don't worry about it kiddo."

• • •

DESPITE TWO WEEKS OF INCESSANT phone chatter among the four suspects, investigators still didn't have the definitive smoking gun they were hoping to generate. They decided to ratchet up the pressure one final time. At 2:09 a.m. on May 4, Oscar Jimenez sent a text message from his undercover telephone number directly to Donna's cellphone: "SO U DONT TAKE ME SERIOUS U THINK IM PLAYING? U HAVE SOME PUTA CALL ME TO SEE IF I'M FOR REAL? IF U THINK WHAT KADIES BABY DADDY DID FOR U CANT COME BACK UR FUCKING CRAZY. I WANT THE $$$$ NOW OR IM GOIN AFTER THE 100K!!!"

Investigators were hopeful the text would be a game-changer, quickly organizing a surveillance team at the Icon Condominiums, hoping Charlie might pay his mother a visit. Which is precisely what the bearded periodontist did the following day. This time, Harvey joined in their conversation, which took place in a remote area near the condo's private, outdoor pool. Two FBI agents posing as interested condo buyers actually walked right by them on the pool deck as the three Adelsons huddled to game out their next move. But the agents weren't able to decipher their words, as the mother, father, and son spoke barely above a whisper.

On his way back home, Charlie called Katie, reading her specific phrases from Jimenez's text. Clearly worried, he then called Donna and instructed her to go ahead and pay the $5,000 blackmail demand after all—the sooner the better. Their message to Sammy, he said, would be that they were paying the money simply to be nice, and that it would be a "one-time-only" payment.

The very next afternoon, May 6, Donna called Jimenez directly. Yet, being the strong-willed, independent woman she was, she changed the game plan 180 degrees from what she and Charlie had agreed upon. For eight solid minutes, the Adelson family matriarch pushed back fiercely against the notion that she was in any way involved in Dan Markel's murder or knew anything about who was. And also made clear she wouldn't be paying a single penny of blackmail.

"I have been so stressed out," she confessed in her thick, New York accent as the call began. She told Jimenez that she'd been picking the brains of a dozen close friends "asking them what I should do because I don't know your friend who is in jail … I'm sorry your friend's in jail, but I don't know what that has to do with me."

"You know exactly what it has to do with," the undercover agent retorted in his own distinct, Hispanic accent.

"I know there's a big reward out there," Donna told him. "And if you need money for your friend, that's the way to get it … If I could help, I would help."

Jimenez explained that Tato had told him the whole story while the two were in jail together in Broward. "All I ask is to send the 5K. Everybody knows what's going on."

"You know you're saying everyone knows," Donna replied. "I know I lost my ex-son-in-law. I did not have anything to do with it. That's why I said ask him what person—"

"That's not what my brother Tato told me," Jimenez interrupted. "He told me everything when we were in jail."

"I am telling you," Donna fired back, her voice full of passion. "It's not me! It's not me! I have had a year of aggravation— a year and a half of aggravation over this. My daughter, my grandchildren. It is not me! … I don't know who caused this. It wasn't me."

"This is not going to go away," the undercover agent declared, "because Tato told me everything."

"But I don't know who 'Staco' is," Donna responded, butchering Luis Rivera's nickname. "You don't understand."

"Listen to me. Let's stop fucking around!" Jimenez barked angrily. "Let's stop fucking around, okay? You know who Katie is. And you know that Katie has somebody that knows Tato. And they took care of a problem for you people… You know who the fuck Katie is… I know you don't know who Tato is. But we know who all of you are. And this ain't going away."

If Oscar Jimenez thought he could bully Donna Adelson into submission, he was sadly mistaken, the 66-year-old grandmother a force to be reckoned with in her own right. "You're looking for some money. Get $100,000 or whatever the reward is," she reiterated. "*It isn't me!* You have got the wrong person."

"You're Donna Adelson?"

"Yes I am," she said projecting confidence. "Yes I am"

"Well, I know— we know who's involved in all this."

Donna sighed deeply, repeating yet again, "If you want the money, you should get it from the police. They can give you a whole lot more than you're asking me for ... I just— I can't do this. I've had too much stress and too much aggravation from this and I don't know what you are talking about. I just don't know. I just don't know!" she cried out, her voice conveying extreme frustration.

"Señora Adelson, you can tell me all you fucking want— I know you know." Jimenez repeated that Tato had told him "everything" when they were locked up together at Broward. "I just wanted to take care of him because Katie was being taken care of with her fucking Tuto."

But Dan Markel's ex-mother-in-law wouldn't yield an inch, telling the stranger she believed was blackmailing her, "If you think you know who this is, then, then go ahead and do it. Because I know it isn't me. *I know it isn't me.* And I can't take this kind of level of stress. I just can't. I know I didn't do anything." She sighed again.

"You make this 5K come to me," Jimenez demanded. "That's all I need. Just do it and get it to me."

Donna sighed one final time, weary from the heated exchange. In a tone signaling resignation—though not necessarily defeat—she told Jimenez, "I'll call you back."

But Donna Adelson never called the undercover agent back. No one did. And despite two weeks of repeated suggestions— and threats—of escalating the situation to the police or the "fucking FBI," that is an action Donna, Harvey, Charlie, Katie, and Garcia evidently decided wasn't in their best interest. What they of course didn't know, however, was that the Tallahassee Police and the FBI didn't need them to report anything, as they were already keenly aware of what was going on. And were now poised to take action of their own.

16.

First Domino Falls

INSIDE A TWO-STORY NORTH MIAMI townhouse—just a few blocks from the Atlantic Ocean—a precious little girl was counting the days as best she could while eating her breakfast, just before preschool. It was Tuesday, May 24, 2016. Kaylee Cecilia Garcia would be turning four the following Monday—and could hardly contain her excitement, her youthful exuberance reverberating off the walls. In just two days, the entire family planned to pile into their black Lexus for a three-and-a-half-hour drive to the Magic Kingdom, where Mickey, Donald, and all of the splendor and mystique of Disney World awaited. They'd already purchased their tickets and locked in hotel reservations through the weekend.

But Pat Sanford and Craig Isom had plans of their own that week that didn't exactly align with little Kaylee's. They too were excited, but for a very different reason. The time had finally come for them to speak directly with the birthday girl's mommy and daddy. And quite likely, to read them their rights, slap on the cuffs, and haul them into custody for the cold-blooded assassination of Professor Dan Markel.

Sanford and a female FBI agent paid a visit that morning to Rapid Capital Funding—a small Miami company specializing in consumer loans—where Sigfredo Garcia was actually holding down an honest job for the first time in years, working as a senior funding analyst. The law enforcement officers flashed their badges at the front desk and were led straight to their prime suspect.

At precisely that moment, Isom and a male FBI agent—both in plainclothes—were pounding on the front door of Garcia's townhouse. Though his "wife" was inside—all alone—she stayed far away from the door, well aware that the men she spied through her kitchen window weren't there for pleasant conversation. The family dog, Thunder, was in the backyard, barking furiously—suggesting that Katie had other "guests" behind her home. Much to her dismay, her desperate calls and texts to her "husband" went unanswered, as his 12-minute conversation with the FBI had already begun.

Standing in a hallway near Garcia's workstation, Sanford began the interview by asking him if he knew a man named Luis Rivera. Garcia immediately assumed a defensive posture, telling the special agent he knew about 19 people by that name.

"We got some information about something that happened a couple of years ago, and your name popped up in it," Sanford revealed. "Have you ever been to Tallahassee?"

"No, I have not," Garcia answered nervously in his Cuban accent. He continued to deflect the agent's questions about Rivera, telling him, "What bothers me is to— why should I know or not know a Luis Rivera?"

"Do you know who Dan Markel is?" Sanford probed, removing any ambiguity about where their discussion was heading.

"It doesn't sound like anybody I know," Garcia replied, making it appear as if he were searching his mind to make sure. Asked if he'd ever taken any trips "up north," he quickly answered, "None whatsoever." Sanford explained that he was simply trying to get his side of the story, but told him he wasn't at liberty to reveal any details about the investigation.

That didn't seem fair, Garcia responded, telling the agents he wasn't accustomed to having someone show up unannounced at his job, flash an FBI badge, and ask him questions. "So obviously, I'm on defense, and I don't know if I should say anything more than I want to say. But, I mean, if I can help, obviously, I'd be more than *happy* to." For some reason, the pitch of his voice rose two octaves with the word "happy."

Perhaps because he wasn't happy at all. Though he wanted to help, he told the agents, "It's just that I feel like I should be a little bit defensive now, because, you know, you guys showed up to my job."

Sanford made clear to Garcia that he wasn't under arrest and that his participation in their discussion was entirely voluntary. "We got some information," he continued, "and we're trying to find out if that information is even right at all, without ruining your life here."

With that prompting, the 34-year-old father of two abruptly changed his story. Sort of. "I travel to Orlando," he acknowledged. "I go to Disney." Which was certainly north of Miami. "I go to L.A. I've gone to Dominican Republic with my family. Stuff like that." But Tallahassee still wasn't registering.

Sanford shifted back to Luis Rivera, describing him as a short Hispanic man with tattoos who was now locked up in jail. The agent gazed into Garcia's eyes, searching for the slightest hint of recognition. But his subject remained poker-faced, eventually saying, "Okay, because, you know, my name is very different." Yet another attempt at misdirection.

"Is your nickname Tuto?" the special agent asked. Garcia begrudgingly acknowledged that it was.

"Do you know Rivera as Tato?"

Garcia acknowledged knowing *a* Tato, but told Sanford, "my uncle's Tato too." Though he admitted knowing a Luis Rivera and knowing a Tato, he refused to concede they were one and the same. "I know several Luis Riveras," he repeated, defensively. "Let's just keep it like that, because I don't know where you're heading with this." In other words, until he knew what the agents were after, he wasn't ready to reveal that he and Luis Rivera had been best friends since childhood.

But Sanford kept pressing, telling the many-time felon he wanted to know "who this guy is and find out exactly what his deal is, if you're tight with him or not, if you've been with him a lot—"

"No," Garcia cut him off. "I'm not tight with nobody." And the only people he'd been with a lot, he added, were his wife and kids. "I'm like daddy of the year actually," he bragged, boasting that he even babysat.

Garcia then pivoted back to the matter at hand, telling the agents he didn't believe it wise to continue talking with them—he didn't want to be "collateral damage," he explained, regarding "something that I have nothing to do with." Sanford advised him that if he had nothing to do with it, it was important for him to clear his name. He asked Garcia if he'd be willing to meet at his FBI office. "We can sit down and I can go over some stuff," Sanford said, "some documents and stuff like that to find out if you know anything about all this stuff."

As someone intimately familiar with the system, Garcia responded reflexively that he wouldn't do that "without an attorney, obviously. I don't, I don't— that just sounds wrong, okay? Because it's like you have a whole bunch of stuff on people that you're saying came and said my name." Which Sanford had actually never said.

If he came into the office, the FBI agent explained, "You can start pointing people out for us."

"I wish I could," Garcia replied, "but I'm not really, I'm not really that guy. I'm not. Do you want me to call— have my attorney to call you guys?"

"Who's your attorney?" Sanford inquired.

"I don't know yet," Garcia sheepishly acknowledged, "but I'm going to call one." Sanford knew that as soon as Garcia indicated he didn't want to speak further without an attorney present, the interview would have to stop. And that he therefore needed to coax him away from that possibility. "I mean, if you didn't do anything wrong, man," he suggested, then an attorney really wouldn't be necessary.

Garcia acted as if he were much more concerned about the reaction his boss was going to have to FBI agents being on the premises than being fingered for a murder. "When I walk back in there," he predicted, "there's a parade of questions that's going to be ridiculous right now." Garcia noted that the security level at his workplace was exceedingly high due to the prevalence of clients' personal financial information and that it wasn't acceptable for non-employees to invade that secure environment. Yet he didn't want to walk outside when Sanford first arrived, he explained, because he noticed the gun under his shirt and thought the special agent might be a disgruntled client. "Big gun, too," Garcia said, seemingly envious.

He told the pair of FBI agents he wouldn't leave with them without an attorney "unless you tell me I'm under arrest and you're taking me to jail." Sanford assured him that wasn't the case.

"Anything I can do to help you, I will be more than happy to help you," Garcia reiterated. "But I'm not going to, like, just put myself in a position where I might not be helping myself."

"Have you taken any trips with Mr. Rivera, with Tato?" the special agent tried again, steering the conversation away from Garcia possibly lawyering up.

"No," Garcia responded, no longer attempting to feign ignorance that Rivera and Tato were the same person—for the first time tacitly acknowledging he knew exactly who Sanford had been talking about the entire time.

"Have you ever been anywhere with him?" the agent asked.

"No," Garcia repeated. When asked if he knew Tato's phone number, he claimed he didn't because, in the era of cellphones, "Like, do you really remember, like, any of your friends' numbers by memory?"

Sanford told him that he didn't want to keep him from his job any longer. Yet Garcia said he really didn't want to go back to work, because he didn't know what to say if his boss asked him what the FBI wanted. Was he going to tell him, he wondered aloud, that "the FBI came and asked me some questions about some Spanish, Latino guy that's short with tattoos. And now they wanted me to know if I've taken trips with him?" They were odd questions, he mused.

The answer to which, he told Sanford, was "no, obviously. But it's still scary to me because I don't know what you guys want. Or what people are trying to tie me into. Because the

FBI don't just come around asking people questions. I watch enough *CSI* to know that."

At that point, Sanford decided he had nothing to lose, telling Garcia someone had called them and provided information about his involvement in "a homicide up in, in North Florida. Part of Florida up there. Did you ever hear about a Dan Markel?"

"A homicide?" Garcia asked, his voice conveying surprise.

"Uh-huh. Yeah. Yeah."

"Said he got killed?" he asked, his tone somewhat bewildered. "No."

"You hadn't heard about that murder or anything?" Sanford pressed, now making his interview subject extremely uncomfortable. "You know anything about— ever hear it on the news or anything?"

"No," Garcia insisted. Which would be his final word on the subject. He told the agents he wanted to speak with a lawyer.

•••

MEANWHILE, THE MOTHER of Sigfredo Garcia's two children was anxiously pacing around their townhouse, nearly paralyzed by fear. While Isom and his FBI colleague were standing outside her front door, one of Tuto's coworkers, Mike Perez, called her from her "husband's" cellphone. Katie told Perez how scared she was. She was whispering, hoping the officers outside the door couldn't overhear what she was saying. Katie had no idea that other agents were listening to her every word through a wiretap authorized by a Florida judge.

Perez informed her that Tuto was being questioned by the "feds." To help allay her fears, he agreed to drive by her townhouse to find out who was knocking on her door. He called back about ten minutes later from just outside her building, telling Katie he was now certain it was the feds— two of them in plainclothes. She seemed terrified, asking him whether they were going to kick the door in. Perez assured her they couldn't do that without a warrant and wouldn't take such an extreme action with only two officers on site.

"What is going on?" Katie said helplessly. Perez told her he believed it had something to do with her and Tuto's association with Tato. "Lay low," he advised, telling her the best approach was to make the officers believe no one was home.

Finally, Tuto called her back. "What the fuck?" she barked, both perturbed and confused. "Like I'm freaking out. What the hell is going on?"

"I have no idea," her "husband" said. "Some special agent came to talk to me right now... They said somebody called anonymously and said something about a trip, an 'M,' a homicide or something. I don't know man."

"They're just like fucking stalking," Katie told him, referring to the two officers outside their home. "Like don't they need to fucking call us first and fucking let us know?"

Tuto assured her that the men standing on their front doorstep would need a warrant to get inside. He told Katie he'd talk about it more when he got home, informing her that the agents at his workplace had asked questions about people he didn't even know. He'd put an end to the questioning, he said, by telling them he wanted to speak with a lawyer. And as soon as he hung up with his "wife," Sigfredo Garcia frantically began making calls to actually find one.

•••

LATER THAT AFTERNOON, while under tight surveillance the longtime couple was blissfully unaware of, Garcia walked into a Walmart and purchased two Straight Talk wireless phones—"burner phones"—one for him and one for Katie. Shortly thereafter, agents tried contacting each of them on their old cellphones, but neither answered. Moments later, their surveillance camera showed the "husband" and "wife" leaving their home together. Their townhouse remained vacant that night—except for the family dog. By late afternoon the next day, the only time the front door had opened was when two friends dropped by to retrieve Thunder.

That same Wednesday evening, however, Garcia returned to pack up a bunch of suitcases, loading them into the trunk and back seat of the Lexus. He pulled out of the parking lot and began driving north on Interstate 95, heading to Katie's brother's home in Tamarac, in Broward County—where Katie and the children were already safe and sound. About halfway there, he pulled off the highway and drove up to a gas pump at an Exxon station in Hallandale Beach.

The moment his driver's-side door cracked open, approximately ten law enforcement vehicles appeared from nowhere—entering the gas station from multiple directions—and surrounded the Lexus. In the blink of an eye, Garcia was swarmed by a phalanx of FBI agents and local police officers, several with guns drawn.

A pair of officers grabbed him, pulled him out of the driver's seat, and threw him to the ground, handcuffing the newly arrested perp while his face was pressed against the asphalt. As he was being read his rights, a familiar face caught his eye—that of Pat Sanford, who was smiling ear to ear. Just to his side, and equally delighted, stood Craig Isom, who was now seeing before his very eyes the culmination of his police department's painstaking investigative work.

Over the next two hours, while Garcia sat handcuffed in the back seat of a squad car, officers scoured the Lexus for any incriminating evidence—luggage and children's toys strewn all over the gas station's parking lot. Among other things, they found 50 $100 bills. As well as a small plastic baggie of cocaine in Tuto's wallet. Though he'd been arrested more than 20 times before, never had there been a show of force quite like this. Then again, Sigfredo Garcia had never previously been arrested for the ruthless killing of another human being.

Nearly two years had passed since Dan Markel's brutal slaying. At long last, the first domino in the long march toward justice had fallen.

17.

Switching Sides

A FULL YEAR BEFORE Sigfredo Garcia's arrest, Luis Rivera was taken into custody in Broward County. His arrest, however, had nothing to do with Dan Markel. Rather, King Tato was corralled as part of a massive federal operation aimed at decapitating the Latin Kings—one of 29 South Florida residents indicted for a wide range of criminal activity, including drug trafficking, kidnapping, robbery, burglary, and murder. In January 2016, after pleading guilty to federal conspiracy charges, Rivera received a twelve-and-a-half-year sentence and was transferred from his county jail cell to the Coleman Federal Correctional Complex just north of Orlando—almost exactly halfway between Miami and Tallahassee. Poetic justice, perhaps.

Two days after Garcia's arrest, Craig Isom and Pat Sanford paid a visit to the Coleman facility to meet with Rivera, who by that point was well aware that his best friend since childhood was now behind bars for the murder of Dan Markel.

After being read his Miranda rights, Rivera adamantly denied any involvement in the homicide, telling the investigators he'd never traveled north of Orlando or Tampa. But when they showed him a still image of his ATM transaction in a greenish Prius the evening of the murder—unwittingly posing for the camera—Rivera reluctantly acknowledged that the photo showed both himself and Garcia. The gang leader then changed his story, admitting that he'd rented the Prius and traveled with Garcia to Tallahassee. The reason for their lengthy journey? To explore the Florida State campus, he said, fully aware the gentlemen seated across from him weren't buying a word. Pressed again on whether he was at the scene of the crime, Rivera clammed up, neither admitting nor denying that he was.

A warrant for his arrest for first-degree murder was signed a few days later. Rivera was formally arrested on June 28 and moved to the Leon County Detention Center in Tally for processing and further proceedings. The State Attorney's Office planned to try him on October 24, three weeks before Garcia's trial. Both were facing a possible death sentence. Behind the scenes, however, Rivera's court-appointed lawyer, Chuck Collins, was working diligently to reach an agreement with prosecutors not only to keep his client off death row, but to preclude a trial altogether. Through his deft maneuvering, the defense lawyer secured a plea deal almost too good to be true.

Under the agreement, Rivera would plead guilty to second-degree murder and would share with law enforcement everything he knew about Dan Markel's homicide, commonly known as a "proffer." He'd also be required to testify truthfully at any resulting trials. For his cooperation—and for being the first to flip and turn State's evidence—he'd be sentenced to only 19 years, to be served "concurrently" with his existing federal sentence. In other words, for Rivera's role in snuffing out Dan Markel's life, only six-and-a-half years would be tacked onto his existing sentence.

Yet State Attorney Willie Meggs and his Chief Assistant Georgia Cappleman considered that outcome a good deal for the government. Cracking a tight-knit conspiracy often necessitates making a deal with one of the co-conspirators, who can provide an insider's retelling of the crime—in all of its gory detail. Though the TPD had done yeoman's work establishing that Tato and Tuto had driven up from Miami with every intention of killing Dan Markel, the details surrounding who had hired, paid, and assisted them were far less clear. By making this deal with Rivera, the investigators and prosecutors hoped those additional pieces of the puzzle would soon fall into place—enabling them to bring the ringleaders of the murderous plot to justice.

•••

A SMALL INTERROGATION ROOM at the Jefferson County Sheriff's Office, about 30 miles east of Tally, was the setting for the most consequential event in the two-plus years since Dan's murder. It was Friday, September 30, 2016. Luis Rivera sat in one of several seats around a wooden table. His lawyer, Chuck Collins, was seated just to his right with Craig Isom and Pat Sanford directly across the table, the pair chomping at the bit to hear what King Tato had to say.

For his part, Rivera was just as eager to disgorge the horrific secrets that had been tormenting his soul—keeping him up at night—since July 2014. He'd tell the same basic story a second time a few days later while being recorded on video, with Chuck Collins's father and law partner, David Collins, beside him.

Clad in a blazing-red, jail-issued jumpsuit, the bushy-haired, heavily-bearded, handcuffed gang leader confirmed that he and Garcia had made two trips to Tally, the first in early June 2014. Initially, Rivera believed the job would be a robbery, not a murder. Asked why, he replied, "Because I'm a jack boy. I rob drug dealers." He told the investigators he'd never killed anyone, despite his lengthy criminal record and leadership role with the Latin Kings. "I done beat people with bats, hit them with sticks, and shit like that," he readily acknowledged in his Puerto Rican accent, but had never before participated in a murder. They left on a Wednesday evening and returned on a Friday, he said. For the first trip, he told Isom and Sanford, Garcia had rented a black Nissan and was the one chiefly responsible for the driving.

Before they left Miami the first time, while planning out their trip at Rivera's apartment, Garcia told him, "We getting hired, *but to kill somebody.*" Rivera learned he'd be earning $35,000 simply for riding along. Why did Garcia even need him? Because he didn't want to go by himself, Rivera explained, and didn't trust anyone else to go with him.

"Who's fucking hiring you?" Rivera had asked his best friend at the time.

"Katie told me this 'lady' is going to hire me," Garcia had replied. "But I want you to go with me." Rivera mulled it over for a moment. "All right, for the drive, all right. Fuck it. I will take the drive," he'd agreed.

They left around 10:00 p.m., he said, and arrived somewhere between 5:00 a.m. and 6:00 a.m. that Thursday morning. Rivera told Isom and Sanford that he was drinking and smoking pot the entire ride to Tally. During their drive, Garcia showed him a piece of paper that contained Dan Markel's photo and a typewritten address and also told him their intended victim's name.

The partners in crime headed to Tallahassee without a map, Rivera recounted, and weren't using GPS for directions—for obvious reasons. Eventually, however, Garcia had to stop, confessing that he couldn't remember how to get where they were going. The bigger problem, Rivera revealed, was that his friend was drunk. They stopped at a gas station and purchased a roadmap. Garcia glanced at it quickly and then threw it in the glove compartment. From that point on, Rivera said, Garcia didn't need to look at the map again, recalling precisely how to get to Dan Markel's house from memory. Based on the way Rivera described Garcia's familiarity with where he was going, Isom and Sanford assumed that he'd come to Tallahassee once before—sans Rivera.

Upon arriving in Tally, Rivera continued, they rented a hotel room. That first morning, after scoping out their intended victim's house, the two sat together in the rental car at Winthrop Park, facing Trescott Drive. When they finally saw Dan's black Accord approaching, they "followed him all the way to the school. He dropped his kids off. Boom, I lost him," Rivera told the investigators. "I guess he was going to the gym that morning."

They went back by his house several times, he said, but each time his garage door was closed; they couldn't determine whether he was home. He and Garcia ended up going to Hooters where they "drank beer like crazy." They went back to the hotel, he added, "did pot and drank—just hanged out." The duo followed Dan to the preschool the next morning as well, but never saw him come back out. So they returned to the hotel, drank, and did cocaine Garcia had purchased from a Black guy in a four-door Chevy.

The 33-year-old former gang leader told Isom and Sanford that Garcia had been given $5,000 in cash in advance of that first trip. His lifelong pal let him hold onto $500, just in case he ran out doing stupid things like buying coke. As it turned out, only $600 remained following that initial trip.

"Where did he get the money from?" Sanford inquired.

"He said he got the money from *the lady*," Rivera answered. "He still haven't told me her name yet." He then corrected himself, telling the special agent that Garcia had actually received the money from Katie, who in turn had received it from "the other lady."

Why did he believe someone wanted Dan Markel dead? "Because *the lady* wants her two kids back," Rivera explained, now making it crystal clear the "other lady" was none other than Wendi Adelson. "She wants full custody of them kids. Because he had all the custody. That was the plan. That was the deal. That's what we went to go kill that man for." Garcia had filled him in on all of those details, he said, before they got on the road for their first trip.

As they were driving around Tally, he told Garcia that if this lady had so much money, "We should just go rob her. That was my intention," Rivera noted. "Fuck this guy. I don't got nothing against that guy. I don't even know that guy." But Garcia pushed back, telling him they had to kill the lady's ex-husband—that was their mission.

Sanford asked how Garcia knew so much about the lady and her desire to get custody of her kids. "Katie," Rivera replied. "I guess Katie told him everything." He was sure Katie knew everything because he overheard her talking with her "husband" while he and Garcia were in the rental car. Garcia wanted to make sure the lady was going to have their money on time. "Tell her she better have that fucking money," Rivera overheard him telling Katie over the phone.

"Did you know it was Katie because of what he was saying," Sanford asked, "or could you actually hear her voice?"

"No, it was Katie," Rivera confirmed. "I could hear her voice." He told the investigators he overheard her telling his pal, "Make sure you do everything right; don't do nothing stupid." Katie was "the one in the middle doing everything," he added. She called her "husband" several times during the drive up to Tally. Rivera kept telling him, "Yo, get off the phone, bro. Why do you keep talking to her? Ain't nothing to talk about." That's how they were going to get caught, he warned his friend. "But he always kept talking," Rivera explained, "every time she would call."

During the drive up, Katie told Garcia to call her when they completed the job. "She thought it was going to happen that same night that we went up there," Rivera recounted. Garcia did call her the first evening, he said, but only to report, "Nothing happened today. Fuck it. This shit is sour. It's not— We couldn't even find the guy."

On one of the occasions they were staking out Dan's home from the nearby park, Garcia asked Rivera to go into the house and kill him. But he refused, he proudly told the officers. "I wouldn't have enough balls to fucking shoot somebody for some kids, man." In fact, he took credit for aborting their mission altogether, boasting, "I didn't let that shit happen," ultimately telling Garcia it just wasn't worth it. "My mind was like, for some kids, we are going to kill this guy for some fucking kids? Are you serious? Why can't she just get full custody?"

Isom wanted to know about the weapons they'd taken with

them to Tally. There were two, Rivera explained: a short-nose, black .38-caliber Smith & Wesson revolver he'd purchased from a 19-year-old Black kid in his neighborhood for $150 and Garcia's long-nose, blue steel .38-caliber Taurus. Garcia wanted to use the Taurus to kill Dan, but Rivera thought it was too big for the job, telling his buddy, "That's a big gun. What the hell? Shit, are you trying to blow somebody's brains out? You are crazy." When Rivera handed him the smaller gun, Garcia cleaned it with alcohol and a bandana to remove all fingerprints. They went to a gun store in North Miami, Rivera told the investigators, where he purchased 12 .38-caliber bullets—six for each gun.

•••

ABOUT A MONTH AFTER that initial trip, Rivera said, Garcia told him, "Man, I got to do this." But Rivera didn't want to go back. He thought about it all day. He told the investigators he blamed Katie for what happened, because she had his pal "all messed up, all confused." They were living apart at the time, he noted, because she'd kicked him out. Garcia was living in an apartment near Biscayne with a 40-year-old Black man nicknamed Jibaro. Isom and Sanford would later learn that, like Rivera, Jibaro was a Latin King named Anthony Ortiz—King Little Anthony.

Meanwhile, Katie was living in Miami Beach with her kids. When she needed to be somewhere, she'd drop them off at her "husband's" apartment. "Garcia would leave," Rivera explained, "go get fucked up, and go to Shrimp's house. Be at Shrimp's house and leave the kids with Jibaro."

"Who was Shrimp?" Isom asked.

"Tatia, I call her Tatia," Rivera explained. "But I just called her Shrimp. That was like his girlfriend." The investigators would learn that Shrimp was a stripper, whose real name was Stefanie Carmona. Rivera told them that Katie couldn't stand it when Garcia stayed with Shrimp. She'd "harass him. Every time he was over there, she would go pass by, drive by. 'Oh, mother fucker. I see you!' Throwing pictures of the house, sending pictures to his phone."

But at the same time she was reacting with intense jealousy to her "husband" being with Shrimp, Katie was having her own relationship with "the dentist," Rivera pointed out. He recalled thinking, "Like you are fucking this guy and then you are over here harassing my dog. Let my dog live his life as you do." In discussing the messy situation with his best friend, Rivera told him, "You will be one day with Shrimp … and then spend one night with Katie. Then she kick your ass out the house and she go with this guy. Come on man!" Katie had him had him "so messed up that he was drinking every day," Rivera said. "Every day he was drinking and every day he would do coke."

"Who is the dentist?" Sanford asked, interrupting Rivera's train of thought, testing him to see if he knew Charlie Adelson's name.

Rivera told the investigators that he didn't know the dentist's name, but believed Katie had been working for him. He was certain "she was fucking a dentist," which made Garcia furious. "This bitch over here cheating on me," he'd lament to Rivera.

One afternoon, he and Garcia took off early from Coastal Masonry—before his friend was fired for the final time— and ended up at a restaurant in Garcia's pickup truck. It was lunchtime. From a distance, they spied on Katie sitting with a guy Garcia told him was "the dentist." He was so jealous, Rivera said, "he wanted to get the car and smash right through 'em." "That's fucked up," he told his pal. "And you are over here stalking this ho. Like come on, you are not an ugly guy, man. You can get whoever you want. Like leave her."

Rivera offered his opinion that Katie had been the driving force behind their second journey to Tally, speculating that she'd been telling Garcia, "If you want me back, you gotta' do this shit." In retrospect, he was peeved his friend had let his "wife" manipulate him. He told Garcia at the time, "I really know why you are doing this for. You are doing this because of your stupid-ass wife … It was all fucking Katie's fault man we in this shit. Katie."

Even though he strongly believed that killing Dan Markel was a bad idea, he went back to Tally with Garcia on the second trip "because it was my best friend. And I didn't want him to take anybody else and get him all fucked up."

•••

AFTER RIVERA COMPLETED his workday on Wednesday, July 16, 2014, Garcia told him they needed to leave for Tallahassee and handed him $350 to rent a car. Rivera told Isom and Sanford that he explained to the man at the car rental place that he needed a reliable car to get to Orlando. Moments later, he was behind the wheel of the greenish Prius.

Before Rivera described their second trip any further, Isom drilled down on the financial arrangements. Rivera indicated that even before the first trip, it was his understanding that the total amount being paid for the hit was $100,000. They were dividing it "40-something" to Garcia, $35,000 to himself, and the rest to Katie. In retrospect, though, he believed Katie wound up with somewhere between $50,000 and $60,000, based on everything he'd been hearing about her acquisitions while he was locked up at Coleman.

Rivera told the investigators they'd taken only one weapon on the second trip—the short-nose, Smith & Wesson revolver he'd purchased in June. This time, he drove the entire way. They were actually pulled over at one point, he noted, which was scary because he was on probation and could have been taken to jail immediately. But after examining his license and writing up a speeding ticket, the officer merely told him to slow down and wear his seatbelt. "I looked at Garcia and I told him, 'This mother fucker didn't take me to jail.'" Getting pulled over, he said to Garcia, was "a sign man. We should just turn around."

"Nah, man. Fuck that!" his buddy responded. "We up here." So they plowed ahead to Tally and ended up at the same hotel—in the same room—they'd stayed in the prior month, arriving late that evening. "We started drinking, doing coke," Rivera added. "I barely didn't sleep." Garcia, he said, had been doing cocaine since leaving Miami. He was still doing coke when Rivera fell asleep around 2:30 a.m.

They drove straight to Dan's neighborhood that Thursday morning, driving to a park area just behind his house. Garcia got out and walked up to the rear property line. "He said he seen something, but he wasn't too sure if it was somebody." So they drove around to the front of Dan's house.

As they were driving down Trescott Drive in one direction, Rivera told the officers, Wendi was walking directly toward them in the other. "I remember her clear as day with the two boys," he said, telling them he saw her face clearly. After he passed her, Rivera kept looking at Wendi in his rearview mirror, asking his buddy, "Man, what's up with this lady? Why is she looking so much?" To which Garcia responded, "Oh, that's *the lady*. That's Wendi."

"Oh, that's her name," Rivera thought to himself at the time, finally able to attach the name "Wendi" to the "lady" Garcia had been telling him about—the one who was paying them to kill Dan Markel. He asked what she was doing there. Garcia told him she was there "to make sure that everything is all right" because Dan was supposed to leave town the next day. "So it's got to get done the next morning before he leaves," he told Rivera. But Rivera wasn't content with that answer, especially as he watched the lady—through the rearview mirror—begin talking on her phone.

He asked a second time why she was there. Garcia agreed to call Katie to find out, eventually making the call from the hotel parking lot. Rivera told Isom and Sanford that he overheard their entire conversation. Katie told her "husband" that Wendi was just confirming they were really there and "that she wasn't paying him for nothing." And that she'd also come to see the kids. "Just make sure you get that shit done," Katie instructed her "husband" as the call ended.

Isom asked if Garcia knew, even before calling Katie, that

the woman they spotted on Trescott Drive was Dan's ex-wife, Wendi. Rivera said he did. Although he initially said Garcia had met Wendi before, he backtracked, telling the investigators he wasn't 100% certain. And despite the revelation about a "Wendi sighting," neither Isom nor Sanford showed Rivera a photo to determine if she was actually the woman he'd seen.

After speaking with Katie, the pair had the rest of the afternoon to kill. "We was driving around looking for coke," Rivera noted. Lo and behold, they bumped into the same drug dealer who'd supplied them back in June. "Follow me," the Black guy told them. But while Rivera was driving, all of a sudden he heard a loud *boom*—a gunshot. He nearly jumped out of his seat. Garcia, who'd been fiddling with the short-nose revolver, had accidentally fired a bullet into the floorboard. The Prius began slowing down almost instantly. "We don't got no gas!" Rivera exclaimed. "How the hell we don't got no gas?"

Garcia looked through the hole in the floor, realizing he'd shot clear through the gas line. "You shot the line you idiot!" Rivera yelled. "Are you serious?" They pushed the vehicle off the road. The drug dealer circled back and offered to drive them to Auto Zone. Garcia went with him, Rivera explained, while he remained behind in the Prius. Garcia came back with a new hose, jacked up the car, and repaired the gas line—good as new. They followed the Black guy to a trailer park. Rivera waited in the car while Garcia went to get some more coke.

The drug dealer then secured them a new hotel room—closer to Dan Markel's house—where the three men partied like they were Hollywood celebrities. That evening, Rivera spotted an owl in the parking lot, snapped a picture on his phone, and posted it to his Instagram page.

A few minutes later, Garcia's phone was ringing. "Tell him to take that shit down," Rivera overheard Katie say. She asked her "husband," "Is he stupid or what?" Rivera told the investigators that he took the picture down, but wondered why he was the stupid one when Katie and Garcia had been "talking on the phone all fucking day," creating a trail far more incriminating than his Instagram post.

With that extensive buildup, Luis Rivera finally began telling the law enforcement officers about the day that would change his life—and countless others—forever.

•••

THE LIFELONG FRIENDS WERE UP early that Friday morning, Rivera actually showering for the occasion as Garcia swigged what little booze remained from their evening of partying; he also was snorting "bumps" of cocaine. "Don't worry," he told Rivera. "Everything all right." His soon-to-be accomplice, however, didn't share his confidence.

They left the hotel and drove straight to Winthrop Park—just beyond the intersection of Trescott Drive and Betton Road—the same park they'd used for surveillance during their first trip. They sat in the parking lot facing Trescott, with Rivera behind the wheel, no more than a half mile from Dan Markel's home. They waited. And watched.

Just after 8:30 a.m., they spotted a black Honda Accord that headed toward them, then turned right onto Betton Road. Rivera pulled into the street and began following—from a distance—the entire five miles to Creative Preschool.

While Dan was at the school, Rivera was driving in circles, waiting for him to reemerge. When he finally came back through the front door, Tato and Tuto were in pursuit again, following Dan for nearly ten miles on I-10 East. The Accord exited onto Thomasville Road. So did Rivera, continuing their pursuit until the black sedan pulled into the parking lot at Premier Fitness. The pair watched as their target, dressed in a red T-shirt and black athletic shorts, exited his vehicle and entered the building.

They found a parking place with a perfect sight line to the gym's front entrance—and waited once more. Just after 10:30 a.m., they saw Dan leave the building and walk to his car. When his Accord left the gym's parking lot, Rivera and Garcia were close behind, following southbound on Thomasville

Road for three miles.

As they approached the outskirts of Betton Hills, Rivera noticed the Accord turning left before reaching Betton Road. Rather than following Dan, he continued to Betton Road, turned left, and then left again onto Trescott. As he approached Dan's house, Rivera saw the Accord barreling toward him from the opposite direction—then turn right into Dan's driveway. The garage door was up. As the Prius reached the driveway and began turning left, the Accord was edging its way into the garage. It pulled to a stop, engine still running.

Rivera pulled up just a few feet behind its rear bumper. The second he came to a stop, Garcia jumped out of the passenger seat and zig-zagged between the cars to the Accord's driver's-side door. Dan, who was talking on his cellphone, glanced upward at the stranger standing beside him. Garcia held the .38-caliber revolver up to the window and pulled the trigger—quickly firing two shots—then raced back to the passenger side of the Prius, excitedly telling Rivera, "Let's get out of here."

They began their 500-mile journey back to Miami. At some point, Garcia instructed him to pull off the highway at a bridge. A body of water was off in the distance. Garcia scampered away, jumping over a guardrail and tossing the gun toward the water. He raced back to the Prius and they reentered the highway. Just a little later, Garcia called Katie, telling her, "Everything is done." Rivera was able to hear her response: "I know," she said. He was puzzled. "How the fuck does she know?" he wondered. "How would she know if this shit is done?"

Garcia told his "wife" to make sure the money would be there when they returned. "Don't worry about it," Rivera heard her say. "You will have it tomorrow morning, first thing. The sun will come up and you will have it."

The following morning, Rivera recounted, he was at a barbershop when his cellphone rang. "Where the fuck is Tuto at?" Katie asked, her tone conveying frustration. "Stupid mother fucker won't answer the phone. Who going to come get the money?"

Upon their return to Miami, Garcia had taken the Prius after dropping Rivera off at the apartment he shared with Jessica Rodriguez. Rivera felt pretty certain his best friend would have ended up at Shrimp's house. After hanging up with Katie, he called Shrimp. Sure enough, Garcia was there, "drunk sleeping" according to Carmona. "Wake his ass up," Rivera instructed the stripper. "Tell him Katie looking for him." Rivera told the investigators he next called Jibaro—King Anthony—telling him to pick up Garcia and get him to Katie's home ASAP.

Still at the barbershop, Rivera's phone rang again. Now it was his baby mama on the line. "Babe," Jessica Rodriguez said, "Katie and Tuto are here. I got a bag in my hand," which she indicated Garcia had handed her. "It feels like a brick."

"Don't touch it!" Rivera demanded. "Don't even look at it. I'm on my way." He told Rodriguez not to let Katie and Tuto leave and raced home. When he arrived, Katie was holding his newborn baby, Lulu. "What's up?" he greeted them. "Where the bag?" Garcia pointed to a plastic grocery store bag lying on the floor. Rivera grabbed it, pulled out the stacks of money, and stuck them in his pocket. "Leave Katie here, man," he told Tuto. "Let's ride."

The lifelong friends sat together in Rivera's old, beat-up Mercedes, just outside the apartment, where he carefully counted out his money, all $100 bills. They were stapled together in $1000 stacks—$37,000 in all, $2,000 more than Garcia had promised.

Isom asked Rivera what he believed the money was for. "For the murder," he replied.

"Money for another drug deal, money for—"

"Nothing else," the former gang leader insisted. "The money is for the murder. That's it."

"Any other possibility besides that?"

"That's the final answer. And that's the answer. The money was for the murder."

Isom asked whether Rivera had any discussion with Garcia about Garcia's share of the money. Rivera told them he didn't, but that Garcia "had his money in his pocket the same day." As for who'd delivered the bag of money to his home, he told the officers it was Katie.

Rivera opened up to Isom and Sanford that he was affected emotionally by what went down in Tally. "And I was so mad. I was thinking about the murder. And it was just hitting me, hitting me." It was so bad that Rodriguez called Tuto and told him to come over to "calm this nigger down. I don't know what's wrong with him." When he arrived, Garcia told his friend to "chill out" and "stop thinking about that shit." Rivera couldn't understand how he could be so callous: "I didn't even do it. How the fuck can you walk around here like that? Something that you did, and you are out here like everything was all right?"

Rivera told the investigators that he couldn't sleep at night, calling the entire sequence of events a "nightmare." "I kept thinking about that man and them kids. It really hurted me man," he confessed, becoming outwardly emotional for the first time. "It really do."

•••

SATURDAY, OCTOBER 1, 2016, was a warm, muggy fall day in South Florida. Katie Magbanua began the day beaming with pride as she watched her four-year-old daughter Kaylee—dressed in a darling, pink tutu—perform a ballet recital. The cute little girl gave her mom a big hug when she was done, smiling and giggling with childlike joy.

When the performance ended, Katie dropped her daughter off at Garcia's sister's apartment so she could run a few errands. She pulled into a nearby strip mall to shop for clothing for Kaylee and her brother Ethan. When she completed her shopping, she trudged back through the parking lot and opened the trunk of her Lexus—the same one in which her "husband" had been arrested four months earlier. She put the bags of clothing in the car and got in herself, then pulled out and began driving away.

As she approached the shopping center's exit, Katie was slowed by some congestion. She waited for what seemed like an eternity for her turn to pull into the road.

Suddenly, out of nowhere, she noticed what seemed like an army of uniformed police officers descending toward her from multiple directions—guns drawn. From behind the wheel, she instinctively threw her hands in the air as officers screamed at her to put the vehicle in park. But Katie was frozen in terror, unable to move. An officer opened her door and reached in to place the car in park, screaming at her to get out of the vehicle with her hands held high.

The 31-year-old mother did just as she was instructed, so frightened urine was streaming down her leg. Craig Isom and Pat Sanford stepped forward from behind the uniformed officers. "Ms. Magbanua," Isom announced. "I have a warrant for your arrest for the murder of Dan Markel."

Despite her fright, Katie seemed to be expecting this moment. She asked for permission to call to her attorney, placing the call from one of the two phones she had with her in the Lexus. She was then cuffed, read her rights, and placed in a squad car to be transported to the Broward County Jail.

Still standing in the parking lot—his own heart now racing—Isom felt his cellphone vibrating in his pocket. He pulled it out and held it to his ear. On the other end, a man named David Markus introduced himself as Charlie Adelson's lawyer. "Look," Markus said. "If you have a warrant for my client's arrest, there's no need to ambush him like we understand you just did with Magbanua. I can assure you we will have him surrender to you in Tallahassee. Just let me know in advance and we'll make those arrangements."

Isom told the attorney he appreciated the heads-up and would give his request appropriate consideration. As he hung up, he conjured up the image of the wealthy periodontist being marched to a police cruiser in handcuffs. That was a day the silver-haired, veteran police investigator was looking forward to with immense anticipation. And one he hoped was just over the horizon.

PART THREE
Courtroom

18.

Lawyering Up

AS SHE WAS MAKING the 45-minute drive from her home in Miami to the Broward County Jail to meet with her newly arrested client, Tara Kawass couldn't help but reflect on how her own life's journey had come full circle. Some 18 years earlier, as a 19-year-old college student, she was the one handcuffed in the back seat of a squad car on her way to the Broward County Jail. Her arrest and 48 hours behind bars would ultimately change the arc of her entire life.

At that point in time, Kawass wasn't just young and naïve, 5'4" and 100 pounds soaking wet. She also was an immigrant, having grown up in Kingston, Jamaica. When she arrived as a freshman at Miami's Florida International University (FIU) at just 17, she was a foreigner in every sense of the word, the American experience at once unfamiliar and daunting.

During her sophomore year, a friend in some distress had asked her to cash a handful of checks her parents had sent, claiming she didn't have a bank account. Without giving the matter much thought, Kawass agreed to take them to her bank and cash them—handing the teller in excess of $1,000 in phony checks, unwittingly committing a felony. Two days later, she was back at the NationsBank branch seated across from a police officer, trembling. Kawass wasn't even thinking about jail, but rather, how her strict disciplinarian father would kill her. And even more important, how disappointed he'd be. She panicked, attempting to lie her way out of the jam by claiming she wasn't the one who'd cashed the bad checks.

Minutes later, she was in the back seat of a police car being whisked away to jail. As she reminisced about these events 18 years later, Kawass conjured up a vivid image of the arresting officer's face as he peered at her through the rearview mirror. "You're a very attractive girl," he told her with a vile smirk. "They're going to have their way with you in there." The sheer terror she felt as she was yanked out of the police car and marched into the jail was seared in her memory.

And it got worse. She was taken to a special room where jail employees strip-searched her, body cavities and all. She was then thrown into a cell with other hardened criminals. Between the stench of her new quarters and the paralyzing fear gripping her, time literally stood still, the longest 48 hours of her life. The 19-year-old Jamaican was too petrified to eat or use the toilet. She felt like a caged animal. A feeling that would later fuel her passion to help those ensnared by the iron grip of the criminal justice system—just as she'd been as a teenager.

Her case took three years to wind its way through the system, ultimately requiring Kawass to endure a year of probation and perform 100 hours of community service. Though she ended up pleading guilty only to a low-level misdemeanor, she had to disclose that black mark on her law school applications, before she was permitted to take the bar exam, and to immigration officials when she applied for—and was granted—American citizenship in 2010.

A year or so after that life-altering experience, Kawass was taking a legal psychology class at FIU when a male student barged through the classroom doors in the middle of a lecture, loudly proclaiming that he'd left a book behind after attending an earlier class. The professor had the students search all around them for the lost book, but no one found it, and the student left.

Before returning to his lecture, the professor informed the students that they'd just taken part in an experiment.

There was no lost book. The student who'd stood at the front of the classroom was merely playing a role. The professor projected onto a screen a photo lineup, and asked Kawass and her classmates to identify the student from among five photographs. She had no trouble doing so, concluding the fourth photo from the left was a perfect match. She was certain. But also dead wrong. So were the rest of her classmates. That was the entire point of the experiment. The male student's photo wasn't in the lineup at all.

The epiphany flooding through Kawass's mind at that moment brought her right back to her foul-smelling jail cell, once again demonstrating the imbalance of power between law enforcement and those accused of crimes. Between her own brush with the law, the experiment in her psych class, and her obsession with the TV show *Matlock* as a child growing up in Jamaica, it was inevitable Kawass would find her way to law school and become a criminal defense lawyer.

During her 3L year—also at FIU—Kawass worked as an unpaid intern at the Miami-Dade County Public Defender's Office. She loved everything about it. A job as an assistant public defender was waiting for her when she graduated in 2007. During her seven years in that role, she handled hundreds of cases for indigent defendants accused of homicide—trying about a dozen of them to jury verdicts. Kawass even tried a few high-profile first-degree murder cases, including one in which her client, a high school student named Jason Beckman, was charged with killing his politician father with a shotgun blast to the head while his dad was taking a shower.

Kawass left the Public Defender's Office in May 2014 and began doing a mix of indigent defense work for the Office of Regional Counsel—which handles cases the Public Defender's Office can't—and private defense work for clients who could afford to pay her directly. Though she learned of the murder of a Florida State law professor later that summer, that news had barely been a blip on her radar. That is, until July 2016, when Kawass was contacted by another immigrant whose plastic surgeon had been subpoenaed to provide records of her breast implant surgery.

At the time, Katie Magbanua informed Kawass that the father of her two children had recently been arrested and charged with the murder of Professor Dan Markel—and that he was now awaiting trial in Tallahassee. She told the defense lawyer that law enforcement officers had been pounding on her door, trying to speak with her, the day before her "husband" was arrested.

Katie also let Kawass know about the probable cause affidavit for Garcia's arrest, which by then had been released to the media. The affidavit included numerous references to Katie's supposed involvement in the murder plot. She told Kawass she was scared and that she didn't understand why the State Attorney's Office would have any right to records about her breast augmentation. No way did she want that sensitive information released in such a high-profile case. But Dr. Leonard Roudner's office had informed her that she had only ten days to file a motion to protect the privacy of her records or he'd be forced to divulge them.

Though Katie had engaged an attorney immediately after Garcia's arrest—fearful that hers would be next—she'd lost confidence in his dedication to her cause. She told Kawass she'd heard rave reviews about her passion fighting for wrongfully accused clients. The defense lawyer immediately agreed to represent Katie, filing a motion to quash Dr. Roudner's subpoena just a few days later.

The hearing was held on August 19, 2016, before Circuit Judge James C. Hankinson, who'd recently been assigned to the Markel case. Even though she was a complete outsider and had never before set foot in the Leon County Courthouse, Kawass— with her strong Jamaican accent—was able to persuade the judge to limit Dr. Roudner's production to records revealing the dates of Katie's medical appointments and how she'd paid for her surgery. A small victory, but victory nonetheless.

During her flight home that evening, the Miami defense lawyer felt certain her involvement in the Dan Markel case had just come to a close. A belief she'd hold until receiving Katie's desperate call from a shopping center parking lot explaining that she'd just been arrested and was being escorted to the Broward County Jail.

•••

JUST BEFORE DR. ROUDNER'S OFFICE notified Katie of the subpoena for her records, her "husband" was making his own change of attorneys. On July 12, 2016, another Miami defense lawyer, Saam Zangeneh, took over as Sigfredo Garcia's lead counsel. Zangeneh also was a South Florida transplant, his journey to The Magic City even more circuitous than Kawass's.

Zangeneh's father had served as a high-ranking naval officer. But not for the U.S. Navy. Rather, he was a member of the Imperial Iranian Navy under the Shah of Iran. During the 1970s, when the United States and Iran were close allies, the American government allowed Iranian officers to train at American military bases. Zangeneh's dad had been stationed at the U.S. Naval War College in Newport, Rhode Island, where Saam was born in April 1973—making him an instant American citizen. He and his family then returned to Iran and eventually ended up in London.

While Saam's father was climbing the ranks of the Iranian Navy in England, his maternal grandfather was in Iran raking in huge sums of money as a chemical engineer for BP—at the zenith of OPEC's stranglehold on world oil markets. The entire Zangeneh family was filthy rich, even dining on occasion at the Shah's palace in Tehran.

That would all change in December 1978, with the Iranian revolution that toppled the Shah's government and installed a radical Islamic cleric, Ayatollah Khomeini, as Iran's supreme leader. With the new regime in place, the Zangeneh family's wealth evaporated in the blink of an eye. They were no longer welcome in their own country. Because Saam had birthright citizenship in the United States, his parents sent him to live with his aunt, a college student studying in Evansville, Indiana.

Zangeneh eventually ended up in the D.C. suburbs,

attending George C. Marshall High School in Falls Church, Virginia. He had every intention of becoming a doctor—to fulfill his parents' dream—performing well in school and serving as class president in both his junior and senior years. A scholarship to Virginia Tech lured him to the Appalachian Mountains for college. As a pre-med student, Zangeneh majored in biology and landed a prestigious internship at the National Institutes of Health, where he spent a year conducting biomolecular research.

Everything was going according to his master plan until he found himself running a pharmacology lab in a program affiliated with the Medical College of Virginia. For the first time, he started to question whether a life in medicine was really for him. His supervisor, an Indian immigrant himself, told Zangeneh he was such a good bullshitter, he ought to consider going to law school. So on a whim he believed would lead absolutely nowhere, the pre-med student took the LSAT. And did quite well.

He applied to only one law school—the University of Miami. Why there? Because that's where the exquisite beaches and all the beautiful women were. If he was going to suffer through law school, Zangeneh needed some fringe benefits to make it worth his while. He nearly flunked out in his first year. So he decided to alter his strategy the final two years, rarely attending class, instead studying the material mostly on his own. In May 2001, the first-generation American graduated UM Law with honors.

During his 3L year, an instructor pulled Zangeneh aside during a mock trial, suggesting he consider becoming a prosecutor. At the time, he had a six-figure job offer in hand to work at a cushy Palm Beach law firm, specializing in patent law. But when his best friend from law school landed a job at the State Attorney's Office in Miami, Zangeneh followed him there—ultimately making less than half of what he'd have earned as a patent lawyer.

Within 15 months, he was prosecuting homicides and trying tons of cases. In the two-and-a-half years he served as an assistant state attorney, Zangeneh was lead prosecutor in 20 murder cases. His penchant for unconventional courtroom theatrics even earned him a special moniker: the "Persian Prosecutor." Yet he burned out quickly and decided to hang out his own shingle as a criminal defense lawyer.

Ten-plus years into private practice, the former prosecutor had developed quite the reputation as a defense attorney, using Instagram posts—featuring his flashy suits and closely-trimmed, salt-and-pepper beard—to catch the attention of well-known rappers who found themselves in trouble with the law. He'd appeared on behalf of criminal defendants in over 20 states and even had an office in Puerto Rico. Among his high-profile clients was a Miami man named Derek Medina, who'd been dubbed the "Facebook killer" for posting a photo of his wife's dead body on the social media platform after shooting her. Zangeneh wrapped up Medina's trial in November 2015, six months before his new client Sigfredo Garcia's arrest.

It was actually Garcia's older brother, Noel, who reached out to him in July 2016. Zangeneh had represented Noel Garcia on several prior occasions, and had gladly received his referrals to a wide network of friends and associates. At the time Noel asked him to represent his brother Sigfredo, the defense attorney hadn't heard the first thing about Dan Markel or his July 2014 murder. That would change in a hurry. He agreed to represent Tuto for a pittance, well aware of the intense media exposure the case would generate—banking on the new clients and revenue that would surely follow.

• • •

BEFORE MEETING WITH KATIE at the Broward County Jail, the first call Tara Kawass made was to another Miami defense lawyer named Christopher DeCoste. Like Kawass and Zangeneh, DeCoste wasn't a native Floridian, having grown up in Hingham, Massachusetts, a wealthy suburban enclave on the south shore of Boston Harbor. He received a strictly Catholic-school education, attending the exclusive, all-boys

Boston College High School, where he and his classmates were subjected to a strict dress code and instructed in classrooms with iron bars protecting the windows—an atmosphere uncomfortably similar to prison.

Though he earned excellent grades without much effort, DeCoste was far more interested in athletics. He'd played ice hockey since the age of five and was a solid high school defenseman, playing in one of the most competitive regions in the country. He also played lacrosse in the spring. In both sports, DeCoste's pregame ritual was to sit by his locker with headphones over his ears, amping himself up for battle listening to his favorite tunes.

Villanova University in Philadelphia offered DeCoste a spot on its hockey team, which he gladly accepted. At 6'2" and 220 pounds, he wasn't even one of the bigger players in the conference. Because of the constant travel, he found it difficult to keep up with his classes, particularly as an engineering major. The Boston native had already been considering abandoning hockey when a serious knee injury late in his freshman season made that decision for him.

As a youngster, nobody pushed DeCoste harder than his mom, a small-statured Italian businesswoman who impressed on her son the importance of "getting paid to think"—medicine or law topping the list of her career aspirations for him. Midway through his time in Philly, DeCoste paid a visit to the Stanley Kaplan Center to learn what the admission tests for medical and law school were like. While there, he observed a pre-med student engrossed in a thick MCAT workbook, sweating profusely, looking like he wanted to end his own life. Across the room, a girl who was flipping through a slimmer workbook with the acronym "LSAT" on the cover. She was smiling. That sealed the deal—law school it would be.

DeCoste ended up back in Boston, at Suffolk University, where he excelled from the start. One day during his 1L year, he poked his head into the model courtroom—on which the law school had spared no expense—the cavernous, ornate room as stately as ones found in federal courthouses. As he took a seat on a wooden pew, a student was on the witness stand being questioned by a fellow student, who was standing at a lectern with her notes spread out before her. DeCoste learned they were preparing for an upcoming trial competition. He sat there mesmerized. What he observed made him realize how much he missed—and yearned for—competition, with both hockey and lacrosse now in his distant past. He decided to make trial competitions the focus of his 2L and 3L years.

The thrill of being in the arena came flooding back. DeCoste crammed every hour he could into practicing with the trial team—often late into the evening and on weekends—pouring his heart and soul into his preparation. The harder he worked, the better he got, ultimately becoming one of the most polished student trial advocates in school history.

Just like his experience with the Villanova hockey team, DeCoste and his teammates travelled to competitions—even bringing trophies back to Suffolk after winning a few. During his closing arguments, he felt the familiar rush of adrenaline coursing through his veins—no different from his days skating after loose pucks at top speed. He even readied himself for battle just as he had before athletic events, harnessing his intensity with his favorite songs piped into his eardrums, a ritual he'd later reprise as an actual trial lawyer, eventually with Apple AirPods his acoustical medium of choice.

But on the biggest stage of all—the National Trial Competition—his trial team suffered a bitter defeat in the regional finals at the hands of archrival Harvard. DeCoste was crushed. Seeing his Harvard adversaries accept the mammoth trophy at the awards ceremony was thoroughly demoralizing, the sting of that loss forming a chip on his shoulder he'd carry throughout his career.

The majority of cases he'd worked on with the trial team were criminal, rather than civil. DeCoste found the factual scenarios in the criminal cases far more interesting—sexy even—and decided to begin his career as a prosecutor. With the stellar resume he'd developed in law school, he lined up interviews with some of the biggest prosecutorial offices in the country: Chicago, Brooklyn, the Bronx, Philadelphia, and Miami.

What sold him on Miami? The allure of being able to handle felony cases quickly coupled with a *Miami Vice*-style recruiting video the State Attorney's Office had sent him promoting the glitz and glamour of The Magic City. "It was so cheesy, it was actually great," DeCoste told his new colleagues upon joining the office in 2005, some 18 months after the Persian Prosecutor, Saam Zangeneh, had moved on. DeCoste was literally thrust into the boiling cauldron, handling homicide cases barely 18 months into the job. During his three-and-a-half years as a prosecutor, he served as lead counsel on dozens of homicides, ten of which went to trial. In all, he tried more than 50 cases to jury verdict.

Though he made the most of his time in the State Attorney's Office, DeCoste had become a prosecutor knowing full well his political ethos skewed too liberal to remain one for very long. By late 2008, the Boston transplant had started his own practice as a defense attorney. Most of his clients were indigent—state-court defendants assigned through the Office of Regional Counsel and federal-court defendants assigned through a special "CJA Panel." Though the pay wasn't great, the experience he developed was. Before long, he had a steady diet of murder cases—hundreds over the course of time.

In 2013, however, the 34-year-old lawyer's career—and life—suffered a major setback when he was diagnosed with Hodgkin's lymphoma, forcing him to undergo chemotherapy and radiation. He was scared, and had no clue whether he'd live or die. For the first time ever, he had to put his life in the hands of a complete stranger. That experience connected him with his clients in a brand-new way. Criminal defendants also have to place their lives in the hands of a complete stranger—their lawyer. They too are scared and have so much riding on that stranger's performance.

DeCoste's fight against cancer helped him appreciate first-hand the depth and magnitude of his clients' plight. As his cancer finally went into remission, that valuable lesson further amplified his zeal to pour himself into their cases as if *their* lives depended on *him*.

Five months after completing chemo and radiation, DeCoste met Tara Kawass, the very day she was leaving the Public Defender's Office. He told her he had a felony-murder trial starting in four days and was considering replacing the second-chair lawyer, and asked her to join him at the defense table. Thus began her first week in private practice after a seven-year run as an assistant public defender. It was a week that would end with the jury finding the tandem's client not guilty. And one which left little doubt that the slender woman from Jamaica and former hockey player from Boston—odd couple though they were—made a pretty good defense team. They'd join forces many times in the years ahead, including on the biggest stage of their entire careers.

•••

ON OCTOBER 1, 2016, DeCoste was at his office preparing a case for trial when his phone rang. When he picked up, he heard a female voice with a familiar Jamaican accent. "They just arrested Katie," Kawass said.

"*Who*?" DeCoste asked, not recognizing the name.

"Katie Magbanua," Kawass responded. "Don't you remember what I told you about her and the law professor who was murdered up in Tallahassee?"

That description jogged his memory. After a grueling federal trial that DeCoste and Kawass had handled together that July, she'd mentioned, almost casually, that she'd soon be flying up to Tallahassee on a motion to quash a subpoena for medical records for a client who'd undergone breast implant surgery. As of that point in time, DeCoste hadn't heard the first thing about Dan Markel's murder.

"I need you," Kawass said in an urgent tone. "I can't handle this huge case without you. Can you drop everything and meet me at Broward?"

"I'll hop in my car," DeCoste replied excitedly in his full-on

Boston accent. "Giddy up!" He still knew next to nothing about Dan Markel or his murder. But within just a few months, Chris DeCoste and Tara Kawass would become two of the world's leading authorities on those very subjects.

Based on their initial discussion with the State Attorney's Office in Tallahassee, they quickly surmised that Katie had been arrested merely as a means to pressure her into cooperating. The Filipina immigrant and mother of two certainly wasn't the "big fish" prosecutors were trying to hook. Charlie Adelson was. The prosecutors were counting on Katie's willingness to spill the beans on her ex-boyfriend in order to free herself from jail and reunite with her kids. They were even willing to consider immunity from prosecution in exchange for her cooperation. If she'd just agree to share what she knew, she could be a free woman in a matter of days.

But Katie made clear to her attorneys that she wouldn't be telling prosecutors that Charlie had involved her in a murder plot—because it wasn't true. She told them she knew absolutely nothing about Dan Markel or why he'd been killed. And from their very first meeting with Katie at the Broward County Jail, Kawass and DeCoste believed her—and *in her*. Yet their repeated efforts to convince prosecutors they'd arrested an innocent woman fell on deaf ears.

Thus, the defense team's first order of business was to spring Katie from jail through a motion for pretrial release. With no prior arrests, let alone convictions, DeCoste believed they could make a compelling case for release on bond, as their client was neither a danger to the community nor a flight risk. Indeed, during the four-plus months between her "husband's" arrest and her own, she hadn't left Florida a single time, even though she could have fled to the Philippines, where several of her relatives still lived. The defense lawyers scheduled a hearing, hoping to convince the judge to release Katie on bond.

•••

STATE ATTORNEY WILLIE MEGGS had tapped his chief

assistant, Georgia Cappleman, to spearhead the Dan Markel prosecution from its inception. Cappleman's biography couldn't have contrasted more with the three defense lawyers'. Unlike those transplanted Floridians, the seasoned prosecutor had lived all but a few of her 40 years in Tally—a lifer. Her father, Bill Cappleman, had been one of the most decorated quarterbacks in Florida State Seminole history. After completing his record-breaking college career in 1969, he played for the NFL's Minnesota Vikings and Detroit Lions before settling down and having kids, ultimately ending up just a stone's throw from his old stomping grounds.

His daughter Georgia attended Tally's public schools, culminating with her graduation from Leon High. With her tall frame and athletic genes, she excelled as a volleyball player and as a member of the dance team. Having lived in Florida her entire life, she decided to venture off to Tulane University in New Orleans, where she partied a bit too much and struggled academically as a freshman. After a brief, unsuccessful stop at the University of Florida, Cappleman returned to Tally in the middle of her sophomore year, enrolling in her dad's alma mater, Florida State.

Though she considered herself a pre-med student—and hoped to become an orthopedic surgeon—Cappleman didn't enjoy the rigorous courses in the required curriculum. She changed her major to English. During her senior year, she waited tables at Clyde's, a local watering hole catering to state legislators and lobbyists—many of whom were lawyers. A few of the patrons encouraged her to apply to law school. Though she had no burning desire to be a lawyer, Cappleman didn't know of anything else to do with an English degree. In August 1998, she stepped foot inside Florida State's law school for the very first time.

Not only had she gone to law school essentially by default, Cappleman found her way to the State Attorney's Office with a similar lack of intentionality. During her 2L year, one of her courses included a short internship in that office. She liked the experience enough to accept a second internship the summer between her 2L and 3L years and to continue part-time as a 3L. A job as an assistant state attorney—with an actual salary—was waiting for her upon passage of the bar exam in 2001.

Over the course of her 15 years as a prosecutor, the two-time Florida State grad slowly worked her way up the ranks, becoming second in command in 2009. She developed a reputation for being hardworking, tenacious, and thoroughly prepared. She pushed law enforcement officers and junior prosecutors—as well as herself—to pursue leads relentlessly and to never take "no" for an answer when digging for an important piece of evidence. Cappleman cared deeply about victims and their families and was keenly aware of the crucial role she played in helping them achieve justice.

As a matter of style, she couldn't have contrasted more with the Miami-based defense lawyers she'd be squaring off against in the Dan Markel case, who had a penchant for courtroom theatrics and fiery rhetoric—not averse to casting aspersions on law enforcement, prosecutors, or on occasion, even judges. Georgia Cappleman nearly always displayed a calm, poised, and unflappable demeanor—cool as a cucumber under pressure—showmanship simply not part of her craft. She was able to roll with the punches better than most trial lawyers, living by the motto, "Never let them see you sweat." As she told one interviewer, "I just try to look like a duck on the surface of the water, even though underneath, it's a lot of frantic movements."

No stranger to high-profile cases herself, as of December 2016, the veteran prosecutor had been involved in nearly 150 jury trials, including some of the biggest murder cases in Tallahassee history—one of which was eerily similar to Dan Markel's. Adam Frasch was a successful, jet-setting podiatrist from an affluent neighborhood who shared two children with his model/actress wife Samira. They too had been in the midst of a nasty custody battle. In February 2014, her body was found at the bottom of her swimming pool. The autopsy revealed she'd sustained blunt-force trauma to the head before drowning. Cappleman would ultimately convince a jury to find

Frasch guilty of first-degree murder. She also obtained a first-degree murder conviction and the death penalty against Gary Michael Hilton, dubbed the "National Forest Serial Killer" for murdering at least four people in national parklands in three states.

In addition to her work as a prosecutor, Cappleman taught classes as an adjunct professor at the law school on several subjects, including juvenile justice, sexual assault, domestic violence, and the death penalty. She also coached law students competing in criminal trial competitions—some of the same ones DeCoste had participated in while at Suffolk Law. Amazingly, though, as involved as she was teaching and coaching future criminal lawyers at Florida State, she'd never met—or even heard of—its most well-known criminal law professor and scholar. Beginning in July 2014, however, Georgia Anne Cappleman would spend nearly every waking hour thinking about Dan Markel, the fellow professor she'd never gotten to know.

•••

IN THE 1992 COMEDY *My Cousin Vinny*, Vincent Gambini (Joe Pesci) is a newly minted personal injury lawyer from Brooklyn who winds up in rural Alabama together with his fiancée, Mona Lisa Vito (Marisa Tomei). Even though he's never tried a case, Gambini makes the thousand-mile journey to defend his teenage cousin, Bill (Ralph Macchio), against a murder charge premised on a witness's mistaken identity. What makes the movie so hilarious is how conspicuously out of place the New York couple appears in Podunk, Alabama, and how alien Gambini is to the prosecutor, judge, court officials, and prosecution witnesses, all of whom seem hell-bent on sending his innocent cousin to the gas chamber.

When Tara Kawass and Chris DeCoste arrived at the Leon County Courthouse for Katie's bond hearing the morning of December 9, 2016, an eerie feeling swept over them—as if they'd walked into a scene straight out of *My Cousin Vinny*.

They were surrounded by people speaking with deep, southern drawls—a dialect they seldom encountered in Miami. Even more concerning was the familiarity Cappleman and courtroom personnel seemed to have with one another, as if they were having a long-overdue family reunion. As they took their seats beside their client Katie Magbanua—attired in unflattering, jail-issued garb—the two defense lawyers hoped and prayed Judge Hankinson would turn out to be fairer to them than Judge Chamberlain Haller (Fred Gwynne) had been to Vincent Gambini.

They had their doubts. Like Cappleman, James C. Hankinson had attended law school at Florida State and had been a lifelong prosecutor—for 22 years—before ascending to the bench in 2002. Kawass and DeCoste had learned from their reconnaissance that the bespectacled, slow-speaking jurist tended to favor the prosecution when ruling on motions and objections—dubbed by some as "Hang'em Hankinson"— though opinions of him varied among Tally's defense bar, with some giving him high marks for impartiality. He was quite accustomed to presiding over high-profile murder cases, the Markel case no more media intensive than many he'd tried before. Indeed, when Cappleman was trying the Adam Frasch and Gary Michael Hilton cases, it was Judge Hankinson who was "calling balls and strikes" from his perch on the bench.

The long-serving jurist was extremely knowledgeable about criminal law and procedure, often quoting cases and statutes verbatim solely from memory. He believed trials should move at a brisk pace—if only to permit jurors to complete their civic duty as quickly as possible. Judge Hankinson was a stickler for punctuality and didn't take kindly to lawyers who were unprepared or lacked what he considered to be appropriate courtroom decorum—a "no-nonsense judge" to his inner core. He had an uncanny ability to sniff out improper questions within the first few words—often ruling them out of bounds and admonishing the offending attorney before opposing counsel could even object. Indeed, when James C. Hankinson was on the bench, there was little doubt in the courtroom as to who was in charge.

•••

THE BAILIFF CALLED THE bond hearing to order. The chatter between the lawyers was spicy right out of the chute, with Kawass and DeCoste accusing Cappleman of withholding evidence and engaging in gamesmanship. Playing to the TV camera and reporters behind him, DeCoste asserted that the prosecution had dumped an avalanche of materials on the defense team at the very last minute—12 pounds in all— in attempt to pressure Katie. Not to cooperate, he said, but to lie. Yet his complaints fell on deaf ears, Judge Hankinson announcing that he was ready to get on with the matter at hand: whether sufficient proof of guilt existed to keep Katie behind bars until trial.

Cappleman called just one witness, Investigator Craig Isom, who provided a *Reader's Digest* version of the mountain of evidence investigators had amassed about the murder plot— and Katie's involvement. The lead prosecutor played several of the wiretapped phone calls between Katie and Charlie and her and Garcia, and had Isom provide a blow-by-blow description of the conversation the mother of two had with her former lover at Dolce Vita.

Of the 34 objections DeCoste lodged to Cappleman's questions, Judge Hankinson overruled all but two. And during DeCoste's cross-examination, the judge sustained several objections Cappleman didn't even assert, scolding the out-of-town attorney on multiple occasions for posing improper questions. To the defense team from Miami, it sure felt as if they were in Judge Chamberlain Haller's courtroom, with the deck stacked completely against them—and their client.

When it was their turn, Kawass called one of Katie's brothers, Erik, to the witness stand. Erik testified that, prior to her arrest, his sister had been the main person taking their cancer-stricken mother to chemotherapy treatments and that Katie had also been attending to the special needs of her ten-year-old son, Ethan, who was autistic and had a speech delay. He told Judge Hankinson that his sister could stay with him in Gainesville—much closer to Tally—if she was released on bond. During cross-examination, Erik revealed that he and Katie had multiple cousins still living in the Philippines, though neither he nor his sister had been there since 1992. Since her arrest, Erik testified, Katie's children were being cared for by their brother Francis and his wife in Fort Lauderdale.

Cappleman asked the judge to deny Katie's bond request and to keep her in custody "for the short time remaining until her scheduled trial in February." Kawass argued that her client, having never before been arrested, presented no danger to the community and wasn't a flight risk because her entire family lived in Florida. This time around, Judge Hankinson didn't find the former assistant public defender quite so persuasive. He denied bond, assuring that Katie would remain behind bars until trial.

As sheriff's deputies led his client from the courtroom—her hands cuffed and feet shackled—DeCoste's frustration boiled over. He told a reporter that he and Kawass were "stunned" by the judge's ruling. "In this case," he sneered, "justice took a back seat to ego and politics a long time ago."

•••

AS IT TURNED OUT, Katie Magbanua wasn't tried in February 2017 after all. The two months Cappleman predicted she'd remain in jail following the December 2016 hearing morphed into nearly three years, each continuance occurring at her own attorneys' request. Kawass and DeCoste were simply buried by an avalanche of discovery documents and electronic data supplied by the prosecutors—over 12 terabytes—the information seemingly spewing at them from a gargantuan firehose. Digesting that giant mountain of material took considerable time and energy. They also decided to take sworn depositions of dozens of individuals appearing on the State's witness list, a few of whom were located thousands of miles away.

Then, in March 2018, a mammogram revealed that Kawass had breast cancer, making her the second member of Katie's defense team whose body had been ravaged by the dreaded disease. A double mastectomy and six months of chemotherapy would follow. Though Kawass offered to find another lawyer for Katie so she could proceed to trial more quickly, her client refused, explaining that Kawass was the only one who truly believed in her. The incarcerated mother even sent her attorney get-well cards from her jail cell. The two-time FIU grad lost three-quarters of her long, wavy, jet-black hair, her last chemo treatment occurring in October 2018. She finally returned to work full-time that December.

Meanwhile, the passage of two additional years hadn't resulted in the arrest of anyone bearing the last name of Adelson, much to the frustration of the TPD—as well as to Dan Markel's family and friends. A few weeks before Katie's arrest, the police department had intentionally leaked a probable cause affidavit laying out in exquisite detail all of the evidence it had amassed against Charlie. The *Tallahassee Democrat* ran a story about the contents of the affidavit, laying bare the simmering feud between the TPD and State Attorney Willie Meggs over whether to charge members of the Adelson family with Dan's murder.

Investigator Isom and his TPD colleagues strongly believed that ample evidence existed to prosecute both Donna and Charlie for their roles in the homicide. That included not just the circumstantial evidence arising from the divorce proceedings and the pattern of telephone calls around the time of the murder, but also all of the communications involving Donna, Charlie, and Katie immediately following the April 2016 bump. But neither Isom nor Police Chief Michael DeLeo could convince Meggs, or his successor, Jack Campbell—who took office in January 2017—to pull the proverbial trigger on prosecuting Wendi's mother or brother.

The hope of all involved—prosecutors, police investigators, and Dan's family and friends—was that pressure for Katie to flip would mount with each passing day in the rigid confines of her jail cell, away from her children. And that, once she turned State's evidence and began to cooperate, prosecutors would no longer have just circumstantial evidence, but direct evidence of Donna and Charlie's involvement in the murder plot. Katie and her lawyers were well aware that a deal far better than Luis Rivera's was waiting for her if she agreed to cooperate. But as her months behind bars turned into years, it became clear the UCF grad and mother of two had no such intention.

That seemed like it might suddenly change, however, the Friday before the September 23, 2019 trial date. Cappleman fielded a call that afternoon from Kawass and DeCoste, who were already in town preparing for battle. They told the assistant state attorney that their client wanted to meet with her.

For three years, the defense lawyers had repeatedly insisted that Katie was innocent and was being wrongfully prosecuted. Though Cappleman had assured them on multiple occasions that her office had no interest in prosecuting an innocent person, there was too much incriminating evidence for her to take their claim of innocence very seriously. Indeed, prior to receiving their call that Friday afternoon, the defense attorneys had never extended her an invitation to discuss the case directly with their client.

The veteran prosecutor interpreted their eleventh-hour invitation as a signal that Katie had something of value to offer. And if that turned out to be the case, it wasn't too late to negotiate a deal in exchange for her cooperation. Which made it worth Cappleman's while to spend her Friday evening not with her family, as she'd intended, but rather, in one of her least favorite places on earth—the Leon County Detention Center, Katie's home for the last three years.

At about 8:00 p.m., Cappleman and her investigator, Jason Newlin, sat in a small meeting room across the table from Kawass, DeCoste, and a wide-eyed Katie Magbanua, who'd just been aroused from a nap. Cappleman and Newlin said they were all ears to hear whatever Katie might want to share—expecting her to say something along the lines that she'd unwittingly become a pawn in Charlie Adelson's plan to assassinate Dan Markel and didn't comprehend what was going on until it was too late.

But that isn't even close to what Katie told them. Rather, in very few words, she declared that she was innocent and knew nothing at all about Dan Markel's murder. She professed to having no idea why investigators and prosecutors believed the evidence suggested otherwise and even expressed her willingness to take a polygraph exam to prove she wasn't involved. Somewhat taken aback, Cappleman and Newlin pressed her on some of the more incriminating evidence against her. Her answers left them entirely unconvinced. They thanked Katie and her lawyers for their time and left the jail—frustrated and disappointed—wondering why they'd been summoned to meet with Katie if that was all they were going to hear.

The entire group would be going to trial the following Monday morning after all. Though the defense lawyers had asked Judge Hankinson to sever Katie's trial from Garcia's, that motion had been denied. A jury of their peers would therefore sit in judgment on both "husband" and "wife." In a trial that would be front-page news in Tallahassee—and the talk of the town—for three solid weeks.

19.

Laying it Out

THE TRIAL TOOK PLACE in courtroom 3G of the Leon County Courthouse, a modern, five-story structure with a sleek, curved entranceway and attractive glass-and-stone facade, ringed by stately moss-draped oak trees and prominently located across the street from the Florida State Capitol. The sprawling complex, occupying two entire city blocks, is home to numerous county offices and agencies, including the Second Judicial Circuit State Attorney's Office.

Thus, not only did Georgia Cappleman have the luxury of sleeping in her own bed each night of the lengthy trial, during the daytime, she was just footsteps from her office and an army of staff ready to respond to her every need. The seasoned prosecutor enjoyed a home-court advantage in every way imaginable over the Miami-based defense lawyers, who were holed up at nearby hotels for nearly a solid month—preparing each evening in cramped rooms littered with pizza boxes, dirty dishes, and their own laundry.

Though Katie wasn't facing the death penalty, because Garcia was, the jury had to be "death qualified"—with prospective jurors agreeing they didn't harbor moral convictions that would preclude them from meting out the ultimate punishment. The intense publicity surrounding the case further complicated, and lengthened, the jury-selection process, which lasted three full days. In the end, ten women and two men, as well as two alternates—ranging in age from 19 to 63—were empaneled to hear the evidence, a broad demographic mix of Tallahasseans who would spend three weeks together, earning a whopping $30 per day.

The windowless courtroom they reported to is shaped like a long, narrow shoebox, its climate control set to a temperature more befitting a Polar icebox. The room is so narrow, it's barely wide enough to accommodate both the prosecution and defense tables. No more than 60 to 70 spectators can be crammed into the well-worn, wooden gallery pews. The only spacious portion of the entire courtroom is the jury box, which contains 14 comfortable, black-leather chairs and is slightly elevated from the floor to maximize viewing angles.

The trial began in earnest on Thursday, September 26, 2019. Early that morning, the courtroom was abuzz in activity, a "pool" camera operator setting up at the front of the gallery with newspaper and TV reporters vying for seats just behind him. Ruth and Phil Markel and Dan's sister Shelly claimed seats in the third row, behind the prosecution table, where they'd sit throughout the trial beside their victim advocate. Several of the slain professor's colleagues from Florida State and friends from the community were sprinkled throughout the packed audience. The anticipation and nervous energy permeating the courtroom was palpable. That was particularly true at and around the three counsel tables.

Seated at the prosecution table—closest to the jury box and facing the bench and witness stand—were Cappleman and Assistant State Attorney Anna Norris, also a Tally native. Norris had eight years of experience as a prosecutor and had herself tried more than 100 cases to jury verdict. Other prosecutors and paralegals, who would come and go as the trial proceeded, milled about the prosecution table like bees hovering around fragrant spring flowers.

Tara Kawass's younger sister, Kristen, primarily an appellate lawyer, sat with Kawass and Chris DeCoste at the defense table closest to the prosecutors, which also faced forward. Accompanying Saam Zangeneh at the second defense table—which was at a right angle to Katie's defense table and faced the jury—was another Miami defense lawyer, Mauricio "Mo" Padilla, who'd served as second chair to Zangeneh in several prior cases.

Though they were still residing at the local jail, the defendants seated beside their lawyers had received extreme makeovers, now barely resembling the mugshots that for years had been splashed across the TV news, documentaries, and pages of the *Democrat*. Garcia's dark hair was neatly cropped close to his scalp, his face silky smooth. Though he didn't ordinarily wear glasses, he was wearing a pair of black, wire-framed glasses that made the many-time felon appear almost professorial. A sharp-looking, charcoal-gray suit and bright blue shirt covered Garcia's muscular frame. A sheriff's deputy even helped him fasten his light-colored, patterned tie which, as intended, softened his image even more.

Katie also was sporting a pair of glasses—hers with a thicker black frame around the lenses, with stylish, silver arms extending to her ears. She was dressed in a professional-looking black pantsuit, her lush, jet-black hair flowing freely down her back. A gold wedding band encircled her left ring-finger, implying that she and Garcia were actually married. Based solely on her appearance, the Filipina immigrant easily could have passed for a candidate interviewing for a position as vice president of a bank—rather than a jailed inmate standing trial for murder.

Though they hadn't ever been legally married, the two defendants had been through an awful lot together over more than 15 years—as a young couple scraping by in Orlando during Katie's college days, the birth of a son and then a daughter, and a tumultuous, on-again, off-again romantic relationship. A murder trial before a jury of their peers, however, would be their biggest challenge yet. Because of the circumstances, an occasional glance from Katie to Garcia, or from him to her, was all either could do to offer the other comfort and support.

Twelve complete strangers would soon decide whether

they'd ever return to a life together, or whether, in Garcia's case, he'd ultimately have any life at all.

•••

"ALL RISE!" THE BAILIFF CRIED OUT, as the Honorable James C. Hankinson entered the courtroom and ascended to his seat on the bench. The 12 jurors and two alternates were led single-file to their seats in the jury box—chairs that would soon become as familiar to them as those surrounding their own kitchen tables. The judge reminded the jury that the two defendants had been charged with first-degree murder, conspiracy to commit first-degree murder, and solicitation to commit first-degree murder. After reciting some standard preliminary instructions, he invited an opening statement on behalf of the State of Florida.

Georgia Cappleman strode confidently to the stately, mahogany lectern, where she recounted for the jury how Jim Geiger's tranquil summer morning on July 18, 2014, was suddenly disrupted by the harrowing events at Dan Markel's home next door, culminating in the law professor's death some 14 hours later. She marched through the timeline of Dan's activities that morning, describing the surveillance footage of the silver-pine-mica Prius following his car to the gym and on his route back to his Betton Hills home.

Cappleman told jurors that while trying to determine who might have wanted to harm the professor, investigators learned that Dan and his ex-wife Wendi Adelson had been "embroiled in a very contentious divorce and continued litigation." Taking some liberties with the facts, she stated—incorrectly—that Wendi had moved to South Florida with her sons and that the court had to order their return to Tally. The prosecutor told the jury that Wendi's mother, Donna, "despised Dan Markel and was desperate for Wendi and these two kids to move down to where she was located in South Florida." And that her brother, Charlie, had made "references to hiring a hitman to kill Dan Markel."

The assistant state attorney described for jurors how investigators pieced together the evidence, using cell tower dumps to identify Garcia and Rivera as the hitmen who killed Dan. She pointed to the unlikely love triangle between Katie, the father of her children, and a wealthy dentist named Charlie Adelson. Whose sister Wendi, she said, "had a problem. And her problem was named Dan Markel. And the solution to that problem was Magbanua, Garcia, and Rivera."

The veteran prosecutor walked jurors through Garcia and Rivera's first trip to Tally six weeks before the eventual homicide, telling them "it was intended to be a murder trip, but it ended up being more of a scouting trip." Garcia had told Rivera, she said, "they needed to kill this guy so that his wife could get their kids" and that they were being paid $100,000 for the hit. Rivera had overhead Katie on the phone telling his pal, "Don't do anything stupid." But on the second trip, Cappleman noted, they each did something pretty stupid—Garcia shooting a hole in the gas line of the rented Prius and Rivera posting a picture of an owl on Instagram.

She listed the numerous benefits Katie, Garcia, and Rivera each ended up with in the months following the murder. Cappleman then described the bump between Donna and the undercover agent, previewing the phone chatter among Donna, Charlie, Katie, and Garcia over the ensuing days—noting how the undercover agent's phone number passed through all four co-conspirators. She concluded by telling jurors they'd be "convinced beyond a reasonable doubt that the State is not pulling a fast one on you, but rather, that Katherine Magbanua was hired to solicit Garcia, who in turn solicited Rivera to come to Tallahassee and to execute Mr. Markel in cold blood."

Though her opening remarks left little doubt the prosecution believed Donna and Charlie were the masterminds—and funding sources—behind that execution, Cappleman didn't offer any explanation as to why those two white, wealthy individuals weren't seated in the courtroom alongside the Brown-skinned defendants. It would be up to the defense lawyers to provide their own explanations.

• • •

SAAM ZANGENEH APPROACHED the lectern in a snazzy, bluish-gray, pinstriped suit—one of a closetful of extravagant, custom-tailored ensembles he'd showcase during the trial. He held up seven fingers, telling jurors that was the deal prosecutors had given Luis Rivera to turn State's evidence—seven years for his role in Dan's murder—the "deal of the century." Pointing directly at Cappleman and Norris, he asserted that their "real targets" were Donna, Charlie, and Wendi Adelson. And to get to them, he posited, they first needed to go after the "low-hanging fruit," starting with Rivera.

Zangeneh argued that Rivera was "the prosecution's parrot," to whom they'd "spoon-fed" his testimony. He pointed out that though cell tower records proved that Rivera had traveled from Miami to Tally about a month before the murder, "there's no such records for Sigfredo Garcia." Indeed, when Rivera was handed a traffic citation during *that* trip—not the second one as he'd said in his proffer—Zangeneh added, the state trooper found no one else in his vehicle.

Jurors would be hearing "speculation," the defense lawyer suggested, as to why the Adelsons wanted to hurt Dan Markel. But that, he said, had nothing to do with "this case," which was built solely on Rivera's statements. "Because the only person that can put Sigfredo Garcia at the scene, the only person who can tell you that Sigfredo Garcia got out of the car and purportedly shot Dan Markel, is who? It's the guy who got the seven years—the guy who got the deal of a lifetime."

"It's *crazy* how much he changes his story," Zangeneh continued, alluding to the inconsistencies in Rivera's statements over time, telling jurors it made no sense that Rivera would have received $35,000—as he claimed—simply to drive to Tally twice while Garcia did the actual shooting. "You know, two and two has to equal four," he declared, his facial expression conveying utter disbelief.

He pivoted to Katie, telling the jury his client loved her.

"That's his wifey." But they were going through a "rough patch." Garcia "was not happy that this dental playboy that drives around in a Ferrari with nice hair and big muscles and a long, long wallet was with his wifey." The prosecution wanted jurors to believe the unbelievable, he asserted, that Garcia, "whose heart was broken," decided to help the very man who was causing his misery.

Zangeneh told jurors that it made far more sense for Charlie to have solicited Rivera to help with the Dan Markel problem. Why? Because Rivera was the *primero* of the Latin Kings, its leader, with a criminal network extending from Key West to the Panhandle, routinely engaged in robbery, drug dealing, and homicide. King Tato himself was a known drug dealer, he said, "a pharmacy from soup to nuts, from steroids to cocaine." The defense attorney speculated that the gang leader had likely been supplying Charlie with drugs, which naturally would have led Wendi's brother "to solicit this murder for hire from Luis Rivera."

When Rivera turned State's evidence, Zangeneh explained, the government believed Garcia and Katie "would be the next to crumble to get to the Adelsons. That's what everybody thought. But yet here we are. They've maintained their innocence, and we're here in trial."

Less than a minute before walking back to his counsel table, the former Miami prosecutor finally acknowledged that his client had been in Tally, with Rivera, the day of the murder. But that was only for a drug deal, he contended—without elaborating—similar to many such deals King Tato had involved his buddy Tuto in previously. He insisted that Rivera was the one who had shot and killed Dan Markel, having secured "the services of his organization to supply the gun and to supply another henchman." Ending as he began—with seven fingers held high—Zangeneh reiterated that the only person who would testify that his client had killed Dan Markel was Luis Rivera.

•••

FOR TARA KAWASS, her opening statement would mark the culmination of a roller-coaster ride that had begun with Katie's desperate call from a shopping center parking lot on October 1, 2016. At the time, the defense lawyer couldn't possibly have fathomed how the next three years would unfold—or that her client would spend virtually that entire time in the confines of the Leon County Jail.

Kawass's hair—still thinned out from her recent battle with breast cancer—was pulled back tightly into a clip, as it would be throughout the trial. Unlike the two lawyers who'd preceded her, her mouth barely reached the small microphone extending from the lectern. But what she lacked in physical stature, Kawass more than made up for with her passionate tone, frequent and forceful hand gestures, and fiery language. The feisty defense lawyer was a bundle of energy and blur of motion from behind the lectern.

"Prosecutorial desperation," she began, her words enunciated in her distinct, Jamaican accent. "That is the only reason why Katherine Magbanua is sitting before you today, charged with a crime that she had absolutely nothing to do with. The prosecution's relentless obsession with arresting the Adelson family has led to this day, this moment, in this courtroom, where an innocent person is being accused of a crime that she did not commit."

She told jurors they'd be learning a lot about Katie, "a hardworking woman, who loves her children and just wants to provide a good life for them … one of the strongest women I have come to know." Her "major downfall," and the only thing she was guilty of, Kawass said as her eyes rolled to the back of her head, "is having *horrible* taste in men."

Which led her straight into a recitation of Katie's on-again, off-again relationship with Sigfredo Garcia. By 2013, she said, Katie "was done with Sigfredo." Then, into her life walked Charlie Adelson. Kawass pushed back against the State's theory that Katie was the "only link" between the Adelsons and the hitmen, pointing to cellphone records revealing that Garcia had made at least one call directly to Harvey Adelson,

17 days before the murder.

Katie's attorney laid bare the enormous elephant pervading the proceedings, telling jurors that members of the Adelson family "are not in this courtroom today" because "the State hasn't even arrested them or charged them with anything." Cappleman, she said, didn't want jurors to think about that, "because it's not good for their case. *You have to think about it*," Kawass insisted. Why? Because Katie was charged solely out of "the prosecution's desperation and blinding desire to arrest Charlie Adelson and his parents," the government fully believing she'd rat them out. But to the prosecutors' great surprise, she continued, "Katherine doesn't have the information they want."

Common sense, Kawass added, would lead jurors to the inescapable conclusion that "Katherine was just a pawn in Charlie Adelson's plan to kill Dan Markel. And now the prosecution is trying to use Katherine as a pawn to get Charlie Adelson." It made absolutely no sense, she argued, that Katie would have coordinated the murder of a man she'd never met "for a guy that she has known for less than a year." Nor did it seem reasonable, she contended, that Katie would have asked the father of her kids "to commit a murder for her new boyfriend."

The defense attorney tore into Luis Rivera like a Pit Bull devouring a juicy steak, calling him a "liar" and "multiple-time convicted felon," someone who "even on his best day, can't keep his story straight." And who repeatedly "takes pleas to save himself." A murderer who, Kawass noted, would be set free through the prosecution's deal "probably before he's even 50." The prosecutors, she asserted, knew that much of what Rivera was saying wasn't true—like supposedly seeing Wendi on Trescott Drive with her two boys the day before the murder, when the boys were actually at preschool. Asking jurors to believe only the parts of his statements that fit the prosecution's theory—and to disregard the parts that didn't— was "offensive," Kawass snarled.

The State had dug up and "ripped apart Katherine

Magbanua's life," she told jurors, including her "phone records, her taxes, her medical records. And nothing, no direct evidence that she was involved. *Zero*. And that's because she wasn't involved. How far are they going to go, members of the jury, before they stop?"

Which was precisely why, the defense attorney stressed, "we don't leave these decisions in the hands of the government, because they are so blinded right now that they can't see the truth." Kawass implored jurors to look at the evidence with their "unbiased eyes." Katie was "grateful to have you here today," she added, because she'd been "waiting three years for this day. For people to take a look and see what the truth is in this case. She had absolutely nothing to do with this. She did not know. She's innocent. Find her not guilty. Thank you."

•••

CAPPLEMAN BEGAN THE prosecution's evidence with a parade of witnesses who described the events of July 18, 2014: Jim Geiger, police officers who responded to the crime scene, Stewart Schlazer—the charter school teacher who was speaking with Dan the moment he was shot—the general surgeon who treated him upon his arrival at the hospital, and the medical examiner who conducted his autopsy.

The lead slugs extracted from Dan's skull were passed around the jury box as if they were fascinating artifacts unearthed from an archaeological dig, rather than lethal instruments that ended a fellow human being's life.

Robert Yao, an expert witness in bullet path trajectory, testified that the bullet that penetrated Dan's left cheek had been fired at a downward angle, "which is more indicative of somebody being taller and aiming downward toward the victim from outside the car."

In view of the location of the bullet hole in the driver's-side window, measured at 49 inches off the ground, Yao testified that the gun was more likely fired by an individual who was 6'1"—Garcia's measured height at the time of his arrest—than

5'4", Rivera's height.

Craig Isom occupied the witness stand for much of the second day of trial. For more than five years, the seasoned investigator had poured himself into Dan's case—the most comprehensive, time-consuming investigation of his entire career. He was chomping at the bit to tell the jury everything he and his team had done to solve the crime. The silver-haired, round-faced man's large frame was covered by a loose-fitting gray suit and light-gray shirt—his girthy neck exposed through a wide-open collar. Isom introduced himself as a retired police investigator, having concluded his 28-year stint with the TPD in September 2017.

After getting her witness to tell jurors that he'd reviewed Dan and Wendi's divorce file as part of his investigation, Cappleman approached Isom with State's Exhibit 75, a massive, white, three-ring binder containing the entire 575-page court file. But rather than delving into those important pleadings in any depth, the lead prosecutor simply had Isom describe Wendi's relocation motion and Dan's subsequent motion seeking to restrict Donna's visitation with her grandsons. In less than five minutes, she moved on from the contentious divorce proceedings—without showing jurors a single page from the white binder.

Though Cappleman asked Isom about Donna's email diatribes tearing into her ex-son-in-law, she had him summarize only one of them—again without letting jurors review the email for themselves. Instead, the prosecutor spent 30 minutes having the retired police investigator narrate the surveillance footage from Premier Fitness and city buses, which the jury did get to see in living color, both on a giant projection screen and on monitors arrayed throughout the jury box.

Isom shared with the jury how the SunPass transponder information provided by the FDOT zeroed in on the exact Prius that had been in Tally the morning of the shooting. And how his investigators followed that lead to a Miami rental car company to whom the vehicle was registered.

Cappleman projected onto the screen State's Exhibit 82—

Rivera's rental agreement for the Prius—pointing out the word "Brother" in the top-left corner and the telephone number just beneath it.

Isom told jurors that his team was able to use the Facebook account of a "Tuto Dade" to confirm that the telephone number on the rental agreement belonged to Sigfredo Garcia. A photograph from the same Facebook account was then projected onto the screen, depicting Garcia in a white tank top standing cross-armed in front of a shiny, black Dodge Ram pickup truck. Cappleman ended her direct exam with another photo—a still image of the Prius captured by a city bus the morning of the murder—showing what appeared to be a person seated in the front passenger seat. Who, coincidentally enough, also was wearing what appeared to be a white shirt.

Zangeneh used his cross-examination to make some basic—but obvious—points. Isom confirmed that neither the Premier Fitness nor city bus video footage captured a clear image of the Prius's license plate and didn't assist investigators in determining who was inside the vehicle. But the one-time Persian Prosecutor also asked Isom to speculate on a pretty far-fetched theory. Noting that the Prius wasn't seen on the gym's surveillance footage for a chunk of the time Dan was working out, he asked, "So you wouldn't be able to tell the members of this jury whether or not a drug transaction took place in the parking lot of Premier?" Isom readily agreed.

Zangeneh also had the retired investigator acknowledge that Tally was no stranger to gang activity, so much so that a gang unit existed within the TPD. Which, in the defense lawyer's view, somehow confirmed his theory that Dan's murder had arisen from gang-related activity organized by King Tato.

Chris DeCoste handled Isom's cross-examination for Katie's defense team, an opportunity he'd been eagerly anticipating for years. There was nothing he relished more—and no greater thrill he experienced as a trial lawyer—than methodically shredding into small, meaningless pieces the work of homicide investigators. He planned to use Isom as a prop to illustrate all of the mistakes he and his law enforcement colleagues had made. The defense team wanted jurors to believe that Isom and his team had merely latched onto what they already believed to be true—so-called "confirmation bias"—Katie's arrest based largely on their preconceived notions of her involvement, rather than on actual evidence.

DeCoste handed Isom the giant white binder containing the divorce file, to make the obvious point that Katie's name didn't appear anywhere within its 575 pages. He used photographs of Wendi, Donna, Harvey, and Charlie arrayed across a large posterboard to make an even more obvious point—that none of the Adelsons had been arrested, even though Isom and his team believed that the murder plot had originated with some or all of them.

The Boston transplant also got Isom to agree that Rivera had access to the TPD's investigative reports prior to making his proffer statement—reports that revealed his team's belief that Katie had been the conduit between Charlie and the hitmen. "You have no way of knowing whether Luis Rivera was just regurgitating what you had written in your reports as to what you thought the theory of the case was, right?" DeCoste asked in a sharp tone.

"I have no way of knowing what he had access to at that point," Isom responded.

"You know that those reports are handed over in discovery, right?"

"Yes."

"No way for you to know whether he's telling the truth or not?"

"No," Isom conceded.

The longtime investigator also admitted that Rivera's initial proffer statement hadn't been recorded, prompting the defense lawyer to ask, "We have no way here in this courtroom today to view Luis's words, Luis Rivera's words on September 30 and point out the inconsistencies with his other statements, do we?" Isom sheepishly acknowledged the point. He also reluctantly conceded that Katie's arrest had involved a large

SWAT team of ten to 15 officers—some with guns drawn—and that she'd been so frightened she urinated on herself. He further agreed that Katie's arrest had come within 24 hours of Rivera's initial proffer—which would help DeCoste argue later that, absent Rivera's statements about Katie's involvement, the State didn't believe sufficient evidence existed to connect her to the murder.

The defense attorney tried to make it appear that Isom and his colleagues hadn't objectively investigated Katie, focusing first on the Lexus sedan in which she was arrested. Isom agreed that Katie's ownership and use of the Lexus fit his working theory "that she's somehow involved in this." DeCoste got him to concede that the TPD had never investigated the vehicle's condition, whether it had been involved in accidents, the number of miles on the engine, and hadn't even taken pictures of it.

Showing the State's witness the car title, the defense attorney got Isom to confirm that Katie had paid $1,700 for the 13-year-old vehicle, and that there were 160,000 miles showing on its odometer.

"So the only evidence that you have on this Lexus," DeCoste asked, "is that it was a legitimate purchase, right?"

"Yes," Isom agreed.

As for Katie's breast augmentation, the retired investigator conceded that he didn't know where she'd acquired the cash used to pay the plastic surgeon. "You didn't investigate the possible source of that cash, right?" DeCoste pressed him.

"No," Isom admitted. "Cash is very hard to trace."

"Unexplained cash would be good for your theory, right."

"It fits," Isom agreed. But he pushed back against the insinuation Katie's lawyer was making. "I didn't have this theory and then try to make it fit like a square peg in a round hole. That's not the case."

DeCoste had Isom confirm that the murder weapon had never been found, despite Rivera drawing a map—in crayon—of where he claimed it had been disposed of. And despite investigators making three or four attempts, with Rivera riding along, to locate it.

"Possibly he didn't want you to find it?" DeCoste asked.

"Very possible," Isom conceded.

The former Miami prosecutor saved his best point for last, forcing Isom to admit that he'd become aware Katie had been working as a "bottle girl" for two upscale South Florida nightclubs, Hollywood Live and Club Fate. And that law enforcement hadn't subpoenaed records from either or spoken with the clubs' owners, managers, or other employees to determine whether she'd been making significant cash tips. Isom even admitted knowing "that there's a lot of cash that gets floated around" at those types of establishments.

Yet he denied it had been an "oversight" not to have conducted a deeper investigation into Katie's work at those clubs. His denial, however, quickly backfired. Whipping out the transcript of Isom's pretrial deposition, DeCoste had him acknowledge that, when asked the identical question just months before, Isom had testified that the failure to investigate Katie's work at those clubs "was just an oversight." A wry smile washed over DeCoste's face as Isom squirmed in his seat—just a bit embarrassed—the defense lawyer's successful impeachment of the witness reminiscent of his days honing his trial skills in Suffolk Law's model courtroom.

DeCoste ended his cross-examination by trying to convince Isom—or at least the jury—that his entire theory hinged on a dubious fact, asking him whether investigators had concluded Katie was involved simply because "there is no evidence directly linking Garcia and Rivera to any of the Adelsons?"

"That sounds accurate," Isom readily admitted.

"So if during this trial we're able to establish that there is communication between those parties," DeCoste asked, "then you would agree with me that Katherine Magbanua is not involved, right?"

"No," Isom responded firmly, not falling for the defense lawyer's overly simplistic logic.

Though he didn't get the answer he'd hoped for, Chris DeCoste had to be pleased with his cross-examination overall.

Much as he'd planned, he got Isom to admit several points fitting neatly within his and Kawass's defense themes.

It was up to Georgia Cappleman to try to repair some of that damage through her redirect examination. She began right where DeCoste left off, having Isom acknowledge that there was evidence of a call between Garcia and Harvey Adelson and that investigators were well aware of that communication when they charged Katie with murder. "I mean, there's other parts to this case," the lead prosecutor asked, "other than did every single piece of communication funnel through her?"

"Correct," Isom confirmed.

"All right. So, for example, we've got a wiretap that we're going to talk about later, right?"

"Yes."

"And part of our— your decision to make an arrest had to do with what was her conduct on that wiretap, yes?"

"That's correct," Isom agreed, accepting the words Cappleman was spoon-feeding him with her leading questions.

"And we've got phone records putting her in the middle of this, right?"

"Yes."

"Financial evidence putting her in the middle of it?"

"Yes."

Over DeCoste's vehement objections—all of which the judge overruled—Cappleman essentially testified, with an occasional affirmation from Isom, that during the month in which Dan was killed, Katie had "deposited significantly more cash than any other month that we looked at surrounding the time of the homicide." And that, at that particular time, she wasn't even working for the nightclubs.

The assistant state attorney also pointed out that Katie had never reported any income on her tax returns from having worked as a bottle girl. As for the Lexus, Isom agreed that no evidence had been found establishing that Katie had paid even a penny for it.

In Florida, after the attorneys complete their questions, jurors get to pose their own. They do so by writing them down on a piece of paper and having the written questions handed to the judge. One juror wanted to know what recordings were made of Rivera's prior statements. Isom indicated that he recorded the former gang leader using a body cam when Rivera accompanied him and fellow investigators in a police van. "And he showed us how he got to the house and he pointed out different things ... So you'll probably— I'm assuming you'll see that sometime." Yet Isom would turn out to be wrong about that prediction.

Cappleman followed up by asking if it was common procedure not to record the first interview of a suspect who decides to turn State's evidence.

Isom told jurors that there wasn't anything unusual or unethical about not recording the first such interview. The prosecutor also got him to respond to the notion that Rivera had been "spoon-fed" what to say during that interview, Isom telling the jury that no one from the State Attorney's Office had ever suggested to Rivera or his lawyers what they wanted him to say.

Yet with his final questions, DeCoste succeeded in getting Isom to admit that it had been the prosecutors' idea, not his, for Rivera's initial proffer statement not to be recorded. "Legally, you do not have to answer to them, right?" the defense attorney asked.

"No, legally I do not," Isom agreed.

"You could have recorded that if you wanted to?"

"Yes," Isom conceded.

Weary from his time on the witness stand, the retired investigator stepped down, feeling confident he'd established several key points for the prosecution and that he'd deflected the defense lawyers' pointed questions reasonably well. His testimony, though imperfect, had served its intended purpose and likely held the interest of most jurors.

Meanwhile, just outside the courtroom, another witness was patiently awaiting her turn to testify. And there was little doubt that jurors and spectators alike would be on the edges of their seats to hear what this particular mother of two had to say.

20.

An Adelson in the Courtroom

BY THE SECOND DAY OF TRIAL, the name Wendi Adelson had become nearly as familiar to jurors as that of Donald J. Trump. Though the 45th President wasn't about to barge through the courtroom doors, Dan Markel's ex-wife was. She'd flown in from Miami in compliance with the State's subpoena compelling her testimony. Her own lawyer, John Lauro, had hashed out an immunity agreement with the State Attorney's Office which ensured that the former clinical law professor could testify freely without fear her words might later be used against her.

More than five years had elapsed since Wendi last stepped foot in the Leon County Courthouse—when she and Dan were seated at opposite sides of the courtroom with their divorce lawyers by their sides. Just a few months following that contentious February 2014 hearing, their family court proceedings came to a screeching halt—rendered moot by Dan's murder. The very same murder that occasioned her appearance in Courtroom 3G on this particular fall afternoon.

With Lauro by her side, the Coral Springs native entered the courtroom sporting a heather-gray dress with black, embroidered stitching that encircled her neck and bisected her body from top to bottom. A black blazer further enhanced her lawyerly appearance. Now 40 years of age, the mother of two didn't look a day over 35, her long, silky, highlighted blonde hair cascading freely down her back, elegant wisps resting gently against her blazer's left lapel. Whether it was her skillful use of makeup, expensive surgical enhancements, or good genes, not a single wrinkle, blemish, or mole marked her velvety-smooth skin.

Though Cappleman had called Wendi as a witness for the prosecution, the State's lead counsel had precious little idea what she'd actually say. In every sense of the word, Wendi Adelson was a hostile witness, with little incentive or desire to help the prosecution prove its case. Her entire family had been under the microscope of investigators and prosecutors for more than five years—her mother and brother the subject of an elaborate FBI sting operation, their telephone conversations wiretapped and homes surveilled.

Wendi had presumably read the probable cause affidavit against Charlie, laying the foundation for both his and Donna's eventual arrest and prosecution. She had no doubt learned of Cappleman's opening statement, in which the prosecutor had told jurors that her brother had ordered the hit on her ex-husband. Quite naturally, she wouldn't have viewed the assistant state attorney as anything other than an enemy hell-bent on destroying her family. Yet despite her disdain for her interrogator, Wendi remained calm and poised throughout her direct examination—seemingly enjoying her moment in the spotlight—at times smiling and giggling as if she were gossiping with a close friend.

Nevertheless, a pattern emerged early on in her questioning, in which the lead prosecutor would ask a seemingly straightforward question that Wendi would then evade, spin, or answer in a manner that strained credulity. She disagreed that her family members were "wealthy" or "millionaires." She testified that she actually enjoyed living in Tallahassee and had no desire to move to South Florida when she and Dan first split up in September 2012. Asked if her parents were "very involved" in trying to facilitate her relocation, Wendi would only agree that they were "supportive" and disputed that they'd been overly involved in her "personal business."

After Cappleman had Wendi confirm that Judge Hobbs, the family court judge, had denied her January 2013 petition to relocate, the assistant state attorney declared, "You were upset about being stuck in Tallahassee" — more of a statement than a question. Yet to her surprise, Wendi rejected that notion altogether, testifying that she'd been *relieved* the judge had ruled against her because she was so happy at her job at Florida State. Though it made no sense she'd been pleased *her* petition had been denied, Cappleman was too flustered to press the issue. Shifting her focus, she asked, "Would you consider your divorce with Mr. Markel to be a nasty divorce?"

"I think most divorces aren't very pleasant," Wendi responded, sidestepping the question.

"But this one was like *really* unpleasant, right?" Cappleman pressed her.

"I found getting divorced to be unpleasant, yes," the Brandeis grad reluctantly acknowledged, but without agreeing the level of unpleasantness was anything unusual. She professed to not remembering fighting with Dan over things as small as a tennis racket or that he'd threatened to press kidnapping charges against her or go after her law license.

Without showing her the actual pleading, Cappleman had Wendi focus on Dan's final, March 2014 motion—in which he complained about his ex-wife's alleged violations of the marital settlement agreement, including her failure to allow the boys to Skype with him. Wendi told jurors she didn't recall any of the motion's specifics. Although she knew Dan was "frustrated about the Skyping," she chuckled, "It's hard to Skype with two toddlers."

As to whether Dan had pressed Judge Hobbs to restrict Donna to supervised visitation with Ben and Lincoln—or had contended Donna had been disparaging him, telling their boys that he was stupid and was "trying to take my Sunshines away" — Wendi claimed she couldn't recall. She even testified that she didn't remember if Dan had sought sanctions against her. But she did admit that she'd probably shown Dan's motion to her mom. Which was the most important point Cappleman was trying to make, to help establish Donna's motive.

"Is it fair to say that your parents are very protective of you?" the prosecutor inquired.

"I think that's fair to say," Wendi conceded.

"Is it fair to say that your brother is very protective of you?"

Once again, Wendi agreed. The assistant state attorney then reminded her of a statement she'd made to Craig Isom during her five-hour interview the day of the shooting—that her parents were very angry with Dan. Cappleman asked if that had been an accurate statement.

"At that point in time, during our divorce, I do think they were angry with him," Wendi acknowledged. "They felt like he had treated me badly." But she pushed back against the question's underlying premise, that Dan's motion had fueled her family's desire to harm him, telling the prosecutor, "I don't think anyone took that motion very seriously." Cappleman asked whether Dan himself had taken the motion seriously, which prompted an odd giggle from his ex-wife. "If he wrote the motion," Wendi conceded in a light-hearted tone, "he was probably taking it seriously."

The assistant state attorney approached the witness stand with State's Exhibit 80, a collection of four emails Donna had composed during the divorce proceedings. To help the jury understand Donna's reference to "Jibbers," Cappleman had Wendi confirm that Jibbers was a nickname she'd assigned to Dan. She told jurors she came up with that nickname when he was "being really difficult and causing me a lot of pain." Though she didn't intend for it to be derogatory, Wendi admitted to never calling her ex-husband Jibbers to his face.

Surprisingly, however, after taking the time to introduce Donna's emails into evidence, Cappleman didn't ask Wendi a single question about their content—or tone—or show them to the jury. Just like the caustic language contained in the divorce pleadings, jurors would never get to see for themselves the venom Donna had spewed in her lengthy diatribes.

"Did Charlie Adelson like Dan Markel?" the veteran

prosecutor asked, shifting her focus. "And again, I'm referring to the time before his death."

"He would listen to me when I would tell him things I was upset about at the time with the divorce," Wendi answered, another deft misdirection. "So whether he liked him or didn't like him, he certainly was supportive of me."

Cappleman pressed her on the point. "But he never expressed *any* dislike?"

"No," Wendi insisted, shaking her head side to side—an answer belied by numerous pieces of evidence.

"Did he mention hiring a hitman to kill your husband?"

"No," Wendi replied, carefully parsing the prosecutor's words.

Cappleman rephrased her question. "Did he ever joke about he looked into hiring a hitman but buying you a TV as a divorce present would be cheaper?"

Aware the prosecutors had a transcript of her interview with Craig Isom—in which she'd made that exact statement—Wendi conceded the point, sharing with jurors that Charlie "would make jokes that weren't very funny about all kinds of things." Cappleman drilled down deeper, asking, "Did Charlie ever say that he considered all possible options to take care of the problem, the problem being Dan Markel?" Wendi denied that he had. And also denied that her brother had taken her out for a "celebration dinner" following Dan's death.

Dissatisfied with that last answer, the assistant state attorney asked Wendi if she'd vomited while out to eat with Charlie shortly after the murder. To that simple question, the former clinical law professor and novelist provided a long-winded response, sharing how she'd "barely eaten for a full month just out of grief and shock." When she finally went out to a restaurant for the first time, Wendi testified, she wasn't used to having alcohol, "and I threw up at the table, the only time in my life I've done something like that. But it was certainly not a celebration."

Seemingly out of the blue, Cappleman asked the million-dollar question: "Were you involved in any way in a plot to kill

Dan Markel?," a question on which Dan's friends and family members—and the Tally community writ large—had been fixated for five years.

"No," Wendi answered stridently. She told jurors that she didn't know who'd been involved in the homicide, signaling her confidence that the prosecution's theory of how the plot unfolded—and the roles her family members had played—was dead wrong.

Cappleman then pivoted to Katie Magbanua. Wendi shared with the jury that Charlie had introduced her to Katie at a dinner in South Florida. During Father's Day weekend a month before the murder, she testified, she'd also gone to the beach with Katie and one of her friends near her parents' South Beach condo. Cappleman projected an image onto the screen of Wendi lying on her stomach, propped up by her elbows— her right shoulder pressed against Katie's left—the bikini-clad women smiling for the camera. In the photo, Wendi was sandwiched between Katie and her friend Yindra Mascaro.

Wendi explained that she'd "met many, many girlfriends of my brother's over the years. I didn't get any indication that it was a serious relationship." Charlie had never been married, she told jurors, though he'd fathered a child with one of his girlfriends—a boy born in December 2017.

The veteran prosecutor shifted gears again, asking the witness about her liquor purchase the day of the shooting. Wendi confirmed that she'd purchased a brand of bourbon pronounced "bullet." Asked why she'd gone all the way to ABC Liquor on Thomasville Road when other liquor stores were much closer to her home, she responded, "I don't know many liquor stores. That was the first one that popped up."

Cappleman asked whether she had visited the "crime scene" before arriving at the liquor store. Wendi looked at her quizzically, then answered, resolutely, "I did not visit the crime scene."

"You did not pull up to the crime scene tape on Trescott Drive?" Cappleman asked, her tone incredulous, fully aware that, hours after the shooting, Wendi had told Craig Isom she'd done just that.

"No," Wendi insisted, doubling down on her answer. "I was driving on Centerville Road and sometimes I would take a shortcut through Trescott ... But when I was driving on Centerville Road, I saw some sort of tape or obstruction and so, I didn't turn." Though Cappleman could have impeached Wendi with either the transcript or video of her marathon interview with Isom, for some reason she chose not to. Indeed, during the entire trial, jurors would never see a single minute of Wendi's videotaped interview, which by then had been viewed tens of thousands of times on YouTube and had been featured in multiple TV documentaries.

Wendi testified that she'd been the one to schedule the Best Buy repairman to fix her TV on July 18, 2014, even though Donna's telephone number was on the service ticket as the contact number. She acknowledged that her mom had suggested offering Dan one million dollars to persuade him to allow her relocation to South Florida, but told jurors that no such offer had ever been made. Incredibly, Wendi refused to admit that, following Dan's murder, she'd permanently relocated to South Florida—insisting that her living situation over the past five years had been fluid and that she'd been exploring employment options "in many different places."

"Did you change your children's last name from Markel to Adelson?" Cappleman asked abruptly as she neared the end of her direct examination.

"I did," Wendi admitted. She told jurors she'd done so unofficially when registering them for school just a few weeks after Dan's slaying—to "keep them safe"—and that she later legally changed their surname to Adelson. That decision, she explained, was in response to her children's faces being plastered across national TV news broadcasts—unblurred—and their names being bandied about in newspapers. Wendi also admitted to legally changing Ben's middle name, which had honored Dan's deceased maternal grandmother—his Bubbie Helen.

•••

THE DEFENSE LAWYERS had many questions of their own. For some reason, Saam Zangeneh appeared particularly interested in the types of cars the Maestro owned. Wendi testified that she was pretty sure he drove a Mercedes and knew "he had one really fancy car," but couldn't recall whether it was a Porsche or a Ferrari. She agreed with the defense lawyer that her brother was successful, handsome, and had a lot of girlfriends. As to whether he used steroids or illicit drugs, she claimed to have no idea.

Completely out of left field, Zangeneh asked his fellow UM Law alum, "Do you know when Luis Rivera started serving your brother drugs?" — as if actual evidence had been presented of such an arrangement and only the timeline remained in question.

"I don't know anything about that," Wendi responded, clearly taken aback by the insinuation. Barely five minutes into his questioning, Zangeneh passed the witness.

Tara Kawass handled the cross-examination for Katie's defense team. Right out of the gate, she asked Dan's ex-wife if she knew who'd killed him. Wendi told jurors she didn't. Asked if Charlie had "anything to do with killing Dan Markel," Wendi answered with slightly less conviction. "I don't believe so," she testified. If the brother and sister had discussed the subject, Wendi didn't say. Amazingly enough, none of the attorneys bothered to ask.

In response to Kawass's questions, Wendi testified that she didn't follow any media coverage about Dan's murder and advised her parents not to either, claiming she'd received "constant death threats" arising from the news coverage. Not only did she tell Katie's attorney that she hadn't seen Cappleman's opening statement, Wendi professed to being blissfully ignorant of the prosecution's theory that her family members had orchestrated the murder plot — which seemed pretty far-fetched if John Lauro had been doing his job as her lawyer.

Kawass asked Wendi about her decision to divorce Dan. The prosecution witness explained that she'd asked her husband for a divorce several months before leaving the marital home in September 2012. At the time, "he told me that if I— if I tried to get divorced from him, that I could leave with the clothes on my back and that he would take the kids and that I would be penniless." That was why, Wendi testified, she believed it best to announce her decision while her husband was out of town. She admitted that, during the divorce process, both of her parents had shared with her their negative feelings about Dan and at times had even called him names.

Kawass also asked about Jeff Lacasse. His former lover told jurors that their relationship started out casually but had been getting more serious until a "big fight" in late June, "and after that point I didn't really want to be with him anymore." The catalyst for the fight, Wendi recalled, was Lacasse's belief that she'd been cheating on him. She had a vague recollection, Wendi said, about a double date she and Lacasse had been on with Charlie and Katie at a South Florida restaurant in March 2014. That dinner and the time at the beach, she told jurors, were the only occasions she'd ever been in Katie's presence.

Kawass was fully aware that Luis Rivera, in his pretrial statements, had claimed he'd seen Wendi and her two boys walking along Trescott Drive the morning before the shooting—which the defense lawyer knew had to be false because the boys were at preschool that morning. She asked Wendi to confirm that Rivera's account couldn't be correct. Wendi agreed that her kids would have been in preschool that morning and stated that she couldn't recall a single occasion since her separation from Dan in which she'd been walking along Trescott Drive.

Katie's defense lawyer also had Wendi confirm that she was testifying under a grant of immunity, following up by asking, "So that means that anything you say today can't be used against you if the State decides to arrest you later on?"

Upon hearing that question, a smile washed over Wendi's face, as if Kawass had intended it as a joke. Instead of answering, Wendi laughed, telling the attorney in a cavalier tone, "The State isn't going to decide to arrest me." That salty interchange marked the seminal moment of her testimony, if not the entire trial, the one-time law professor broadcasting to law enforcement, prosecutors, and the world at large that she—and perhaps her family as well—were untouchable.

Kawass broached the topic of the payout on Dan's life insurance policy, trying to establish that Wendi and her family had benefited financially from his death. But that wasn't correct, Wendi explained, because the proceeds were "put away for the kids. I've never seen it." Nor, she said, did she have any control over the money, which had been placed in a trust under the control and supervision of Dan's sister, Shelly.

Kawass ended her questioning by asking Wendi about the status of her children's relationship with Dan's parents—both of whom perked up from the gallery, eager to hear their former daughter-in-law's answer. Ruth and Phil Markel hadn't been permitted to see their grandsons in three years, since the State Attorney's Office inadvertently released to the media an email Ruth had sent Cappleman on September 30, 2016—the day before Katie's arrest. Aware that dominoes might begin falling rapidly, Dan's mom had asked the prosecutor to ensure that a "tight plan for emergency placement" of her grandkids was in place in the event Wendi and members of her family were taken into custody.

From the witness stand, Wendi acknowledged that, "Two years after Danny died, I stopped visitation." But also testified that she was ready for visitation to resume and had been "in discussion the last few weeks" with Dan's parents to make that happen. As they listened to those words, Ruth and Phil gasped incredulously, shaking their heads, as the "discussion" their former daughter-in-law was now testifying about was not, in their view at least, a serious effort to allow their visitations with Ben and Lincoln to resume. Indeed, following the trial, they never heard another word on the subject.

When the baton passed back to Cappleman for redirect examination, she had Wendi confirm—a second time—that she personally had prohibited her former in-laws from visiting with their grandsons, which Wendi told the jury was because of "what they did."

At the behest of one of the jurors, Judge Hankinson asked Wendi to elaborate. "Well, they were allowed to see the grandchildren for two full years," she explained. "And I used to cook meals for them and arrange playdates. We had sleepovers. And then I found out that Ruth Markel had reached out to a foster care agency to try to place my children with that agency. And I became worried that they were trying to take my children away from me. And so, after that time, I didn't feel a level of trust that they could spend time with the kids. I was afraid they were trying to take them from me."

During Cappleman's follow-up questioning, however, Wendi admitted that she knew Ruth's email seeking possible emergency placement of the children was premised on her belief that Wendi might be arrested along with her parents and brother. The prosecutor pressed her: "So they were not trying to take your children unless there was an event where you were unable to care for them?"

For the first time in her testimony, Wendi became visibly agitated, pushing back against the premise of Cappleman's question. "Because there's no event in which I would be unable to care for them," she testified—again, believing that her own arrest was an abject impossibility—"that feels like trying to take away my children."

The lawyers' and jurors' questions now fully answered, Wendi Jill Adelson stepped down from the witness stand. With John Lauro by her side, she walked back out through the courtroom doors, where reporters greeted her with their own questions. The high school valedictorian and Truman Scholar put her head down and continued marching forward, ignoring each and every one. In a couple hours' time, she'd be on a plane back to South Florida, where three people with a vested interest in her courtroom adventure were sure to have questions of their own.

• • •

CAPPLEMAN CALLED TPD OFFICER Bill Brannon to establish that Wendi's burgundy Honda Odyssey had driven down Trescott Drive, toward her old home, shortly after the shooting. Brannon told jurors he'd arrived at the crime scene while Dan was being removed from his vehicle and loaded into an ambulance. Yellow tape stretched across the road at two locations, he testified, three to four houses on either side of Dan's. From his patrol car, he guarded the northern perimeter, closest to Centerville Road.

The assistant state attorney showed him a photograph of Wendi's vehicle. Brannon confirmed that it appeared similar to a minivan that pulled up to the northern crime-scene boundary, where he was stationed, and then made a three-point turn, doubling back toward Centerville Road. He also testified that the crime-scene tape wouldn't have been visible from Centerville Road—due to the considerable distance and curvature of the street. In other words, that Wendi's testimony about having seen crime-scene tape while driving along Centerville Road wasn't remotely possible.

The law enforcement officer also told jurors that whoever had been driving that minivan would have had a clear view of Dan's driveway before reversing course and heading away from the crime scene. And that the driver would have been able to see marked patrol cars just outside Dan's house.

"Okay. And did this person in the van get out or attempt to interact with you at all or ask you anything?" Cappleman asked.

"No, ma'am."

"And would your vehicle have been readily visible to the person in the van?"

"Yes," Brannon responded. "I had the emergency lights activated."

• • •

WENDI'S EX-BOYFRIEND JEFF LACASSE took the stand next. Cappleman had the bespectacled, bearded professor—and Dan Markel look-alike—focus on his interactions with Wendi on June 4, 2014, the day Rivera and Garcia departed on their first excursion to Tally. Lacasse told jurors he met Wendi at RedEye Coffee early that afternoon to discuss why she'd bailed on their planned trip to visit his parents in California. That same evening, he recounted, Wendi was a "nervous wreck," so much so that he had to leave her house to purchase Pepto-Bismol. But she wouldn't open up to him about what was causing her such anxiety.

Between that tidbit and Officer Brannon's testimony about Wendi's drive to the edge of the crime scene, Cappleman clearly wanted jurors to speculate that Wendi had advance knowledge that something was about to happen to her ex-husband—both in early June and in mid-July.

In contrast to Wendi's testimony that she'd been relieved when Judge Hobbs ruled against her on her relocation petition—and was happy to remain in Tally—Lacasse testified that Wendi was actually "quite bitter about it." He also told jurors that, five days before the murder—timing he hadn't revealed in his initial TPD interviews—"Wendi and I were speaking, and she asked me if she could share something with me confidentially ... She said that Charlie had explored 'all options' to take care of the problem, and that he had looked into having Professor Markel killed." Wendi had even mentioned the cost of a hitman, which Lacasse recalled being either $15,000 or $50,000. She told him at the time that Charlie had been exploring this option during the summer of 2013, after her attempted relocation was foreclosed by the family court judge's ruling.

Though their relationship ended just prior to Dan's murder, Lacasse testified, Wendi actually took his call a couple of weeks later. During their conversation, she confided in him that she and her brother had gone to what Charlie labeled a "celebration dinner"—at which she vomited.

Toward the end of his direct examination, Lacasse left

the distinct impression that he believed his ex-girlfriend had deliberately arranged the murder to coincide with a trip she knew he was about to take to Tennessee. Had he not changed his plans at the last minute to depart on Thursday evening rather than Friday morning, Lacasse testified, he'd have driven right by Betton Hills almost precisely when the shooting occurred and continued driving all the way to Tennessee—as if he were hightailing it out of state. He let jurors know that Wendi's suggestion to Craig Isom that he be considered a suspect had, in his view, been an effort to frame him for Dan's murder.

During his cross-examination, sticking to his theme that Rivera had been supplying drugs to Charlie, Zangeneh asked the professor if he'd observed Wendi's brother doing cocaine the night they were together in South Florida. Lacasse testified that he hadn't. As for his discussion with Wendi about Charlie's interest in hiring a hitman, Lacasse told Zangeneh, "My stomach kind of flipped. It was a chilling statement." He also revealed that "preceding that was a discussion that if anything ever happened to Danny, she would move to Miami."

DeCoste's questions delved deeper into Charlie's personality and relationships. Lacasse agreed with the defense attorney that Wendi's brother "seemed like somebody that hung out on both sides of the tracks," which he found to be "almost a braggadocio kind of thing." He told jurors that Charlie described his gym friends as "nefarious." As for the topic of hiring a hitman, DeCoste had Lacasse confirm that the timing of when Charlie and Wendi supposedly had that discussion—in the summer of 2013—would have been before Charlie had even met Katie.

Oddly enough, some of the best questions to Lacasse were posed by jurors. One was whether Wendi had indicated she wanted to relocate in order "to have the children full-time." Lacasse responded that, by the time they were dating, Wendi already knew that relocation was "no longer a possibility. But the other side of that coin was how unhappy she was in Tallahassee"—and how frustrated she was by the existing child custody arrangement. The divorce and custody battle, he said, were topics that Wendi raised consistently throughout their relationship.

•••

ASSISTANT STATE ATTORNEY Anna Norris called TPD Sergeant Chris Corbitt to the stand, one of a handful of times he'd testify for the prosecution. He'd later serve as the State's key witness outlining what investigators had learned from cell tower data about the movements of Rivera, Garcia, and Katie in the days before and after the homicide. On this occasion, however, he testified about Wendi's movements following the shooting. Dan's ex-wife, he explained, had encountered the roadblock on Trescott Drive between 12:35 p.m. and 12:45 p.m. Using a map projected onto the screen, he also demonstrated how far out of her way Wendi had gone to purchase bourbon at ABC Liquor. Market Square Liquors, he told jurors, was located in the very same shopping center as Mozaik, the restaurant where Wendi had met her friends for lunch.

With testimony surrounding Wendi's potential involvement in the homicide now complete, the prosecution team was finally poised to call its star witness: a short-statured, heavily tattooed, lifelong criminal who—in his navy-blue uniform, handcuffs, and leg shackles—was being closely guarded by a bevy of armed sheriff's deputies just footsteps from Courtroom 3G. The outcome of the entire trial hinged on what jurors would make of his testimony. As the prosecutors held their breath—and the defense lawyers licked their proverbial chops—King Tato was led through a back door onto the grand stage he'd command for the next two days.

21.

Blue Jumpsuit

THOUGH HE WASN'T PROVIDED a fancy suit and professorial eyewear like his lifelong best friend, the Luis Rivera deputies led to his seat at the witness stand barely resembled the man in the blazing-red jumpsuit who'd spilled his guts to investigators three years earlier. He'd lost considerable weight. His black hair and beard were no longer bushy and unkempt. Rather, his hair was now neatly cropped, close to his scalp—much like Garcia's—his beard relegated to faint, thin strips reaching down his face, joining in a small patch of black fuzz beneath his chin.

The former *primero* of the Latin Kings' North Miami tribe—now Inmate 07850-104 at a maximum-security federal penitentiary in Tucson, Arizona—had been transported clear across the country for his big day in court. His testimony before the jury would mark the sixth time he'd been sworn to tell the truth about Dan Markel's murder, following the two occasions at the Jefferson County Jail with Craig Isom and Pat Sanford, his appearance before the grand jury in Tally, and depositions by Garcia's and Katie's defense lawyers, one of which had taken place in Arizona. Though all of that prior testimony made Rivera a very experienced witness, it also created numerous inconsistencies resulting in part from his memory fading as the years passed by.

To anyone unfamiliar with his backstory, the man on the witness stand hardly seemed to fit the part of a cold-blooded killer. He was so soft-spoken that Judge Hankinson had to instruct him, on several occasions, to move closer to the mic. Though his English was somewhat broken, it was surprisingly coherent considering his limited formal education, his answers articulated with a distinct Puerto Rican accent. As he testified, Rivera was unfailingly polite to whomever was posing questions, answering "yes, ma'am" or "no, sir," sometimes asking the lawyers to "repeat that question please." On the few occasions a curse word inadvertently slipped through his lips, he quickly gathered himself and apologized.

His illiteracy was abundantly apparent from the outset. Asked to spell out his name as he introduced himself, Rivera ticked off the letters "L-I-U-S," without anyone seeming to notice his obvious mistake. The lawyers were frequently frustrated and stymied by his inability to read, unable to show him written documents when they wanted to impeach him or refresh his recollection. Yet somehow his lack of formal education actually made him a more sympathetic witness. Indeed, as he testified, Rivera was so pleasant and good-natured—charming almost—even those familiar with his backstory could easily have forgotten that he was a hardened, lifelong criminal.

Georgia Cappleman needed only an hour to help her star witness hash out the basic facts surrounding the murder and establish each defendant's role. Rivera told the jury that, as far as he understood, his best friend Garcia was legally married to Katie. Though he was obviously well acquainted with her, Rivera testified that he didn't have an independent relationship with Katie because "that was Garcia's woman." But the couple was "on and off," and at the time of the murder, he testified, "she was dating the dentist." The assistant state attorney showed Rivera a photo of himself and his own baby mama, Jessica Rodriguez, together with Garcia and Katie. She also projected onto the screen a photo of Rivera and Garcia, side-by-side, to demonstrate their significant height difference.

The diminutive Puerto Rican told jurors he stood a mere 5'4" whereas Garcia was 6'1".

In early June 2014, Rivera testified, Garcia informed him that he had a job to do in Tallahassee and asked if he'd ride along. He didn't ask any questions about the nature of the job, Rivera explained, because Garcia was his best friend and he trusted him—"whatever he wanted to do, I would have rolled." Garcia told him he'd earn $35,000 for his participation in what Rivera initially believed would be a robbery. But "like halfway there, we just— he said, we are going to have to kill the man for some kids." When Cappleman asked what that meant to him, the former gang leader responded, "It is for a lady. I guess the lady wanted her kids back." On the way to Tally, Garcia showed him a piece of paper containing a picture of Dan Markel.

"The guy that y'all ended up killing?" the prosecutor asked.

"Yes, ma'am," her star witness replied.

On their first trip, Rivera testified, Garcia rented the car and did the driving. Yet when they were pulled over in Gainesville for driving 90 in a 70-mile-per-hour zone, he acknowledged, he—not Garcia—was behind the wheel. Rivera explained that they'd "switched for a minute" because Garcia "told me to drive." Though he told jurors that he and Garcia had arrived in Tally between 5:00 a.m. and 6:00 a.m., the traffic ticket Cappleman projected onto the screen revealed they'd been pulled over at 9:12 a.m.—still some 150 miles shy of their destination.

Rivera testified that Garcia had between $2,000 and $5,000 with him on that first trip, which he assumed he'd received "from the people that hired him." Garcia, he noted, hadn't specifically told him who that was. While at the hotel room they rented, they interacted with a Black man named Shoddrick Nobles, whom neither had ever met before. Rivera told jurors that he and Garcia brought two .38-caliber handguns on the first trip. Asked if they'd planned to commit the murder on that trip, he answered, "We was supposed to, but we couldn't find him." Though they followed Dan "all the way to a daycare, we kept losing him." Garcia was driving. "By the time we made a circle," Rivera testified, "I guess he had pulled out and left."

"Who was supposed to be the shooter on this first trip?" Cappleman asked.

"I was going to be the shooter," Rivera acknowledged.

"Did you make a suggestion to change the plan from shooting to something else?"

"Yeah. I found out— for the kids. I ain't going to shoot nobody in front of no kids." He suggested to his pal that they "go rob the lady"—meaning Wendi—instead. Garcia made clear they had no choice, telling him, "We have got to go take care of Markel." Yet they returned to Miami having done neither.

Eventually, Garcia called him and told him the time had come to return to Tally "to finish that job." This time, Rivera testified, he was the one who rented the car—a green Prius. Cappleman projected the rental agreement onto the screen and walked Rivera through the document—having him confirm that he used the word "brother" to refer to Garcia. Rivera told jurors that Garcia had actually been with him, waiting outside in another car, while he paid $300 in cash for the rental vehicle. The lead prosecutor then projected the registration form from the Budget Inn onto the screen, pointing out Rivera's name and address.

She then pivoted to the events of July 17, the day before the shooting. Rivera testified that he and Garcia "woke up, took a ride toward Markel's house that Thursday morning, and went around the house. As soon as we went around the house, we came back around, and we seen a lady walking through" who was on the sidewalk with two children. He was convinced she'd seen them as well, telling jurors, "I was driving, and as I looked in my rearview, I seen her looking."

He asked Garcia why the woman was looking at them. "That's the lady with the kids, man," his friend replied. Rivera was concerned about her having spotted them, and even more worried when he saw her making a call through the rearview mirror. Garcia then called Katie, he said. "The lady just seen you," she told him. "Y'all get out of there."

Cappleman abruptly changed the subject, not wanting Rivera to dwell further on the "Wendi sighting"—which she knew was incorrect. Records from Creative Preschool established that Ben and Lincoln were in school that morning, not on Trescott Drive. Indeed, the lead prosecutor would later stipulate to that fact, making it clear for jurors that her star witness was confused, mistaken, or even fibbing about this important detail.

Cappleman had Rivera confirm that he'd posted a picture of an owl on Instagram. Almost immediately after he did, he testified, Katie called Garcia, causing his friend to demand that he "take that shit down." He also confirmed that he and Garcia met up with Shoddrick Nobles again on the second trip and arranged to buy drugs from him. While that was going on, he testified, "I was driving, and Garcia pulled a gun out and shot a hole right through the car." He explained how Garcia and Nobles had gone to Auto Zone together to purchase "a little piece of hose to come fix it up." Nobles, he said, helped them get a different hotel room later that evening.

The next morning, the longtime gang leader told the jury, he and his best friend sat in the Prius at a park near Dan's home—with Garcia in the passenger seat. Once they saw his vehicle approach, they followed him to the daycare and then to his gym.

"What happened once Mr. Markel came out of the gym?" Cappleman asked.

"We followed him all the way back to his house," Rivera replied. He told jurors they eventually separated when Dan pulled into Betton Hills from one direction and he drove around to enter the subdivision from the opposite direction—with the two ultimately heading directly toward one another on Trescott Drive. Dan then pulled into his driveway, Rivera recounted, "and I pulled right behind him." He noted that Dan was on the phone.

"As soon as we pulled in," he continued, "Garcia jumped out— jumped out of the car and went around ... in front of the car, right behind his car and in front of the car I was driving. Went to the driver's side and shot him."

"He shot Mr. Markel?"

"Yes, ma'am."

"How many times?"

"Twice."

"Did you actually see Mr. Garcia shoot Mr. Markel?"

"Of course." He told the jury that the gun Garcia was holding was "just inches away" from his intended victim when he shot Dan.

"Do you see the person in the courtroom who shot Mr. Markel?" the assistant state attorney asked.

"Yes, ma'am."

"Could you please point that person out and describe what he is wearing?"

Rivera pointed in Garcia's direction, telling jurors that he was "wearing a tux"—apparently unable to discern the difference between formalwear and an ordinary suit.

Cappleman asked what had happened to the murder weapon. Rivera told the jury that Garcia had dumped it in a lake, near a bridge, on the way back to Miami. Though he'd ridden around with law enforcement officers after turning State's evidence—trying to locate the discarded firearm—Rivera told jurors they weren't able to find it.

The veteran prosecutor saved her most impressive exhibit for last—the ATM surveillance camera image showing the lifelong best friends in the rented Prius the evening of the murder. Rivera pointed to himself in the driver's seat and Garcia, in his long-sleeve white shirt, in the passenger seat.

The State's lead counsel then backtracked to Garcia's call with Katie during the return trip to Miami. With the windows rolled up, Rivera testified, her voice was loud enough for him to hear through the receiver on Garcia's cellphone. He recalled Garcia telling his "wife," "'Hey, the shit is done.' She goes, 'I already know it is done.'... And then we asked for our money. 'Like, where the money at?' She said, 'You will get it tomorrow.'"

Cappleman asked if he knew where Katie was getting the money from. "Not really," Rivera replied, "but we know the lady—Wendi—was paying it." Garcia told him the total amount being paid was $100,000, of which he was keeping $40,000 and Rivera was being paid $35,000. The remaining $25,000, he testified, was for Katie.

The morning after the murder, while he was at a barbershop in Miami Beach, Rivera told jurors, he received a call from Katie. "Where is Tuto?" she asked. Garcia, he said, was with his girlfriend, Shrimp, a stripper. Katie wanted to know who was coming to get the money. Once he located his friend, Rivera testified, Garcia and Katie brought his portion of the money to the apartment he shared with Jessica Rodriguez. He drove straight there from the barbershop.

When he arrived, Garcia and his "wife" were already there. The money, he explained, was in a clear plastic bag inside a brown paper bag—which Garcia handed to him while Katie looked on. All of the money was in $100 bills and was stapled together in stacks of $1,000. Rivera told the jury that he didn't count the money because he trusted Garcia, his best friend. While the two sat together in his car—outside their baby mamas' presence—Garcia gave him an extra $2,000.

Cappleman closed her direct examination with a series of questions focused on Katie's role in the murder plot. "So Garcia hired you to do a murder?" she asked. "Didn't he?"

"Yes, ma'am."

"And who hired him?"

"The Adelson family."

"I am sorry?"

"The Wendi family."

"Wendi's family hired him?"

"Yeah."

"And how was Wendi's family connected to Sigfredo Garcia?"

"Because Katie, Katie was dating the dentist."

"Okay. Did Katie know about the murder?"

"Yes, ma'am."

"Did Katie have a role in hiring Sigfredo Garcia?"

"Yes, ma'am."

"How do you know that?"

"Because he told me."

"Do you see the person in the courtroom that you say hired Sigfredo Garcia to do this homicide?"

"The only one I see is Katie."

"All right. Would you please point her out and describe what she's wearing?"

The prosecution's star witness pointed directly at Katie Magbanua, noting she was wearing gray and black. Having identified her and the role she played, Rivera had checked all the boxes he'd been flown in from Arizona to fill in. Cappleman passed him to the defense lawyers for what was certain to be a roller-coaster ride through cross-examination. She and Anna Norris braced themselves and held their breath.

• • •

SAAM ZANGENEH'S QUESTIONING was more akin to a college hazing ritual than a carefully choreographed cross-examination—lasting two grueling hours. A good 30 minutes were devoted to Rivera's leadership role in the Latin Kings and his long history of drug dealing. When Zangeneh began asking about the agreement that led to his federal racketeering conviction, Judge Hankinson finally cut him off—sustaining his own objection—imploring the defense lawyer to move on to more relevant topics. Yet despite the judge's admonition, Zangeneh didn't ask his first question about Dan Markel's murder until 40 minutes into his cross-examination.

When he later meandered back to even more questions about the Latin Kings, Rivera couldn't resist asking what every juror and spectator had to be wondering: "Are we here for the murder case or the Latin King case?"

"I think it's the same thing," the former prosecutor retorted, drawing the ire of a judge who, like everyone else in the courtroom, was growing increasingly impatient with his approach.

The defense lawyer finally scored a point by having Rivera confirm that, for merely tagging along with Garcia on the second trip to Tally, he'd been paid the exact same $35,000 he'd been promised on the first trip—when he was the one who was supposed to shoot and kill Dan Markel. Zangeneh found that notion fairly incredible, and hoped jurors would conclude that Rivera was paid what he'd originally been promised because he *did* pull the trigger on the second trip.

Garcia's attorney also spent considerable time trying to convince jurors that Rivera was only feigning illiteracy, noting that his cellphone records revealed nearly 8,000 text messages during a six-month period. Yet the State's star witness had a ready answer—that iPhones possess technology that allows users to dictate outgoing texts and have incoming texts read to them.

Zangeneh was successful in getting King Tato to admit to numerous inconsistencies between his courtroom testimony and his prior statements. One glaring inconsistency was that he'd previously told investigators he didn't drive at all during the first trip and received the speeding ticket during the second. Another was his testimony that he and Garcia had arrived in the early morning hours on the first trip, though the time indicated on the traffic ticket—9:12 a.m.—established they hadn't arrived until closer to lunchtime. A third was that he'd told the investigators he knew prior to leaving on the first trip that the "job" was to commit a murder, rather than a robbery, though he was now testifying he didn't know that until halfway to Tally.

The defense attorney did his level best to cast doubt on the reliability and accuracy of Rivera's testimony, forcing him to reveal that he'd been diagnosed as bipolar and schizophrenic and that he'd been doing cocaine since the age of 15. Another fruitful area for Zangeneh was the illogic of Garcia having done anything at all to assist Charlie Adelson, the rich playboy who was sleeping with his "wife" and preventing him from reuniting with her. Rivera readily agreed that Garcia was livid with Charlie for dating Katie, so much so that he could "see the anger in his face."

Zangeneh also tried to peddle his theory that Charlie had hired Rivera to do the murder because the gang leader had supposedly been his longtime drug dealer. But Cappleman cut him off at the pass, objecting each time he tried to ask whether Rivera had ever sold drugs to Charlie—objections the judge promptly sustained. "Can we approach sidebar judge?" Zangeneh pleaded, hoping to convince him of the relevance of his questions.

"No. *Move on*," Judge Hankinson demanded, his patience wearing thin.

Late in his questioning, the defense attorney returned to his Latin Kings theme yet again, prompting a testy exchange with the prosecution witness. "Why you keep saying Latin Kings?" Rivera fired back, very animated for the first time. "It ain't got nothing to do with this. You wrong. You're wrong man. This ain't got nothing to do with no Latin Kings. This has to do with me and Garcia. No Latin Kings."

Zangeneh did plow some new territory with a pair of letters Rivera had written Cappleman from jail—apparently in his own handwriting—both dated November 3, 2016, about a month after he'd turned State's evidence. The judge allowed Garcia's lawyer to project the letters onto the screen so jurors could see them. "I told you everything you wanted to know," Rivera had written the prosecutor in the first one. "I helped you break the case." In both letters, he begged Cappleman to help him get moved out of protective custody—solitary confinement—and back into the general population of the Leon County Jail. The isolation, he told jurors, was becoming unbearable.

Though Zangeneh was using the letters in part to demonstrate that the lifelong criminal wasn't actually illiterate, Rivera testified that he dictated the letters to another inmate, and then copied that inmate's writing in his own hand. When Zangeneh tried to read the second letter aloud, Judge Hankinson's frustration boiled over. "We've done this enough," he said tersely. "Put the letter down."

More than 90 minutes into his questioning, Garcia's attorney finally started asking questions about the July 2014 trip at the heart of the case—a subject he'd been avoiding like the Bubonic plague. By then, however, the judge refused to let him propound any questions remotely similar to ones Cappleman had already asked in her direct examination. "We've done that," he groused. "Something new Mr. Zangeneh."

"On the day in question," the defense lawyer tried again, "what time did you start following Mr. Markel?" The judge stopped him in his tracks again, his irritation mounting. "*Something new* I said Mr. Zangeneh."

Zangeneh did break a bit of new ground by having Rivera confirm that his buddy Tuto got out of the Prius while the two were waiting in the parking lot of Dan's gym—to urinate on a bush. Yet that tidbit only confirmed that his client was with Rivera while they were stalking Dan. Perhaps not the wisest testimony to elicit.

Zangeneh ended with his strongest point—though it was too little and far too late—having Rivera concede that he'd avoided a possible death sentence by turning State's evidence. At which point, much to the delight of everyone assembled, the one-time Persian Prosecutor announced that he had no further questions. If his goals had been to sow seeds of doubt about his client's role in the murder, and to eviscerate Rivera's credibility as a witness, Zangeneh hadn't come close to achieving either. Though the needle had certainly moved during his cross-examination, it was likely now closer to Sigfredo Garcia's conviction than to his acquittal.

•••

BY COMPARISON, TARA KAWASS'S cross-examination, though also two hours in length, was more disciplined, methodical—and successful. She was able to get Rivera to confirm several key defense themes on which she and DeCoste had been harping: that Katie had been earning money at nightclubs after kicking her "husband" out of their home; that, despite their breakup, the two were in constant communication because of their kids; and that it was "common knowledge" that Katie had been working for the dentist—Charlie Adelson.

She had the prosecution witness elaborate on Garcia's intense jealousy of Charlie and his anger over the periodontist dating his "wife," sharing with jurors how his friend wanted to run them both over with his truck when he was spying on them as they ate together at a restaurant. "I should just take this truck and smash them and run their asses over while they're eating," Rivera told jurors Garcia had said at the time. He testified that he had to restrain his friend from acting out on his anger.

Another point Kawass used Rivera to make was that both his and Garcia's arrest warrants had been released to the media in June 2016, long before Katie's arrest—and that the State's theory about her client's involvement in the murder was "all over the media." Yet, despite that, she didn't flee.

Like Zangeneh, Kawass pointed out numerous inconsistencies among Rivera's various statements, including a variety of different descriptions he'd provided about when he learned the job in Tallahassee would involve a murder. Rivera claimed that he didn't recall ever telling investigators that he knew the actual nature of the job before leaving for Tally the first time. "I thought we was going to rob somebody," he insisted, telling jurors that he didn't know the job involved a murder until after getting into the car. "We spoke about it going up there."

As for why he'd previously stated he didn't drive during that first trip, he explained, "I thought I got the ticket on the Prius," holding his hands up in an expression of *mea culpa*. "I was confused."

Kawass scored big with a seemingly innocuous question, asking the blue-uniformed witness, "Isn't it true that you knew Markel put his hand up to his face?"

"Yeah," Rivera acknowledged, without realizing the import of his concession. Had he been seated in the driver's seat of the

Prius at the time of the shooting—as he claimed—there was no possible way he could have seen Dan hold his hand up to his face when Garcia pointed the gun at him. If Rivera truly knew that—and wasn't merely parroting what Garcia had told him—he, not Garcia, had to be the shooter.

Kawass unearthed another interesting nugget when she had Rivera confirm what he told her at his March 2018 deposition in Arizona—that he believed his best friend had made another trip to Tally, without him.

"But you never mentioned that in any of your other statements, did you?" she asked.

"Nobody asked me but you," Rivera explained.

Kawass finally turned her attention to the money drop, the most damaging piece of evidence Rivera had supplied against her client. Having testified on direct examination that Katie had called him that morning looking for her "husband," she asked Rivera if the phone records would confirm that—knowing full well they revealed that the first call that morning was from Rivera to Katie, not from her to him. Yet Rivera told jurors he was sure she'd called him first.

As for the money itself, Kawass asked Rivera if he'd pulled the $35,000 out of the bag while on the way out the door of his apartment—as he'd told Zangeneh during his deposition. Rivera testified that was exactly what happened.

"But Jessica will be able to tell us that, right?" Kawass asked, almost daring Cappleman to call Rodriguez as a corroborating witness. Rivera told jurors he was sure his baby mama would recall that, as well as what the brown paper bag looked like.

Kawass scored more points questioning Rivera about the sequence of events starting with when he arrived at Rodriguez's apartment that morning. He initially testified that he couldn't recall if Katie was inside the apartment or outside when he got there. But moments later, he told the jury she was already inside, and greeted him by saying, "What's up Tato?"

"Isn't it true that Katie said nothing else in your presence?" the defense attorney asked.

"I left," Rivera replied.

"Okay. So you can't testify to any statements about Katie saying she even knew what was in that bag, right?"

"She ain't never said nothing," he agreed.

Rivera acknowledged that he didn't deposit his $35,000 in the bank because he didn't want to leave a trace the police could find. Instead, he stashed money at his sister Maria's house, telling jurors he put it in a sealed, "vanilla" envelope. Asked why he hadn't left the envelope with Rodriguez, Rivera explained, "She'll steal that shit. Excuse my language." But he did buy his baby mama a car, he testified, and gave her $2,000 to pay her rent.

"So she'll be able to tell us that—that you gave her money?" Kawass asked, again baiting Cappleman. Rivera again told jurors that Rodriguez would be able to corroborate his testimony.

Her cross-examination now complete, Tara Kawass resumed her seat—satisfied she'd achieved her primary goal of casting serious doubt on the only direct evidence the State could offer against her client. And if jurors didn't believe Rivera's statements about Katie's role in the murder, there was precious little chance, Kawass believed, they'd convict her based solely on the circumstantial evidence.

Cappleman's redirect examination was mercifully brief—just a few questions. She asked Rivera why he ended up not being the one who pulled the trigger.

"Because that man had kids and I didn't want to do it," he told the jury, his pretense of humanity bringing his day and a half of testimony to a close. As deputies led him away from the witness stand, Judge Hankinson quipped to the weary jurors—stating the obvious—"So, not quite as exciting as it looks on TV, huh?"

• • •

THE PROSECUTION CALLED a handful of witnesses to corroborate various portions of Rivera's testimony. The first, Jonathan Grossman, a detective with the Miami-Dade Police

Department, had been asked to inspect the Toyota Prius Rivera had rented from Hybrid Auto Rentals—later purchased by a locksmith and painted white—to determine if a bullet hole existed in the floorboard. Sure enough, Grossman found a hole in the passenger floorboard directly above the fuel line—just as Rivera had described. Cappleman showed jurors a photo of the hole with a lengthy wooden dowel sticking through it.

Keith Leland, who worked at Creative Preschool, told jurors he recalled Dan Markel entering the side entrance of the building the morning of the shooting. While Dan took his children to an outdoor deck, Leland testified, he happened to be looking out a window when he noticed a greenish-silver Prius parked in front of the building.

The State's next witness, Shoddrick Nobles, was a bearded Black man—bald as a billiard ball—who spoke in a deep, baritone voice. A shiny glint from the overhead courtroom lighting reflected off the gold crowns that comprised his upper row of teeth. He'd actually been living in his car when he first met Rivera and Garcia. Unlike Rivera, he made no apologies for the profanity that littered his testimony.

Nobles told jurors that he ran into the two Hispanic men outside their room at the Budget Inn, having never met them before. Garcia asked if he could find him some cocaine. Nobles told jurors he returned with $40 worth of cocaine and partied with his new friends in their room. About a month later, he recounted, the same two men flagged him down on the side of the road, telling him they were having car trouble; they asked for a ride to an auto parts store. In contrast to Rivera's testimony, Nobles testified that he took both men to Advance Auto Parts to purchase a hose. After Garcia fixed the car, the out-of-towners asked him to get them a room at the Rodeway Inn and gave him $60 for his troubles.

Cappleman showed Nobles State's Exhibits 85 and 86—each one a collection of eight-by-ten color photos of Hispanic men investigators had shown him in January 2016 to determine whether he could identify Rivera and Garcia. As he did then, Nobles picked Rivera's photo out of Exhibit 85 and Garcia's photo out of Exhibit 86. The assistant state attorney also showed him a document from the Rodeway Inn confirming that he'd registered for a room from July 17 to July 18, 2014. Though his testimony wasn't a perfect match to Rivera's, it was pretty darn close.

June Umchinda was one of Charlie Adelson's many ex-girlfriends—her relationship with him commencing about a year after Katie's ended. Umchinda finally broke up with the periodontist in June 2017, upon learning he'd impregnated another woman during their relationship. The State had subpoenaed her to share some of her observations during the time she stayed with Charlie at his waterfront home. But it was evident from the outset that she was none too happy to have been dragged hundreds of miles to testify in a murder case about a complete stranger. She appeared most uncomfortable on the witness stand, her answers both evasive and contradictory.

Umchinda recalled that Charlie had been acting "stressed and irrational" shortly after news of Garcia's and Rivera's arrests broke. Because the media was "tracing things back to him," she told the jury, "he was nervous and worried and just not himself." He also slept with a gun.

She testified that she'd observed large amounts of money lying around Charlie's house, which he kept in a refrigerator-sized safe in his bedroom. But Umchinda resisted sharing any additional details, forcing Cappleman to confront her with the transcript of her July 2018 interview with Special Agent Sanford. The prosecutor shared with jurors that, during that interview, Umchinda had said that "there was always stacks of hundreds, like a lot of cash in there ... thousands and thousands of dollars." And further, that all of Charlie's money was "like stapled together, the hundreds in bundles." Those recollections aligned perfectly with Rivera's testimony about the $37,000 he'd received for his role in the murder.

•••

DESPITE TARA KAWASS'S repeated efforts to goad the prosecution into calling Jessica Rodriguez as a witness, Cappleman didn't take the bait. Which was surprising, considering that Rivera's baby mama could have corroborated several key aspects of his testimony.

During her interview with Isom and Sanford the day after Katie's arrest, Rodriguez told the pair that Garcia and his "wife" had come over her apartment not long after the June 27, 2014 birth of her baby Lulu. When Garcia walked through the front door that day, he asked her if Rivera was there. She told him he wasn't. Garcia then handed her a brown plastic grocery bag that had something bulky inside that felt like a brick. The bag was double knotted at the top and very heavy. "This is for Tato," Garcia told her at the time.

Initially, Katie remained in the parking lot, in the driver's seat of her Mazda SUV. Rodriguez told Isom and Sanford that she walked out to the balcony and yelled out, "You're not going to come up and see your niece?" With that prompting, Katie came upstairs and reached out for Lulu, but said she couldn't stay long because she and her "husband" were in a rush. Rodriguez recalled asking her if she was aware of the contents inside the bag. "I don't know," Katie told her. "They're stupid." At that point, she told the investigators, Garcia got on the phone with Rivera, telling him, "Yo, I just came to your house and I dropped it off with Jessica."

Rodriguez told the law enforcement officers that Katie and Garcia had departed before her own baby daddy arrived. Rivera "flew" home, she said—preventing her from peeking inside the bag even though she wanted to. He grabbed the bag the second he walked in. Though he didn't initially tell her what was inside, he later told her it was "money and drugs."

In her deposition seven months before trial, however, Rodriguez had a somewhat different recollection, testifying that Rivera had arrived home before Katie and Garcia left, and that the three left her apartment together—all fully consistent with Rivera's testimony before the jury.

Though there were certainly discrepancies between her

2016 statement and 2019 deposition—as well as differences between her recollection of key events and Rivera's—had she been called as a witness, Jessica Rodriguez could have confirmed that, in July 2014, Garcia had come to her home with a heavy bag that felt like it contained a brick, called Rivera and told him to hightail it home, and that Katie was inside the apartment together with her "husband" and the heavy bag.

Yet in the chess match the trial had become, Cappleman made the strategic decision that Rodriguez's conflicting versions of the money drop made calling her as a witness too risky. Thus, jurors would be forced to rely solely on Rivera's account of what had transpired that morning, without any corroboration from his baby mama. Which may have been precisely what Kawass actually wanted each time she dared Cappleman to call Rodriguez as a witness—employing reverse psychology on the State's lead counsel to sheer perfection.

22.

Mountain of Evidence

AS THE TRIAL ENTERED its second week, the prosecution team shifted gears, focusing almost exclusively on the circumstantial evidence tying Katie to the murder plot. The State subpoenaed one of her best friends, Yindra Mascaro, and flew her in from Miami. Unlike June Umchinda, Mascaro didn't display the slightest discomfort or evasiveness as Assistant State Attorney Anna Norris walked her through her testimony—even though her recollection of key events hardly resembled the picture Katie's lawyers had been painting throughout the trial.

Mascaro told jurors she'd grown up in the same Miami neighborhood as Katie, Garcia, and Rivera. Though they'd lost touch while Katie was in college in Orlando, the two had become reacquainted at Mascaro's 25th birthday party in October 2011, and remained close friends thereafter. Katie was even godmother to her daughter.

Norris led Mascaro through Katie's job history, fleshing out a resume that included short stints at the front desk at SoFi Dental and as a bartender and bottle girl at two South Florida nightclubs, Club Fate and Hollywood Live. Mascaro told jurors she'd been working at Hollywood Live alongside Katie until her friend quit in May 2014 because she was "over the club scene already." She was pretty sure of that timing, Mascaro said, recalling that Katie had quit a couple of months before she had. She testified she was certain that she herself had quit in July 2014, when she learned she'd become pregnant with her second child.

Mascaro also shared with the jury the timeline of Katie's relationship with Charlie Adelson, which began while Katie was working at SoFi Dental in 2013—where the handsome periodontist would come to perform extractions and implants. Charlie, Mascaro testified, owned a nice waterfront home in Fort Lauderdale and had a lot of "toys," including a limousine, multiple vehicles, jet skis, and a boat. In other words, his lifestyle couldn't have contrasted more with the one led by Katie's "husband."

Mascaro told jurors that Charlie had arranged for Katie's October 2014 breast augmentation through a plastic surgeon he knew, Dr. Roudner. She testified that, to the best of her knowledge, Katie never worked for either Charlie or the Adelson Institute. Their romance, she said, ended in early 2015. Katie reunited with Garcia that May while they were both at a gathering watching the Mayweather-Pacquiao fight on TV. The couple lived together from then until Garcia's arrest a year later. But even though she was no longer romantically involved with Charlie, Katie continued to receive gifts from him, Mascaro testified, including a Lexus sedan she described as "pristine."

Before wrapping up her direct examination, Norris asked about a special request Katie had made the *same day* Dan Markel was shot. Mascaro shared with jurors that Katie asked her to watch her kids that very evening and that the siblings ended up spending the night. Before coming to get them the next day, Katie called to let her know that Charlie's brother-in-law had been in an accident and that he anticipated traveling to Tallahassee to visit his sister.

During her cross-examination, Kawass got Mascaro to acknowledge that she was merely approximating that Katie ceased working at Hollywood Live in May 2014. The defense attorney then asked a question she'd quickly come to regret—

how much money the two women were earning in the clubs. Mascaro told jurors that on a "good night," they'd receive between $400 and $500 in cash tips, whereas an average night would be more in the range $100 to $200. And further, that she and Katie worked in the clubs only a couple of nights a week.

If Mascaro was correct about those facts and figures, even had Katie continued working in the clubs as late as August 2014, her maximum earnings for a single month would have been less than $5,000. Yet the jury was about to learn that her post-murder cash deposits eclipsed that figure by a wide margin. Kawass also asked Mascaro how often she watched Katie's kids—seemingly expecting her to say that it wasn't unusual for her to do so. Yet that question backfired as well, with the prosecution witness telling jurors that she "rarely" did so.

Yindra Mascaro stepped down from the witness stand, left the courtroom, and headed home to Miami. Though her appearance was brief, the damage she'd just inflicted on her good friend's defense was most significant indeed.

•••

THE STATE THEN CALLED a pair of Adelson Institute employees, Clariza Lebredo and Erika Johnson. Like June Umchinda, neither woman appreciated being parachuted into a trial hundreds of miles from home. Anna Norris found herself trying to pry information from them like an interrogator questioning hostile prisoners of war. Lebredo told jurors she'd been Harvey Adelson's dental assistant for 40 years. Until 2016, she testified, Donna Adelson was the office manager— "the boss." She told the jury she had no knowledge of Katie ever working for the dental practice.

Norris had Erika Johnson testify about a visit two FBI agents paid to the office on June 1, 2016. They had a subpoena seeking copies of all of Katie's employment records. Johnson immediately called her boss, Charlie, who initially told his assistant, "I wouldn't give anything." Though Johnson was aware of his romantic relationship with Katie, she told jurors she'd never seen Katie at the office working as an employee.

Norris next called Sergeant Chris Corbitt back to the stand to share with jurors tedious—but critically important—evidence from the tower dumps and cellphone records. Together, he and the assistant state attorney methodically marched through a colorful PowerPoint presentation that illustrated his findings.

On June 2, 2014, Corbitt testified, Katie's cellphone pinged a tower near Comfort Rent A Car at the very time her "husband" was there renting a Nissan Altima—the car he exchanged the following day for the Hyundai Sonata that actually made the June trip to Tally. Katie's phone pinged the same tower again four days later, when the Sonata was being returned. Even more illuminating, at 10:25 p.m. on July 15, 2014—the evening before Garcia's and Rivera's second trip to Tally—the GPS embedded in the silver-pine-mica Prius signaled its presence in the parking lot of Katie's North Bay Village apartment community.

Though there was no data indicating that Garcia's phone had pinged cell towers during the June 4-5 trip, Corbitt showed jurors a map illustrating the towers his phone pinged during the July 16-18 trip—both on the way to Tally and coming back to Miami. At 12:30 p.m. on July 18—about 90 minutes after the shooting—Garcia's phone connected with Katie's for a 20-second call. That was consistent with Rivera's testimony of Garcia briefly calling his "wife" to let her know the job was done, and her replying, "I know." Corbitt testified that the cellphone data revealed that, at the moment that call connected, Garcia's phone was in Alachua County, about 90 minutes by car east of Tally. A perfect match.

Corbitt told jurors that he'd identified two different phone numbers associated with Luis Rivera, an older number and a newer one. Norris asked if any records existed indicating whether Katie had ever called the older number. The police sergeant told jurors that she'd done so on precisely three occasions: June 5 at 10:59 p.m. and July 17 at 11:40 p.m. and 11:41 p.m. Which, coincidentally enough, were the only two occasions prior to his arrest King Tato had ever been to Tallahassee.

Corbitt showed jurors on the PowerPoint how the cellphones of Rivera, Garcia, and Katie appeared to congregate near Jessica Rodriguez's apartment at about 9:45 p.m. the evening of the shooting. He testified that at 10:20 p.m. that same evening, Katie's cellphone connected with Charlie's— once again, pinging a tower near Rodriguez's apartment.

Beginning at 9:44 a.m. the next day—the morning of the money drop—the call detail records revealed that Katie had repeatedly reached out to her "husband" by phone and text. None of the attempts succeeded, Corbitt testified, because Garcia's phone had apparently been powered down or disabled after 5:12 a.m. Katie also reached out to Rivera's newer phone number three times that morning between 10:22 a.m. and 10:31 a.m., a number she'd never previously contacted. She and Rivera connected for about a minute and a half at 10:23 a.m.

Jurors were shown a chart displaying 43 different communications between 9:44 a.m. and 11:23 a.m. that morning, which indicated who was making the calls, who was receiving them, and their duration. The first call that actually connected was from Katie to Anthony Ortiz aka King Anthony aka Jibaro. They spoke from 9:47 a.m. to 9:49 a.m. Ortiz then attempted, unsuccessfully, to get ahold of Garcia. Ortiz and Rivera exchanged text messages and then spoke on the phone at 10:35 a.m.—just after Katie and Ortiz completed a second call. Though Ortiz could have shed light on what was going on that morning, jurors would never hear from him—King Anthony had been dead for more than two years, the victim of an unfortunate motorcycle accident.

Norris had Corbitt use a map she projected onto the screen to illustrate where Katie was as she made those calls. Using a red dot to depict her location, the police sergeant illustrated how Katie traveled south from an area not far from Charlie's Fort Lauderdale residence and continued toward Rodriguez's home—implying that she'd retrieved the money and was heading to Rodriguez's apartment to deliver it. Based on the cellphone data, it appeared that Katie was at or near Rodriguez's home from 10:00 a.m. until about 11:30 a.m. that morning. All while her kids were presumably still with Yindra Mascaro.

Though Chris DeCoste fired dozens of questions at Corbitt, he was able to make only four points of any consequence. First, that the initial call between Katie and Rivera the morning of the money drop was from him to her, not her to him as Rivera had testified. Second, that when their cellphones connected, Rivera was not at a barbershop on Biscayne Blvd. as he'd testified. Third, that Corbitt couldn't say with any level of certainty that Rivera, Garcia, and Katie were in exactly the same place, at the same time, the morning of the money drop.

DeCoste's final point related to a handful of text messages in the more than 300,000 Corbitt had reviewed from Charlie's iCloud account—an April 25, 2014 exchange that began when Katie asked Charlie, "Did Tuto call ur phone"? Corbitt confirmed that Charlie had initially responded, "No," and later joked, "Actually he did. He envited [sic] me to go deep sea fishing—he was so nice!!!" Katie had replied that she was "serious," because Tuto was "Fukin driving me crazy." DeCoste asked the sergeant if he could rule out the possibility that Garcia and Charlie had been communicating through other devices or apps. Corbitt responded that he couldn't.

•••

THE STATE'S NEXT WITNESS, Mary Hull, a financial analyst with Florida's Department of Financial Services, had received an equally tedious assignment: analyzing the voluminous financial records of the key players—the Adelsons, Rivera, Garcia, and Katie. She testified about Rivera's and Garcia's purchases of cars and motorcycles between July and October 2014, as well as the January 2016 retitling of Harvey Adelson's Lexus into Katie's name. Though the title included a $1,700 figure for the sales price, Hull told the jury that there were no corresponding entries in Katie's or any of the Adelsons' bank accounts consistent with that amount.

Hull also testified about the 44 paychecks Katie received from the Adelson Institute between September 2014 and Garcia's arrest in May 2016—all signed by Donna Adelson—and how records the State had subpoenaed from the dental practice revealed not a shred of evidence that Katie actually worked there. The checks Katie received and deposited, she noted, totaled nearly $18,000.

Hull testified that statements from Charlie's and Katie's credit card accounts disclosed that the lovers were in Key West together in late June 2014 and again over the July 4th weekend. Charlie's American Express Card statements documented the purchase of two airline tickets for Katie to travel to the Dominican Republic in March 2015. Norris also showed jurors an October 2015 text in which Charlie asked Katie, "Do you want me to get a cruise for you and your mom?"

The financial analyst reviewed with jurors records relating to payments for Katie's October 18, 2014 breast implant surgery. Of the $4,595 paid, she found entries for only two payments on Katie's Visa card, totaling $195. The remaining $4,400, Hull testified, had been paid in cash. Yet her search through Katie's bank records revealed only $2,180 in cash withdrawals during the ten months prior to her surgery and no evidence at all of any cash advances on a credit card. The clear implication was that Charlie, not Katie, had paid Dr. Roudner for the surgery.

Norris walked Hull through text messages in which Katie had asked Charlie for financial assistance in May 2015—after she'd reunited with her "husband"—in which Katie complained, "I have a shyt load of things to pay for." In response, Charlie indicated that he'd loan Katie whatever she needed. And in November 2015, according to his American Express Card statement, he paid over $1,600 for repairs to her Mazda SUV.

Hull prepared numerous Excel spreadsheets and graphs to calculate and illustrate the money Katie had deposited into her JPMorgan Chase and Bank of America accounts. During 2014 alone, she deposited nearly $74,000, despite her sporadic employment. Of that amount, nearly $47,000—some 63%— was comprised of cash deposits, which Hull testified ranged from $200 to $2000. Some days, she told jurors, Katie deposited funds into both accounts through different ATMs.

In the 12 months preceding the murder, Hull testified, Katie had made cash deposits totaling $15,600—an average of $1,300 per month. Yet in the five weeks between July 21 and August 27, 2014, her cash deposits skyrocketed to $17,300. Norris showed the jury a graph illustrating how much Katie's post-murder deposits deviated from her norm, the line representing August 2014 towering above all other months. It was an impressive exhibit.

Hull also analyzed Charlie's financial records, which were equally noteworthy. Between 2013 and 2016, she testified, the traveling periodontist was earning an eye-popping $3 to $3.5 million a year.

During his cross-examination of Hull, DeCoste was able to get before the jury a text message exchange between Katie and Charlie from September 17, 2014, in which Katie had told him, "I'll let you know my availability so you can know, more or less, how many hours I can dedicate." He got the financial analyst to agree that the message implied his client was about to begin a new job; and also, that Hull had no idea what the source of cash was for his client's bank deposits.

• • •

THOUGH SERGEANT CORBITT and Mary Hull were certainly important witnesses, the volume and complexity of the data they spewed at jurors was overwhelming—at times, mind-numbing. Fortunately for the men and women seated in the jury box, the information imparted by the next witness, Oscar Jimenez, was significantly more accessible—and entertaining.

Within minutes of the retired, undercover FBI agent taking the oath, jurors were at the edges of their seats watching footage of the April 19, 2016 bump in front of the Icon Condominiums in South Beach. Jimenez told jurors that the goal of the operation was to make Donna Adelson believe that he was trying to extort money on behalf of Luis Rivera. Cappleman played Jimenez's telephone conversation with Erika Johnson nine days later, in which he told Charlie's assistant that Donna needed to let him know what she thought about the paperwork he'd handed her.

The undercover agent's testimony set the stage for Special Agent Pat Sanford to take the witness stand. Like Craig Isom, the FBI agent had been working on Dan Markel's murder case since July 2014. He was just as eager to see his efforts bear fruit as was Isom. Because he had so much territory to cover, Sanford was on the witness stand a solid day and a half.

Early in his testimony, Sanford swatted away various themes the defense attorneys had trumpeted throughout the trial. Cappleman had him dispel the notion posited by Zangeneh that Charlie Adelson had directly solicited Rivera to commit the murder. There was no evidence of a single communication between the two men, the special agent testified, even after a meticulous "cross-reference scrub" between all phone numbers either had ever used.

To refute the idea that investigators had spoon-fed Rivera the information he shared during his proffer statement, Sanford pointed out how former gang leader told them he'd received a speeding ticket during the *second* trip to Tally. When he and Isom heard King Tato say that, Sanford testified, they knew he was confused, as they'd learned from a DMV sweep that the ticket had been written in early June, not July. But they didn't correct Rivera, he told jurors, to ensure they *didn't* influence what he was telling them. Rivera also shared with them information they didn't already know—such as how the gun had accidentally discharged in the Prius, blowing a hole through the floorboard and disabling the gas line. And how the $100 bills Garcia and Rivera received for the hit had been stapled together.

Sanford then picked up where Jimenez left off, walking jurors through the incessant phone chatter among Donna, Charlie, Katie, and Garcia following the April 2016 bump. Though jurors had been watching Katie and Garcia from afar for nearly two weeks, to that point of the trial, they had no idea what their voices sounded like. That was about to change. Within a few hours, they'd be able to recognize each without the slightest difficulty—as well as which profanity-laden adjectives and nouns the "husband" and "wife" preferred.

Though Judge Hankinson denied Cappleman's request to play Donna's three calls with Charlie upon returning to her condo following her encounter with Jimenez—concluding the communications constituted inadmissible hearsay—he did allow her to play 28 wiretapped recordings among the alleged co-conspirators during the four weeks following the bump, more than two hours of audio in all. Collectively, the recordings provided jurors a flavor of how frantic Donna, Charlie, Katie, and Garcia had been to address and resolve "Sammy's" escalating blackmail threat. The lead prosecutor had Agent Sanford confirm that, despite the many times one of the participants had suggested—or threatened—to go to the police or the FBI, no one had ever approached law enforcement to report the attempted extortion.

Cappleman badly wanted to introduce into evidence a written transcript of the conversation between Charlie and Katie at Dolce Vita. Sanford had personally assembled the transcript after listening to the audio component of the surveillance footage on more than 100 occasions through high-quality, noise-canceling headphones, using special software to reduce extraneous noises. Outside the presence of the jury, Cappleman had Sanford walk Judge Hankinson through his Herculean efforts to accurately transcribe the dialog at the noisy Italian restaurant.

Though the judge didn't sustain many of the defense lawyers' objections, on this occasion he did, finding that Sanford didn't have the requisite training or expertise to decipher any better than jurors what Charlie and Katie were actually saying. Judge Hankinson told the lawyers he'd devoted considerable time to that effort himself—using his own headphones—but was unable to make out virtually anything Charlie or Katie had said during their hour-long conversation. If he supplied the transcript to jurors, the judge noted, they'd quickly have succumbed to the temptation of reading the written words in lieu of listening to the audio component of the video. Which under the law, he said, would be improper. A rare, but crucial victory for the defense.

Cappleman was permitted to introduce into evidence the audio recording of Sanford's interview with Garcia the day before his arrest. Jurors listened intently—eyes fixed on the defendant—who was listening to himself deny having ever been to Tally, having ever taken a trip with Luis Rivera, or knowing anything at all about Dan Markel. The lead prosecutor ended her direct examination by having Sanford provide a blow-by-blow account of Garcia's arrest in Hallandale Beach, in the same black Lexus that—at the time of the murder—had been Charlie Adelson's.

• • •

DURING HIS TWO HOURS of cross-examination, Chris DeCoste focused relentlessly on the theme he'd been trying to drive home during his withering attacks on all of the State's law enforcement witnesses—that the investigation into Dan Markel's murder hadn't been objective, with investigators viewing the evidence through "dirty windows." He asked Sanford what the letters in the acronym FBI stood for, which, unsurprisingly, drew the answer, the "Federal Bureau of Investigation."

"You would agree with me that the purpose of the Federal Bureau of Investigation," DeCoste continued, "is to investigate, by its name, right?" Sanford agreed that was one of the bureau's purposes. Nor did he quibble with the notion that its goal was to do so objectively.

The defense attorney questioned Sanford about his theory of the murder conspiracy, using an oversized posterboard containing photos of the Adelsons, Garcia, Rivera, and Katie to illustrate his points. "And you believe that that is the group, more or less, that caused the death of Dan Markel?"

"Correct," the special agent replied.

"Adelsons wanted it to happen, right?"

"Correct."

"Rivera and Garcia did it?"

"Yes."

"And the connection is through Katherine Magbanua?"

"That's correct."

One by one, the Boston native asked whether any of the four Adelsons had ever been arrested or charged. When he got to Donna, Sanford replied, "No, not yet," piquing the interest of anyone who was paying attention. But when DeCoste asked the obvious follow-up question—if Donna was about to be charged—the judge sustained Cappleman's objection before Sanford could utter a single syllable.

DeCoste spent considerable time on Katie's work at the nightclubs, using a photo posted on her Facebook account depicting his client with three other women doing a "brand promotion" in May 2013. Sanford acknowledged that Katie had also received a check from Club Fate in June 2015.

"And you have no evidence there was a break in employment there, right?" the defense attorney asked, implying that Katie had worked in the nightclubs continuously between May 2013 and June 2015.

"I have no evidence there was a break," Sanford agreed, noting that he also had no evidence that Katie had worked continuously at Club Fate for two solid years. But DeCoste forced him to concede that he'd never spoken with anyone associated with the nightclub to investigate that important question.

Sanford also acknowledged that the jury had heard only a small sample of Katie's communications during the time the wiretap was in place, agreeing that there had been 359 wiretapped calls in all. He also conceded that Katie had likely communicated via WhatsApp and FaceTime during that time—and that law enforcement was unable to capture her communications on either platform.

In all of the wiretapped calls, DeCoste declared, "Not once

does she say anything about being involved in a murder." Sanford admitted that was true. He also agreed that Katie had been communicating fairly regularly with Charlie even before the April 2016 bump—despite the pair no longer being involved in a romantic relationship.

DeCoste briefly returned to Katie's cash deposits, noting that evidence existed that she'd been receiving cash from Garcia for their children as well as cash tips from the nightclubs. "You still maintain, 'Well, it's still off-the-books cash—it came from the murder,' right?"

Sanford responded that investigators hadn't been able "to trace that cash back to anything, especially off of her tax returns. It was not there."

"The Federal Bureau of Investigation, right?" DeCoste asked, setting up his next point.

"That's correct."

"Not the Federal Bureau of Imagination?" Though Cappleman lodged an objection to the obviously improper question—which Judge Hankinson promptly sustained—the defense lawyer's wry smile suggested he was thoroughly enjoying his joust with the FBI agent. Even if that meant drawing the ire of a judge he didn't consider the least bit impartial.

DeCoste pivoted to the more than two dozen wiretapped recordings Cappleman had played for jurors, first trying to make the point that although Charlie appeared desperate to meet with Katie, she appeared reluctant to meet with him. Sanford disagreed with that characterization, pointing out that Katie was actually the one to suggest using WhatsApp to discuss the blackmailer's demand—not Charlie.

The former Miami prosecutor asked Sanford whether Katie was ever captured in a wiretapped call saying, "'They're onto us. They know.' She doesn't say that, right?" The special agent conceded the point, for whatever it was worth. And also, that Katie repeatedly lamented how someone was harassing "you people," not how someone was harassing "us."

"But again, it's the government's belief," DeCoste pressed

him, "that because she didn't call the police, she must have been involved?"

"That's part of it," Sanford agreed.

DeCoste had the special agent confirm that the wiretap had picked up Charlie talking about purchasing guns, buying steroids, and intimating that he'd been falsifying medical records—trying to paint the picture that, as between him and Katie, Charlie was the one predisposed to criminal conduct.

DeCoste stressed how, months before the murder, his client had texted Charlie asking whether Tuto had called his phone. In view of that text, he asked, "You can't say that there wasn't communication via WhatsApp, other phones, other means in between Charles Adelson and Sigfredo Garcia?" Sanford conceded that he couldn't say that with 100% certainty.

Based on Katie's April 2016 text itself, DeCoste asked, "There's a clear belief that Katherine Magbanua thought Sigfredo Garcia is going to be calling Charles Adelson, right?"

"Yes," Sanford acknowledged. "At some point I believe she thought he would have tried to call him. Yes."

"And the reason is because he objected to the relationship with Charles Adelson?"

"That's correct."

"He desperately wanted her back," DeCoste asserted. Once again, Sanford conceded the point.

Katie's lawyer pivoted to the day of her arrest, getting the FBI agent to agree that he'd traveled to South Florida because he wanted her to cooperate. "You have this big show of force, slap the cuffs on her, and want to talk to her, right?"

Sanford finally pushed back, telling the defense attorney, "That is not the reason for the big show of force."

"Federal Bureau of Investigation, right?" DeCoste asked. Not the Federal Bureau of Intimidation?" This time, Judge Hankinson pounced before Cappleman could even lodge her objection, admonishing DeCoste that his blatantly argumentative questions wouldn't be tolerated. "I'm not going to warn you again, Mr. DeCoste," he said angrily, intimating that the next time would result in a contempt citation. Yet the defense attorney didn't seem the least bit chastened that he'd incited the judge's wrath yet again.

"Let's talk about evidence of innocence, of Katherine's innocence," DeCoste transitioned, getting the witness to agree that there had been significant media publicity following Garcia's and Rivera's arrests. "Katherine didn't flee, right?"

"I believe she did," Sanford retorted, surprised by any suggestion otherwise.

"Wouldn't that mean she's gone?" DeCoste asked. That question gave Sanford an engraved invitation to inform jurors that Katie had indeed fled her apartment and stopped using her cellphone the day after the FBI questioned Garcia at his workplace and Isom was rapping on her front door. A point Cappleman had never even made during her direct examination.

"You're talking about the one time that— not yourself, but that two men went and knocked on her door and didn't identify themselves as law enforcement," DeCoste said. "That's the time you're talking about, right?"

"With their badges," Sanford replied. "And she knew they were law enforcement," pointing out how Katie said as much during her frantic telephone conversations that morning.

"And you can't say that the reason why she moved out of her apartment," DeCoste asked, "is because now the person that she was sharing it with has been arrested by you, and she can't pay for it?" Yet Sanford testified that Katie had fled the apartment the day *before* Garcia's arrest.

DeCoste inquired about the trip Katie and Charlie had taken to Key West around the July 4th holiday—just before the murder—asking the agent if he'd learned that was the "good-bye tour" signaling the end of their romance. Sanford told him that he had no information suggesting that was the purpose of their trip to Key West. But he did agree that investigators had indications the couple had broken up prior to the homicide.

DeCoste posited his theory of what had actually transpired. "I'll ask you a hypothetical. Charles Adelson is communicating with Sigfredo Garcia. One wants his brother-in-law murdered, the other one wants the girl that he loves back. The exchange is $100,000 and the murder; in exchange, I'll break up with the girlfriend. What evidence do you have that says that didn't happen?"

Cappleman promptly objected before Sanford began to answer. "Sustained," Judge Hankinson barked, staring at the defense lawyer with evident disdain. Yet DeCoste couldn't have cared less. He'd just used one of the State's key witnesses as a prop, explaining to jurors precisely what he wanted them to believe.

During her brief redirect examination, Cappleman made a pretty good point of her own, projecting onto the screen the June 2015 check Katie had received from Club Fate—the one DeCoste himself had placed into evidence. She had Sanford point out to jurors what was written in the memo line: "4/1 – 5/1/2015 TIPS." The check was for only $985—a far cry from the $17,300 in cash deposits Katie had made in the five weeks following the murder.

Not only that, the very existence of the check implied that Katie didn't even receive her tips in cash. Rather than supporting the notion that the surge in Katie's cash deposits following the homicide was due to her work at the nightclubs, the check from Club Fate seemed to be powerful evidence to the contrary.

•••

THE STATE'S EVIDENCE WAS nearly complete. Cappleman called another FBI agent to the stand—the one who'd rushed into Dolce Vita with his hidden camera upon seeing Katie and Charlie enter the restaurant. After having the witness lay a proper foundation, the veteran prosecutor played several minutes of the video for jurors, who quickly learned that, unlike the video and audio of the bump, the quality of the Dolce Vita video—particularly the audio—made it virtually worthless. Which is precisely why the State's lead attorney had so desperately wanted them to be able to follow along with

Agent Sanford's transcript in hand.

Prior to the State resting, Craig Isom and Mary Hull each made brief encore appearances. Cappleman had Isom describe the crime scene immediately following the shooting, solely to establish that Wendi couldn't have possibly seen the yellow crime scene tape all the way from Centerville Road—as she'd testified. The retired police investigator also told jurors that Wendi had acknowledged to him during her interview that same day that, just hours earlier, she'd driven down Trescott Drive all the way to the outer perimeter of the crime scene.

Anna Norris brought Mary Hull back to the stand to share with jurors her findings from reviewing Katie's tax returns. Her 2014 return indicated employment at SoFi Dental and the Adelson Institute. And in 2015, in addition to the Adelson Institute, Katie indicated she'd been employed by a dermatologist named Dr. Obed. The names Club Fate and Hollywood Live were nowhere to be found on either return. Also of significance, Hull testified, Katie's reported wages were only $15,390 in 2014 and $18,402 in 2015, as compared to her cash deposits of $46,820 in 2014 and $27,480 in 2015. And those cash deposits didn't even include her biweekly checks signed by Donna Adelson.

After answering Zangeneh's and DeCoste's questions, Hull stepped down from the witness stand, prompting Georgia Cappleman to rise to her feet and utter the words everyone had been waiting to hear: "Judge, at this time, the State rests." It was now up to the defense lawyers to put on their case. And for Garcia and Katie to make the ultimate decision: would they take the witness stand and testify in their own defense?

23.

Rolling the Dice

THE TENTH AND FINAL DAY of evidence fell on Wednesday, October 9, 2019, which—had his life not been brutally extinguished—would have marked Dan Markel's 47th year on earth. It also was Yom Kippur, Judaism's holiest day, one Dan certainly would have been observing by attending synagogue and fasting to atone for his sins.

It also happened to be a very important day for Katie Magbanua, but for very different reasons. She'd been up especially early that morning, a fellow inmate meticulously weaving her long, jet-black hair into an austere French braid. The judge had given her the evening to mull over whether to take the stand in her own defense, an opportunity her "husband" had declined the prior afternoon. Which wasn't terribly surprising.

Defendants in criminal cases rarely take that gamble. Though there is certainly risk in not testifying—that jurors will hold a defendant's silence against her—the risk of taking the stand is far greater. Why? Because of the difficult questions a skilled prosecutor will force a defendant to answer. Completely on her own, without a defense lawyer whispering suggestions in her ear. A single answer prosecutors can demonstrate to be untruthful can unravel a defendant's testimony—indeed, her entire defense.

And it isn't merely the defendant's verbal answers that can signal dishonesty or consciousness of guilt. Nonverbal cues can be just as important—and damning. Jurors may interpret a defendant's uncomfortable facial expressions, awkward hand gestures, or darting eye movements as signs that she is manufacturing her testimony rather than telling the truth. Slight hesitations, stumbles, and mistakes so common in everyday communication take on a whole different complexion during a criminal defendant's testimony.

Because the burden of proving a defendant guilty "beyond a reasonable doubt" is so high, defense lawyers generally prefer to poke holes in the prosecution's evidence than take the gamble that jurors will believe—much less like—their client. Nearly all of the evidence pointing to Katie's involvement in the murder was circumstantial, the only direct evidence coming from a former gang leader who'd turned State's evidence to save himself from the death penalty. Tara Kawass and Chris DeCoste had plenty to work with to convince jurors they had ample reason to doubt Katie's guilt. Putting her on the stand would invariably shift the jury's focus away from the gaps in the evidence to Katie herself, placing nearly all of their eggs in the basket of her perceived credibility.

All that said, defendants daring enough to take the risk of testifying sometimes reap a significant reward. Not only because a few can actually pull off a solid performance, but also because of the element of surprise. Criminal defendants so rarely testify, prosecutors are often left flat-footed when they do. Unless the prosecution assumes that something that happens less than 10% of the time will happen 100% of the time—and prepares accordingly—a criminal defendant who chooses to testify can actually enjoy a tactical advantage.

Preparing an effective cross-examination of a murder defendant is hard, tedious work, especially in a case involving voluminous evidence spanning a period of several years—as in the Dan Markel case. And to be fully prepared, Georgia Cappleman and Anna Norris had to assemble two such cross-examinations. Though Sigfredo Garcia had already taken a pass on his chance to tell his story, the prosecution team was anxiously awaiting word on whether his co-defendant would as well—and was moments away from finding out.

•••

AT 9:00 A.M., JUDGE HANKINSON instructed Kawass to call her next witness. As she rose to her feet—to the surprise of virtually everyone assembled—Katie's attorney announced, "Your Honor, at this time the defense calls Katherine Magbanua to the stand." An eerie hush fell over the courtroom as Katie, sporting a conservative black pantsuit and white V-neck blouse, maneuvered between the counsel tables and approached the witness stand, where she stood to take the oath. The jailed inmate and mother of two would be taking the huge gamble after all.

Jurors had been eyeing Katie from afar since jury selection had begun 16 days earlier, trying to get a sense of who she was and what made her tick, cogitating over the ultimate question: did the immaculately dressed, olive-skinned woman have enough ice water in her veins to orchestrate the savage murder of a man she'd never met? They were already intimately familiar with her impeccable command of vocabulary words not taught in schools—their ears likely still ringing from the vulgar profanity that spewed from her lips during the wiretapped calls. But now, those who would be deciding Katie's fate would be hearing from her directly—almost close enough to touch—as she answered questions they'd been pondering since the trial began. They'd even get to ask their own.

Katie admitted to being nervous, her facial expression more deer-in-the-headlights as her testimony began than one of comfort or confidence. She appeared meek and timid—almost obsequious—hardly how one would envision a murderess. The 34-year-old UCF grad was unfailingly polite, answering questions "yes, ma'am" and "no, ma'am," much as Luis Rivera had, even saying "bless you" into the mic whenever she heard a juror or spectator sneeze.

Yet unlike Rivera—who oozed personality—Katie's testimony came off as wooden and flat, Kawass leading her with answers instead of letting her client tell her own story. The defense team had clearly made the calculated decision that Katie would be better served by short, crisp answers than an attempted charm offensive that might backfire.

Less than a minute after stating her name, Kawass asked Katie "the most important question. Did you have anything to do with the murder of Dan Markel?"

"No, ma'am," Katie replied, her words enunciated softly, barely escaping her lips.

"Did you get the father of your children, Mr. Garcia, to commit a murder on behalf of Mr. Charlie Adelson?"

Katie's eyes darted to Garcia the instant her lawyer mentioned his name. "No, ma'am," she answered, with just a bit more volume.

Kawass began walking through her client's relationships with both Garcia and Charlie. Katie described her early days with Garcia in Orlando while she attended college, telling jurors they were "great." Though they'd never been legally married, she testified that they considered themselves husband and wife. But they'd fight and break up, largely because she'd find evidence on his cellphone revealing that he'd been cheating on her.

By late 2013, when her daughter Kaylee was about 18 months old, she'd kicked her "husband" out of their home after finding out about yet another incident of infidelity. "I was done," she recounted. She started dating Charlie soon thereafter, having met him while she was working as a receptionist at SoFi Dental. Once he learned she was unattached, she told jurors, Charlie took the liberty of putting his number on her cellphone.

Over time, Katie testified, their relationship grew into one of girlfriend and boyfriend. They communicated every day through text messages and phone calls, the latter often ending with the words "I love you." But the romance was never truly serious, she explained, the couple never discussing marriage or even the prospect of living together. In fact, Katie confessed, she occasionally still had sex with Garcia despite her ongoing relationship with Charlie. Both men, she noted, were well aware of the other's role in her life. Charlie even encouraged her to get back together with her "husband" because he was the father of her children.

Kawass pivoted to July 1, 2014, which was the same day the call detail records revealed Garcia calling Harvey Adelson's cellphone—the call that helped investigators piece together his connection to the murder plot. Katie told jurors she had plans to go out on a jet ski with Charlie that day. He picked her up in the same black Lexus that eventually became hers, the jet ski hitched to the back. Garcia had taken the kids from her just before Charlie arrived.

About a block away from her apartment, Katie said, Garcia suddenly darted in front of them in his blue Volvo—cutting them off in the middle of the road—causing Charlie to slam on his brakes. The Volvo was turned sideways, blocking the entire street. Garcia jumped out of the car, seething—standing between the two vehicles screaming—leaving their kids in the Volvo's back seat. Instead of escalating the confrontation, Charlie drove away, doubling back in the opposite direction. Though Garcia's cellphone connected with Harvey's at 5:20 p.m. that same day, Kawass didn't ask Katie whether she knew anything about that call.

Instead, she transitioned to Katie's work doing liquor brand promotions and as a bottle girl at Club Fate and Hollywood Live. Katie explained that "bottle service" involved taking liquor bottles to VIP sections of the clubs "with sparklers, make a big scene, like, take pictures, like, dance a little bit," the idea being to make customers "feel special." Dressing provocatively, she told jurors, inspired guests to tip generously.

In stark contrast to Yindra Mascaro's testimony, Katie testified that a "good night" could generate $1,000 to $1,500 in tips and that she sometimes worked more than twice a week. Curiously, her lawyer didn't pose a single question about *when* Katie was earning those tips, which presumably was her motivation behind the entire line of questions. The well-dressed defendant admitted that she didn't report her cash tips to the IRS because "none of the girls really did it."

Kawass asked several questions about her client's interactions with Charlie's sister, Wendi Adelson. Katie became more animated talking about her Father's Day beach outing with Wendi and Yindra Mascaro—for the first time speaking freely and naturally. She told jurors she had no recollection of Wendi discussing anything about her divorce and that the two never spoke with one another apart from the two times they were together. She also acknowledged having met Donna and Harvey Adelson.

The defense attorney transitioned to the day of the shooting. Katie testified that she didn't have any knowledge that her "husband" was leaving town and that he'd never mentioned Tallahassee in their conversations. She claimed not to remember anything she was doing on July 18, 2014. But she did recall Charlie saying something about his ex-brother-in-law being in an accident, though not one involving a shooting or a murder. "I would remember *that*," Katie told jurors.

Kawass quickly segued to Luis Rivera. Katie testified that she knew King Tato only through her "husband" and had never been close with him. Outside of interactions that included Garcia, she said, she'd never hung out with Rivera or spoken with him on the phone and didn't even store his number as a contact. But when Kawass tried to get Katie to agree that the number the call detail records revealed her calling with a 934 prefix—Rivera's old number—belonged to someone else, her client stared at her with a puzzled expression, asking, "Wasn't that Luis's number?" The very opposite of the point her lawyer had been trying to make.

As for the records revealing her calls with Rivera the morning of the money drop, Katie testified that she was probably trying to find Garcia. Leading her witness—as Kawass did throughout her direct examination with hardly any objections—the Jamaican-born lawyer declared, "Now it's clear from the records that you didn't call him first. He called you." Katie nodded in agreement.

"Were you ever trying to deliver money to Luis Rivera and Mr. Garcia at Jessica Rodriguez's house?" she asked.

"No, ma'am," Katie answered. She also denied retrieving money from Charlie that had been stapled together. Kawass had her confirm that she'd been to Rodriguez's apartment several times before that morning. And reminded jurors the prosecution hadn't brought Rivera's baby mama to the courtroom to testify—tacitly goading Cappleman yet again to do just that as part of her rebuttal evidence.

Kawass walked up to the witness stand to show her client a printout of a text message exchange she had with Charlie on July 19, 2014—to refresh her recollection as to what she'd been doing the morning of the supposed money drop. Katie carefully flipped through the pages. Her memory refreshed, she testified that she'd been at the pool with her son Ethan "around 11:00" that morning. Which is when Corbitt testified the cellphone revealed its presence in the area of Rodriguez's apartment. And when, according to Mascaro, Ethan and Kaylee were still with her. Though Katie acknowledged that Mascaro had watched her kids on occasion, she couldn't recall if that particular day had been one of them.

Kawass moved on, asking Katie to describe why she started working for the Adelsons. Examining a text message her lawyer placed before her, Katie explained that on June 24, 2014, she asked Charlie to assist her in obtaining free health insurance for her children—from the State of Florida—by placing her on the Adelson Institute payroll at a minimal salary. She acknowledged that their arrangement was a ruse intended to defraud Florida's Department of Children and Families into providing insurance she wasn't eligible to receive. She also admitted that she never actually worked for the Adelson Institute, despite the 44 checks she received from September 2014 to May 2016.

However, Katie claimed that she *did* work directly for Charlie. Yet when Kawass asked her to describe their arrangement, her answer was a confusing mishmash. "I was kind of like his assistant," she testified. "If he needed any help with, like, off of— a patient or something was— or, you know, he needed help with, I would, I would help him with that. And he had, like, rental places too. So I spoke to him about that too."

When her lawyer asked if she assisted in collecting the rent, Katie told jurors that Charlie wanted her to, but that his tenants were too difficult. She testified to doing "odd jobs" for Charlie, but without specifying what they were. Kawass didn't even ask if she'd ever called any of Charlie's patients—which the two had talked about, seemingly in jest, during the wiretapped calls—likely because her client's answer would have been that she hadn't.

Apart from cash tips and checks from the Adelson Institute, Katie told the jury that she also periodically received money from her mother and from Garcia, presumably for the kids. Though he didn't have a job, her "husband" would sometimes show up with cash, which she suspected had come from illegal activities. When Kawass asked if she'd been aware that Garcia was selling cocaine, Katie answered in the negative, explaining that she didn't ask him where the money was coming from because "it's for my kids."

As for her breast implants, Katie testified that she'd been wanting them since high school and that Charlie had referred her to Dr. Roudner. She claimed that she'd been saving up cash since seeing the doctor for an initial consultation in early 2014. By October 18, she finally had the $4,000 she needed to proceed and even received a discount for paying in cash. By that time, Katie told the jury, she wasn't seeing Charlie very much because he'd been "ghosting" her—not answering her calls as much. It was her "husband," she revealed, not Charlie, who took care of her during her recovery from the surgery.

Kawass briefly returned to Katie's work in the nightclubs, showing her—and then the jury—a photo taken at Club Fate in April 2015, depicting her client as a voluptuous blond in a skimpy black dress that barely covered her artificially enlarged breasts. Notably, however, the defense lawyer didn't ask if she'd been working there during the summer of 2014. Kawass actually had Katie confirm that her tips—with a "P"—grew larger after her breast augmentation, presumably because of her enhanced sex appeal. But that didn't jibe with her skyrocketing cash deposits in July and August of 2014, when her sex appeal—and breast size—had been more limited.

Katie also testified about a bad motorcycle accident in which Garcia had been seriously injured in January 2015. She told jurors that Shrimp was on the bike with him and that her "husband" had received a legal settlement following the accident.

Which led Kawass to her next subject: the Lexus. Katie told jurors she began borrowing the luxury vehicle from Charlie after her own auto accident in April 2015, which had totaled her Mazda SUV. She testified that she eventually paid her ex-boyfriend $1,700 in cash for the Lexus, which she knew at the time was below value. He'd given it to her at that price as "a favor," she said. Another favor from Charlie, Katie testified, was his recommendation for an office job with his housemate, Dr. Jerome Obed, a dermatologist. She told jurors she worked the front desk for Dr. Obed and did clerical work. Much of the money he paid her, she admitted, was "under the table," to allow her to continue receiving free public health insurance for her kids.

Kawass asked a slew of questions about Katie's communications following the April 2016 bump, most of them of a leading nature. Cappleman finally lodged an objection—which was promptly sustained—but the pattern of the defense lawyer supplying all of the expected answers continued virtually unabated. Katie told jurors that when she met with Charlie at Dolce Vita, he never showed her any piece of paper like the one he described his mother receiving. Though they spoke for an entire hour, the only thing she was able to recall was that "he just started going off on scenarios, and I kind of just lost him." She was confident, she said, that Charlie didn't inform her that the blackmailer had said anything about a homicide or his ex-brother-in-law. Katie explained that the reason Charlie had asked her to call the telephone number on the piece of paper was because the blackmailer had said "ex-girlfriend or my name."

"Why didn't you call the police?" Kawass asked, well aware jurors had likely been ruminating over that very question since listening to the wiretapped calls.

"It really wasn't my place to call the police," Katie answered, explaining that the police would have thought she was "crazy" if what she reported was that "I have a friend's mom that's getting threatened that might have said my name."

Her attorney had her focus on the 23-minute call in which she and Charlie were each threatening to go to the cops or the FBI. Listening to the call to prepare for trial, Katie testified, she found it "very embarrassing. I just—I mean, I didn't even know I could say that many bad words in, in a 23-minute span." When Kawass asked if she'd have stopped using her phone altogether had she actually been involved in criminal activity, Katie answered, "Of course"—as if her continued use of her phone was the magic fact upon which the entire case could be resolved.

Katie claimed that she'd spoken in code about the number she wanted Garcia to call—disguising it as the price of their son Ethan's clothing—because "I might have been around my children or at work." And when she told both Charlie and Garcia the phone number for "a property," she was employing code because "I was probably next to Yindra at work." As for Charlie stating that he didn't know the name "Tuto," Katie confirmed that he knew that the names Tuto and Garcia were interchangeable because she'd referred to her "husband" by both names in Charlie's presence many times before.

Kawass walked Katie through Garcia's arrest—as well as her frightful morning with law enforcement officers banging on her front door. She told jurors that, at the time, she didn't believe Garcia had been involved in a murder and that the only packing she'd done prior to his arrest was for the family's upcoming trip to Disney World. There was a lot to pack, she explained, because they planned to be gone the entire weekend. After her "husband's" arrest, Katie testified, she moved into her brother Francis's home in Broward County, never fleeing despite intense media scrutiny focused on her suspected involvement.

Kawass desperately wanted Katie to tell the jury that the State Attorney's Office had offered her immunity to flip on Charlie and turn State's evidence, and that she'd refused. However, prior to trial, Judge Hankinson had ruled any such question out of bounds based on the rules of evidence. Nevertheless, the defense lawyer attempted to back her way into that subject by asking Katie to describe what it was like being in jail. Cappleman objected and the judge told Katie not to answer.

"Are you aware that the government wants Charlie Adelson?" her lawyer tried again. Katie nodded affirmatively as Cappleman objected—loudly. "Sustained," the judge ruled.

"Were you aware that the government has said that you have the key to your own freedom?" Kawass asked, with Cappleman objecting mid-question in her attempt to drown out her adversary's words. Once again, Judge Hankinson told Katie not to respond. The lawyers then gathered around the judge for a sidebar, as the lead prosecutor protested what seemed to be an obvious end-run around his prior ruling.

But the judge didn't see it quite the same way—permitting Kawass to continue with her line of questioning. Asked what it meant to her that she held the key to her own freedom, Katie answered, "That it's up to me to get out of jail."

"Okay, and how would you do that?" Kawass asked.

"If I gave up Charlie."

"Do you have information that Charlie Adelson was involved in this?"

"Do I have information?" Katie asked, regurgitating the question. "I mean, based on everything that we've been seeing," she said somewhat tentatively. "But I don't have personal information."

"Based on everything you've seen," Kawass asked, "do you think Charlie Adelson was involved in this?"

"*Yes,*" Katie replied.

"And the last time you saw your kids was when?"

"That's not relevant," the judge interjected before Katie could respond. "Anything further Ms. Kawass?"

"Are you innocent?" she asked, to which her client provided an altogether unsurprising response: "Yes."

Though it didn't seem that way at times, Katie's two hours of direct examination was actually the easy part. What would come next would be considerably more challenging. Kawass and DeCoste girded themselves for what they felt sure would be a rough-and-tumble ride through cross-examination. During which their client would actually have to come up with the answers all on her own.

•••

SAAM ZANGENEH HAD ONE primary mission during his questioning: to establish that his client despised Charlie, couldn't stand Katie being involved with him, and would never have done anything to help him. All notions Katie readily agreed with. Garcia's attorney also had her confirm that Charlie had used illicit drugs in front of her and that Rivera was a drug dealer, trying to bolster his theory that King Tato was someone Charlie likely would have called when he needed drugs—or a murder. His cross-examination lasted all of ten minutes.

Georgia Cappleman confidently took her place behind the mahogany lectern clad in a bright red suit, her long blonde hair flowing freely down her back. Though she'd tried more than 100 cases to jury verdict, in only a few did she get to experience the adrenaline rush of confronting a murder defendant on the witness stand. A solid cross-examination held the potential to deliver a knockout blow—and a guilty verdict for the State of Florida and the Markel family. She was ready, her cross-examination meticulously outlined in the materials she set upon the lectern. This was one prosecutor who wasn't about to be caught flat-footed.

She began right where Zangeneh left off—with Garcia's intense hatred of Charlie. Katie agreed that her "husband" was desperate to get her back. But wouldn't agree that he'd do "anything" for her, "because sometimes I ask him simple tasks, and he can't even do that."

"What about for $100,000?" the assistant state attorney asked in a biting—almost sneering—tone. "Would he do things for that?" Incredibly, Katie answered that he wouldn't.

"Did Mr. Garcia even know that Mr. Adelson was the one behind this whole thing?" Cappleman asked. Katie stared at her quizzically, asking what time the prosecutor was referring to. "Ever?" Cappleman clarified, her voice amplified.

"I believe not," Katie replied.

"Because you didn't tell him who it was, did you?" That was a trick question, much the same as "When did you stop beating your wife?," the goal of which was to have Katie answer "no," that she'd never told Garcia that Charlie was the mastermind behind the murder plot. Which would have implied that she knew, yet didn't tell him. But Katie was well prepared, rejecting the prosecutor's premise altogether, insisting, "I didn't know who it was."

"You told him it was Wendi, didn't you?" Cappleman persisted. Katie shook her head side-to-side. "No," she answered, this time not pushing back against the notion that she actually knew who'd solicited the murder.

The State's lead counsel tried to get Katie to agree that she had control over her "husband" and "wore the pants in that relationship." But the defendant would only concede that Garcia "listened to certain things, but there's a lot of things that he just wouldn't listen to as well."

Cappleman asked why Katie's phone records revealed her presence in the vicinity of Comfort Rent A Car if she hadn't been there when Garcia rented a vehicle in June 2014. "It was around other businesses," she replied. "I don't know what I did that day."

Answering the assistant state attorney's rapid-fire questions, Katie agreed she'd lied on her tax returns, lied to the

Department of Children and Families, and concealed from her "husband" and Charlie that she was having sex with the other at roughly the same time, offering only, "I didn't think that I had to tell either one that I was sleeping with the other." She also freely admitted to lying to Charlie on several occasions during the wiretapped calls.

"And you testified on direct that the reason you went to Mr. Garcia for assistance," Cappleman asked, "is not because he had something to do with this murder, but because he's your child's father and that's who you go to when you have a problem, right?"

"Well, at that specific time, yes," Katie agreed.

"And that's why you solicited him to commit this murder, right?" Cappleman asked forcefully.

"You would insinuate that, yes," Katie replied, her composure beginning to unravel. "But that's your opinion. That's not what happened."

The veteran prosecutor was relentless, framing up the same question in a slightly different package, asking Katie if she approached Garcia to "help this lady get her kids back in Tallahassee" or solicited him "to commit a murder of Dan Markel?" Katie gently nodded her head side-to-side, quickly regaining her composure. "No, ma'am," she said softly.

Cappleman asked why, during the wiretapped calls in which Charlie feigned ignorance as to who Tuto was, Katie hadn't pointed out, "you know who Tuto is. Tuto is my baby daddy." Katie danced around the question several times, but the prosecutor refused to move on until she answered it directly. The best Katie could muster in response was "that it sounded weird that he's saying a different name when he knows Tuto's name." Still not satisfied, Cappleman pressed her again. This time, Katie answered, "I just didn't ask"—which was even less responsive than her prior answers.

The assistant state attorney finally left that particular question aside, but remained laser focused on the wiretapped calls. She asked why Katie was helping Charlie in the first place if the problem involved only him and his family. To which

Katie provided a rambling, largely incoherent answer: "I can't tell you why," she began. "Like, I did— I mean, he's asked me weird stuff before. But somebody mentioned my name, and that's what piqued my interest. I was like, why would somebody approach your mother saying my name? And then I didn't know about Tuto's name until later on."

Cappleman transitioned to the Dolce Vita meeting, getting Katie to admit that she *did* remember parts of her conversation. She testified that the "scenarios" Charlie raised with her were "that it could be the cops or it could be somebody ... extorting his family for money." When she completed that sentence, Cappleman asked the obvious follow-up: "You didn't ask him why the cops would be running an undercover operation on his mother?" To which Katie supplied her stock answer: "No, ma'am." The same answer she gave when asked if she recalled Charlie reading a phone number to her from a piece of paper.

The seasoned prosecutor then asked the next logical question, inquiring what "leverage" might have existed to make Charlie so paranoid. Katie replied that he "might have said something, but, like I said, he just goes on and on about stuff." Cappleman asked whether Charlie told her that the person who approached his mother, if not the cops, might need to be killed—a phrase she lifted from the transcript Agent Sanford had prepared from the Dolce Vita recording. "No, ma'am," Katie replied once more, telling the prosecutor, "I would remember something like that."

Cappleman shifted gears, now grilling the defendant about the gifts Charlie bestowed on her—inquiring first whether he'd purchased a trip for her and her "husband" to go to the Dominican Republic. "No," Katie answered. That trip, she said, was actually for her and her children to visit her mother-in-law. Yet she readily agreed that Charlie had paid for it. In response to more rapid-fire questions, Katie denied that Charlie had let her borrow his Ferrari or paid for repairs to her Mazda or any of her credit card bills, a cruise for her and her mom, her breast augmentation, teeth whitening, or insurance. She claimed not to recall Charlie providing her with $1,400 in cash six days after she texted asking for money.

"Well, what makes you so special that Charlie Adelson wanted to give you all these things after the end of your relationship?" Cappleman asked pointedly, ignoring Katie's denials. "Why is he giving you all of this stuff?"

"I don't know," Katie answered with a bewildered expression—now accepting the premise that Charlie *had* provided her the many benefits Cappleman had ticked through. As for being put on the Adelson Institute's payroll, Katie reiterated that Charlie had done so as a favor to help her acquire health insurance for her son—who needed treatment for his disability—rather than as a payoff for a murder or a means to keep her happy. She acknowledged that she was still sleeping with Charlie in September 2014 when he put her on the payroll, despite her earlier testimony that he began "ghosting" her shortly after the murder.

Cappleman asked why, on the wiretapped calls, the two had discussed her physically going to work at the Adelson Institute's Tamarac office when she wasn't actually doing that. Katie had a ready answer: "Because he did *want me* to go to the—in the office to clean up a bit, but I never, I never did it." Less than a minute later, however, she gave the exact opposite answer when Cappleman asked if she'd ever gone into the dental office on the weekends, testifying, "I believe I have, like, probably— but not often, like once or twice only."

"And what was the purpose of that visit?"

"He wanted me to clean up in the office," Katie replied. "I probably just stopped at— by at the office. Don't recall what I did. It's been a couple of years." She readily conceded that she never called any dental patients, despite the wiretapped calls in which she and Charlie were openly discussing her doing precisely that.

Cappleman next asked Katie about her work as a bottle girl. The jailed inmate double downed on her testimony that she was earning as much as $1,500 in tips on a "good night." That was at Club Fate, she told jurors, the fancier of the two nightclubs, but also the one that had written her checks that bounced. She clarified that the checks represented tips for credit card transactions—which were *in addition* to the cash tips she received directly from customers. Cappleman asked how many times she'd received $1,500 in tips in a single night. Though Katie believed it had been at least five, she didn't want to be boxed into a corner, telling the prosecutor, "I can't give you, like, a specific number."

The assistant state attorney used Yindra Mascaro's testimony to press Katie further, asking whether she agreed with her good friend's assessment that a "good night" would generate $400 to $500 in tips. Katie disagreed, for three reasons: first, that such a meager level of tips might have been a good night *for Mascaro*, but not for her; second, Mascaro never worked at Club Fate, where the tips were better; and third, Mascaro didn't do bartending, whereas she did.

Cappleman asked the defendant whether she had any schedules or other documentation to confirm she'd been working at either nightclub around the time of the homicide. Katie claimed that her text messages would corroborate that she was—though her attorneys never introduced any such texts into evidence. Asked who her boss, coworkers, and customers were at the time, she testified that she couldn't remember any of their names.

The lead prosecutor finally asked the money question—if it was even possible to make $13,000 in just one month as a bottle girl, which was the sum total of Katie's cash deposits during August 2014. Surprisingly, Katie freely admitted that she couldn't have earned that much in a single month. But that was beside the point, she contended, because she was likely saving up her cash before making those deposits—and also noted she was getting cash from her "husband." That latter point, however, only begged the question of where *his* cash was coming from following the homicide, especially since, according to her testimony, he didn't have a job.

Cappleman projected onto the screen the graph Anna Norris had used with Mary Hull, asking Katie if it was merely a coincidence that the "striking spike" in her cash deposits occurred "at exactly the time of this homicide." Katie stared at the projection screen with a blank expression without uttering a word—almost as if she was stalling for time to formulate a credible explanation. "From your diagram, I can see that," she finally said, not challenging the data it conveyed. "But I don't recall that." With so much riding on her answer, she couldn't come up with any reason why her soaring cash deposits coincided so perfectly with the murder she professed to knowing nothing about.

The veteran prosecutor asked whether, on the day of the shooting, Wendi or Charlie had let her know via WhatsApp that Dan Markel had been shot. Though Katie denied any such communication, Cappleman's goal in asking the question was merely to plant the seed that her response "I know" — following Garcia's report, "it's done" — was informed by a heads-up she'd received from a co-conspirator. Since there wasn't a record of any such cellphone communication, Cappleman wanted jurors to speculate that the tip had come through an encrypted message.

She then asked Katie if she'd talked to Rivera "on the day of the money drop." Instead of responding, "What money drop?"—to demonstrate her ignorance of any such event— Katie appeared more focused on making sure the jury understood that it was Rivera who placed the initial call to her and not the other way around, a fact her lawyers had harped on repeatedly. Her response didn't suggest any lack of familiarity with the money drop itself. And as to whether it was merely a coincidence that the only time she and Rivera had ever spoken on the phone was that very day, Katie was unable to provide an intelligible answer.

Cappleman neglected to cross-examine Katie about her testimony that she was at the pool with her son Ethan at 11:00 a.m. that same morning, which is what she told jurors on direct examination after Kawass showed her a text message exchange from Charlie's iCloud account. Yet the actual texts didn't support that testimony at all. Rather, at 11:18 a.m. that morning, Katie had merely written that she'd "probably" be going to the pool *later*—not that she was already there or had any definite plans. It wasn't until 3:54 p.m. that she texted Charlie that she'd just returned from the pool. In the heat of battle, neither of the prosecutors noticed that Katie and Kawass had taken significant liberties in their interpretation of the texts.

Cappleman turned to the time period just before Garcia's arrest, forcing Katie to admit they went to Walmart to purchase "burner" phones just after law enforcement officers descended on his workplace and their townhouse. But she pushed back against the suggestion that she "dumped" her cellphone or stopped using it—pointing out that she still had it at the time of her arrest months later and only used the burner phone to speak to her "husband."

Seemingly out of nowhere, Cappleman asked, "Isn't it true you've been offered some kind of big payoff if you refused to cooperate against Charlie Adelson?" Katie's eyes widened, seemingly shocked by the insinuation. She denied any such offer.

"Do you remember telling anybody that you would be able to stay home after you get acquitted and have a tutor for your kids to be homeschooled at the house?"

"No," Katie responded with a confused look. "I've never made that comment."

"Did you ever show your breasts to some people and tell them that you got them courtesy of the professor?"

"Definitely never happened," Katie answered, her expression one of disgust. She also denied asking someone whether God would forgive her for what she'd done.

Cappleman then highlighted the inconsistency between Katie's testimony on direct examination that Charlie "faded into the background around the time Mr. Markel was killed" and her concession during cross-examination that the two were still having sex as late as October 2014. Katie tried her best to reconcile those answers, but what came out of her mouth was convoluted at best: "I mean, I guess I didn't realize it until now, like, the whole him— as Ms. Kawass was saying, about the ghosting me. I didn't realize that until now, like— that he was."

Her questioning complete, Georgia Cappleman resumed her seat beside Anna Norris at the prosecution table. In just 45 minutes, the lead prosecutor had covered a giant swath of territory. With the exception of the Lexus sedan Katie had inherited from the Adelsons—which somehow escaped her attention—she'd hit on every key point the prosecution's witnesses had raised throughout the trial. Though Katie had survived her onslaught without a game-changing gaffe or revealing admission, Cappleman's cross-examination had been crisp and effective. Exactly what she'd been hoping for.

•••

KAWASS'S REDIRECT EXAMINATION focused more on garnering sympathy from the jury than shoring up her client's weaker moments during Cappleman's interrogation. Katie reiterated that the Adelsons hadn't put any money aside for her in exchange for her silence. In fact, quite the opposite was true. During her three years of incarceration, she testified, her family had gone into severe debt to support her. "It's damaged my whole family."

Her lawyer asked if the Adelsons could "pay you any amount of money to keep you away from your children?"

"Never," Katie replied, nodding her head side-to-side with vigor.

"And you have been aware from the beginning who they want?"

"Yes, ma'am."

"Why won't you just lie and tell them that Charlie was a part of this?"

"I wish I could," Katie replied, gazing at the jury box, "because I wouldn't be incarcerated, and I'd be free, and I'd be with my children."

"And why haven't you done that?"

"Because I'm telling the truth," she insisted.

Jurors had a few questions of their own, mostly about Katie's work doing liquor promotions and as a bottle girl. They asked if she reported her tips directly to the nightclubs. She hadn't, Katie said, because none of the other girls did. Another juror wanted to know why she didn't report her tips on her tax returns. To which the defendant replied, "I would have to pay back a lot of money for it." In other words, because she'd owe taxes on her earnings—just like all of them.

Moreover, if she reported all of her tips, Katie told jurors, she wouldn't have been eligible for the free health insurance she was receiving from the State. She was perfectly willing to admit that she was a tax cheat and an insurance fraudster, but hoped jurors wouldn't hold that against her in deciding whether she also was a murderess.

After more than three hours of questioning, Katie resumed her seat between Kawass and DeCoste. All in all, jurors were no doubt struck by the contrast between what they'd just witnessed and what they'd heard earlier that week in a slew of Katie's wiretapped calls. The ultra-demure image she tried to project from the witness stand bore little resemblance to the persona established through her vulgar, often angry tirades with the two men in her life. The dichotomy between "in-court Katie" and "out-of-court Katie" was too stark to ignore.

Beyond that, jurors had seen a witness who appeared confused or flustered virtually any time she wasn't being spoon-fed answers by her own lawyer, and whose responses to difficult questions were often evasive, convoluted, or outright gibberish. If the goal of her defense team had been for Katie's testimony to be a game-changer in their favor, they'd likely failed in that endeavor. If it had moved at all, the needle was now likely pointing more in the direction of her conviction than acquittal. Certainly not what she and her lawyers had been hoping to achieve when they took the gamble of having her place her hand on the Bible just a few feet from the citizens who'd be deciding her fate.

• • •

AFTER KAWASS ANNOUNCED that Katie had no further evidence to present, Anna Norris recalled Sergeant Corbitt as the State's only rebuttal witness, using him to introduce into evidence text message exchanges between Katie and Charlie about teeth whitening, car repairs, credit card payments, and loans. All to show that, despite her denials, Katie had indeed received those benefits from her former lover long after their romance concluded. The prosecution then rested for a final time.

At which point, Judge Hankinson sprang his own surprise — on jurors. Closing arguments would begin the next morning, followed by jury deliberations. And if they didn't reach a verdict by early evening, jurors would spend the night — and the weekend if necessary — sequestered in a local hotel on the State of Florida's nickel. In accommodations just a bit more luxurious than rooms rented by the likes of Luis Rivera and Shoddrick Nobles. A little extra incentive to reach a unanimous verdict as quickly as possible.

24.

Last Word

IT HAD BEEN TWO WEEKS to the day since Georgia Cappleman stood before jurors outlining the evidence they'd see and hear during the trial. Since that time, the jury had heard from more than 40 witnesses, reviewed nearly 200 exhibits, and listened to some 30 recorded conversations. They'd seen numerous video recordings, some crystal clear, and one—the Dolce Vita footage—clear as mud. It was now time for the assistant state attorney to explain how all that evidence fit together, and why it left no reasonable doubt that Sigfredo Garcia and Katie Magbanua had been involved in a coordinated plot to assassinate a man they didn't know.

Cappleman queued up a PowerPoint presentation she projected onto the screen behind her, a large photo of a smiling Dan Markel at the center of the first slide. She began by tugging at jurors' heartstrings, telling them, "On July 18, 2014, this community suffered a blow when a revered law professor, colleague, son, father, brother, and friend was gunned down in broad daylight in his own home." She asked, "What enemy or enemies had Mr. Markel made that set into motion such a brutal act?" None other than his own family, she lamented. What had he done to provoke them? Nothing more than "wanting to be a good father, refusing to let his children be taken away from him."

As she continued to speak, it became obvious the veteran prosecutor was drained from all of the work she'd poured into the case. She'd typed out her entire argument—the printout contained in a three-ring binder resting on the lectern—and at times was merely reading it aloud, only occasionally making eye contact with jurors. Cappleman plodded through the first half of her presentation in a monotone, nothing approaching the energy and passion to be expected during a closing argument in a trial of such magnitude. She fumbled with the remote clicker several times—advancing to the wrong slides— taking timeouts to let jurors know she was having technical difficulties as she tried to find her place.

She also was racing against the clock. Judge Hankinson had allotted each attorney two hours to make their closing arguments. Cappleman had the unenviable burden of explaining the evidence, guiding jurors in applying the judge's instructions, and then coming before them a second time to rebut the defense lawyers' arguments—all within two hours. Which is what made the first part of her argument so puzzling.

For a solid 20 minutes, the State's lead counsel read aloud entire paragraphs from the divorce pleadings, as well as from Donna Adelson's emails to her daughter, to help jurors understand that Wendi's testimony that her divorce from Dan was merely "unpleasant" was a "severe understatement." It was almost as if she'd realized—only after having rested her case—that the jury hadn't gotten to read a single word from those exhibits. Yet they were critically important to understanding how livid Wendi's parents were with their ex-son-in-law.

Cappleman finally arrived at her central point—that Donna had paid handsomely for Wendi's divorce lawyers, "engaging in all these bitter legal battles," yet "Wendi and the boys were still here in Tallahassee." As Wendi had told her boyfriend Jeff Lacasse, "She was never going to be able to move to South Florida unless something happened to Danny. And she was right." Within 48 hours of the murder, the prosecutor reminded jurors, Dan's ex-wife had moved in with her parents and, over time, "systematically erased their father from these boys' lives."

Cappleman pivoted to Wendi's activities on July 18, 2014, showing the jury on the PowerPoint how she traveled miles out of her way to the crime scene, purchased Bulleit whiskey—intimating that Wendi was well aware by then that bullets had penetrated her ex-husband's skull—and then drove all the way back to a restaurant near her home. Wendi didn't get out of her minivan at the crime scene, ask questions, or make any phone calls, she reminded them. "And then she told you guys that she just observed the crime scene tape on her way by Centerville Road, which is not possible."

The lead prosecutor advanced the PowerPoint to a slide showing small photos of Harvey, Donna, Charlie, Wendi, and Dan arrayed across the top row, Katie centered below Charlie in a row by herself, and Garcia and Rivera on the bottom row, with arrows between the pictures implying that Charlie had retained Katie, who in turn solicited Garcia, who then involved Rivera. Cappleman told jurors that other individuals on the slide "also bear responsibility for the murder of Professor Markel," but that their job was to focus solely on Katie's and Garcia's roles.

"That being said," she acknowledged, "it's natural for you to wonder what's going on with these other people—when and how they will be charged." Cappleman noted that a lot had been made of her "personal feelings about charging the Adelsons," telling the jury with a smirk, "Maybe you think I'm eager to do this again in the near future." Yet all that mattered, she said, was the evidence relating to the two defendants standing trial. "Anyone else is for another day or for another jury."

Some 30 minutes into her presentation, Cappleman finally began homing in on the murder, reminding jurors that when Garcia called Katie on the way back to Miami and told her "It's done," that his "wife" had responded, "I know." The assistant state attorney confessed that she had no idea how Katie would have known so quickly that the murder had been completed, for some reason not cultivating the seed she'd planted when asking Katie about a possible WhatsApp message from Wendi or Charlie.

As best she could, Cappleman tried to deflect the withering attacks she knew the defense lawyers were about to level on Luis Rivera's credibility. She acknowledged that King Tato was a "bad dude" who'd made a deal with prosecutors "to save his own butt." His Latin Kings affiliation, she contended, was relevant only because it made him a suitable candidate to assist with a violent crime. As to the insinuation prosecutors had "spoon-fed" him his testimony, she pointed out how the defense lawyers were also contending that his testimony was "terrible and inconsistent"—telling the jury they couldn't have it both ways.

More importantly, if she'd been spoon-feeding Rivera what she wanted him to say, why on earth hadn't he provided any evidence about the Adelsons' role in the homicide? After all, the State's theory was that Donna and Charlie were the masterminds behind the crime. Rivera's inability to say anything about their involvement, Cappleman argued, established that Rivera had told the jury only what he actually knew—without fabricating details he didn't.

"You don't have to rely on Luis Rivera," she added, because "the whole case doesn't hinge on him," as he merely confirmed "what you already know" from the circumstantial evidence. But in her very next breath, Cappleman labeled him the "linchpin" who tied all the evidence together, now trying to have things both ways herself. And though she acknowledged there had been inaccuracies in his testimony, she didn't pause long enough to reflect on a single one. Rather, she merely asked jurors to consider that Rivera had made "ten statements in this case over a three-year period about events that happened over five years ago."

The veteran prosecutor anticipated that Garcia's and Katie's lawyers would argue that Rivera—not Garcia—had been the one to pull the trigger and had fabricated his entire story to save himself from the death penalty. To convince jurors that wasn't so, Cappleman projected onto the screen the ATM surveillance camera image taken the evening of the murder. Rivera, she pointed out, was in the driver's seat of the Prius with Garcia in the passenger seat, which was consistent with the city bus video footage filmed minutes after Dan was gunned down. "You're not going to be the shooter and the getaway driver," she asserted—as if that notion were an unyielding principle of criminal behavior. The bullet hole in the window of Dan's Honda Accord—now displayed on the projection screen—also indicated a "taller shooter," she said, alluding to the expert testimony that had Rivera been the shooter, the bullet would have penetrated the car window closer to the ground.

The phone evidence also was compelling, Cappleman told jurors, noting that the entire second trip to Tally lasted about 36 hours and that, during that time, there were 21 phone events between Katie and Garcia, including 12 calls. She walked jurors through the cell tower data confirming that both Rivera and Garcia were in Dan's neighborhood on July 17 and the video footage from Premie Fitness and city buses showing the Prius before and after the shooting—pointing out Garcia's white shirt in the passenger seat. And the very first phone call he made following the murder, she reminded the jury, was to none other than Katie.

The two-time Florida State grad segued to the "flurry of activity" the next morning. Katie had repeatedly tried to get ahold of Garcia, she recounted, but couldn't connect with him because he'd "dumped his phone." Her cell records showed she'd traveled to the area where Charlie's home was located. Cappleman stressed that at 10:22 a.m. there was phone contact for the first time ever between Katie and Rivera. Her phone records revealed that she was later at Rivera's apartment and that she, Garcia, and Rivera had met up for the "money drop. All of their phones are consistent with being there."

"Why does Katherine Magbanua have to be the connection?" she asked. Apart from Rivera's testimony that she was, Cappleman pointed to several pieces of circumstantial evidence: Katie was sleeping with both Charlie and Garcia at the same time; there was "zero evidence or proof of communication whatsoever between any Adelson and Mr. Rivera"; nor was there evidence of any communication between any Adelson and Garcia except for a one-minute connection with Harvey Adelson's phone on July 1, 2014—a call that obviously hadn't been answered, and yet another mysterious detail Cappleman didn't even attempt to explain.

The assistant state attorney distilled the voluminous financial evidence into a few easily digestible chunks. She reminded jurors that Garcia had purchased two cars and a motorcycle in the three months following the murder and that Katie had received a steady stream of payments from the Adelson Institute beginning in September 2014—netting her nearly $18,000. She showed jurors a chart of Katie's frequent ATM deposits in the months following the murder and reminded the jury of her breast implant surgery.

On the screen behind her, Cappleman then displayed Mary Hull's graph illustrating the mammoth spike in Katie's cash deposits immediately after the homicide. "Ms. Magbanua says she earned this cash working off the books in a night club," the prosecutor said dismissively. Yet she offered no evidence of any such income other than "a photograph of her scantily clad at what appears to be a nightclub." And Yindra Mascaro, Cappleman helped jurors recall, had testified that Katie hadn't worked at any nightclubs after June 2014.

"Her being put on the payroll at the Adelson Institute," she asserted, "is a sham." Katie had testified that she was working only for Charlie—not the Adelson Institute—but hadn't shed any light on what tasks she supposedly performed for the periodontist. And if she'd been working for Charlie and not the Adelson Institute, Cappleman asked rhetorically, "Why would the Adelson Institute be paying her?" And why would she have received the title to Harvey Adelson's Lexus in January 2016, long after her relationship with Charlie ended?

"All of these things post-murder," she emphasized, "and all of them post-relationship with Mr. Adelson." That was "very unusual treatment" for an ex-girlfriend. "When you look at this financial picture in comparison to the homicide date," Cappleman argued, "it's pretty undeniable that she had this huge benefit that coincided *dead on* with the murder of Mr. Markel."

The lead prosecutor pivoted briefly back to July 18, 2014, pointing to another telling piece of circumstantial evidence— that Katie had asked her friend Yindra Mascaro to keep her children overnight that very evening. While her kids were with Mascaro, she reminded jurors, the cell tower evidence revealed that Katie was at Rivera's residence. The next morning, "she's traveling south talking to Charlie Adelson for 25 minutes." The same morning she told Mascaro that Charlie's ex-brother-in-law had been in an accident.

Cappleman then transitioned to the April 2016 bump and the incessant phone chatter that followed, highlighting the significance of Donna not reporting the extortion attempt to law enforcement. Instead, "she goes straight to Charlie Adelson who goes straight to Katherine Magbanua who goes straight to Sigfredo Garcia. This is exactly what this undercover operation was designed to ferret out."

The prosecutor flashed onto the screen a photo of Donna and Charlie seated side-by-side at the waterfront near the Icon Condominiums tower the following day, pointing out that Charlie never heard his mother refer to Katie by name—only that the stranger trying to blackmail her had mentioned an "ex-girlfriend." Despite his bountiful supply of exes, Charlie had called only one—Katie. Who promptly met with him at Dolce Vita to discuss how to handle the blackmailer's demand.

Cappleman played for the jury the recorded call between Katie and Garcia, in which her "husband" initially told her, "I'm not making that fucking phone call," but then reluctantly agreed, "I'm going to take care of this fucking problem … 'cause the less you know, the better off you are." She reminded the jury how Katie had employed encoded language to convey the blackmailer's telephone number, offering the incredible explanation that she needed to disguise the number "because my kids were around or my coworkers were around."

Meanwhile, Garcia was lying to Katie about having called the number, Katie was lying to Charlie about having done so herself, and Charlie was lying to Donna about the problem being under control. Very odd behavior for innocent people, Cappleman insisted.

As she neared the end of her opening argument, the assistant state attorney played a small sample of the 23-minute phone call between Katie and Charlie, in which the Filipina immigrant angrily spewed profanities, pushing back against her ex-boyfriend's request to "find out who the fuck it is." The woman whose voice was captured on that recording, Cappleman asserted, was the real Katie Magbanua, not to be confused with the well-dressed, prim-and-proper woman who'd taken the witness stand in her own defense and denied any knowledge of the murder.

Concluding her remarks, the veteran prosecutor told jurors that the case "involved the most premeditated murder imaginable ... stalking and following and planning and trips and stuff going back a year" all of which "came to fruition when Garcia fired those two shots into Mr. Markel's vehicle and devastated so many lives in an instant." She asked them to use their common sense and to convict both Garcia and Katie of first-degree murder and conspiracy to commit first-degree murder.

• • •

THOUGH GEORGIA CAPPLEMAN had the unenviable burden of trying to synthesize and explain two weeks' worth of evidence in just two hours, Saam Zangeneh's mission was even more daunting: trying to convince the jury that the evidence confirming his client's presence at and near the crime scene wasn't what it seemed. Not surprisingly, he didn't need his full two hours, completing his argument in just 53 minutes.

Yet what Zangeneh lacked in substance he tried to make up for in swagger and style, performing like a thespian on stage—reveling in his moment in the spotlight—arguing with passion and gusto. He constructed his entire argument around a metaphor, telling jurors that the prosecution was trying to get them to buy "the Sigfredo Garcia house." His job, he said, was to be the "inspector," pointing out problems with its foundation, wiring, plumbing, and roof.

Its foundation, Zangeneh contended, was Luis Rivera, making Cappleman pay the price for referring to him as the "linchpin" of the State's case. Rivera, he reminded the jury, was the "head of a criminal organization," the "first crown" of his North Miami Latin Kings tribe for nearly 15 years. "This is not a charitable organization," he said with a smirk. "This is a violent gang." That mattered, he argued, because King Tato had ample criminal connections to have pulled off a murder without any assistance from Sigfredo Garcia.

Zangeneh used one of the letters Rivera had written to Cappleman from jail to bolster his argument that he *had* been spoon-fed his testimony. He zeroed in on Rivera's statement, "It is ridiculous that I am in confinement only because I helped you," asserting that was precisely what he'd done—helped the prosecution rather than telling the truth.

Oddly, the one-time Miami prosecutor devoted more than ten minutes of his argument to picking apart Rivera's testimony about the *first* trip from Miami to Tally—the one that *didn't* end with Dan Markel having two bullets in his head. He told the jury that no records existed to establish his client was on *that* trip, contending its real purpose was a drug deal between Rivera and Shoddrick Nobles. "There's holes and questions on this trip that have to be screaming," he insisted.

As Cappleman had predicted, Zangeneh posited that Rivera had been the triggerman. "Do you think he would have gotten the deal that he got if he admitted to being the shooter?" he asked rhetorically. He argued that Rivera's position in the Prius's driver's seat made him—not Garcia—the logical one to commit the murder because he had the shorter distance, and more direct path, to the driver's seat of Dan's car. He demonstrated for the jury how Rivera would have walked up to the law professor's Accord and fired his weapon, gangster style with his shooting hand held high—thereby explaining the height of the bullet hole. "A gangster killed Dan Markel," Zangeneh declared. And that's exactly what Rivera was. "Two and two has to equal four."

Rivera's story also didn't make sense, he said, because being a hitman is a "one-man job. You don't see movies where you have two hitmen go do something. It's one guy with a briefcase and gloves. That's what you see. You don't see a tag-team hit squad."

Though Zangeneh didn't dispute Charlie's involvement in the murder, he suggested that Wendi's brother could have hired Rivera directly, noting that they lived in the same geographic area, that Charlie was a known drug user, and that Rivera was a convicted drug dealer. He speculated that the periodontist could have asked his girlfriend, Katie, if she had any connections to get "some coke or some weed," and that she likely would have connected him with King Tato. "Rivera comes by and a deal is struck," Zangeneh contended with a shrug of his shoulders—as if the entire case were as simple as that.

The defense lawyer pivoted to "the wiring," returning to his house metaphor. His client, he said, "could not stand Charlie Adelson," reminding the jury of two separate incidents—one in which Garcia wanted to ram his car into the restaurant Charlie and Katie were dining at, and a second when Garcia angrily confronted the couple on the street when they were headed out with the jet ski. He asserted that Garcia wouldn't have agreed to kill another human being without at least knowing who was behind the request. And even for a $100,000 payout, Zangeneh insisted, his client never would have done so for Charlie Adelson, the dentist who was "banging" his "wife."

"Now let's talk about the plumbing," he transitioned. "What stinks." Six-and-a-half years in a state prison "because he said my client did a murder." That certainly stunk. Something else that smelled, he told jurors, was Investigator Shawn Yao's testimony about the height of the shooter, reminding them that Yao had initially concluded from the 49-inch height of the bullet hole that whoever fired the gun had to be between 5' and 6' tall. That range included Rivera, but excluded Garcia. Two weeks before trial, however, Yao "came up with a new theory," he said with evident disdain, solely to make the height of the shooter fit Rivera's testimony.

Nearly 45 minutes into his argument, Zangeneh finally turned his attention to the most damning evidence against his client—which confirmed Sigfredo Garcia's presence in Tally on July 18, 2014. The cell tower evidence, the defense lawyer declared, didn't "conclusively" place Garcia's phone at Premier Fitness, though he provided jurors no explanation for that position. He claimed that the ATM surveillance video revealing his client in the Prius's passenger seat—wearing a long-sleeve white shirt—didn't match the city bus video, contending that the passenger in that footage had been wearing a short-sleeve white shirt. Yet he didn't show jurors images from either to allow them to compare the two so they could draw their own conclusions.

That left only one source of evidence placing Garcia in Tally the day of the murder, Zangeneh argued—Luis Rivera— "and I believe we've made our position on him very clear." He quickly backtracked, however, realizing he'd forgotten about Shoddrick Nobles—who not only testified that Garcia was buying drugs from him and partying with him, but had also identified him from a photo lineup. "I forgot about him," Zangeneh sheepishly acknowledged. He reminded jurors that Nobles lived in his car and was a drug dealer who the State didn't prosecute for providing his client drugs, much less bust him on a probation violation. "He got a pass because his testimony fits their story." But the defense lawyer offered jurors no explanation as to how Nobles was able to pick his client out of a photo lineup if he'd never met him.

Wrapping up, the former prosecutor insisted that there was "substantially more evidence against the Adelsons than there is against Sigfredo Garcia." The State, he said, was "chomping to get the Adelsons," and "rightfully so." But as to his client, Zangeneh asked jurors not to buy the house the State was trying to sell them and to come back "with the right verdict."

•••

KATIE'S DEFENSE TEAM SELECTED Chris DeCoste to make their final pitch to the jury. The one-time trial-team superstar was on his game from start to finish—articulate, passionate, and at times spellbinding—his full-throated argument delivered with a robust, yet pleasing, Boston accent. Periodically, he paused to glare at the prosecutors—seated just a few feet to his right—his hostile expression conveying utter disdain and contempt. Unlike Cappleman, the polished defense lawyer rarely looked down at his notes, his eyes locked on all 14 jurors throughout the hour and 40 minutes he stood before them.

"The less you know, the better," he began. "That's what Sigfredo Garcia said to Katherine Magbanua in 2016 over the wiretaps. It's also what this government wants from you, because the more you know about this case—the more facts— the more you realize that the pieces don't fit and that *she's innocent.*"

Before diving into the heart of his argument, DeCoste took a step back to humanize the victim, calling Dan Markel a "brilliant scholar, devoted father, and amazing son." In a nod to Ruth and Phil Markel, who were looking on from their familiar seats in the gallery, he told jurors, "No parent should ever have to bury a child, let alone sit in a courtroom and watch the first-degree murder trial—the gruesome first-degree murder trial—for their son."

Echoing the lead prosecutor, he asserted that the Adelsons were responsible for Dan's murder and "must be brought to justice." But as to his client, DeCoste argued, the State hadn't conducted an objective investigation. Rather, "they tried to build a case around her to force her to cooperate so that they could get what they've been going after for years—the Adelson family." There would likely be another trial, he predicted, to determine the fate "of one or all of the Adelsons, but you're not that jury."

DeCoste swiveled to face the prosecution table, his eyes shooting daggers and his volume escalating. "If the government wants to charge the Adelsons, *charge them*," he said, his hands slashing down forcefully for emphasis. "It appears the government has more evidence against them than the defendants in this courtroom." What happened to the slain law professor, he acknowledged, "was tragic, but convicting an innocent woman doesn't fix that. Nor does it in any way honor the memory of Professor Dan Markel."

To illustrate the State's failure to investigate his client objectively, DeCoste told a story he said his father had shared with him when he was a boy. His dad had been driving in the Midwest, he recounted, amid sprawling patches of farmland. Alongside the road, he spotted a barn. A boy with a bow and arrow was standing between the road and the barn. His father noticed a few circular targets painted onto the side of the barn, with an arrow sticking out of one of the bullseyes.

His dad pulled over, hoping to witness the boy's precision as an archer. As he looked on, the youngster shot an arrow into the side of the barn, but wildly missed all of the targets. Yet he didn't appear the least bit fazed by the careless shot. Instead, the lad calmly walked up to the side of the barn with a can of paint and painted a new target around the arrow he'd just fired. DeCoste told jurors that was precisely how the government had investigated Katie. "The idea was to paint the target around her to force her to cooperate."

The target metaphor, he said, also explained the government's misplaced focus on the phone calls between Katie and Charlie, who she was dating, and Katie and Garcia, with whom she shared two children. Of course she was in frequent communications with them. Those calls were perfectly natural, DeCoste argued, not smoking guns pointing to her involvement in a murder.

Regarding her cash deposits, he told jurors, "They presented it to you as *unexplained* cash—trying to paint those circles around the arrow brighter and brighter, thicker and thicker." Even though the investigators knew that

Katie was working at nightclubs and making cash tips, they performed "zero investigation" to determine when and how much. "No subpoenas sent out. No interviews." Why didn't they investigate? he asked. Because they'd have found an explanation for the cash deposits, and "those circles around that arrow start to evaporate."

Curiously, DeCoste contended that the dramatic escalation in his client's cash deposits during the weeks following the murder was actually evidence of her *innocence*. Why? "If you're receiving money from a murder, who in their right mind is going to deposit it?" he asked with a tone of incredulity. "Those are acts of an innocent person." The State was trying to fault his client, "a young mother, for working multiple jobs, trying to do anything she can, even if it means taking money from Mr. Garcia that may not be from honest places … for the support of her children."

As for her breast enhancement, "There is zero evidence—*zero*," he asserted, "that it was paid for from the proceeds of a homicide." The title conveying the Adelsons' Lexus to Katie was objective evidence she'd purchased it legitimately, he declared, the entire transaction no more significant than "an ex-girlfriend buying an old used car from an ex-boyfriend." He mocked the prosecution for suggesting that Katie would have been compensated for her role in a murder with a 14-year-old vehicle with 160,000 miles on its odometer.

DeCoste explained the checks Katie had received from the Adelson Institute with similar logic, telling jurors it would have been "foolish," had she been involved in a murder, to create a "paper trail" of "employment records, tax documents. That would be a crazy thing to do if you want to distance yourself from somebody should anybody ever get investigated or arrested in the future." Indeed, that is how he explained nearly all of the incriminating evidence against his client—by flipping it on its head to suggest that it pointed to her innocence, rather than guilt—hoping the jury would believe that a criminal would have successfully covered her tracks, rather than leaving them behind for investigators to find.

The Boston transplant argued that the government was "splitting hairs" by questioning why Katie's checks had come from the Adelson Institute rather than Charlie directly. She *was* working for Charlie, he insisted, reminding the jury that she'd texted him the day before the first check was written with her "availability so you know more or less how many hours I can dedicate." He pointed to the wiretapped recordings in which Katie mentioned calls she was making to Charlie's patients.

DeCoste argued that the wiretap evidence—as a whole—also pointed to Katie's innocence. "Hundreds of calls. Hundreds of texts. Not one thing—*not one*—not one thing of her being involved in this murder, only her needing to know less." Katie's testimony that Charlie was "definitely involved" in the murder wasn't based on any personal knowledge she absorbed as an insider, he reminded jurors, but rather, on seeing "what all of you have seen during this trial." Cocking his head toward the prosecution table—and pointing directly at Cappleman—DeCoste reiterated, "You want to charge him, *charge him*."

The defense lawyer tried to turn another piece of incriminating evidence on its head, contending that Charlie never would have asked Katie to call the blackmailer if she'd been involved in the homicide out of concern "she could say something wrong, do something wrong, to incriminate him." Rather, Katie was a logical choice to make the call, he asserted, because "he knew she didn't know anything."

DeCoste made short shrift of the Dolce Vita video footage. "Can't understand any of it, much of it," he said. And as far as Katie was concerned, "That wasn't a conversation about a conspiracy of the murder of his brother-in-law. It was just another day sitting down with Charles where he's talking about how his family is getting harassed."

The defense lawyer knew jurors would likely wonder why Katie—were she truly innocent—hadn't gone straight to the police upon learning someone had inserted her name into an attempt to blackmail the Adelson family. His simple explanation was, "Katherine wasn't bumped or harassed or called or texted. It wasn't her place. It wasn't her place to be calling the police because it wasn't directly against her."

But he then reminded jurors that Katie actually told Charlie that she *was* going to go to law enforcement—undermining the very point he'd just made—having been recorded on the wiretap as saying she was going to go to the "f'ing FBI." Incredibly, DeCoste paused to tell jurors that Katie "hates that she swore" and "won't even spell out swear words"—as if jurors hadn't already gleaned from the wiretapped recordings that "fucking," "fuck," "motherfucking," "bullshit," and "asshole" were words firmly entrenched in her everyday vocabulary.

Halfway through his argument, the former prosecutor projected a photo of Luis Rivera—taken by a newspaper photographer during his testimony—onto the screen, telling jurors that investigators had improperly dismissed numerous problems with the longtime gang leader's "story." He reminded them that the government determined it didn't have enough evidence even to arrest Katie until hearing Rivera's proffer—let alone to prove her involvement in the murder. Yet once King Tato mentioned her name, they rushed to slap the cuffs on her the very next day.

"Katherine is innocent," DeCoste proclaimed. "She is innocent of all three of these charges." The only way the jury could convict her, he argued, was "to believe Luis Rivera, a man who cannot be trusted" and whose testimony was a "convoluted mess full of contradictions." Rivera, he contended, provided only two things to support the charges against Katie—"that he heard some phone calls, and that on July 19, Katherine paid money."

As for him overhearing Katie's voice on phone calls with Garcia, that was an "easy lie," DeCoste asserted, because he had the phone records at his disposal. "Plus, he knows Sigfredo Garcia's habits of communicating with the mother of his children."

He pointed out that Rivera also got critical facts demonstrably wrong. As an example, he testified that during the June 2014 trip to Tally, Katie and Garcia were "constantly" on the phone. "The answer to that," DeCoste retorted, "to quote Shoddrick Nobles: *Nope!*" The phone records revealed only one 29-second phone call between the "husband" and "wife" during the entire car ride from Miami to Tally.

"Let's go to 7/19—another easy lie." Rivera testified that Katie had called him while he was at the barbershop. "Again, *wrong*," DeCoste declared. The phone records established that it was actually the other way around. This wasn't a minor detail, he insisted. "It's a *huge* detail, because these are the pieces of evidence that Luis Rivera is giving, and Luis Rivera is the sole witness against her." He wasn't only wrong about who initiated that call, the defense attorney emphasized, he also was wrong about where he was when he and Katie spoke—not at Ray's Barbershop, as he testified, but miles away in Miami Beach.

Rivera's testimony against his client, DeCoste told the jury, was the product of a "desperate" deal with the government. Rivera was desperate to avoid the death penalty and the government was desperate to make progress in the case. The Latin Kings gang leader knew he'd secure a deal only by naming someone new—who the government didn't already have within its grasp. And that's the only reason, DeCoste asserted, why King Tato had implicated Katie in the murder plot.

Rivera was so desperate for a deal, he added, he even "tried to give them Wendi Adelson, testifying that she was at Dan's house with the children the morning before the murder." But even the government agreed—and stipulated—that Rivera's testimony on that point was incorrect, as the children were actually at preschool that morning. His lie about Wendi proved "he doesn't care about sending somebody away for his own good. His life is about taking from other people, and he gets a deal by taking from *her*," DeCoste said passionately, pointing at his client.

He told jurors Rivera had lied to them about something even more basic—that he couldn't read or write, reminding them he had a driver's license. How could he have passed his written exam if he couldn't read or write? he asked rhetorically. "That guy can read. Don't be fooled."

DeCoste deftly sifted Rivera's testimony through the jury instruction explaining how to assess the credibility of a witness, noting that he was a five-time felon, his testimony had been littered with inconsistencies, and prosecutors "had him by the neck" if he deviated from his story. "He's pretty much checking every box on the jury instructions of why you should not trust him." Then, with a theatrical flair, the former trial team superstar pulled Rivera's photo off the machine that had projected it onto the screen for 25 solid minutes, crumpled it into a ball in his left hand, and tossed it into a garbage can—telling jurors that was exactly where the former gang leader's testimony belonged.

DeCoste claimed that prosecutors had pressured Katie to cooperate with them and expected that pressure to pay dividends. "What they didn't count on, however, is that Katherine Magbanua is innocent. And here we are in trial."

The prosecution had even stooped so low, he scowled, as to imply that Katie had refused to cooperate based on the promise of some kind of "payoff," a suggestion DeCoste found offensive because there's "no amount of money that you could pay a mother of two to risk never seeing her children again." Did they seriously believe "Katherine sacrifices seeing her children so that Wendi can be with hers? They can't see it, they can't understand it," he said—now becoming emotional—gesturing forcefully with his right arm. "That she's innocent and she wasn't involved."

So how did the murder go down if Katie wasn't involved? DeCoste fleshed out his theory: Charlie "wanted the murder to happen" and had money. Garcia "wanted Katherine Magbanua back" and had the means. He pointed to the April 2014 text message exchange between Katie and Charlie establishing that she believed Tuto was trying to contact her new boyfriend directly. It didn't take much of a leap from those text messages to conclude that the wealthy periodontist had hired Garcia without Katie's knowledge or involvement.

Though the cellphone records didn't reveal any direct communications between the two, DeCoste speculated, "Maybe—wild thought—they were communicating through other means because he was talking about *a murder.*"

The July 1 confrontation in the street, he asserted, was one of the most critical pieces of evidence in the entire case—and yet one the prosecution couldn't explain. Why was Garcia so angry? Because he and Charlie had a deal, DeCoste posited, that if he'd eliminate Dan Markel, Charlie would end his romantic relationship with Katie. But Garcia hadn't followed through with his end of the bargain when he drove up to Tally in June. And as of July 1, it was now clear to him that Charlie was reneging on his, flaunting his continuing relationship with Garcia's "wife."

It was no coincidence, DeCoste stressed, "That right when the murder finally happens, Charles Adelson—and we know it from the messages, we know it from Katherine Magbanua—ghosted her, broke up with her." The murder was not *through* Katie, he insisted. Rather, it was *about* Katie.

DeCoste pointed out that his client, who was born in the Philippines and spoke the language, didn't flee even after Garcia and Rivera were arrested for the murder. Even with the widespread publicity about the case, dragging her name through the mud. And even after a probable cause affidavit leaked to the media detailed her supposed involvement. "Somebody guilty would have left," he told jurors. "She stayed."

The government, DeCoste said, had provided Katie "the key to her own freedom." Yet she hadn't used it to get out of jail. Why not? "There is only one reason why a single mother of two young children would sit in custody for three years in confinement, risking it all." He paused for dramatic emphasis. "She's innocent. That is the only explanation."

Like Zangeneh, DeCoste tried to convince the jury that Rivera had been the shooter, not Garcia. What was his basis for that contention? That Rivera "told you how Dan Markel was on the phone, how Dan Markel put his arm up," details he couldn't have known if he'd been sitting in the Prius when Garcia shot him. "He knows that because he's the one that pulled the gun on Dan Markel and killed him."

"Ladies and gentlemen, this is what a wrongful prosecution looks like," the defense attorney stated in a solemn tone, bringing his argument to a close. "It's within your power to stop it from becoming a wrongful conviction." He proclaimed Katie's innocence one final time, reminding jurors that she'd been in custody for three years. Barely above a whisper, he told them, "It's time for her to go home."

•••

HAVING BITTEN HER TONGUE through two-and-a-half hours of blistering attacks on her and her law enforcement colleagues, Georgia Cappleman had no difficulty summoning the energy and passion that had been largely absent from her first argument. During her final 20 minutes behind the lectern, the seasoned prosecutor was full of emotion, her eyes laser-focused on the men and women who would shortly step into the jury room to decide the case.

She focused first on DeCoste's argument. "They have attempted to inflame you against me to invoke your sympathy on behalf of their client," she said, noting how her adversary had dwelled on Katie being in jail, unable to see her children. Incredulous, Cappleman reminded jurors, "*She's on trial for murder* … Dan Markel will never see his kids again, and he didn't get a choice in that." Pointing toward Katie's defense table, the prosecutor asserted, "She had a choice, and this trial is about her choices."

Cappleman appeared sincerely perplexed as to how anyone could argue that no evidence existed of Katie's involvement in the murder, imploring jurors to listen carefully to the wiretaps, which left little doubt she was "right in the middle of this thing." As to DeCoste's repeated reference to her "innocence," she asked, "What possible motive would I have to prosecute an innocent person? In what universe would that assist me in getting the Adelsons?"

She transitioned briefly to the "overwhelming" evidence against Garcia. "He shot Dan Markel, a man he didn't even know." Once again, Cappleman expressed incredulity, this time over the notion that Garcia wouldn't have been stupid enough to party with Shoddrick Nobles in his hotel room if he was about to commit a murder. "They shot this man in broad daylight in Betton Hills," she reminded jurors. "They don't care about being stupid." All Garcia cared about was the money, which "he blew immediately to impress and win back Ms. Magbanua. His conduct is the very definition of 'cold-blooded.'"

Cappleman noted how Katie's lawyers, throughout the trial, had "bent over backwards to tell us" she had been working for the Adelson Institute, though only remotely on the weekends. Yet Katie had freely admitted from the witness stand that she'd never worked for the Adelson family's dental practice, contending instead that she'd worked for Charlie as his personal assistant. "Why is Donna stroking the checks if she's working for Charlie?" Cappleman asked, a question DeCoste never even attempted to answer.

The prosecutor reminded jurors of the $100,000 reward for information leading to an arrest. Katie had in her possession the telephone number of someone she had reason to believe was actively extorting the Adelson family over Dan's murder. "Do you think this woman wouldn't have turned that number in, *in a heartbeat*," Cappleman asked, "and collected that reward if she didn't have anything to do with it?" Similarly, there was no reasonable explanation for her using encoded language to describe that phone number had she merely been an innocent bystander, the State's lead counsel stressed, pouncing on a subject DeCoste hadn't addressed a single time during his entire argument.

Cappleman quoted an exchange she had with Katie during cross-examination: "Did you talk to Luis Rivera on the day of the money drop?" Rather than telling the prosecutor she didn't know anything about a "money drop," Katie had simply answered "Yes," implying that she knew about the money drop.

This time around, Cappleman dedicated more time addressing Rivera's credibility as a witness, telling jurors, "The man has a sixth-grade education and reads on a third-grade level and they want you to believe he understood the evidence well enough to falsify the testimony, get all these little, intricate things correct." The notion that this poorly educated man was a "smart guy," she added, was preposterous, reminding jurors that he'd even misspelled his own name after taking the oath. And that he'd been careless enough to rent a car in his own name knowing he was about to commit a murder.

Cappleman asked jurors to consider the significance of Rivera turning State's evidence on his best friend since childhood and his "wife." "Why would he do that" if they weren't involved in the murder? And if the gang leader, as Zangeneh speculated, had been hired directly by Charlie? Would he really send his innocent best friend to death row in order to protect Charlie? Did that make any sense?

The assistant state attorney also answered the question of why Garcia would gladly have committed a murder for a man he despised, telling jurors, "You'd be surprised how much people would set aside for the right amount of money. He also would do anything for Katherine Magbanua, and she was the one asking." It also wasn't clear that Garcia even realized that Charlie had been the mastermind behind the hit, she noted, having told his best friend they were in Tally to commit a murder "for Wendi."

Cappleman had her own metaphor for jurors to ponder during their deliberations, telling them the Dan Markel murder conspiracy was like a train, with each co-conspirator isolated from all but one of the others: Donna's only connection with Charlie, his with Katie, hers with Garcia, and his with Rivera. "You can't get from the engine to the caboose without going through the middle," she declared, "and the middle is Katherine Magbanua."

She impressed on jurors that, just because Katie "didn't come to Tallahassee or pull the trigger herself, does not mean that she is not *just as guilty* as the ones who did. She hired Garcia, who in turn hired Rivera, and she's the conduit between Dan Markel and the man that put a bullet in his head. Without her, none of this happens." Pointing directly at Katie, Cappleman reiterated, "Without her, we're not sitting here today."

The veteran prosecutor spoke her last few words with the picture of a smiling Dan Markel back on the projection screen, coming full circle to where she began. She implored jurors to focus on the totality of the evidence, which would bring them back to what the case was really all about: "justice for Dan Markel. And there is only one verdict that speaks the truth in this case, and that does justice in this case, and that is a verdict of guilty as charged for both defendants. Thank you so much."

Georgia Cappleman raised her fists in the air, triumphantly, as if she'd crossed the finish line in a marathon. Which, for all intents and purposes, she just had.

25.

Civic Duty

JURY DELIBERATIONS MARK a seismic shift in the trial process. Before closing arguments are completed, jurors are instructed—multiple times per day—that they may not discuss the case with anyone. That restriction doesn't merely prevent them from communicating with friends, family members, and the media. It also prohibits jurors from discussing the case even amongst themselves—the thought being that deliberations should be based on the complete presentation of evidence, not just bits and pieces, and that jurors should keep completely open minds until they have seen and heard everything.

Thus, for three solid weeks, during breaks, at lunch, and while they waited in the jury room as the judge and lawyers hashed out matters beyond their purview, the citizens serving on this particular jury—all strangers when the trial began—discussed everything under the sun other than what had happened to Dan Markel. They bonded discussing the jobs they had to put on hold—as nurses, teachers, researchers, and government employees—as well as their families and pets. Several had young children at home and two were actually pregnant, one not yet showing and the other unmistakably nearing her due date.

Finally, the two men and ten women who now bore one of society's most weighty civic obligations were at liberty to share with one another the thoughts that had cascaded through their minds—and filled a plethora of juror notebooks—as they watched the evidence unfold before them.

Something else that had changed the moment the jury-room door closed was the balance of power. From the outset of the trial, members of the jury had done precisely as they were instructed by the judge and the bailiff—showing up, taking breaks, and grabbing meals only when others told them they could. And now? They were the ones suddenly in charge—the judge, bailiff, courtroom officials, and lawyers all at their beck and call. If they had a thought, question, or concern, they even had a direct line—through the bailiff—to the Honorable James C. Hankinson.

The third thing that had changed abruptly was what was transpiring on the other side of the jury-room door. In virtually the blink of an eye, Courtroom 3G was transformed from the frenetic pace and activity resembling a professional sporting event to what now could most accurately be described as the atmosphere of a maternity ward's waiting room. The prosecutors, defense lawyers, and defendants milled aimlessly about their respective counsel tables—both defendants now shackled at the feet with metal chains for good measure—anxiously watching time pass by. Ever so slowly.

For Phil, Ruth, and Shelly Markel—who'd been living the nightmare of Dan's vicious slaying for more than five years—each minute the jury remained out felt more like an hour. Though they knew the end was near, they had no way of knowing what the outcome might be, which made each passing minute all the more excruciating.

For the lawyers, after thousands of hours of tedious, mind-numbing work over several years, apart from the anxiety they shared with everyone else, a sense of helplessness and loss of control was even more pervasive. They'd each done everything within their power in their attempt to persuade jurors of the righteousness of their respective causes. But they now had no further ability to shape the outcome, and were entirely at the mercy of whatever whimsical thought or spur-of-the-moment belief any particular juror might conjure up as the deliberations proceeded. For professionals accustomed to being in total control, their abject inability to influence what was now happening inside the jury room was enough to make them queasy.

•••

ONLY TWO MEMBERS of the jury had attained their sixtieth birthday. One of them, Douglas Rusmisell, was selected as foreperson as their first official act of business, just as a massive cart containing the trial exhibits was being wheeled into the room. It was already after 4:00 p.m. The hope that they'd be able to avoid a night in captivity at a downtown hotel was fading as quickly as the daylight. The group had already decided to eat dinner in the jury room to jam as much work into the remainder of the evening as they possibly could.

The members of this particular jury took their civic obligation seriously, cutting corners to reach a speedy resolution the furthest thought from any juror's mind. To a one, they wanted to proceed carefully and deliberatively, with the aim of reaching a unanimous verdict fully consistent with Judge Hankinson's instructions. In the early going that Thursday afternoon, they worked as a synchronized team of 12—unified in purpose and mission.

They made the logical decision to begin with the case against Sigfredo Garcia, as the evidence presented against him seemed simpler to digest and synthesize. The group focused on several important pieces of evidence: the Premier Fitness surveillance footage and city bus videos revealing what appeared to be two men in the greenish Prius the morning of the murder; the still images from the JPMorgan Chase ATM camera depicting— with crystal clarity—Rivera and Garcia in the same Prius in South Florida early that evening; and Jim Geiger's eye-witness account of a Prius-like vehicle hurriedly backing out of Dan's driveway seconds after he heard gunshots. Collectively, that was enough to convince the group that both men had been involved in the shooting. They also concluded that Garcia, clad in a white shirt, had been in the passenger seat as the Prius fled the crime scene. His phone number scribbled onto the car rental agreement further cemented his involvement.

But, as several jurors correctly observed, under the law Judge Hankinson had provided them, Garcia's mere presence at the scene of the crime didn't necessarily make him guilty of first-degree murder. Nearly half of the jury doubted Rivera's testimony about Garcia being the triggerman, accepting Saam Zangeneh's argument that King Tato had every incentive to lie to save himself from the death penalty. The only other evidence helping decipher which of the two was actually the gunman came from the State's weapons expert, who merely indicated that it was more likely the shooter was taller rather than shorter. Which wasn't very convincing either. Nor was Cappleman's argument that the shooter and the getaway driver couldn't possibly have been the same person. For the moment at least, the jury appeared stymied.

Perusing their written instructions, one of them pointed out that it really didn't matter who the shooter was. If both Rivera and Garcia had been in Dan Markel's driveway with the intention to kill him, she said to the others, they were equally guilty of first-degree murder—no matter which of them actually pulled the trigger. Though that seemed well and good, another juror posited the scenario that Garcia might have believed they'd come to Tally merely to rob Dan, and only learned of the intent to kill him after Rivera fired his gun. How, in that instance, could Garcia be guilty of first-degree murder? That brain teaser led to Rusmisell's first—of what would become several—written questions to Judge Hankinson. He wrote out a second seeking more clarity on the judge's instructions regarding the crime of conspiracy to commit murder. Rusmisell knocked on the jury-room door and handed the note to the bailiff to deliver to the judge.

While awaiting a response, the 12 jurors engaged in a free-wheeling discussion about the evidence—which quickly devolved into their respective impressions of Wendi Adelson.

Virtually all of them were turned off by how Dan's ex-wife appeared to be dripping with white privilege—beautified by expensive cosmetic work—and how she was living a very comfortable life despite all the misery that had transpired in the wake of Dan's murder. They were especially repulsed by how Wendi had done everything within her power to erase her ex and his family from Ben and Lincoln's lives. Jurors found her testimony evasive and dishonest, especially her statement that she hadn't driven down Trescott Drive to the crime scene—which they knew from other evidence wasn't true. Many were particularly disturbed by her cavalier response— and laughter—at the notion she might someday be charged. One juror even scribbled in her notepad, "She's a lying bitch."

Not only did they agree amongst themselves that Wendi likely had some foreknowledge about the murder plot, given the opportunity, the group wouldn't have had the slightest difficulty convicting her mother and brother of first-degree murder. It made no sense to jurors that anyone else would have hired two hitmen to drive all the way from Miami to execute Wendi's ex-husband. That Katie and Charlie were in a sexual relationship at that very time made the connection between the Adelsons and the killers as clear as a crisp blue sky.

To a one, jurors felt deeply frustrated they weren't given the opportunity to pronounce judgment on the wealthy masterminds behind Dan's savage killing—who were still living their best lives, driving fancy sports cars and enjoying the view from cushy, waterfront homes. It was difficult for them to grasp why the only three individuals the State seemed willing to prosecute were members of minority groups from underprivileged backgrounds—mere underlings who'd done the Adelsons' dirty work. Something about that seemed very, very wrong. But they realized they held no power to bring members of the Adelson family to justice, a job they hoped would present itself to another jury, just like them, in the near future. For now, they had their own job to do, and wanted to do it well.

• • •

THE BAILIFF KNOCKED on the door, handing the foreperson a handwritten note from Judge Hankinson, essentially telling jurors that he couldn't answer their question because it asked him to apply the facts to the law, which was their job. He'd answer most of their questions in much the same fashion—which jurors found frustrating. They decided to take a stab at figuring out whether the State had proven its case against Katie Magbanua.

The group quickly concluded that Rivera's testimony had been riddled with too many inconsistencies to rely solely on his account of Katie's involvement in the homicide. Many were bothered by the sweet deal he'd received to turn State's evidence. Not a one believed he was actually illiterate. If they were going to convict the jailed mother of two of first-degree murder, jurors wanted to ground their decision on other, more reliable evidence.

Naturally, they discussed Katie's own testimony, each sharing notes they'd jotted down while she was on the stand. As they went around the room, it became clear that none of them believed her broad, self-serving claim of innocence. Indeed, as a whole, the jury believed her testimony had been largely untruthful.

The most powerful pieces of evidence against her, as many articulated when given the chance, were her large cash deposits following the murder and the checks she'd received from the Adelson Institute. All 12 believed that the cash and checks constituted evidence of a payoff. Yet one of the more outspoken jurors—a college-educated, 25-year-old woman—pressed the group on the State's burden of proof. Katie receiving a lot of money from the Adelsons, she noted, didn't by itself prove her direct involvement in the murder. She told the other jurors she didn't believe the evidence presented had been clear enough—or strong enough—to convict Katie of murder. The cohesiveness that marked the beginning of the panel's deliberations began to deteriorate.

Another juror chimed in, focusing the group's attention on the money drop the morning after the shooting, reading from her notes that Katie had traveled to Charlie's home to retrieve the money and was then at Jessica Rodriguez's apartment delivering the payoff. *That* proved Katie's direct involvement, didn't it? she asked the others. But the outspoken, 25-year-old juror pushed back, telling the others there was no such proof, only Rivera's uncorroborated testimony that Katie showed up with the money.

"That's not true!" several others retorted, pointing to Sergeant Corbitt's testimony about Katie's cellphone pinging towers near Charlie's home and then later, by Rodriguez's apartment. "We all saw it on the maps," one of them said. She noted how colored dots and arrows had been used to depict where Katie's, Garcia's, and Rivera's cellphones had pinged nearby towers, eventually all congregating around the apartment Rivera shared with his baby mama.

"Show me," the 25-year-old juror requested. "Show me the maps that demonstrate that Katie was there." Other jurors began rummaging through the large stack of exhibits on the cart, trying to find the maps the prosecution had projected onto their screens during Sergeant Corbitt's testimony. But they were nowhere to be found. Rusmisell grabbed his notepad and scribbled out another note to the judge: "Is Corbitt's cell tower mapping available for our consideration?"

It was getting late and looking most unlikely that jurors would be able to avoid their night in captivity. When the bailiff returned with the judge's response, their fate was sealed. Judge Hankinson advised that the computerized maps they'd seen on their screens during trial were merely "demonstrative aids and are not available as exhibits." He told them they needed to recall Sergeant Corbitt's testimony as best they could. As Rusmisell finished reading the note aloud, the group sat together in stunned silence. Deeply frustrated. Two weeks of testimony and hundreds of exhibits left them with only their notes and their memories regarding what was now emerging as the most critical piece of evidence in the entire case. They gave up for the night at 8:30 p.m., opting for a fresh start on Friday morning.

When they arrived at the 12-story Sheraton Four Points, adjacent to Florida State's campus, jurors were led to the elevators by a bevy of sheriff's deputies clad in forest-green uniforms. The elevator doors opened on one of the hotel's upper floors, which had been cordoned off just for them. A half dozen officers stationed throughout the hallway ensured the group remained isolated from the rest of the world. Each juror was allowed to make a phone call, but only while being closely guarded by a uniformed officer. By far the worst news of all was that breakfast would be served at 5:00 a.m. sharp— the dining area being opened just for them to avoid contact with anyone who might try to influence their decision.

•••

AFTER THEIR RIDICULOUSLY early start, jurors were back on the bus to the courthouse, arriving just before 8:00 a.m. on Friday morning. They resumed their deliberations over the three charges against Sigfredo Garcia: first-degree murder, conspiracy to commit first-degree murder, and solicitation to commit first-degree murder. Rusmisell held a preliminary vote on the first-degree murder charge. Eleven were in favor of conviction. But the 25-year-old woman seemed even more entrenched now. Though she told the others she was having trouble convincing herself the State had proven Garcia's premeditation, something else was bothering her. And it had little to do with the legal meaning of the word premeditation.

The holdout juror hadn't had a good night of sleep at all, tossing and turning in her uncomfortable hotel room bed. Over and over again, her mind had wandered to Ethan and Kaylee Garcia. Whether their biological parents would ever again be involved in their lives was a decision now resting in her and her fellow jurors' hands. Not only did that make her decision incredibly weighty and consequential, she believed it also presented a searing moral dilemma.

Though their life together had been hardscrabble for many years, by the time of Garcia's arrest, the holdout reasoned, the "husband" and "wife" had turned a corner, finally on the straight-and-narrow path. As best she could tell, Tuto's days as a criminal appeared to be behind him; he was even holding down an honest job for the first time. Regardless of whatever they might have done in the past, she believed, the longtime couple was now parenting their kids lovingly under one roof as fully contributing members of society.

Under those circumstances, the young woman asked herself, was it morally and ethically permissible for the criminal justice system to yank Ethan and Kaylee's parents away from them—forever—leaving them to grow up as orphans in foster homes? It was bad enough that Dan Markel's kids had to grow up without a father. What purpose would it serve, she wondered, to take another pair of innocent children's parents away from them? That moral conundrum was eating away at her as she tried her best to straddle the line between doing right morally and doing right legally.

The atmosphere inside the jury room became more and more tense as the morning wore on. Eleven jurors did their level best to persuade the college-educated woman that causing a hung jury wouldn't solve anything. That another jury—just like them—would have to start all over again, with the exact same evidence. And after all the time, energy, and resources the prosecutors and defense lawyers had poured into the case, it wasn't fair to them—or even Katie and Garcia—to tell them the jury simply couldn't make a decision.

To the majority, it was becoming evident that the holdout's personal feelings were clouding her judgment. They begged her to review the evidence objectively, without factoring into her thinking what would happen to the Garcia children. Yet despite the immense pressure her fellow jurors were heaping on her, the moral and ethical dilemma the woman had wrestled with into the wee hours was making it impossible for her to vote "guilty" as to either defendant.

But finally, after lunch, she relented, agreeing she'd vote to find Garcia guilty of first-degree murder after all. The others had convinced her that the many-time felon was guilty of that charge because he'd either been the shooter or had to know in advance that he and Rivera were traveling to Tally to commit a murder, not a robbery. And that made the murder just as premeditated for him as for Rivera, whether he'd fired the fatal shot or not. Though she felt physically ill voting in favor of convicting Ethan and Kaylee's dad—especially considering the relative slap on the wrist Rivera had received for precisely the same conduct—her vote made it unanimous. The prosecution wouldn't be forced to try Sigfredo Garcia all over again.

But that still left Katie. The 25-year-old juror was adamant she wasn't going to vote to convict Katie as well—and take both parents away from their innocent children—because the prosecution, in her view, hadn't satisfied its burden. She even persuaded another female juror to side with her as the deliberations over Katie continued. The evidence against the Filipina immigrant was entirely circumstantial, the two told the others, nothing firm enough to "nail her to the wall."

The 12 decision-makers argued and fought for more than an hour, the majority doing everything they could think of to forge an agreement, trying to convince the two now holding out that the cell tower evidence clearly established Katie's presence at the money drop. The holdouts retorted that unless the others could "guarantee" that Katie was there to deliver the money, they couldn't—and wouldn't—vote to convict her. But without Sergeant Corbitt's demonstrative maps to assist them, the majority's efforts to persuade the two dissenters were proving futile. As much as they wanted to secure a conviction against Katie, after three weeks of jury service, the ten in the majority were now even more desperate to go home.

With the climate inside the jury room becoming increasingly uncomfortable—emotions ever so close to boiling over—Rusmisell penned another note, asking the judge, "If we have a hung jury on one person, can we give a verdict on another?" The note the bailiff returned with gave them permission to do just that. Not long thereafter, a juror knocked on the door, handing the bailiff the foreperson's final note—making clear they'd reached a verdict as to one defendant.

•••

THE TENSION PERMEATING Courtroom 3G reached a crescendo, everyone except the judge on their feet as jurors filed in, taking their familiar seats. More than five years after Dan Markel's ruthless killing, they were about to deliver at least a partial measure of justice. In his hand, Rusmisell clutched a verdict form containing three checkmarks and his signature. Only he and his fellow jurors knew the outcome, the defendants, lawyers, and Dan's family members all gazing into their eyes in search of clues. The bailiff retrieved the verdict form and handed it to Judge Hankinson. The moment of truth had arrived.

After cautioning everyone against having any reaction to the verdict, the judge calmly began ticking through the jury's findings on the charges against Sigfredo Garcia, whose hands rested on his counsel table—clasped together as if in prayer— his eyes cast downward. That is, until the judge announced the first verdict, at which point he looked up with a vacant stare: *guilty* of first-degree murder the judge read out, without the slightest hint of emotion.

Accompanying that pronouncement were Katie's barely audible, high-pitched whimpers, which continued as the judge announced that her "husband" had also been found guilty of conspiracy to commit first-degree murder, but not guilty of solicitation. The man with whom she'd spent virtually all of her adult life—the father of her children—was now a convicted murderer, quite possibly on his way to death row.

From the front of the gallery, Phil Markel, seated between his ex-wife and daughter, buried his head in his right hand, overcome with emotion. Ruth and Shelly each stared straight ahead, frustrated that the verdict being announced was impartial justice at best. As the judge polled the jurors—asking each if the verdict as read was correct—Katie grabbed a tissue, her sobbing becoming louder and more rhythmic.

The judge then began delivering what is commonly referred to as the "Allen charge"—also known by lawyers as the "dynamite charge"—instructions intended to motivate a seemingly deadlocked jury to reach a decision in order to avoid a mistrial. He sent the 12 jurors back to the jury room to try once more to reach a verdict as to the charges against Katie, whose head was now buried in a tissue, her whimpering growing louder still. Even Tara Kawass was dabbing her eyes with a tissue, as she rubbed her client's back for comfort.

"All right," the judge said once the jurors had exited. "Mr. Garcia is remanded into custody pending sentencing in this matter. We will start sentencing Monday morning at 10:00. As to Magbanua, we will wait to hear further from the jury." As the judge instructed sheriff's deputies to take Garcia away, the now-convicted defendant leaned over his counsel table, caught Katie's eye, and mouthed the words, "I love you."

Thirty-six minutes later, jurors were back in their seats with sullen expressions, several of them now in tears themselves. They'd devoted three solid weeks of their lives to fulfilling the most important civic obligation they'd likely ever have. After 11 hours of often-heated deliberations, they'd fallen short of completing their mission, hopelessly deadlocked over Katie's guilt or innocence—ten to two in favor of conviction. A hung jury after all.

Left with no other choice, Judge Hankinson declared a mistrial as to Katie, setting a status conference for later that month to start the process all over again—one that would ultimately culminate in a second trial, this time, involving only one defendant. Now it was Katie's turn to be led away in handcuffs, to the jail that had been her home for three long years. And that would remain her home until a new jury of her peers could be impaneled to determine what role, if any, the 34-year-old mother of two had played in the murder of Professor Dan Markel.

•••

THE FOLLOWING MONDAY morning, a second trial began, this one to determine the punishment for Sigfredo Garcia's heinous crime—what lawyers and judges refer to as the "sentencing phase." This time around, Garcia and his attorneys occupied the main defense table, as Katie, Tara Kawass, and Chris DeCoste were no longer part of the action. As uncomfortable as the final stages of their deliberations had become, the same 12 jurors were back in their familiar seats, having had the weekend—in their own homes—to clear their heads and decompress.

Following brief opening statements by Cappleman and Zangeneh, Ruth Markel approached the witness stand, the pain and anguish of the last five years evident in her slow, uneven gate. Her unrelenting sorrow was etched in her face as she began to read from her victim impact statement—delivered on her entire family's behalf—with jurors and spectators alike hanging on her every word. The man just convicted of killing her son looked on with a blank expression, just a few yards away.

The 75-year-old grandmother didn't mention any of the Adelsons by name—despite all she believed they'd taken from her family. Instead, she told jurors, in her pronounced Canadian accent, that "because of the acts of a few, my son Dan's life was cut very short, and I have been forced to experience the unthinkable and to live a life filled with unimaginable pain and heartbreak no mother should ever have to endure." She shared his impressive biography with the judge and jury, from Harvard undergrad, to Cambridge, to Harvard Law, and ultimately, a position on Florida State's law faculty.

Of all his accomplishments, Ruth noted, she was "most proud of the father Dan was to his beautiful boys, Lincoln and Ben. It is hard to capture in words the joy and excitement I felt when Dan became a father and I became a grandmother. I derived even more joy and happiness watching Dan raise his two boys." She described her son as a "present, devoted, loving, supportive, selfless father," and told the jury how much his boys loved him. "He was their hero," she said tearfully.

Due to his extensive travels, Ruth shared, Dan had made friends all over the world, including in Canada, England, and Israel, staying connected with them throughout his life. But once he moved to Tallahassee, she said, he immersed himself in the local community, frequently hosting events in his home and playing significant roles at his synagogue. He became part of the fabric at the law school, "passionate about teaching and the students adored him." His "energy, drive, and sociability," she declared proudly, "enhanced the student body and the faculty."

Ruth segued to the awful mid-July day that would change everything, when "Dan's life was brought to a sudden, abrupt, and tragic end… In one fell swoop, our son, brother, and father of two young boys were all killed." Her life, she said, "was shattered." The grief and pain of a mother who loses a child, she added, "never ends. For me, 'closure' and 'normalcy' are only words in a dictionary, not a reality that I will ever experience again."

She ruminated about her frustrations with the legal process, lamenting how she and her family had waited "more than five years for those involved in Dan's murder to be brought to justice, which has only exacerbated my pain, grief, anxiety, and health." Ruth confessed to finding the legal process "cumbersome to navigate." In the end, she told jurors, it was she who'd received "a life sentence. But I know that even after justice occurs, Dan's murder will continue to torment me for the rest of my life."

The grandmother of five transitioned to Ben and Lincoln— ages four and three when their father's life was extinguished— who she hadn't seen or spoken with in more than three years. "My grandchildren were forever turned upside down as a result of this crime." They'd been "robbed of their childhoods as they are forced to confront and try to understand the unthinkable crime of murder at such a young age."

Dan's mom closed her remarks by telling the judge and jury that not a single day "goes by when thoughts of Danny do not enter our minds. His murder has been horrible for us—

shocking, surreal, hard to understand. Danny is never coming back," she said emotionally, wiping away another tear, "but we continue to hope and pray for justice." As she stepped down from the witness stand, a somber silence blanketed the courtroom, interrupted only by the sound of muffled sobs emanating from the jury box and the gallery.

In her ten-minute statement, one thing Ruth didn't touch upon was what she believed to be the appropriate punishment for Sigfredo Garcia for his hideous crime. Her son had written highly acclaimed law review articles articulating his fierce opposition to the death penalty. Yet now, a jury was about to decide whether to mete out precisely that punishment to his killer. The bitter irony of the situation couldn't have been lost on anyone who knew Dan Markel. But if Ruth had her own feelings on the subject, she decided to keep them to herself. And to let the jury make its decision without her guidance or interference.

•••

SIGFREDO GARCIA'S LAWYERS presented evidence from a psychologist, Dr. Julie Harper, who'd spoken extensively with their client and members of his family. Dr. Harper filled jurors in on Garcia's difficult upbringing in a broken and impoverished home, his involvement in the juvenile justice system, and his drug and alcohol abuse beginning as a child. The jury also learned how he'd been shot and nearly died when he was just 23, a harrowing event the psychologist firmly believed had shaped much of the remainder of his life.

She shared with jurors that although Garcia had been very smitten with Katie in their early days, his "wife" could be abusive and demeaning, even hitting him in the face when she was upset with him. Garcia would do everything within his power to make her happy, Dr. Harper testified, often putting Katie's needs above his own. At the time of the homicide, in her view, Garcia had fallen into a major depression over their breakup, often medicating himself with alcohol and other substances, particularly when Katie would withhold the children from him—which she did frequently.

The defense wanted jurors to conclude that Dan's murder had its roots in Katie's domineering influence over her "husband," which was one of the mitigating circumstances they were permitted to consider and weigh in deciding on the appropriate punishment. Because the defense was relying on that contention, during her cross-examination, Cappleman asked the psychologist a fairly obvious question: whether, during her interviews with Garcia, he had admitted that Katie had directly solicited him to commit the murder.

"I don't have that information," Dr. Harper replied. Her answer—which could have amounted to a bombshell revelation and critical piece of evidence for Katie's retrial— landed harmlessly on the courtroom floor.

After hearing Cappleman and Zangeneh argue one final time, the jury began deliberating on whether to impose the ultimate punishment. Though a small handful of jurors argued adamantly for the imposition of the death penalty, the majority voted for life imprisonment, largely because they didn't trust Rivera's testimony that Garcia had been the shooter. They were also persuaded that Katie *had* exerted a dominating influence over her "husband"—even the holdout jurors who refused to convict her, ostensibly because they hadn't been convinced of Katie's involvement in the murder. Positions that were seemingly irreconcilable. Just 45 minutes into their deliberations, Rusmisell informed the bailiff that the jury had completed its work.

For a second time, the 12 jurors filed into the courtroom with a verdict, which the bailiff handed to the judge to read aloud. Judge Hankinson announced that the jury had found two aggravating factors sufficient to warrant the sentence of death: that the murder had been committed for pecuniary gain and also in a cold, calculated, and premeditated manner. But the jury also concluded, he stated, that the State had not proven that those aggravating factors outweighed the mitigating circumstances they were permitted to consider. Which, in plain English, meant that Garcia was being spared the death penalty. The very result the punishment theory scholar he'd brutally murdered would himself have embraced.

The judge thanked the jurors for their lengthy service. As they filed out of the courtroom, Garcia locked eyes on a few, mouthing the words "thank you," the only two words he'd uttered in their presence during the entire trial. When Judge Hankinson formally pronounced his sentence 20 minutes later, Garcia was provided an opportunity to share whatever was on his mind. Yet despite all he'd been through, the convicted murderer had nothing at all to say.

In addition to sentencing him to a life sentence without the possibility of parole for first-degree murder, Judge Hankinson sentenced Garcia to 30 years in prison for his conspiracy conviction, to run consecutively with his life sentence—as if he could somehow serve additional time in his afterlife. Ever gracious, the judge wished him luck as he announced the court would stand in recess. Sigfredo Garcia was led away in handcuffs and shackles one final time, this time unlikely to step foot in a public setting ever again.

Of the five people investigators believed had actively participated in the plot to kill Dan Markel, two had now been convicted and sentenced for their roles—Rivera and Garcia—while one, Katie, remained in jail awaiting a second trial.

As for Donna and Charlie Adelson, though they were still living their best lives, the mother and son—as well as their high-priced lawyers—were well aware that could change at any moment. Though the wheels of justice may have been turning slowly, Georgia Cappleman and her team had every intention to keep plowing forward—relentlessly—until full and complete justice was finally in hand.

But just five months later, the entire planet would grind to a virtual standstill. As would the already painfully long march to justice for Dan Markel and his family.

26.

Big Fish

THE COVID-19 PANDEMIC didn't merely wreak havoc on public health and the global economy as it shuttered businesses and schools all across the nation. As of mid-March 2020, concerns over in-person gatherings also brought virtually all courtroom proceedings to a sudden halt. Courthouses throughout America were closed for all but the most urgent matters. Though judicial proceedings gradually resumed by the summer of 2020—primarily on virtual platforms such as Zoom and WebEx—a host of complicating factors rendered it all-but impossible to conduct jury trials over a computer screen. That was especially true in criminal cases, as anyone accused of a crime is afforded a constitutional right to confront witnesses.

In June 2020, amid the uncertainty over when Katie Magbanua's retrial would finally occur, Judge James C. Hankinson retired following a distinguished 40-year career as a prosecutor and jurist, the last 18 years on the bench. Judge Robert R. Wheeler was assigned to replace him on the Dan Markel case.

After earning both his bachelor's and law degrees from the University of Florida and ten years in private practice, Wheeler had risen through the ranks of the Florida Attorney General's Office, becoming the lead attorney in its criminal appeals division in 2003. By 2007, he was working as a lawyer for Governor Charlie Crist, becoming his general counsel in 2009. Governor Crist rewarded his trusted servant with an appointment to the bench the following year.

Judge Wheeler quickly developed a reputation for integrity and fairness. A June 2021 magazine article that ranked Florida's trial judges for fairness in criminal cases selected him as "Fairest of Them All" out of the 13 judges in Florida's Second Judicial Circuit. From his perch at the front of the courtroom, Wheeler projected a softer, somewhat less commanding, presence than Judge Hankinson.

Though criminal jury trials had resumed by the summer of 2021, public health concerns continued to cast a dark cloud over when Katie's retrial would finally begin. As cancer survivors, both Chris DeCoste and Tara Kawass faced a heightened risk of hospitalization or even death if they became infected with COVID. As much as they wanted to stand before another jury proclaiming their client's innocence, as wave after wave of contagious variants continued to ravage the Sunshine State, Katie's lawyers told Judge Wheeler they simply couldn't proceed.

To illustrate their fears were well founded, DeCoste and Kawass informed the judge that, unbeknownst to them, the Leon County Jail had permitted Katie to come to court and sit beside them during a live pretrial hearing when, as it turned out, she had an active COVID infection—her second bout with the virus. Reluctantly, Judge Wheeler agreed to continue the retrial until February 14, 2022.

•••

GEORGIA CAPPLEMAN HAD obviously been deeply frustrated when jurors at Katie's initial trial announced they were hopelessly deadlocked—her years of hard work ending in a thoroughly disappointing mistrial as to one of the two defendants. As events would later unfold, however, the young juror who had firmly stood in the way of Katie's conviction may have been a blessing in disguise. Between the mistrial and the lengthy delay caused by the pandemic, Cappleman and her colleagues had ample time to game out how they could present their evidence more convincingly. As well as a golden opportunity to correct the biggest problems they'd encountered during the first trial.

Of all of the things that had gone wrong, the most glaring was the prosecution's inability to make any real use of the Dolce Vita video. Not only had Judge Hankinson refused to permit them to hand jurors Pat Sanford's transcript of the dialog between Katie and Charlie Adelson, when they played the video, it was merely to demonstrate that there was too much extraneous noise to make out anything the former lovers were saying. But having read Sanford's transcript, Cappleman strongly believed that at least some of their discussion was highly incriminating and would therefore amount to dynamite evidence at Katie's retrial.

With the extra time afforded by the cascading continuances, she pressed Sanford to use his FBI contacts to find an audio forensics expert who could enhance the Dolce Vita audio sufficiently to allow Katie's and Charlie's voices to be deciphered with clarity. The special agent identified several different experts who took a crack at doing so—each of whom reported it simply couldn't be done. Cappleman was beside herself, immensely frustrated, at times feeling as if she were banging her head against the wall.

She'd even gone to Sanford's office to listen to the recording herself, utilizing the FBI's proprietary software—which allowed the audio to be manipulated as it was being played—where she was able to hear many of Charlie's words clearly despite the background noise. Surely, she believed, there was someone on the planet who could clarify the audio so that jurors seated in the courtroom could hear precisely what she was hearing. She told Sanford to keep trying, refusing to accept "it can't be done" for an answer.

Finally, at the eleventh hour—when it was beginning to look like they would never succeed in clarifying the audio—

the FBI identified a soft-spoken South Carolinian named Keith McElveen, who'd earned bachelor's and master's degrees in electrical engineering from Clemson University. For nearly ten years commencing in 1986, he'd served as a war-crimes investigator for the CIA, traveling extensively all across the globe. One of his assignments had been to analyze surreptitious audio recordings to extract individual voices out of crowds. He found the exercise excruciatingly tedious and frustrating, as the technological tools available to him at the time were rudimentary and largely ineffective.

Keith McElveen would eventually pivot from that frustration to form three different audio forensics companies by his mid-forties. His objective was to design software tools capable of isolating individual voices in noisy "cocktail-party" environments. By 2020, he held 12 patents for technologies capable of doing just that. His latest invention was a hearing-aid undershirt that embedded dozens of tiny microphones, enabling users to better focus on individual conversations in crowds and noisy environments—an application that had enormous potential to help hundreds of millions of people who suffered from impaired hearing.

In November 2021, Sanford met McElveen at a gas station in Georgia, roughly halfway between Tally and McElveen's home in Charleston, handing the former CIA investigator a thumb drive containing the Dolce Vita audio files. In December, Cappleman disclosed the audio expert's name to Tara Kawass and Chris DeCoste on an updated witness list, hopeful that McElveen would have more success clarifying the audio than the others who'd tried—and failed—before him. With Katie's new trial date of February 14 fast approaching, the veteran prosecutor knew this would be their last chance to get anything useful out of the Dolce Vita recording.

By mid-January, however, McElveen reported that he hadn't yet completed his work and needed more time. Surprisingly, *both* sides asked Judge Wheeler to continue the upcoming trial yet again, with Katie's attorneys expressing confidence that the enhancement of the Dolce Vita audio would establish her innocence and "bring an end to this case without the need for a retrial." With both the prosecution and defense pushing for a continuance, Judge Wheeler was left with little choice but to acquiesce, pushing Katie's retrial out to May 16, 2022. What no one knew at the time of the February 4 continuance—not even McElveen himself—was that his forensic work would soon blow the entire case wide open.

•••

THE DOLCE VITA AUDIO that became the central focus of Keith McElveen's existence had been recorded on April 20, 2016—the day after the bump between an undercover FBI agent and Donna Adelson. Poetic justice or not, Wednesday, April 20, 2022, would mark a stunning turning point in the investigation and prosecution of Dan Markel's killers.

Unbeknownst to Katie's defense team, to the media, and to Charlie Adelson and his attorneys, a grand jury was hearing evidence in the Markel case that afternoon at the Leon County Courthouse. Georgia Cappleman was behind a lectern with her witness, Pat Sanford, describing the mountain of circumstantial evidence investigators had amassed—*against Charlie*. The most significant piece of evidence? Charlie's own words, as captured with amazing clarity through McElveen's enhancement of the Dolce Vita audio.

The audio forensics expert ultimately broke the recording into three distinct segments so his software tool could process digestible chunks of the audio, rather than its entirety. Though the software tool had little success clarifying the audio in the first segment, it did a pretty good job reducing—though certainly not eliminating—the background noise in the second and third segments, 41 minutes in all. That said, because Charlie's voice was projected toward the undercover agents' surveillance cameras, and Katie's in the opposite direction, and because his voice was stronger and louder than hers, what was most audible in the final version of the enhanced recording were Charlie's words, rather than Katie's.

A court reporter was retained to transcribe the back-and-forth dialogue that was finally audible. The words contained in the resulting transcript were then superimposed at the bottom of the Dolce Vita video similar to subtitles in a movie or closed captioning on a TV show. Because the court reporter wasn't able to make out most of Katie's words, an ellipsis was used whenever her statements were unintelligible—which was quite often. In contrast, the text at the bottom of the screen revealed nearly everything that came out of Charlie's mouth.

Until Cappleman absorbed the spoken and written words displayed in the final video, her playbook hadn't changed an iota since the 2019 trial—to obtain a conviction against Katie at her retrial with the hope she'd then agree to spill the beans on Charlie to avoid spending the rest of her life in prison. Yet the Filipina immigrant's willingness to spend more than five years in jail and stand trial—not once, but twice—left Cappleman and State Attorney Jack Campbell wondering whether Katie would ever rat out the wealthy periodontist, even following her own conviction.

But after soaking in Charlie's words in the enhanced Dolce Vita video—now hearing and seeing most of them for the very first time—Georgia Cappleman had an epiphany. Charlie's statements to Katie were so incriminating, she reasoned, they were tantamount to a confession. When she played the recording for Jack Campbell, he agreed. With Charlie hoisting himself on his own petard, they no longer needed Katie's cooperation to reel in their big fish. For the very first time since her arrest, the State Attorney's Office concluded that getting Katie to turn State's evidence was no longer a prerequisite to prosecuting Charlie Adelson for murder.

Thus, Campbell gave his chief assistant the green light to take the case against Charlie to the grand jury. After Pat Sanford completed his testimony, and let the grand jurors see and hear for themselves the words that came out of the wealthy periodontist's mouth six years to that very day earlier, the grand jury agreed. Not only had Cappleman secured an indictment against the man she'd always believed had been the mastermind behind Dan Markel's brutal assassination, she'd done so cloaked under a tight veil of secrecy. Which made the next step in the long march to justice for Dan's family and friends as simple as the gentle breeze blowing off the water behind 2518 Whale Harbor Lane.

•••

WELL AWARE THAT CHARLIE ADELSON was a rabid gun enthusiast who had no reservation or compunction about taking human life, those responsible for the operation at his Fort Lauderdale home the next morning weren't about to take any chances. They assembled a well-trained, heavily armed battalion in full riot gear to take the newly indicted defendant into custody. Approximately 20 FBI agents and local police officers gathered a couple of blocks away just before 5:00 a.m. to receive their final instructions, the cover of darkness and element of surprise offering a tactical advantage they hoped would prevent a shootout and bloody scene.

Gradually, they surrounded the home from all sides, sealing off the perimeter—a couple of agents even stationed aboard a boat behind the property to prevent any attempted watery escape. Though movement was detected through Charlie's windows, agents couldn't determine whether the darkened figure was a male or female. Officers positioned behind the rear fence were given the go-ahead to advance. But when they attempted to scale the fence, they were met with a most unwelcome surprise: it was lined at the top with razor wire, leading to some nasty cuts and the decision to retreat.

Their initial plan foiled, the lead agent dialed Charlie on his cellphone to try to coax him to surrender peacefully. But no one answered. Floodlights were then directed against the front of the home, brightly illuminating the entire property and shining into the residence through the windows. An agent grabbed a bullhorn, demanding that Charlie come out with his hands held high. Several officers crouched in defensive positions throughout the front yard—their weapons aimed at the front door—the tension and anticipation reaching a crescendo. Yet nothing happened.

Storming the home with massive force was beginning to look like their only viable option, despite its attendant risks. The lead agent tried calling Charlie one final time before resorting to that approach. Lo and behold, this time he answered, and walked out the front door precisely as instructed.

Rather than a man itching for confrontation or a bloody shootout, what officers observed emerging into the ultra-bright lights was a most amusing sight. Not only was Charlie unarmed, he was nearly naked—a pair of skimpy boxer shorts the only fabric covering his large frame. Shielding his eyes from the glaring light with his forearm, bewildered and confused, he asked, "Am I under arrest?" Officers quickly swarmed him, cuffing his hands behind his back and reading him his rights. They led him back inside to find some clothing and get him dressed.

What the arresting officers spotted through their peripheral vision as they walked their prize through his living space revealed just how lucky they were to nab him without a full-scale battle. Rifles and guns were displayed everywhere, mostly near windows and doors, one even resting on a tripod pointed out a window. The entire operation easily could have devolved into a very different—and deadly—scene. Charlie appeared dazed and disoriented as the officers led him through the house—incoherent gibberish his only audible sounds—likely because he was under the influence of marijuana or some other narcotic.

Finally fully clothed and ready for prime time, the handcuffed arrestee was marched back outside, flanked by officers who'd likely remember this particular perp walk for years. As they approached a squad car and placed Charlie in the backseat, one of the agents standing nearby was soaking in the spectacle with particularly intense interest. Pat Sanford had waited nearly eight years for this very occasion, gladly making the seven-hour drive from Tally with the freshly issued indictment in hand to witness Charlie's arrest with his own two eyes. His hard work, and that of dozens of federal agents and TPD investigators, had finally paid off. For him, the moment was akin to winning the Super Bowl and the World Series all at once.

Within minutes, the police car containing the perceived mastermind behind Dan Markel's vicious slaying was on its way to the Broward County Jail—the same facility where Sigfredo Garcia, Luis Rivera, and Katie Magbanua had all passed through during each one's years-long march to justice.

By 9:00 a.m., news of Charlie Adelson's arrest was reverberating all across the internet, as was the mugshot snapped while he was being processed at the jail. In the photo, his curly brown hair was so long and disheveled—flying wildly in every direction—it wasn't even fully captured in the square frame. His green eyes were bloodshot and glassy, face devoid of expression, beard unkept, and lips pressed tightly together. Hardly the image the 45-year-old millionaire bachelor—or his proud parents or kid sister—would have selected to be featured in the *Miami Herald* or on the TV news later that day.

Fully 2,834 days since the brutal, cold-blooded execution of his ex-brother-in-law, the Maestro was finally behind bars, his life as a Ferrari-driving, steroid-ingesting, playboy periodontist seemingly gone for good.

27.

"If You Want to Arrest Me,
Fucking Arrest Me"

THANKS TO KEITH MCELVEEN'S technical wizardry, many of the words spoken during Charlie's April 2016 conversation with Katie at Dolce Vita were finally audible—for the first time in six years. What was captured by the enhanced audio that had Georgia Cappleman and Pat Sanford sprinting to the grand jury room to seek an indictment against Charles Jay Adelson? Plenty.

The first audible words were Charlie telling Katie, "If they had any evidence, *we would have already gone to the airport.*" Which implied he didn't believe that law enforcement had developed evidence to charge anyone for Dan's homicide— and that he and Katie would already have fled if they had reason to believe they would soon be arrested. He then told her, "Even if they bug your phone … *you're still not talking about any of this.*" That statement was ironic for two reasons: First, at that very moment, Katie's phone *was* bugged. And second, the ex-lovers *were* talking about the events of July 2014—in a public restaurant of all places.

Charlie explained to Katie his understanding of how law enforcement can get suspects to incriminate themselves through a bump. "How do you get people to talk?" he asked rhetorically. "You throw smoke grenades and then you get all of the cockroaches to run out … And everyone's running and everyone's talking and you throw a smoke grenade." He told Katie that "if that was a cop that came and spoke to my mom … it's very smart, because that means my mom hasn't told my dad anything. My mom knows my dad is going to flip out when he finds out."

But as their conversation progressed, Charlie made clear that he believed the bearded man who'd approached his mom was likely a gangster, not a cop. He was troubled by the fact the man knew who Donna was and "knew her routine." He suspected his mother had been approached, rather than his father, because "my dad may be someone who is carrying a gun… You know, you don't want it to turn into a fucking shootout." He told Katie he was going to start carrying a gun in a holster on his back just in case someone approached him. "If someone comes up to me, they'd better be ready to shoot, 'cause I'm gonna shoot 'em. Someone comes up to me asking for money in my house?" And "when the fucking police show up and … there's an oral surgeon standing there with a dead gang member in his fucking driveway, they're not gonna come down too hard on me."

Charlie tried to impress upon his ex-girlfriend the seriousness of their predicament, telling her, "This is happening, and it's serious because these people are going to come back. They didn't go through the trouble of seeking my mom out to hand her that and then go away… They're not going away." He pointed out how much trouble "they" had gone through to arrange the interaction with Donna. The audio then picked up Katie saying, "There's gonna be a point where it's just like, hold on" —

"Well, with a beard or with a badge?" Charlie interrupted, "beard" seemingly a reference to a gangster or bad guy, "badge" an obvious reference to law enforcement.

"Either or," Katie responded.

Focusing on the second possibility, Charlie said, "If a badge comes up to you, tell them, 'Have a nice day, officer.' Listen, if they want to charge me with something, charge me. If not, I don't talk to the cops. Sorry."

"Yeah, I know," Katie replied. "Perfect."

"*If you're gonna charge me, charge me,*" Charlie repeated. In hindsight, his language was most ironic, prophetic even, since those very words—indeed, all of his words on the enhanced recording—were the very reason he was now clad in prison attire, behind bars, at the Broward County Jail.

Charlie then went off on a tangent about the changes in law enforcement techniques over the years, noting how prevalent surveillance cameras had become. The video captured him pointing upward in different directions, counting the number of cameras hanging from Dolce Vita's ceiling. "How many cameras are in here?" he asked Katie. "Five?" Which was two short of the actual number, as Charlie failed to include the two cameras camouflaged in laptop bags at the very next table— pointed directly at him.

"What I'm saying," he added, "is that this person is not going away. They came very equipped *with details*. Where did the details come from? I don't know." He then pivoted to whether they needed to be worried about the bearded stranger providing those details "to the cops." Charlie told Katie they had nothing to be worried about, employing a hypothetical example about him telling the police that his brother Rob had been involved. "They're gonna say, 'Can you prove it?' And I'm gonna say no. 'Do you know *what kind of a gun was used*?' I say no. 'Did you see your brother do *it*?' No... Even if I went in and said my brother said he did *it*, you've got to prove *it*. You've got to put the person at the scene." He was careful not to specify what "it" was that his brother had done, but "it" obviously involved the use of a "gun."

At that point, Charlie's hypothetical morphed into a crime involving a rental car. By then, he likely knew investigators had learned that a rental car had been involved in Dan's murder, as the image of the rented Prius had been blasted out to the news media within days of his slaying. "You have to put *that person* at the scene at the time," he told Katie, apparently to ease her mind, without specifying who "that person" was.

"Let's say you just sat in the car, right? And then I go ahead and commit a crime ... but your DNA is in the car. And I go, 'Yeah, Katie was in my car, and she got out and she did this horrible crime.' Okay, so then they come and get the DNA in the car and go, 'Oh, Katie was in the car.'" That wouldn't prove anything, he reassured her, as her sitting in the car "has nothing to do with me robbing the Burger King. So even if I can prove that, yeah, Katie was with me, can you put Katie at the Burger King?"

Charlie's stream of consciousness continued to wander. What if investigators could put Katie at the Burger King with him? he asked, and then brought her "into an interrogation. They're like, 'Listen, we know that you were in that fucking car and you were in that car such and such day. We know we've got your DNA ... your fingerprints, your fucking hair is all over that fucking car.' That proves, yeah, congratulations, you were in the car. It's not a crime to sit in the car, okay? ... My mom could have sat in that car, too. It's not a crime. They have to prove— they have to put you at the scene at the date." That Donna and Katie were both part of his hypothetical about a rental car being used to commit a crime was most telling.

Charlie's focus then shifted to the undercover agent's mention of "Tuto." He acted as if he had no idea that Tuto was Katie's "husband," about whom they'd spoken many times. And about whom he and Katie had texted with explicit references to "Tuto." He quickly segued to the stranger who'd handed his mother the note, trying to make heads or tails of him based on Donna's description. Charlie told Katie his understanding was that the man was polite and well-spoken, well-dressed, wasn't wearing glasses or a hat, wasn't "strong-skinned," and didn't have a Spanish accent. His mother informed him "he was white, but he could have been Hispanic."

"Either way," Katie chimed in.

Charlie told her that, according to Donna, just looking at the man, he didn't seem like "a thug." Rather, "my mom thought it was like, a process server."

Katie noted that whoever it was had to have "a lot of

knowledge" to know where his mom lived.

Yet Charlie disagreed, telling her that anyone with $19 could go online to find out where someone lived. "And you go online, pull up a picture, and you sit outside and you wait. And you know what their kids look like because, guess what, they're online too." But his confidence suddenly wavered. "So Katie, they'll be back. These people know about … whoever it is *knows information.*"

"And there's not a lot of people that know much about—" Katie began to interject.

"*They didn't mention my name,*" Charlie interrupted again, "which makes me think … these people only know part of the story or they think they know part of the story." He appeared to be saying that whoever was blackmailing his mom didn't know the whole story because, if he did, he would have mentioned Charlie's name alongside Katie's and Tuto's.

What came out of his mouth next was even more illuminating, perhaps Charlie's most incriminating statement during their entire conversation. "Let me ask you a question," he began. "When everybody was there *the next day*, did any of you take any money?" For anyone familiar with the Dan Markel murder investigation, Charlie's statement about "everybody" being "there the next day" with "money" seemed to be a stunningly clear reference to Tuto, Tato, and Katie congregating at Jessica Rodriguez's apartment the morning of July 19, 2014 for the money drop.

Why would Charlie have asked Katie for more information about who was taking money "when everybody was there the next day?" Only one explanation made sense. Because she was physically present at Rodriguez's apartment that morning and knew what had transpired, whereas he wasn't.

"It's not like you're driving around in a Bentley," he added, "cruising around in a mega yacht, you know." In other words, that Katie's possessions following the murder weren't lavish enough to be a dead giveaway that she'd suddenly come into a boatload of money. "Because otherwise, he'd have no idea that *I had anything to do with*—" Though Charlie didn't complete his thought, what he seemed to be saying was that his connection to the murder wouldn't be evident unless those who committed the crime on his behalf were all of a sudden dripping with wealth—just like him.

This time, it was Katie who shifted the focus of their conversation, drilling down again on whether the stranger who'd approached Donna on the street was a blackmailer or a cop, pointing out how he'd been dressed. Which led to Charlie rambling on for several minutes, opining that the man was a thug and speculating about what information he might be able to share with law enforcement.

If the cops questioned the man, he reassured Katie, he'd be forced to concede that he didn't know where the *weapon* was at, *who pulled the trigger*, and that he hadn't been a witness. So, "the question is, how do you know? So, if you didn't witness it, you only heard a rumor on the street that this person did something. Do you know what that's worth? Zero." Meaning they had nothing to be afraid of if the man did report what he knew to law enforcement.

Charlie pointed out that the only way the blackmailer could be useful to the cops would be to "wear a wire, get *this person* talking, and if you can get *the person* to confess on the wire, then you have something that you're charging. You have a confession. You have an admission of guilt."

Though he didn't clarify who he meant by "this person," Charlie was seemingly referring to Luis Rivera. That became even clearer as he rambled on. "Outside of that, there is no evidence, okay? You have a car and you can link *this person* to renting that car that's used at the scene of the crime." Which was a pretty clear reference to King Tato.

And that led him right back to what he'd been telling Katie earlier: "But, you know, you also have to prove that they were also driving that day, too. They didn't rent it and then lend it to a friend." Charlie clearly didn't know that law enforcement already had crystal clear photographic evidence of Tuto and Tato in the Prius the day of the murder as well as GPS evidence of the hybrid's presence near Dan Markel's home—details TPD investigators and the FBI deliberately kept close to the vest.

To prove his point, the bearded periodontist employed another hypothetical, in which Katie had rented a car and he had driven it "to fucking Orlando. I rob a McDonald's in Orlando, I come back, and I go, 'Here's the keys, Katie.' And you go, 'Okay, thanks.' ... My point is, I don't have any knowledge of what went on." The blackmailer, he noted, was either "pretending" to have knowledge, or actually did. It was obvious that Charlie was much more concerned about the latter possibility, and made clear, "I don't want someone paying visits to my parents."

Katie suggested that the purported blackmailer could also be a cop playing games. But Charlie told her that seemed unlikely. "I wish that it was a cop playing games. *Why didn't they know it was me?* ... And they didn't mention me." If it was a cop, he said, it made little sense that they didn't come straight to him. "And I think if [the cops] thought I had something to do with *it*, they would find me and they'd talk to me." Though he didn't say it out loud, it seemed unmistakable, in context, that "it" was code for Dan Markel's murder. That the bearded stranger hadn't mentioned him at all—and instead referred to "your son's ex-girlfriend Katie"—made him believe it *wasn't* a cop.

His next statement was even more incriminating: "Like, go talk to *the person who's involved*, not fucking people who aren't involved." By which he undoubtedly meant himself. And then, almost as if he realized he'd now said too much, Charlie reversed course, saying, "And I'm not involved."

Katie's relationship was with him, he continued, not his family. Which made him perplexed about why his mom was approached rather than himself. "Like, I dated you, not my mom... This person obviously doesn't even know that we dated. That's—*the direct connection* is who was her boyfriend? The 71-year-old guy, Dr. Adelson, or the 37-year-old Dr. Adelson? Yeah, 37. Let's go talk to him, Dr. Adelson. That's who they'd talk to. Not waste your time with Mom. They needed to talk to someone *who knew what the fuck went on.*"

In context, his words seemed to be a clear reference to Dr. Charles Jay Adelson. Who, based solely on the grammatical structure of his sentences, was the one who "knew what the fuck went on."

He returned to his central point: "This person knows information. And even if they are cops," they had said Katie's name. The person also knew that "somebody who had something to do with *it*" — "it" once again seemingly code for murder — "is incarcerated. I don't know anybody in jail."

For the first time in their lengthy conversation, Charlie focused directly on the $5,000 scribbled on the note handed to his mother. He told Katie, "I don't have a problem helping the *community* out" — a seeming reference to either the Latin Kings or the crowd Tato and Tuto ran with — "but I don't want this community to come back next month. And what I think happens if I pay the money, they're gonna be back again and again and again. They've got to make more money. It's not a cop." He'd actually be happy if it turned out to be a cop, he said, "because I've got nothing to hide." Yet that notion was belied by virtually he'd been saying.

Charlie speculated about what would happen if his parents reported the extortion attempt to law enforcement. They'd be asked to take a lie detector test, he predicted, "which they won't do, just for the simple reason that those things give false positives all the time — which unfortunately makes you look bad."

Even more importantly, he said, "If we go to the police, this is gonna put a spotlight on *the investigation*. The FBI. The FBI. We're talking about a bigwig in the FBI, not like a first-year rookie. You're gonna have a 20-year vet with the FBI knocking at *your* door, wanting to speak with *you*, and wanting to speak with *your attorney*." It was pretty obvious that "the investigation" he was referring to involved the slaying of his ex-brother-in-law. He didn't explain why, if he had "nothing to hide" — a phrase he'd used just a minute earlier — speaking with "a bigwig in the FBI" would be such a concern.

Charlie then used another vague term, repeatedly, as an

unmistakable reference to Dan Markel's murder—"this." "*This* made not only national news," he told Katie. "*This* was … in London … *This* was on the BBC news… *This* was on *Good Morning America*. *This* was on [sic] the *New York Times*. *This* was a big story." Once again, he seemed to catch himself, realizing he'd now blabbed too much. He backtracked. "So, well, listen. You didn't do anything. I didn't do anything." Almost as if he wanted his criminal defense attorney to have a few words to cherry pick from their conversation—just in case it was actually being surveilled—to be able to say, "My client denied any involvement in Dan Markel's homicide."

"The next question is, prove it," the Maestro rambled on. "*If you want to arrest me, fucking arrest me.*" He told Katie he wouldn't be sharing his phone with law enforcement. "I'm not gonna sit here and show you the photos of all of the dick pictures I took of myself," he said, feigning embarrassment, noting he had "tons of nude photos" of himself on his phone. "So why don't you come back with a warrant so you can look at all the dick pictures you want of me? I'm serious," he chuckled. "I don't want them laughing at my pee-pee."

Ironically, by the time Charlie made these statements, TPD investigators already had his entire Apple iCloud account in hand—dick pics and all. "I don't like cops and you're not getting my dick pics of myself," he reiterated, "so have a nice day. So that's my answer, okay? If you think I did something, *arrest me, charge me,* and that's it. That's it."

He was so confident the police had no evidence, he told Katie, "If they are cops, I'm happy, because I have nothing to hide"—the second time he'd made that exact statement. "If they're a bad guy, there's two ways of dealing with it. One is to go ahead and contact the Miami Beach Police Department." Katie nodded in agreement. "Yeah," she said. The police would arrange "for things to be set up," Charlie added, to which Katie again replied, "Yeah."

"And when it's set up, they'll be like a fucking SWAT team in place and fucking FBI," he prognosticated. "And they're gonna fucking take this guy down and then he will proffer ten years, 'because we just have you on tape extorting somebody—and now tell us everything you know or else you're gonna serve ten years in prison.'" Once again, Katie verbalized her agreement.

But in his very next breath, Charlie suggested that the blackmailer's arrest would ultimately turn out badly for both of them. "Next thing you know, this person is *singing*. People— other people start *singing*. As soon as they have him, he starts calling *your name* out." Next, his parents would be interviewed by the FBI. "They're gonna ask the story of what happened." Another apparent reference to the murder.

"There's gonna be police at *your* door, at *my* door." It wouldn't be ordinary cops leading the investigation either, Charlie predicted. "It's gonna be fucking big boys flying in to see what they can come up with, okay? And then that's probably gonna make the newspaper." His point in telling Katie all this, presumably, was that they couldn't allow the blackmailer to go to law enforcement because the police or FBI would soon be knocking on his, her, and his parents' door. His prediction was once again prescient, as law enforcement officers actually knocked on Katie's front door just five weeks later.

Charlie's rambling monologue about why they couldn't report the blackmailer to law enforcement set the table for the important favor he was about to ask of his ex-girlfriend.

"I want to give them the money," he told Katie. But he didn't want "them" coming back the following week "asking for $10,000. So this was my idea. I give you money … I want you to call up this person and say that 'I got a call from some friends of mine who say that you reached out to them and that you mentioned my name… These people want to go to the police, because they had nothing to do with what you're talking about, okay? And frankly, I don't know what you're talking about. But the name sounds familiar of who's incarcerated, so I'm going to give you something as charity to help the less fortunate, but … don't ever contact me, my friends, or my family again or we will go to the police.'"

"That way, he gets his money," Charlie continued. "He also

knows that you know everything. That you may have a *friend* who may not be so cool who knows what's going on too who may know people who knows *how to handle* people like this, and that this is a fucking one-time thing." The "friend" of Katie's who Charlie was seemingly referring to was her "husband," Sigfredo Garcia. That would become more apparent in just a moment. He advised Katie to tell the blackmailer that the payment was "charity" to help the "less fortunate" and that the only reason "it's being done" is because she believes in "karma." "The whole time you're talking, you just say, 'I don't know at all what's going on.' You don't use anything other than the words 'help' and 'charity.' ... That's all I was able to come up with."

"If it's the police," he added, "they can't take the money. They won't even come meet you. They fucked up." But if it was a bad guy, "now he's fucking with *his wife*"—the "his" a pretty clear reference to Garcia—"and he's fucking with *him* ... You fuck with the king himself, you'd better kill *him* because *he's* gonna be a big problem. And *he* knows who you are. If *he* can't do it, *he'll* have someone else do it."

It seemed reasonably clear Charlie was telling Katie that her "husband"—"the king himself"—might need to arrange for another killing, this time of the blackmailer. "And so help me God, if they fuck with my family, it's gonna be like, fucking Nazi shit because this will be done. You know what I'm saying. I mean Katie, I don't care what I spend. Okay? I swear to God, Katie." In other words, the Maestro was willing to spend whatever was necessary to eliminate this particular problem if anyone dared to "fuck with" his family.

Charlie then made crystal clear that the "he" he'd just referred to repeatedly was indeed Sigfredo Garcia, asking Katie to confirm that "*he* knows I have you on the salary... You think *he'd* be happy to know that."

"Of course," Katie agreed. Now she was the one who began rambling on, but the audio wasn't clear enough to decipher what she was saying, other than, "he doesn't like," "when I told him," and "that you're helping out because he knows that

I need it." In context, the "he" she was now referring to was clearly her "husband," Sigfredo Garcia.

"He doesn't have any bad feelings towards me, does he?" Charlie inquired. "Our paths never crossed in that I didn't know the two of you when you were together."

"It's not like that," Katie concurred.

"You know it's not where it's like, I fucking was around when you guys were together and then hopped in when you walked out. Like, that's a different story. That's disrespectful." By which Charlie apparently meant that he didn't enter Katie's romantic picture until she'd broken up with Garcia—that Katie wasn't sleeping with him behind her "husband's" back. Katie responded to Charlie's comment at some length, but the audio failed to capture her exact words.

Charlie then reminded his former lover of his continuing support for her and her family over the years. "I mean, Katie, I'd go to the moon and back for you... I don't have to sit here and tell you what I would do... I look for things to do. You don't ask me for shit." He mentioned how he'd taken care of "Noah's birthday," seemingly misremembering the name of Katie's son, Ethan. "I'm the one who is like, 'Hey, I'll sell you the Lexus for a very good price.' ... Like, I don't have to tell you. I show you. There's a difference." All of which was Charlie's way of reminding Katie how much he'd done for her, buttering her up so she'd now do this big favor for him.

"So what do you think?" he asked, seeking her commitment. Charlie reiterated that the blackmailer "needs to know that it's going to go down one of two ways. Like, you're either fucking with me or you're fucking with the police. Pick which one." That was the message he wanted Katie to convey, even though he had zero intention of actually reporting the extortion demand to law enforcement.

Charlie then went back through the entire interaction between his mom and the blackmailer, to impress on Katie, "They did not go through the trouble of finding her and putting that thing together and giving that thing to her" if he planned to go away. "He ain't going away."

He explained why Donna couldn't be the one to handle the situation herself. If his mom arranged a meeting in front of her building, he said, "and he just drives up and she hands him five Gs, what the fuck do you think is going to happen next month? It's gonna be, 'Oh, he needs your help again.' You know what I mean?"

"And the thing is," he added, "if my parents really were *guilty*, they may think they have a big fish on the line that's gonna pay them monthly, and all they have to do is scare this little old lady. And who is she gonna go to? She's gonna go to the cops? *She's guilty as hell.* You have to let 'em know these people are not afraid of going to the cops. They've got nothing to hide. Okay?"

For the next minute or so, Katie did the majority of the talking, but what she said was unintelligible. Eventually, Charlie pivoted back to Garcia, telling Katie he didn't think the people blackmailing his family would want to mess with "his connections."

"Yeah," Katie agreed.

"Is he like so far removed that he's, like he's—" Charlie began a thought.

"Yes, of course," Katie replied, not letting him finish.

Charlie asked if "he" had people he could call.

"Like yeah," Katie confirmed. "Yeah."

"Listen," he reassured her. "You giving somebody some money is not an admission of any kind of *guilt* ... You know how you can say things without saying it? Like, just the way [the blackmailer] said it. Like he said, 'He needs your help. He was there for you. And his family needs your help now.'"

As his mind meandered back to his mom being confronted on the street in front of her condo building, Charlie lamented, "You have to understand, his presence— my mom had diarrhea all night. She's hasn't been eating and she's been up since two o'clock in the morning with diarrhea. Like, how do you think that feels my mom 65 years old and up since two in the morning with fucking diarrhea?" That, apparently, was something the Maestro was unwilling to tolerate—no one was going to get away with giving his mother diarrhea, regardless of what she might have done in the past.

Some 35 minutes into the video, Katie rose from her seat and walked away from their table, presumably to go to the ladies room. She returned less than two minutes later, plopping down across the table from her ex-boyfriend. They briefly discussed some type of gift Charlie had forgotten to bring her, possibly for Garcia's 34th birthday, which was only a week away. He told Katie that when he was leaving his house, "I literally had the bag out and I had it in my car with my car keys... Well, if you want, you guys can swing by my house later."

Charlie pressed her to confirm that she'd perform the favor he was asking. He took a piece of paper out of his pocket and held it in his lap without showing Katie—presumably the printout of the article on Dan's murder the undercover agent had handed Donna. "I want you to ... write the number down, and I'm going to give you cash," he said. He leaned back in his seat to get a better view of the piece of paper and then read aloud the seven digits following the area code: 712-6570.

What was "shocking," Charlie said, was that the bearded stranger was trying to blackmail someone who "had no problem possibly doing *bad things*," rather than someone who was merely "banging their secretary." In context, those "bad things" seemingly included shooting a law professor in the head from point-blank range. "If you're going to blackmail someone," he added, "blackmail someone that's cheating on their wife."

Continuing with that train of thought, Charlie said: "If *this* is what it's actually revolving around, okay. It's actually revolving around this *horrible thing* ... If you're blackmailing somebody who potentially had the ability to get something like *this* done, you've got a fucking set of balls, because they make you shut up real quick." In other words, the blackmailer was messing with people who'd already demonstrated zero hesitation to whack someone, and was now risking precisely the same fate by extorting them. And that made Charlie conclude, "without a doubt ... he didn't come there alone. He came there with someone else. You know what I'm saying?"

He reiterated the danger of paying off the blackmailer, even though that was precisely what he was telling Katie needed to be done. "So what if his homeboys want some money? … We just get a bunch of scumbags knocking on my door going, 'Somebody needs help.' Well guess what? I don't have anything to do with *what happened down there*. You don't. I don't know anyone who does. I don't know who Tuto even fucking is, okay? Like I don't know these people … Go to the fucking police. I don't care. Go to the police. Tell them what you know. I'll tell them what I know—nothing. Because I don't." Yet each of these statements was belied by Charlie's incessant ramblings over the prior 40 minutes.

Though the topic of money was discussed repeatedly during the recorded conversation, the $100,000 reward for information leading to the apprehension of Dan Markel's killers was never raised a single time. Which was telling in and of itself. Charlie's words made clear that whoever was blackmailing his family knew "information" and possessed "details" about the murder. As he was putting on his reading glasses to review the check the waitress had laid on their table, he even expressed his view that the extortion demand was coming from the "inside." But if that was true, and he and Katie had nothing to do with the murder, why wasn't the focus of their entire discussion how to report the extortion demand and claim the $100,000 reward?

The former lovers got up from their table, walking directly in front of the surveillance cameras that had been filming their conversation for more than an hour. As they came through Dolce Vita's front doors into the bright afternoon sunlight, Charlie Adelson and Katie Magbanua had absolutely no reason to suspect that the conversation they'd just had would emerge as the most crucial piece of evidence in the murder case prosecutors in Tallahassee would ultimately bring against each of them. Or that the jury chosen for Katie's May 2022 retrial would be listening to the words they'd just exchanged at the pizza and gelato restaurant over and over and over again.

28.

Whole New Ball Game

THE JURY IMPANELED for Katie's retrial was significantly more balanced than the ten women and two men who'd been unable to decide her fate at the first trial—an even six men and six women. This time around, none of the jurors were pregnant. Two were Black and one was Hispanic, with nearly the entire panel under the age of 50. There was a good mix between blue-collar and white-collar workers—even a licensed attorney among the 12.

For the thousands who tuned into the retrial's daily livestream, a number of changes from the 2019 trial became immediately apparent. For starters, the bench was now occupied by Robert Wheeler rather than James Hankinson. Though the people seated at Katie's defense table remained exactly the same, the second defense table was gone altogether, Sigfredo Garcia now serving his life sentence at the Holmes Correctional Institution, about 20 miles south of the Alabama border—and nearly 600 miles from his hometown of Miami Beach. Because Anna Norris had transitioned into private practice in late 2019, Assistant State Attorney Sarah Kathryn Dugan—affectionately known to her colleagues as "SK" or "Doogie"—was now seated beside Georgia Cappleman at the prosecution table.

Like Cappleman, Dugan was a native of North Florida, having grown up in a rural area about an hour north of Tally, barely south of the Georgia border. She'd spent her college and law school years in two of Florida's biggest cities—at the University of Miami for her undergraduate studies and Florida Coastal School of Law in Jacksonville. Dugan had been most intrigued by her courses in criminal law and procedure. A judicial externship the summer before her 3L year with a judge who held criminal court convinced her that she wanted to be a prosecutor. The State Attorney's Office in Tallahassee offered her a position in 2013, the year before Dan Markel's murder. She'd been rising through its ranks ever since.

Over the nine years she'd been a prosecutor, Dugan had been involved in some of the most significant cases coming through the Second Judicial Circuit, trying numerous first-degree murder cases to verdict either as first- or second-chair prosecutor. Though she'd had very little involvement in the Markel case, that changed in a hurry upon Anna Norris's departure. Cappleman gave her an even larger role than the one Norris had played at the original trial—starting with the responsibility of delivering the prosecution's opening statement.

Dugan told the jury that Katie had been the "link" between the people who wanted Dan Markel's murder done and the person who pulled the trigger. Katie's "connections," she said, made her the perfect candidate to solve the Adelsons' problem. She recounted how various clues had led investigators along two separate paths that ultimately collided. The first related to motive, running from Wendi to Donna to Charlie and centering on their mutual desire to relocate Wendi and her kids to South Florida. The second path began with the rented Prius spotted in Dan Markel's driveway—which led investigators to Rivera, Garcia, and the woman who gave birth to his children. The only thing the two paths had in common, Dugan asserted, was Katie, the "middleman" who allowed the Adelsons to insulate themselves from Dan's killers.

For a solid ten minutes, the experienced prosecutor provided jurors a blow-by-blow preview of the newly enhanced Dolce Vita audio, now the centerpiece of the prosecution's case. What did Dugan find most important about the recording? That Katie didn't seem to question anything Charlie was saying. Not why the police would be running an undercover operation on his family. Or, alternatively, why someone would be blackmailing them. She noted how Katie didn't flee the restaurant as Charlie's ramblings became more and more descriptive—and incriminating. Why not? Because, she told jurors, Katie was well aware of everything Charlie was talking about, as she'd been a direct participant in the plot to kill Dan Markel.

When Tara Kawass replaced Dugan at the lectern, it quickly became apparent that she and DeCoste had dramatically overhauled Katie's defense, jettisoning the theory they'd advanced for years, that "prosecutorial desperation"—rather than actual evidence—had led to Katie's arrest. And that Katie was being prosecuted solely to pressure her into turning State's evidence to reel in the big fish law enforcement and the State Attorney's Office were after—Charlie Adelson. Kawass's 40-minute opening was devoid of any such contention.

The defense team had seemingly concluded that the new jury wouldn't accept that Katie was being prosecuted solely to get her to flip on Charlie with the wealthy periodontist now behind bars. Late in the first trial, DeCoste had teased a theory of a possible direct connection between Charlie and Garcia—that Garcia could have agreed to kill Dan Markel not just for the money, but to get Charlie to terminate his relationship with Katie. Even though there was no actual evidence that had occurred, at the time, it seemed plausible enough to help establish reasonable doubt as to Katie's involvement in the homicide.

But what Tara Kawass was about to tell the fresh faces seated in Courtroom 3G's jury box went much further than that. She promised jurors she and DeCoste would prove a direct, active, and tight-knit conspiracy exclusively between Charlie and Garcia—which had occurred behind Katie's back.

Notably, with their shift in theory, the defense no longer considered the government—and Georgia Cappleman—the villain in their narrative. That role was now assigned to the Maestro himself. And with Garcia already convicted of first-degree murder, unlike at the prior trial, Kawass had no hesitation acknowledging that he was one of Dan's killers. She began her opening by telling the jury that she and the State actually agreed on two critical points: that Charlie had contracted the hit on Dan Markel and that Rivera and Garcia had carried it out. The only thing the two sides didn't agree on, she said, was whether Katie knew about the plan. "If she didn't, she's not guilty on all three counts."

Kawass asserted that every action Katie took, and "every word that came out of her mouth, actually proves to you that she had no idea what was going on." She argued that the FBI and the police had "planted" Katie in the middle of their investigation through the bump and the wiretaps. "Had they not said her name," she told jurors, "all of the conversations would have been completely different, and we wouldn't be here today."

The former assistant public defender tore into Charlie Adelson more ferociously than she had Luis Rivera during the first trial, sharing with jurors that the playboy bachelor had "an endless amount of young, beautiful women for him to manipulate and play with. Because that's what women are to Charles Adelson. Just toys. And the one toy that he ended up playing with is Katherine Magbanua." Charlie, she said, was a "master manipulator"—a refrain she'd employ repeatedly—"someone who uses people to get what he wants, even without them knowing it."

Kawass fleshed out the defense team's theory as to how the murder went down. On February 14, 2014, she recounted, Dan Markel had filed a motion to prevent Donna Adelson from seeing her grandkids without supervision. A month later, Garcia followed Katie when she left her apartment to meet Charlie for dinner and then spied on them as they sat together at an outdoor table. When Katie left to drive home in her own vehicle, Kawass contended, Garcia confronted Charlie about his ongoing relationship with his "wife." It was during that confrontation, Kawass told jurors, that Charlie seized the "opportunity," forging an agreement to pay Garcia $100,000 and to end his romance with Katie if Garcia agreed to kill Dan Markel. "The deal was hatched in that moment."

Kawass told jurors that Charlie's iCloud account revealed that he reached out to Katie the very next morning to ascertain whether Garcia had told her anything about the agreement he'd reached with Charlie. "The texts are going to show you, she had no clue," the defense lawyer explained. "She was even confused about why he was asking her about this." Then, in April 2014, Katie went through her "husband's" phone when he left it unattended. What did she discover? Charlie's cellphone number in his contacts. She immediately reached out to Charlie, asking him, "Did Tuto call your phone?" That text helped prove their secret agreement, Kawass asserted.

She described for jurors the July 1, 2014, roadway confrontation near Katie's apartment, suggesting that Garcia was "pissed" because Charlie hadn't upheld his end of the bargain to terminate his relationship with Katie. That same day, Kawass noted, Garcia called "the Adelsons"—without acknowledging that the call had actually been to Harvey, not Charlie, and simply rolled to voicemail.

Kawass offered a brand-new explanation for Katie's soaring cash deposits following the July 2014 murder, telling jurors the money had come from Garcia's share of the payoff for the murder. Katie's "husband" finally had some money, she said, to demonstrate he wasn't a deadbeat dad. Kawass contended that her client "had no idea that it came from the proceeds of a homicide."

The wiretaps, she argued, would show nothing more than the "master manipulator at work." Of over 400 recorded calls, Kawass said, the prosecutors would be "cherry picking" only the ones they believed helped them. She devoted only two minutes of her opening to the Dolce Vita audio, sharing that she'd been excited to learn of its enhancement because she knew it would demonstrate Katie's innocence. But that didn't happen, she said, because Katie's voice is inaudible throughout the recording. "You are going to be hearing a conversation," she predicted, "that leaves you with more of a question mark than answers."

Kawass told the jury that Charlie ended up keeping his end of the bargain, "ghosting" Katie about a month after the murder and giving her "the brush-off." In the end, he and Wendi got exactly what they wanted, namely her relocation to South Florida with her kids. Garcia got what he wanted, a bunch of money and the end of Charlie's relationship with his "wife." For her part, Donna was likely at home watching TV, "probably watching this trial," Kawass said derisively as she looked into the courtroom's TV camera, as if she could actually see the Adelson family's matriarch sitting on her living room couch through the camera lens.

What about Charlie? Kawass revealed that he'd finally been arrested, just a month before the trial. Pointing to a well-dressed, bearded man at the rear of the gallery, she noted that the periodontist's lawyer was actually in the courtroom, "watching, taking notes. Preparing for whenever Charlie's going to trial." She ended her opening statement with a "guarantee" that "at the end of this case, you will see clear as day that Ms. Magbanua did not know and that she's innocent of these charges."

The defense team had a set of exhibits prepared to demonstrate the difference between the prosecution's theory and theirs, which they trotted out during DeCoste's cross-examination of Craig Isom. The first exhibit, illustrating the State's theory, had a row of photos of the Adelsons at the top, Katie in the middle under Charlie's photo, and Garcia and Rivera below Katie. It depicted Katie as the "middleman" between the Adelsons and the hitmen.

The second one, depicting the defense's new theory, removed Katie altogether, with a vertical line connecting Charlie directly to Garcia. Throughout the prosecution's case, Kawass and DeCoste projected these exhibits onto the screen repeatedly as they cross-examined law enforcement witnesses — to reinforce their contention as to how the conspiracy actually played out.

Based on their new theory — and Kawass's statement they would *prove* its accuracy — it seemed pretty likely that the defense team's star witness would be none other than Sigfredo Garcia, this time in a blue jumpsuit, rather than a sharp-looking suit. Why? Because if Katie had been walled off from Charlie's tight-knit conspiracy with Garcia, as Kawass now claimed, only two people on the planet could testify to that fact: Charlie and Garcia.

But having recently been charged with Dan's murder, the bearded periodontist enjoyed a Fifth Amendment right to ignore a defense subpoena. It wasn't remotely conceivable that he'd be shuffling into Courtroom 3G, in his own blue jumpsuit, to testify on Katie's behalf. Therefore, the only person on earth capable of supporting the defense team's new theory — who could convince jurors that Katie wasn't involved — was the father of her two children.

Indeed, at the defense team's request, Sigfredo Garcia had been transported from his prison cell near Alabama to the Leon County Detention Center so he'd be available to testify once the prosecution rested its case. After all, what did the many-time felon and convicted murderer have to lose? He'd been at the beck and call of Katherine Diana Magbanua since his early twenties. Now that his own guilt had been adjudicated and his appeal dismissed, why wouldn't he do everything within his power to help her beat the murder rap and return home to their kids?

•••

AS GEORGIA CAPPLEMAN listened to Tara Kawass preview the defense team's new theory, she couldn't help but chuckle at how preposterous it all seemed. Though he was the least educated of the entire bunch — represented by defense lawyers on the public dole — it didn't take Luis Rivera long to realize that it made far more sense to cop a plea and share what he knew than to face a jury and a possible death sentence. A deal King Tato was able to make without providing the goods on anyone bearing the last name of Adelson.

In stark contrast, now nearing six years since his arrest, Sigfredo Garcia had *never* approached the State Attorney's Office to negotiate a plea deal. If there really had been a tight-knit conspiracy solely between him and Charlie, with Saam Zangeneh advising him, would Garcia truly have decided to roll the dice at trial, and a possible death sentence, rather than make a deal? Despite being able to serve up the big fish prosecutors were after on a sizzling hot platter?

Indeed, until Charlie's arrest, Katie's lawyers had contended that their client had been arrested solely to help the government arrest and prosecute Charlie. If Garcia actually possessed the very evidence that could achieve that objective, why on earth wouldn't he have raced to the State Attorney's Office the moment Katie was taken into custody, when Zangeneh easily could have negotiated a two-for-one deal? One that could have sprung Katie from jail, gotten Garcia a much lighter sentence, and given law enforcement and prosecutors precisely what they'd been after since Dan Markel's murder—direct evidence of Charlie Adelson's involvement in the homicide.

Would Sigfredo Garcia have allowed the love of his life and mother of his kids to rot in jail for nearly six years if, as Tara Kawass was now telling jurors, he had evidence the entire time that could have exonerated her—and nailed Charlie to the wall? The whole scenario, in Georgia Cappleman's view, was utterly laughable. The reason why Garcia had never tried to make a deal, she firmly believed, was because the only truthful evidence he could have offered would have implicated the mother of his two children, not Charlie Adelson.

• • •

NUMEROUS WITNESSES MADE encore appearances at the second trial. Among them was Wendi Jill Adelson. Oddly, the 43-year-old former clinical law professor strolled into the courtroom—flanked by two seasoned lawyers this time—in the very same heather-gray dress and black blazer she'd worn at the first trial. Though she was seemingly trying to make some sort of statement with her choice of attire, her intended message wasn't entirely clear.

While her outfit may have been precisely the same, the circumstances couldn't have been more different this time around. As of the fall of 2019, the Adelson family seemed to be untouchable, some even wondering who they'd bribed to avoid prosecution. But now, as Wendi was swearing to tell the truth a second time, her brother was behind bars sporting an orange-and-white striped jumpsuit. Though she'd ultimately succeeded in relocating from Tallahassee to South Florida—once the father of her children was out of the picture—Charlie had been forcibly relocated in the opposite direction, Florida's capital city his new home for the foreseeable future. For her part, Donna Adelson had to be on pins and needles every time she heard a knock at her door—her heart likely skipping a beat whenever the phone rang unexpectedly—wondering how soon she'd be the next domino to fall.

As she plodded through her direct examination, Cappleman had Wendi focus extensively on the massive divorce file—which had somehow swelled between the two trials from 576 pages to more than 700—this time having her read portions of the contentious pleadings directly to the jury. Wendi denied that relocation had been the most important part of the divorce case *to her*, though admitted it had been important to her mother.

For some reason, she felt it important to hurl gratuitous potshots at her long-deceased ex-husband, telling jurors, while smirking, that Dan had been "sanctioned" by the family court judge for misbehavior—which wasn't actually true. "Danny fired or alienated all of his attorneys," she laughed. She told jurors her ex had hired three or four different lawyers, whereas she'd employed only one until near the end of their legal battle—when the actual score was three to three. She also claimed that it had been her, not her parents, who'd paid for her legal counsel.

Asked if her mother was a "controlling person," Wendi sighed, casting her gaze upward. "I think my mom is and was very invested in my life," she finally offered. "I don't think of her as a controlling person." She wouldn't agree with Cappleman that Donna "despised" Dan, telling jurors that her mom was merely "disappointed" with the way he treated her. Yet just minutes later, Cappleman had Wendi pick out all of the names Donna had called her ex-son-in-law in her scathing emails, including "asshole," "bully," "zealot," and "jackass." She acknowledged that her mom "was very upset" when the family court judge denied her petition to relocate. And told jurors that she was the one who'd come up with the nickname "Jibbers" at a time she felt "incredibly terrorized" by Dan.

Wendi agreed that the divorce pleadings were "venomous"—but only on Dan's part, not hers. As to her ex-husband's February 2014 motion to restrict Donna's access to Ben and Lincoln, she testified that "nobody took it very seriously" and that Donna wasn't the slightest bit worried about the motion being granted. She denied being involved in a plot to kill Dan or having foreknowledge of any such arrangement.

"But you suspected that your family was involved?" Cappleman asked.

Upon hearing that question, Wendi's face scrunched up. She shook her head side-to-side emphatically. "No, I did not suspect that my family was involved," she disagreed.

The veteran prosecutor pointed her to statements she'd made during her interview with Craig Isom the day of the shooting. "I think I speculated about lots of things during the six hours I spent with law enforcement *without an attorney present*, trying to help them solve this murder," Wendi retorted. "Yes, I said all kinds of things." She boasted how she'd "told law enforcement they could search my vehicle and signed away all my rights."

As she testified about her activities the morning of the murder, Wendi corrected the most glaring misstatement she made at the first trial—that she saw crime-scene tape from Centerville Road as she passed by Trescott Drive and never turned onto her former street. This time, she agreed she had, though denied suspecting that anything significant had occurred that morning. She told jurors that she made a three-point turn once she saw the crime-scene tape because she figured an electrical storm had caused a problem further down the street. She confirmed that Dan had been scheduled to leave town the following day, but adamantly denied knowing how his killers knew that.

As her direct examination neared an end, Wendi told the jury that she wanted all parties culpable for Dan's murder held accountable—even if it involved her own family. Cappleman reminded her that she told Craig Isom her "answer would be different" if her family members had been involved.

"I'm sure while I sat for six hours completely traumatized that I said all kinds of things," Wendi pushed back in a snippy tone. "I think you're taking my words out of context, but sure," she said, her eyes shooting daggers in the lead prosecutor's direction.

This time around, it was Chris DeCoste who drew the lucky straw of cross-examining Dan's ex-wife. The former trial team superstar came out swinging, like a boxer trying to end a fight with a first-round knockout, pummeling the reluctant prosecution witness mercilessly. DeCoste's tone was biting—almost sneering—as he lobbed questions at Wendi like Russian artillery shells raining down on Ukrainian apartment buildings halfway around the world.

He began his questioning trying to get Wendi to accept that the entire murder trial was actually all about her and her failed marriage. But she wouldn't agree.

"You disagree that your ex-husband is dead because of your family?"

"Yes, I disagree," Wendi responded.

"These jurors are here for weeks doing their civic duty because of your marriage, right?"

"No."

"Katie's going through this ordeal because of that marriage, right?"

"No."

"Dan Markel's parents are going through absolute misery because of your failed marriage," DeCoste declared, walking back toward the gallery and pointing to Ruth and Phil Markel in the fourth row. "Isn't that right?"

"No, that's incorrect," Wendi responded.

When DeCoste asked her to confirm that Dan had been a "great" father, his ex-wife was only willing to concede that he'd been a "very good" dad.

"Those boys were his *world*, right?" the defense lawyer pressed her, the word "world" thundering throughout the courtroom. But again, Wendi refused to express full agreement. "As well as his work, yes," she answered, deliberately diminishing the value Dan had placed on his role as Ben and Lincoln's dad.

DeCoste led her through the fiasco of non-kosher food being served at their wedding—which she told jurors had been a simple "misunderstanding"—and her Pearl Harbor-style exit from their marriage. She denied that she "complained constantly to anyone who would listen" about her marriage.

"You agree that you complained to the one person who would actually do something about it?" DeCoste asked.

With an odd giggle, Wendi told him she didn't understand what he was asking.

"Your big brother, Charles Adelson," the defense lawyer clarified, "you complained to him about how bad Professor Markel was and how much you hated him and didn't want to be in a marriage with him?"

"I definitely talked to my brother about how unhappy I was in my marriage, if that's the question," Wendi agreed. "Then, yes."

"Can you think of one person in this world that would actually hire two people to go kill Professor Markel other than your family?"

Sensing how improper that question was, Wendi looked up

at the judge, begging him to intervene. By that point in her cross-examination, it had become crystal clear to everyone in the courtroom that Georgia Cappleman had no intention of coming to Wendi's aid with an objection, despite DeCoste's irrelevant, argumentative, and speculative questions. But instead of drawing the line, Judge Wheeler told her to answer the question.

"I'd love to," Wendi said with a wide grin, "except it calls for an unbelievable amount of speculation." She told DeCoste that it was the "prosecutor's duty," not hers, "to figure out who's responsible."

"Tell this jury, who on this planet would have wanted to kill Professor Markel?" DeCoste pressed her, now sensing he had carte blanche to torture her with whatever questions he wanted to ask. Not only was Cappleman not objecting, neither were Wendi's high-priced lawyers—who sat in their wooden gallery pew mute as they watched their client being slaughtered in broad daylight. "I have no idea," Wendi finally said with a shake of her head, her words barely above a whisper.

DeCoste's tone suddenly shifted, now showering praise on the former high school valedictorian and Truman Scholar, walking her through her impressive biography—leading to his point that Wendi was a "smart woman." Or, as Bostonians like to say, "wicked smaat." When he alluded to her status as a published author, in perhaps the most bizarre moment of her more than two hours on the witness stand, Wendi responded with an over-the-top southern accent: "Now you're just embarrassing me," she claimed, seemingly channeling Scarlett O'Hara from *Gone with the Wind*. She feigned discomfort over DeCoste's flattery, telling jurors she didn't like talking about herself.

"You're a smart woman, right?" he asked, his tone becoming more stern.

"I *am* a smart woman," Wendi replied, hers somewhat biting.

"There's information about this case *everywhere*. You'd agree with me on that?"

Yet Wendi told jurors that, upon her lawyer's advice, she hadn't read articles, listened to podcasts, or watched TV shows about the murder case. She claimed she'd never discussed her ex-husband's slaying with any of her family members.

"How can you say you love those boys if you don't care who killed the father that they loved?" DeCoste asked. Wendi told jurors that she "of course" cared and had refrained from looking at information about Dan's murder solely because of the legal advice she'd received.

But DeCoste continued to pound away. "Are you afraid that when you look at it, you're going to realize that your brother did this?"

With a harsh facial expression, Wendi responded, "I'm not afraid of that." She told the jury her job wasn't to solve the murder case. It was to take care of her boys. "I don't see how it helps take care of them to go reading and watching and soaking up all of the horrible information that's out there."

Katie's lawyer kept at her, like a lion pawing at its suffering prey. "You don't realize that you could be helpful in finally untangling this, to give this jury the truth about what happened to Professor Markel?"

For a few seconds, Wendi stared at DeCoste with an incredulous expression. She couldn't tolerate his abuse any longer, beginning a soliloquy that lasted nearly a full minute. "I've done nothing but help in this process," she began. "I came here and testified. I spoke to the police for six hours without anyone present. I signed over my cellphone, my car, my house—everything. My computer." Her eyes now hurling daggers toward the defense lawyer, she asked, "What else do I have or know that you haven't seen?"

Yet DeCoste's questioning grew even more belligerent. "Do you honestly expect this jury to believe that you haven't confronted your brother about all of this?" With firm conviction, Wendi told jurors she hadn't ever done so.

"Or maybe you don't need to because you know the truth in this case," he asserted. "You already know it. That he went behind your back, right?" Wendi leaned into the mic, uttering the words, "Did not happen."

"You understand that until you expose your brother and explain what he did—that he went behind everybody's back, that he hired a hitman to murder your ex-husband—you'll remain guilty in the eyes of the world?"

"I can't speak to the eyes of the world," Wendi retorted, her answer tinged with disdain. "I can only know that I have done nothing wrong."

DeCoste asked her about a double date she went on with Jeff Lacasse, Charlie, and Katie in March 2014—during Florida State's spring break. The defense team wanted jurors to believe that Garcia had followed Katie to the restaurant and then confronted Charlie and forged an agreement with him just before he drove home.

Wendi testified that she and Lacasse met Charlie and Katie for an early dinner at the outdoor patio of Yardbird in Miami Beach. Her ex-boyfriend would shortly confirm that during his testimony. But Wendi denied ever telling Lacasse that her brother had looked into hiring a hitman. She also denied being aware that he was leaving for an out-of-town trip the same day, and at the same time, the murder occurred. "I don't think I knew when he was leaving town," she told jurors.

DeCoste suggested that the only reason Wendi was testifying under a grant of immunity was because she "feared" being charged with Dan's murder. But she pushed back hard. "I don't fear being charged for a crime I didn't commit," she said, shaking her head. "No." The defense lawyer tried to get her to admit she felt "tension" with the prosecutors. "They recently had your brother Charles Adelson arrested, and he's in custody, right?" Wendi acknowledged that, in view of her brother's arrest, it was "very uncomfortable to be here." She also pointed out how media attention surrounding the case was keeping her from employment and "lots of things in my life."

Shifting gears, DeCoste asked about whether planning had begun for her son Ben's *bar mitzvah*, as his thirteenth birthday was only two months away. Wendi testified that the coming-of-age ceremony had already occurred, telling jurors she'd even invited Ruth and Phil Markel, without revealing if they'd actually attended.

"When was the last time they saw face-to-face their grandchildren?" DeCoste asked, attempting to force Wendi to share with the jury that she'd been preventing such contact for years—as she'd acknowledged during the first trial. But Wendi surprised everyone in the courtroom—except Dan's parents—by revealing that Ruth and Phil had visited with their grandsons on April 20, just weeks before the retrial commenced. Though the purpose for the visit was fairly transparent—to help Wendi appear more humane at this trial than the last—it was still rather remarkable that, after six years of forced isolation, Dan's parents had finally gotten to see their grandsons face-to-face.

Despite that revelation, DeCoste went for the jugular, asking Wendi to admit that she'd been keeping her children from the parents of her murdered ex-husband, but had "no problem letting them hang out with your brother Charles, who's now sitting in custody for first-degree murder?"

"Well, they can't see him *now*, can they?" Wendi shot back, trying to retain her composure despite her evident anger at Katie's attorney.

DeCoste's next questions cut straight to the bone. "For years," he began, Ruth and Phil "weren't able to see their grandchildren despite their pleading with you to see them." He was again pointing toward Dan's parents in the gallery. "But you let them hang out with your *murdering brother*, right?" Once again, neither Cappleman nor Wendi's attorneys lodged an objection.

At this point, Wendi abandoned any pretense of being polite and respectful. She told the jury how Ruth and Phil had seen her kids "for years," but then threatened to have them placed in foster care. "My brother never threatened to put my children in foster care, and if he had, the visits would have stopped with him too."

She grew even angrier as DeCoste suggested to jurors that she didn't love her boys because she didn't care about what had happened to their father. He exhorted her to "look at the evidence and help figure it out, so that more lives aren't ruined by this." Finally, Judge Wheeler interceded, telling the defense attorney he needed to ask questions, not make statements.

"Please end the madness and share the truth," DeCoste continued, undeterred. "Would you please share the truth with this jury?"

"I've been sharing the truth since I walked in here," Wendi insisted, glancing toward the jury box. "I've done nothing but share the truth."

"You know what happened here, right?"

"*I do not know what happened here*," Wendi pushed back. "And if I did, I would have shared it with the police eight years ago." By this point, her facial expression could no longer conceal her disdain for Katie's attorney, who seemed to be delighting in making her suffer.

DeCoste ended with another flourish, trying to get Wendi to admit that she'd vomited at Charlie's "celebration dinner" because of "what he'd done." She denied that was the reason she'd thrown up. And also denied knowing that the murder "didn't involve Katie."

He implored her to "finally tell the truth. Why don't you just admit to this jury that you're guilty?"

"*Because I'm not guilty*," an immensely frustrated Wendi Adelson told jurors, finally bringing to a close 30 minutes of sheer torture. From beginning to end, DeCoste's blistering cross-examination bore little relevance to the guilt or innocence of the defendant who was actually on trial—an entertaining sideshow in the quest for justice, but sideshow nonetheless.

When Georgia Cappleman completed her brief redirect examination, the Brandeis grad slinked away from the witness stand, joining her lawyers on her way to the door, and marched out of the courtroom fuming over how she'd been treated. Luckily for Wendi, the bar at Tallahassee's relatively small airport was fully stocked. Her flight back to Miami would offer a second opportunity for whatever stiff drink—or drinks—her experience in Courtroom 3G had made necessary.

•••

LATER THAT AFTERNOON, Georgia Cappleman trotted out her star witness, Luis Rivera, who was now sporting even more tattoos, inked all across his beefy neck. This time around, he was required to wear handcuffs the entire time he was on the stand. His testimony on direct examination was largely a reprise of what he told jurors during the first trial, yet with one notable exception—that the photo he'd posted on Instagram Katie had instructed him to take down was of a *lion*, not an owl, the Sunshine State's capital city apparently a haven for the ferocious African carnivores.

Cappleman used Rivera to chip away at the defense team's new theory, having him tell jurors about the occasion he and his best friend were in Garcia's pickup truck spying on Katie having dinner with "the dentist." She wanted jurors to conclude that this was the same occasion that involved their double date with Wendi and Lacasse at Yardbird. Rather than confront the dentist, Rivera testified, Garcia drove away and the two spent the remainder of the night together. Furthermore, Garcia had never mentioned to him anything about having had direct contact with the dentist, something Rivera told jurors his friend would assuredly have shared with him.

This time around, Chris DeCoste handled Rivera's cross-examination, his questioning of the former gang leader and convicted murderer far less aggressive than his cross of Wendi Adelson. He took his best shot at getting Rivera to buy into the new defense theory. "Mr. Rivera, I need you to tell this jury the truth," he began. "Garcia came to you to commit this murder, but he didn't mention Katie, right?"

Rivera immediately pushed back. "Katie been involved the whole time, dog ... She's involved. *She's the mastermind.* She was in the middle of this."

"They laid it out for you who they wanted?" DeCoste pressed him, implying that Craig Isom and Pat Sanford had spoon-fed him Katie's name.

"No," Rivera disagreed. "I gave them the truth, bro. I'm not going to go back and forth with you man. I gave them the truth. It was Katie and Garcia. It was all three of us involved. That's the truth man." When DeCoste tried to get him to admit that he "took Katie's innocence," King Tato was emphatic. "No, I'm not taking her innocence. She's guilty just like all three of us are guilty, man."

DeCoste returned to the day the blue-uniformed witness and his best friend had been spying on Katie and her new boyfriend, suggesting that Garcia had confronted the dentist, "and that confrontation turned into a negotiation—between him and Charles Adelson. Right?"

For a moment, Rivera stared at the defense lawyer with a puzzled expression. "You think they spoke?" he asked in a bewildered tone. It was clear he considered such a scenario ridiculous. Rivera also got the better of DeCoste on his final question, when the defense lawyer declared, "The government told you Katie was involved, right?"

Rivera chuckled and smiled. "No sir," he replied. "She's been involved the whole time… Whatever she tells him to do, he jumps and do it. That's his weakness. Her, right there," he said, swiveling his head in Katie's direction.

•••

AS HE DID DURING the first trial, Sergeant Chris Corbitt walked jurors through an extensive PowerPoint presentation illustrating the calls, text messages, and pings emanating from the cellphones that belonged to Wendi, Charlie, Katie, Garcia, and Rivera at critical points in time. He showed jurors a text message exchange in which Charlie had asked Katie to spend the evening with him on July 18, 2014. Corbitt testified that her phone was seemingly turned off when she arrived at Charlie's home. It next showed activity the following morning, when it was pinging towers in a southerly direction between Charlie's home and Jessica Rodriguez's. All of which was consistent with Katie delivering money she'd received from her millionaire boyfriend.

Corbitt scored even more points for the State during DeCoste's cross-examination. At the first trial, the prosecution had been caught off-guard when Katie testified that she'd been at the pool with her son Ethan the morning after the murder, relying on text messages Kawass had placed before her. Between the two trials, Corbitt had committed those very same text messages to memory. Thus, when DeCoste suggested that texts found in Charlie's iCloud account confirmed that Katie was at the pool that morning with her kids, Corbitt told jurors that the texts revealed no such thing, and invited the defense attorney walk through them with him. DeCoste, however, declined his invitation and moved onto other topics.

Sarah Kathryn Dugan wanted to make sure jurors got to see those texts for themselves. During her redirect examination of Corbitt, she projected them onto the screen, asking the veteran police officer what they actually showed. Which was that Katie had indicated at 12:18 p.m. that she'd "probably" be going to the pool *later* and that, at 4:54 p.m., she'd just gotten "back from the pool." Corbitt further testified that her cell tower pings were consistent with her being at Yindra Mascaro's residence at 11:23 a.m. that same morning. Her entire text exchange with Charlie about going to the pool occurred after she'd presumably retrieved her kids from Mascaro—and after the money drop.

Corbitt also testified that both Garcia and Katie had left voicemails for *Harvey* Adelson on July 1, 2014. Dugan showed him a text from Katie to Charlie the following day, in which she said, "Leaving a message was so childish." Her text left little doubt she'd been fully aware her "husband" had mistakenly left Harvey a nasty voicemail and that she was embarrassed he'd done so.

Dugan also showed Corbitt a similar text from March 12, 2014, the day after the double date at Yardbird. Katie's text to Charlie read, "He's acting like a child," which was a pretty clear reference to her "husband's" jealous rage after having spied on her with the dentist. Her text stood in stark contrast to the notion that Charlie and Garcia had gotten together that evening behind her back. The final text Corbitt was asked about was from August 2014, in which Katie told Charlie, "Go on with your life. Have a great life." The defense had suggested the text evidenced a "breakup." Yet Corbitt told the jury that the records he reviewed showed the two talking several times a week long after that text.

•••

ONE OF SEVERAL BATTLES the two sides waged prior to the second trial was whether the new jury would be permitted to see video footage of Katie's testimony from the first trial. The prosecution was entitled to show jurors her prior testimony, no different from any other pretrial statement by a criminal defendant. On the other hand, the judge ruled that the defense team *couldn't* play video of her testimony in lieu of calling her as a live witness. Because Cappleman believed that Katie's cross-examination this time around would be far more devastating—the prosecution team having had almost three years to prepare—she decided not to share the video of Katie's prior testimony with the new jury.

With one small exception. Midway through the State's case-in-chief, Cappleman played a 30-second segment of the audio portion of Katie's October 2019 testimony. At the time, the lead prosecutor had asked the defendant, "Did Mr. Garcia even know that Mr. Adelson was the one behind this whole thing?" To which Katie had replied, "I believe not." That answer, of course, belied the notion that her "husband" and Charlie had plotted Dan Markel's murder together in a tight-knit conspiracy. A pretty significant needle to find in the three-hour haystack of Katie's prior testimony.

•••

ONCE AGAIN, KATIE'S good friend Yindra Mascaro proved to be a powerful prosecution witness. She told jurors that Katie had been getting so little support from Sigfredo Garcia prior to 2016, she had to take him to court for child support—which was directly at odds with Kawass's opening statement, in which she'd contended that Katie's surge in cash deposits came from money her "husband" had provided her from his share of the $100,000 payoff.

Mascaro's testimony also severely undercut the notion that Katie had discovered Charlie's telephone number on Garcia's phone when she rifled through his contacts in April 2014—which Kawass told jurors about as she fleshed out the new defense theory during her opening statement. The prosecution witness testified that Katie confided in her that Garcia had actually gone through *her* phone to find Charlie's number—following their July 2014 roadway confrontation—because he wanted to give "the dentist" a piece of his mind. Mascaro told jurors that Katie was "really embarrassed" that her "husband" had inadvertently left his nasty voicemail on Harvey's phone, rather than Charlie's.

Her most consequential testimony came almost as an afterthought. After acknowledging that she didn't recall precisely when Katie had asked her to keep Ethan and Kaylee overnight, a light bulb went off in Mascaro's head. She told Dugan she'd taken a picture of the kids that night and posted it on Instagram. Until that moment on the witness stand, Yindra Mascaro had never mentioned that photo—nor had she been asked for evidence that might reveal the specific night she kept Katie's kids. During a brief recess, she scrolled through her Instagram posts. When the trial reconvened, Dugan put her back on the witness stand, at which point Mascaro confirmed that the date Katie had her watch her children was indeed July 18, 2014, the same day Dan Markel was shot in his garage and killed. Quite the revelation indeed.

One of the State's new witnesses was a gentleman named Ramzi Naber, who owned Club Fate from 2012 to 2014. Virtually everything he said from the witness stand was at odds with the defense argument that Katie's spike in cash deposits following the murder arose at least in part from tips she'd made working at nightclubs. Naber repeatedly shared with jurors how *unsuccessful* his establishment had been after the buzz surrounding its opening wore off, with employees earning only $400-500 per weekend. He testified that 90% of Club Fate's patrons paid with credit cards, not cash, and that the credit card tips were later paid to employees via check. Though he recalled Katie working for him—describing her as a "shooting star" due to the short duration of her employment— he testified that her records, and those of her fellow employees, had been destroyed by water damage following a storm.

Despite the reverse psychology Tara Kawass employed to sheer perfection at the first trial, this time around, Cappleman decided to risk having Jessica Rodriguez share with jurors what she knew about the money drop. The professional manicurist quickly settled into her testimony, proving to be articulate and confident—smiling frequently—as devastating to the defense as was Yindra Mascaro. Rodriguez told jurors that, shortly after returning home from the hospital in early July 2014 following her daughter's birth, Garcia showed up unexpectedly at her front door. When she opened it, he was holding a bag, telling her it was a package for Tato. Though Katie wasn't there with him, she explained, Garcia's "wife" was in the parking lot in her car. She guilted Katie into coming upstairs to see her "little niece."

Rodriguez described the package as a brown paper bag on the inside of a plastic grocery store bag that felt like "a brick." When Katie finally entered her apartment, she turned to Garcia to make sure he'd delivered the package. Rodriguez recalled Katie being fidgety and in a rush, though she also seemed interested in what was in the bag. She testified that she found Katie's fascination with the bag odd, because it appeared from its size and shape that it was likely drugs, and she'd never known Katie to tolerate anything involving drugs. Rodriguez told jurors that she called Rivera to tell him to come home, and that her baby daddy raced home, arriving before Garcia and Katie had left.

Jurors now had four different pieces of evidence that seemed to confirm Katie's involvement in the money drop: Katie's flurry of calls that morning to Garcia and Rivera, her cell tower pings showing her driving toward Rodriguez's apartment and then stopping there—with no further cellphone activity for about an hour—Rivera's testimony establishing her presence during the money drop, and now Rodriguez's testimony as well.

•••

ONCE MARY HULL WALKED jurors through her PowerPoint slides illustrating the mountain of financial evidence against Katie—including the massive spike in her cash deposits following the murder—the stage was set for them to learn about the bump between the barrel-chested, undercover agent and Donna Adelson, the phone chatter that ensued, and the meeting between Katie and Charlie at Dolce Vita. After Oscar Jimenez and the undercover agent involved in the Dolce Vita recording testified, Keith McElveen explained the tedious forensic work he'd performed to enhance the audio component of the surveillance video. Though the former CIA investigator had helped blow the entire case wide open, his time on Courtroom 3G's grand stage was limited to a mere 19 minutes.

Special Agent Pat Sanford replaced McElveen on the witness stand, walking jurors through the sequence of events following the bump. Unlike Judge Hankinson in the first trial, Judge Wheeler allowed the prosecution to play the three wiretapped calls between Donna and Charlie immediately following the bump. Black headphones arrayed across the front of the jury box were soon on every juror's head—as well as the lawyers', Judge Wheeler's, and Agent Sanford's—as the calls between Donna and Charlie were played followed by Charlie's subsequent call to Katie.

The time had finally come for jurors to see for themselves the centerpiece of the prosecution's case—the enhanced Dolce Vita video—which was projected onto a large screen near the bench and smaller screens in the jury box. Though the prosecution had fought hard to include the written text at the bottom of the video, in a pretrial ruling, Judge Wheeler had excluded both the closed captioning and the written transcript prepared by the court reporter. Consequently, jurors wouldn't get to see with their eyes the words that came out of Charlie's and Katie's mouths as grand jurors had a month earlier. Listening carefully through their headphones, they'd try to make out as best they could—with just their ears—what the former lovers were actually saying to one another at the noisy Italian restaurant.

Once jurors laid their headphones aside, Cappleman had Agent Sanford confirm that, during her October 2019 testimony, Katie claimed that she hadn't learned anything about Dan Markel's murder until after her "husband's" May 2016 arrest—which occurred after the Dolce Vita meeting and all the wiretapped calls. If that statement was to be believed, the woman jurors had just watched and heard—as Charlie rambled on about what to make of the blackmail attempt and the favor he was asking—had been completely unaware of Dan Markel's murder.

And that was equally true for the 20 or so additional wiretapped calls jurors would spend the remainder of the afternoon listening to, including calls in which Charlie had discussed his intention—never fulfilled of course—to collect "the reward money." If Katie hadn't even known about Dan Markel's murder, she wouldn't have had the foggiest clue what "reward money" Charlie was referring to. Yet not once did the wiretaps record her asking, "What reward money?"

As Cappleman prepared to play another wiretapped call—and with the hands on the courtroom's clock signaling 5:30 p.m. that Wednesday afternoon—she could sense that jurors had heard enough. The lead prosecutor rose to her feet to announce that the State of Florida was resting its case.

•••

JUST A DAY EARLIER, Chris DeCoste had signaled that the defense intended to call numerous witnesses, whose testimony he projected would span more than ten hours of court time. With Memorial Day weekend just 48 hours away, it now appeared inevitable that the trial would spill over into a third week, with closing arguments likely the following Tuesday. Judge Wheeler asked the defense to have its witness list assembled by first thing Thursday morning. By then, the question that had loomed over the second trial since its inception would finally be answered: would Sigfredo "Tuto" Garcia swear to tell the truth and, for the very first time, provide his account of the cold-blooded murder of Professor Dan Markel?

29.

Will Tuto Speak?

AS IT TURNED OUT, Sheriff's deputies would never make the four-mile drive from the local jail to the Leon County Courthouse to accompany Sigfredo Garcia for his big day in court. When Chris DeCoste announced the batting order of defense witnesses on Thursday morning, May 26—six years and a day following Tuto's arrest—Garcia's name was noticeably absent, the convicted murderer having been transported from his prison cell in the western Panhandle to Florida's capital city for a purpose he'd never fulfill. Despite Tara Kawass's promise in her opening statement that the defense would prove the existence of a tight-knit conspiracy between Garcia and Charlie Adelson, neither man would take the stand to tell jurors that had actually transpired.

The first person to take note of the glaring omission on the defense's witness list was Georgia Cappleman, who'd been preparing her cross-examination of Dan Markel's assassin for weeks. The veteran prosecutor was loaded for bear with questions and exhibits designed to tie Garcia in knots and expose him not only as a vicious killer and lifelong criminal, but a man who wouldn't hesitate to lie, cheat, and steal for his beloved "wife," Katherine Magbanua.

Though that showdown would assuredly have been the crescendo of the second trial—and a media spectacle rivaling

Wendi Adelson's appearance—it was now clear it would never happen. Why not? Because Garcia simply refused to come to court to tell the jury what he knew—likely because it wasn't even remotely consistent with what Katie's lawyers hoped he'd say. In the days leading up to the trial, he'd even been captured on recorded telephone calls telling them not to have him transported to Tallahassee.

•••

THE DEFENSE LED OFF with TPD Sergeant Sherry Bennett, who DeCoste called to the witness stand ostensibly to discredit Jessica Rodriguez's testimony about the money drop the day after the shooting. Yet Bennett's testimony appeared to do just the opposite, reinforcing Rodriguez's statement that Katie had been present in her apartment just a few feet away from a grocery bag filled with money.

DeCoste played an audio recording of Bennett's telephone interview of Rodriguez on September 30, 2016. In the recording, Rivera's baby mama told the police officer—just as she told the jury—that Katie and Tuto had arrived at her apartment together shortly after her youngest child was born to deliver a bag she assumed was filled with money and drugs. The only significant difference between her 2016 interview and her 2022 trial testimony was that, in the former, she recalled that Katie and Tuto had already departed by the time Rivera arrived home, as compared to her testimony at trial that Rivera had shown up before they left.

DeCoste had TPD investigator Michael Dilmore testify about his digital scrub of Garcia's cellphone to establish that he'd apparently been in communication with Rivera in May 2016, while King Tato was in federal prison, and that Garcia's and Charlie's phones had a common contact—"Sully Mech." The defense apparently wanted jurors to believe that "Sully Mech" was somehow connected to their supposed tight-knit conspiracy. Yet they would soon learn otherwise.

The Boston transplant next recalled Craig Isom to the stand

to have the retired investigator acknowledge that it had been an oversight not to do a fuller investigation of the nightclubs at which Katie had worked. And also to highlight inconsistencies among Luis Rivera's numerous sworn statements. DeCoste also had Isom confirm that Rivera had implicated both Wendi and Katie, but that unlike Katie, Wendi had never been charged with Dan Markel's murder.

Jason Newlin, Cappleman's investigator at the State Attorney's Office, was up next. DeCoste asked several questions about Rivera's Instagram post the convicted killer testified he'd taken down upon Katie's instruction, getting Newlin to concede the obvious: that a lion and an owl are different animals. The defense lawyer grilled him over why no one had reached out to Facebook, the company that owns Instagram, to obtain Rivera's social media post. Yet Newlin had a ready answer. "If you don't send a preservation letter within seven days, you don't get it. It's gone." By the time Rivera told investigators about his Instagram post—of an owl—two years had elapsed since he'd removed it. It would have been futile to request it, Newlin testified.

Another topic that arose during his testimony was the meeting the defense team had arranged between Cappleman, Newlin, and Katie at the jail the Friday evening before the 2019 trial commenced. DeCoste used that meeting to demonstrate that Katie had willingly agreed to meet with the prosecution team without a request for immunity or any restrictions on what they could ask. Yet on cross-examination, Cappleman got Newlin to agree that the eleventh-hour jailhouse meeting was "a joke" that had been arranged "so the defense could tell the jury we were invited out there." The meeting, he testified, "didn't go anywhere."

The defense also called a brand new witness named Ryan Fitzpatrick, who'd been a good friend of Charlie Adelson's for 15 years before the two had a falling out over a business deal gone bad. Fitzpatrick told jurors that Charlie was extremely close with his mom, talking on the phone with her multiple times per day. No one in the Adelson family, he testified, had anything positive to say about the late Dan Markel. He agreed with Tara Kawass that Charlie was a manipulator. But also described him as "brilliant."

Fitzpatrick told the jury that Charlie was "paranoid"—suspicious of everyone—and had security cameras installed around the perimeter of his Fort Lauderdale home. He testified that his periodontist friend regularly used steroids and marijuana. That only became worse, he said, after Charlie's name became associated in the media with Dan Markel's murder. Though he never talked about the murder, Charlie told his friends he was innocent and that any speculation otherwise was "nonsense." Yet according to Fitzpatrick, over time, all of his male friends abandoned him. One statement he vividly recalled Charlie making was, "You can get away with murder. You just have to keep your mouth shut." Pretty darn ironic considering the reason he was now behind bars.

Fitzpatrick also testified about his cash deals with his longtime friend—in which he'd been paid in stacks of $100 bills stapled together, always $1,000 per stack.

•••

ONCE RYAN FITZPATRICK stepped down from the witness stand, the only remaining mystery was whether Katie Magbanua would once again take the witness stand in her own defense. The defense team was well aware that putting her on the stand a second time would be far riskier than the first. When she'd testified in October 2019, the prosecution didn't have the slightest clue what she'd say and had to react to her testimony on the fly, the element of surprise giving the defense somewhat of a tactical advantage.

But that advantage now belonged to the prosecution, which had two-and-a-half years to scrutinize every word Katie uttered from the witness stand and conceive of ways to discredit her and diminish her credibility. Moreover, the prosecution now had several additional pieces of evidence to employ as weapons: Ramzi Naber's testimony, Jessica Rodriguez's, and, most significantly, the enhanced Dolce Vita recording.

Nevertheless, Katie and her defense team decided she had no choice but to testify. Throughout the trial, they'd been telling the jury that she'd been completely unaware of the plot between Charlie and Garcia—that the two men in her life had conspired behind her back. Because Garcia wouldn't be confirming that account with his testimony, there was only one witness left who could—Katie herself.

Outside the presence of the jury, Judge Wheeler questioned her to make sure she truly wanted to testify, even though she had the absolute right not to. Katie confirmed that she did. The judge then declared an early luncheon recess, announcing that her testimony would begin immediately following the break.

By that point, there was only one person in the courtroom whose heart might have been beating more rapidly than the defendant's: Sarah Kathryn Dugan. Because Georgia Cappleman had taken on the onerous task of preparing for Garcia's cross-examination—as the defense made it seem highly likely that he'd testify—she delegated Katie's cross to Dugan. Thus, rather than having a leisurely meal, Dugan spent the 75-minute lunch break scrambling to refine her outline and gather her exhibits for one of the most consequential cross-examinations of her career.

•••

AFTER THE LUNCHEON RECESS ended and jurors were back in their familiar seats, Katie raised her right hand in the air and agreed to tell the truth and nothing but the truth a second time. When Tara Kawass asked how she was feeling, the jailed mother of two admitted, with a nervous laugh, that she was "freaking out" with so many eyes on her.

With her attorney's help, Katie walked jurors through her biography, starting with her graduation from high school in Miami Beach. At that point, she testified, she moved to Orlando to attend UCF, where she and Garcia lived together essentially as "husband" and "wife" during her four years in college—

with him working three jobs and staying out of trouble. "It was great," she recalled.

Yet what Katie was now telling jurors departed dramatically from her actual life story. Following her high school graduation, she'd gone to community college in Miami, not UCF in Orlando. Though she briefly lived together with Garcia in Miami, she kicked him out because of his criminal activities and drug use. When she moved to Orlando in August 2005 to commence her junior year at UCF, Sigfredo Garcia wasn't even part of her life. It was only after he'd been shot on the streets of Miami and nearly died—an event chronicled in the *Miami Herald*—that Katie agreed to take him back. The couple lived together in Orlando for less than 18 months, not four years as Katie testified. The notion that her relationship with Garcia had a blissful origin wasn't anywhere close to the truth.

After their daughter Kaylee was born in May 2012, she testified, their relationship took a turn for the worse, her "husband" often disappearing and his drinking escalating significantly. "Half the time it was me screaming at him," she acknowledged, "and he just doesn't respond, or he'll leave." She claimed that she didn't even know Garcia had been involved in criminal activities, never sharing with jurors that he'd been wrestled to the ground by police officers and arrested—in her presence—just outside their apartment in October 2012.

Kawass asked her client about her double date with Charlie, Wendi, and Jeff Lacasse at Yardbird—after which Charlie and Garcia had supposedly contracted for the hit on Dan Markel. Katie told jurors that nothing about that dinner stood out in her memory, other than her and Charlie arriving, and leaving, in separate vehicles. Kawass didn't ask her if she later learned that Garcia had been spying on her that evening. She also never inquired whether Katie had gone through her "husband's" phone and discovered Charlie's phone number among his contacts—which she'd told jurors during her opening statement was an important piece of evidence supporting the existence of a direct link between the two men.

The defense lawyer began ticking through some of the

evidence that had been presented during the prosecution's case. As to why her phone had been pinging a cell tower near the Miami International Airport in June 2014 while Garcia was renting a car from Comfort Rent A Car, Katie's answer was that her good friend Kenya lived in the same area and that she was probably visiting her at the same time. She told the jury she'd never taken Garcia to rent a car.

Kawass pivoted to the July 1, 2014, altercation between Garcia and Charlie after her rich boyfriend arrived in his Lexus to take her jet skiing. Katie testified that when she got to Shrimp's house to retrieve the kids from Garcia later that afternoon, she heard her "husband" leaving a nasty message on Harvey Adelson's cellphone. She recalled him walking away from her and having to chase him into the street. The only reason she left her own message on Harvey's cellphone later that day, Katie told jurors, was because she felt so embarrassed about the message Garcia had left. All of which was fully consistent with Yindra Mascaro's testimony—but utterly at odds with the notion that Garcia's call that afternoon signified a direct connection between him and Charlie.

Forty minutes into her questioning, Kawass asked Katie whether she had anything to do with the murder of Dan Markel or knew anything about it. To which her client responded, "No, ma'am"—two words she repeated often in response to her lawyer's questions. Katie told jurors that nothing about the date July 18, 2014 stood out in her memory, though she didn't dispute that she could have dropped her kids off with Mascaro that day and spent the evening with Charlie.

In an oddly phrased question, Kawass asked, "Did Charles Adelson ever give you $100,000 in stapled money to give to the father of your kids, who you weren't even with?" Katie denied that he had. By this point in her direct examination, she and her lawyer had settled into a familiar pattern of Kawass essentially testifying and Katie simply agreeing to her statements. For instance, when her attorney declared that she hadn't been trying to locate Garcia or Rivera the morning of July 19, 2014 to arrange the money drop, unsurprisingly, Katie agreed.

Though she acknowledged that she hadn't actually been working for the Adelson Institute—despite the 44 checks she received from the dental practice—Katie claimed she'd been helping Charlie as his "personal assistant," setting up a website and appointments and doing "odd jobs." All so she could receive free health insurance for her kids. Asked about the wiretapped calls in which Charlie had made statements about Katie going into the office to clean up, she confessed with a laugh, "I lied about it. I told him that I did, but I really didn't." Though she testified at the first trial that she never collected rent from Charlie's tenants, she told the new jury the opposite—that she did collect rent for him.

During her opening statement, Kawass had suggested that the spike in Katie's cash deposits following the murder was consistent with the father of her children providing her money from *his share* of the payoff, without his "wife" becoming aware of its origin. Yet when she asked Katie about that topic, her client had no memory of Garcia ever giving her a large quantity of cash. Nor did Katie challenge Mascaro's testimony that she had to take her "husband" to court to force him to pay child support. And because Garcia himself wouldn't be telling jurors that he'd been responsible for the dramatic increase in Katie's cash deposits, the trial would conclude without a scintilla of evidence supporting that contention.

Kawass finally transitioned to the meeting between Katie and Charlie at Dolce Vita. Once again with leading questions, she had Katie confirm that, during their conversation, Charlie had never uttered the words "Tallahassee," "murder," "Dan Markel," or "Wendi's ex-husband." Katie testified that if Charlie had used the word "murder," she'd certainly have recalled that. She told the jury that she agreed to call the number Charlie provided her merely because "I thought they were saying my name." And testified that she believed that the scenarios Charlie was describing "had to do with drugs or someone trying to extort money from his family or someone Tato might know."

The defense attorney walked Katie through her arrest,

making sure jurors knew that urine had been streaming down her leg and that a platoon of officers had surrounded her, guns drawn, to take her into custody. Kawass then asked a most unorthodox question—what Katie had told *her* when they first met at the jail following the arrest. Katie testified that at their initial meeting, she told Kawass, "… I knew nothing." For any lawyer tuned into the livestream of the proceedings, it was certainly an odd moment, because a client's intentional disclosure of communications with her lawyer ordinarily waives of the attorney-client privilege. From that point on, the prosecutors could have asked Katie about additional conversations with her lawyers over the prior six years, though they never did.

Tara Kawass ended her direct examination laser focused on Charlie Adelson, asking her client if she believed he was guilty. "Yes, ma'am," Katie answered emphatically, agreeing that her ex-lover "should be prosecuted for his involvement in the murder of Dan Markel."

"Do you think he should come forward and let the jury know that you had nothing to do with this?" her attorney followed up. Once again, Katie answered with a resolute "Yes, ma'am." But she then went off script without warning, embarking on a 30-second speech about her displeasure that it had taken three years following the last trial to bring charges against Charlie when she'd made clear, during her prior testimony, that there was more than enough evidence to arrest him. She claimed that there was nothing new in the enhanced Dolce Vita video that she hadn't shared from the witness stand during the first trial. That led to Kawass's final question—whether Katie's 2019 testimony was "consistent with the Dolce Vita video?"— yielding one final, and altogether unsurprising, "Yes, ma'am."

•••

SARAH KATHRYN DUGAN began her cross-examination with a commanding, take-no-prisoners style, which became progressively more controlling and forceful as she worked diligently through her outline. Her questions were tinged with a biting, sarcastic edge, her disdain for the defendant palpable.

She started with the defense's contention that Katie's relationship with Charlie had ended just after the murder, with him supposedly "ghosting" her. She asked Katie about the inconsistency between Charlie "ghosting" her beginning in August 2014 and then putting her on the payroll as his "personal assistant" the very next month. The best Katie could come up with to square those seemingly irreconcilable facts was that she and Charlie had remained friends despite their breakup.

Dugan peppered her with questions about the tasks she'd supposedly performed to earn more than $17,000 in paychecks. Nearly all of which elicited "I can't recall" and "I don't remember" responses until Katie finally threw out one concrete example—telling jurors she set up an appointment to have a website designed. Quick on her feet, the prosecutor reminded her—and the jury—that the appointment she set up with a website designer had been made in August 2014, before she'd even begun drawing a paycheck. Backed into a corner, Katie told jurors that Charlie would also call or text if he needed her to perform "odd jobs." Yet Dugan projected onto the screen several texts that made clear she didn't even know when her "boss" was working and when he was away on vacation.

The assistant state attorney had been paying careful attention when Katie testified that she'd collected rent from Charlie's tenants. She had Katie double down on that answer, asking, "So you collected rent from these tenants?"

"Yes," Katie reiterated. At which point, Dugan pounced, fully aware she'd now caught the defendant in a bald-faced lie. She whipped out the transcript from the 2019 trial that documented Katie's testimony that, although Charlie wanted her to collect rent from his tenants, they were so difficult, "I just didn't do it."

"I just asked you if you collected rent, and you said that you did," Dugan declared. "And that was a lie, wasn't it?"

At first, Katie tried to shift the blame for her misstatement to the prosecutor, telling her, "I should have told you to refresh my memory, instead of saying that." But Dugan didn't let her wiggle out of her predicament. "Well, is that a yes?"

"Yes, ma'am," Katie replied, sheepishly admitting that she'd lied about collecting rent from Charlie's tenants. The first of several occasions the skilled prosecutor would draw blood during her aggressive cross-examination.

She asked Katie why Charlie was doing such a huge favor of putting her on the payroll. "Why would he do that for *you*?"

Katie professed not to know why.

"Isn't it because he's keeping you happy because you did a really big favor for him in July of 2014?" Katie answered with her stock "No, ma'am."

"And you did hang that over his head sometimes, didn't you?"

"Not that I can recall," Katie responded. Her answer led Dugan precisely where she wanted to go next. She projected onto the screen a text from Katie to Charlie from April 2015, in which Katie told her ex-boyfriend, "Next time don't be such a dick to someone that has done something for u." The prosecutor asked Katie what favor she'd done for Charlie. "I don't know what I was referring to," Katie replied.

Dugan had her clear up the mystery as to why a phone number for "Sully Mech" had been stored in Garcia's contacts. Katie explained that "Mech" stood for "mechanic" and that Sully was the auto mechanic Charlie had referred her to when she needed repair work done on her Mazda or Charlie's former Lexus. Not quite the evidence DeCoste made it seem during his questioning of Michael Dilmore.

Dugan grilled Katie relentlessly over her skyrocketing cash deposits following the homicide, projecting onto the screen Mary Hull's graph depicting the perfect alignment between the "big cash spike" and when Dan Markel was killed. "Where did this money come from?" Dugan pressed her. To which Katie responded, "There's like jobs that you guys didn't account for."

"Where were you working in July of 2014?" the prosecutor asked.

"I don't know if I was in Fate or Hollywood Live," Katie answered. "And I told you before that Sigfredo had given me cash." But Dugan reminded her of Yindra Mascaro's testimony, that Mascaro herself had quit Hollywood Live in July 2014 and that Katie had quit two months before. She forced Katie to admit that she wasn't working at Hollywood Live then, or at Club Fate, since she'd been working there before Hollywood Live.

"Where were you working in July of 2014?" Dugan asked a second time, still trying to get an answer. This time, Katie responded that she didn't recall. "That was back in 2014," she said, implying that it was implausible that anyone could remember where they'd been working eight years earlier.

"Where did this money come from?" Dugan asked again, pointing on the screen to the August 2014 spike in her cash deposits—noting they were more than twice as much that month as any other. The best Katie could muster in response was, "I wish I could remember. I don't even remember what I did yesterday." A very peculiar statement considering she'd been in Courtroom 3G all day—with the people who'd soon be deciding her fate—on trial for murder.

Dugan kept after her, her tenacity beginning to get under Katie's skin. "You don't remember depositing $13,200 in August of 2014" or "depositing $17,000 from the day of Dan Markel's murder to the end of August 2014?" Her words were dripping with incredulity.

"No, ma'am," Katie replied. "When I look at the records that you have, it's crazy," she acknowledged. She even agreed with Dugan that a sudden surge in cash deposits more than twice her historical pattern should have stuck out in her mind. "That would definitely be memorable," she admitted. But once again, she told Dugan, "Ma'am, I wish I knew and could recall and remember, but I don't."

"And you don't think that's something you would remember?" Dugan asked one final time. Twisting herself into a grammatical pretzel, Katie's answer was defiant: "I *would* remember that." As if it were Hull's graph that contained faulty information, rather than Katie's own words.

Dugan asked how much of the cash spike had come from funds Katie had received from Sigfredo Garcia. "I wish I could remember," the defendant lamented. "Because you're asking me exact amounts, and where I worked, and—"

The prosecutor interrupted, asking Katie to agree that her "husband" didn't provide "much money that often." That it wasn't "like a steady thing." Surprisingly, Katie accepted that characterization.

"If he showed up and handed you $5,000, $10,000, $13,200," Dugan pressed her, "that's something that you'd remember, right?" She tried to get Katie to acknowledge that such large amounts would have been "abnormal." Initially, Katie disagreed, telling jurors, "It *wouldn't* be abnormal." Seconds later, however, she conceded that even $1,000 would have been a "significant amount" and that she didn't remember Garcia ever making such large payments.

Katie was the very last witness who could have provided support for the theory that Garcia had confronted Charlie Adelson after he left Yardbird, where Garcia had supposedly been spying on Katie, Charlie, Wendi, and Lacasse. But in answer to Dugan's questions, she told jurors that she had no indication that her "husband" ever learned that she was even going to Yardbird that night.

The assistant state attorney finally segued to Dolce Vita, focusing first on what had transpired in Charlie's car before the two entered the restaurant. "Did he search you for a wire?" she asked. "No," Katie replied, telling Dugan she didn't even remember being in Charlie's car.

The next 45 minutes of Katie's cross-examination were borne of Judge Wheeler's pretrial ruling that prevented jurors from seeing the closed-captioned version of the enhanced Dolce Vita video. In what amounted to a brilliant trial strategy, the prosecution decided to share with jurors the words they would have seen at the bottom of the video had the judge allowed it—by inserting them into Dugan's questions. The prosecutor played clip after clip from the video, 14 segments in all. Each time Katie and the jurors set their headphones aside after hearing a clip, Dugan repeated key language from the audio to set up her next questions, reading directly from the text jurors weren't permitted to see. Though Kawass forcefully objected to the prosecution's seeming end-run around the judge's pretrial ruling, he overruled her objection.

Thus, not only did jurors get to hear through their headphones—a second time—what the prosecution considered to be the most critical portions of the Dolce Vita audio, which was helpful in and of itself, they also received the benefit of the prosecutor's translation. Even more significantly, after listening to the audio a second time herself, Katie, with just a few exceptions, agreed that Dugan's interpretation of the audio was accurate. If the defense lawyers harbored any intention of arguing during their closing that the words captured by the secret recording were unintelligible, their own client's embrace of Dugan's quotations foiled any such plans.

Though Katie mostly agreed with Dugan's interpretation of Charlie's words, over and over again she testified that she had no idea what her ex-boyfriend was talking about, unable to tell jurors: why Charlie was using examples that involved a rental car and a gun; what it was the cops had no evidence of; why he thought someone was trying to blackmail his family; what event he was talking about that had made international news and been featured on *Good Morning America*; or why someone brought in for questioning would be "singing" and calling out her name. The juxtaposition between Katie's calm demeanor as she listened to Charlie ramble on with one incriminating statement after another six years earlier, and her inability to answer any of Dugan's questions now, was too stark to ignore.

The assistant state attorney focused intensely—and at great length—on the clip in which Charlie had said that the blackmailer was "fucking with him, he's fucking with his wife, if he's fucking with the king himself, you better kill him, because he's going to be a big problem; he knows who you are, and if he can't do it, have someone else do it." And that, if the blackmailer dared to "fuck with my family, there's going to be some Nazi shit. I don't care what I have to spend." Dugan wanted to know why, upon hearing those words, Katie never raised her voice or ran out of the restaurant.

"Like it's nothing that made me like, 'Oh my God! Like what are you talking about?'" Katie replied. "'Like, why are you even talking, period?'" As she articulated her answer, her demeanor grew more animated and expressive than at any other time during her testimony. Helping to make the very point Dugan was trying to get across. In the video jurors had just seen, and audio they'd heard, the woman seated across from Charlie Adelson *never* became animated.

Why hadn't she been more alarmed by the words she was hearing? The best answer Katie could come up with— believable or not—was because Charlie was always talking about "some weird stuff." And though the jailed mother of two denied that her ex had been alluding to Sigfredo Garcia with the words "him," "his wife," and "if he can't do it," she fully agreed that, less than a minute later in the audio, Charlie was talking about Garcia when he said "our paths never crossed" and "I didn't know the two of you would be working out."

After having Katie and the jury listen to the next clip, Dugan asked about Charlie's statement that "you giving money to somebody is not an admission of any kind of guilt." "*Guilt of what?*" the prosecutor asked forcefully.

To which Katie supplied her stock "I don't know" answer, testifying that she had no idea what Charlie meant. Dugan suggested that Katie had expressed concern to her ex-boyfriend that she'd look guilty if she paid the $5,000 he was asking her to give to the blackmailer. "If that's your assumption," Katie said, "but I didn't do any of that."

The next clip Dugan had the defendant and jurors listen to was the one in which Charlie asked, "When everybody was there the next day, did anyone take any money? It's not like you're driving around in a Bentley, cruising around in a mega yacht." Katie confirmed that she heard those same words coming through her headphones. "What did you understand that to mean?" Dugan asked. Amazingly, Katie responded that, "Now it kind of makes sense." But she then caught herself and backtracked, telling jurors, "Nobody ever got money."

"Isn't he saying, when everybody—you, Tuto, Tato—were together the next day after the murder, when you gave them the money, none of you took it and did anything extravagant, right?"

"I guess, that's what it's assuming, that's what it makes it look like to me," Katie conceded. "I see it now." A blockbuster admission. Promptly followed by another.

"He's checking to see, y'all weren't too flashy with this, that would draw attention to you," Dugan declared. "Right?" Katie nodded her head in agreement, saying, "Okay." Thus, not only did Charlie's words appear to be an unmistakable reference to the money drop the day after Dan Markel was gunned down in his garage—and his attempt to confirm that neither Katie nor her companions had been making any public displays of their newfound wealth—the defendant was now embracing that very interpretation. Perhaps the most devastating moment of Dugan's entire cross-examination.

Nearing the end of her questioning, the assistant state attorney ticked off a cacophony of coincidences Katie was asking the jury to accept if she had nothing to do with Dan Markel's murder: that her phone just happened to be pinging a cell tower serviced by Comfort Rent A Car when Garcia was there renting, and later returning, a car used on the first trip to Tally; that the only time she'd dialed Rivera's phone number that entire summer was during the hitmen's two trips to Tally and on the morning of the money drop; and that her phone just happened to be pinging a tower consistent with her being at Rivera's apartment that same morning.

"But those are just all coincidences?" Dugan asked. "You didn't have anything to do with this murder—that's what you're saying?" Katie leaned into the mic to answer. "Yes, ma'am," she said defiantly, glaring uncomfortably at the prosecutor.

"Aren't you mad at Garcia and Charlie for doing this," Dugan asked, her question dripping with sarcasm, "and you're innocent, and you're having to answer for it?"

"Yeah, I've been upset," Katie agreed. But Dugan then reminded her of a phone call she'd had with Garcia just days earlier—recorded by the jail—that demonstrated she wasn't upset with him in the slightest. The prosecutor asked her to confirm that she'd been in tears, telling Garcia, "I can't talk to you, I can't touch you, I can't see you, I can't feel you."

"Yeah, he's the father of my kids," Katie retorted, her eyes now firing poison darts at Dugan. "I'm going to love him forever." Indeed, jurors with a discerning eye might have glimpsed another expression of her unyielding love for her "husband": a gold wedding band encircling the ring finger on her left hand.

Dugan expanded the list of coincidences that, according to Katie, bore no relationship to Dan Markel's slaying: $17,000 in cash deposits during the six weeks following the murder, being put on the Adelson Institute's payroll, her $4,000 breast augmentation, all the favors Charlie had done for her after their breakup, his calling just her, out of all of his ex-girlfriends, following the bump, and "the fact that your 'husband' committed a murder for your boyfriend."

"You either have the worst luck or you did do this," Dugan declared, finally reaching the punchline, her contempt evident in her acerbic tone. Though Kawass's objection was sustained, the prosecutor had made her point.

"I see why I'm in the middle, I'm smack in the middle," Katie acknowledged, her eyes growing wide. "I see it. That's why I'm fighting for my life."

Dugan then reminded her—and the jury—how Kawass had claimed in her opening statement that the defense would reveal "definitive proof" of a link between Garcia and Charlie. Calling their bluff, she asked Katie, "What is it? ... What's the link between Garcia and Charlie?"

"That they knew each other or they spoke to each other," the defendant answered.

"How?" Dugan pressed her, still searching for the "direct link" nearly two weeks into the trial.

"I don't know," Katie confessed, her voice growing louder. "Apparently, everything's being done behind my back. That's why."

On that note, Sarah Kathryn Dugan resumed her seat at the prosecution table, following a masterful, methodical, and merciless cross-examination. Though she hadn't landed a knockout blow with a single punch, the cumulative effect of her relentless jabs and uppercuts had clearly left Katie—and her entire defense—banged up and on the ropes.

Over the next 25 minutes, Kawass did her level best to clean things up as best she could, once again, providing virtually all of the testimony through leading questions—Katie's answers consisting of one "Yes, ma'am" after another. What was their primary explanation to deflect the significance of the Dolce Vita audio clips Dugan had played? That "everything was taken out of context." And that Katie would have been "pissed off and reacting a completely different way" to what Charlie was telling her if she *had* been involved in the homicide, fearing that she might be "about to go down for a murder."

Kawass also played the sympathy card, having Katie share with jurors that her mother couldn't take the trip Charlie had offered her because she was battling cancer—the Filipina immigrant tearing up for the first time during her four hours on the stand. Over Dugan's objection, she told jurors that her mom passed away while she was in jail awaiting trial.

Asked to explain why she was having such a difficult time remembering things that had transpired in 2014, Katie again tried to garner sympathy, telling jurors, "I've been incarcerated for six years and I had COVID twice and I just— I can barely remember anything."

The final question Kawass asked was why Katie had elected to testify in her own defense. "Because I want them to know the truth," she answered, beginning a long-winded response. "It has to come out from me. All this speculation and all of this evidence and how everything's been— I've been living this for six years. And I just— If I didn't come up here and didn't talk to my jury," she said, shrugging her shoulders, "I don't even know. I don't know what the outcome would be."

With those final words, the evidence was now complete. Judge Wheeler announced that the trial would reconvene the following morning—the Friday before the extended Memorial Day weekend—for closing arguments and jury deliberations. With any luck, there would be just enough time for this jury to avoid the fate suffered by the last one, both in reaching a unanimous verdict and in avoiding an evening—and part of the long holiday weekend—in captivity.

30.

Game, Set, Match

DONNING A BRIGHT RED SUIT, Georgia Cappleman stood perfectly centered before the jury, laser focused on convincing the 12 men and women staring back at her that Katie Magbanua had knowingly and willingly brokered the murder of a man she'd never met. Among the observers seated in the gallery and watching with intense interest that fateful Friday morning were Ruth, Phil, and Shelly Markel as well as the two men who'd devoted large chunks of their careers—and buckets of blood, sweat, and tears—to bringing Dan's killers to justice, Pat Sanford and Craig Isom. This time around, there were no PowerPoint malfunctions slowing the lead prosecutor down as she marched methodically through her closing argument.

"This is Dan Markel," she began, a gigantic picture of the smiling law professor projected onto the screen behind her. "This is what he looked like before this defendant sent her friends up to see him." The PowerPoint then advanced to the second slide, revealing a photo of Dan's bloody face following the shooting. "And this is what he looked like afterwards," Cappleman said somberly, the horror depicted by the gruesome photo slowly filtering across the courtroom.

She quickly turned to the question of motive, reminding jurors of Wendi's petition for relocation, Donna's vitriolic emails, and Dan's motion to restrict his mother-in-law's access to his children. Though Donna had proposed bribing her ex-son-in-law with $1 million, the Adelson family ultimately received "a bargain," Cappleman said derisively, paying just $100,000 to achieve their objective. How did Katie Magbanua fit into that picture? She was "the woman who knew people who could get a thing like this done."

The veteran prosecutor noted how "TV" had become a code word associated with the homicide. Charlie had joked about purchasing the TV as a divorce present for Wendi because it was cheaper than hiring a hitman. Donna had scheduled a service appointment for the very same TV to ensure her daughter had an alibi the morning Dan was killed. And in one of her conversations with Charlie the day of the bump, Donna had informed him that the TV would cost "about five," a reference to the $5,000 blackmail demand.

Cappleman zeroed in on the evening of July 18, 2014 and the following morning, pointing to the cell tower evidence revealing Katie's arrival at Luis Rivera's apartment at 9:46 p.m. after she dropped her children with Yindra Mascaro—a fact Mascaro confirmed from her social media posts. What was Katie doing that evening that required her kids to be somewhere else? Heading to Charlie Adelson's house, the prosecutor asserted, to retrieve the money to pay Garcia and Rivera. She reminded jurors of a text earlier that day in which Katie and Charlie had arranged to spend the night together. And that Katie had powered her phone down for about 11 hours.

When it finally powered on the next morning, Cappleman recounted, the cell tower evidence showed Katie traveling south away from Charlie's home and "toward the money-drop location." The entire time, she said, Katie was engaged in a flurry of communications with phone numbers belonging to Rivera, Jessica Rodriguez, and Sigfredo Garcia—all of which came to a sudden halt at 10:31 a.m. Why? Because, as Sergeant Corbitt had testified, they had all congregated in the same location—for the money drop—a fact both Rivera and Rodriguez confirmed from the witness stand. And then, at 11:23 a.m., cell tower pings showed Katie near Yindra Mascaro's home, presumably picking up her kids, telling her good friend upon arrival that "Charlie Adelson's brother-in-law was in a car accident."

Nearly 45 minutes into her argument, the State's lead counsel pivoted to the bump, the wiretaps, and the enhanced Dolce Vita recording. She paused to remind jurors that Katie had testified she didn't even know about the murder until a month later, when Sigfredo Garcia was arrested. "She's supposedly doing and saying all these things," Cappleman said—her hand gestures conveying sheer incredulity—"with no information whatsoever that there *was even a murder.*"

She quoted several of Charlie's incriminating statements at Dolce Vita, starting with his suggestion that the man who'd approached his mom was either someone trying to blackmail his family "or it's the cops working undercover." Why hadn't Katie respond to that statement, the prosecutor wondered aloud, by asking her ex, "Why are the cops approaching your mother? ... Did your mother do something that the police would be investigating?" She threw her hands up, palms facing the ceiling—her expression one of utter bewilderment.

Cappleman reminded the jury that when Charlie said, "This person knows information," the surveillance video actually picked up Katie responding, "There's not a lot of people that know much about—" Yet when Dugan asked during cross-examination what Katie had been trying to say before the audio trailed off, "She doesn't know. She can't tell you. No memory of it ... No memory of a man coming to you and trying to get you to have contact with some thugs that approached his mother to blackmail her about a murder."

She segued to Charlie's hypothetical scenario of the blackmailer being arrested, questioned by law enforcement, and, "The next thing you know, this person is singing. He starts calling your name out." The assistant state attorney pointed at Katie at the defense table. "Why would a bad guy be calling *her name* out if she knows nothing?" She and Charlie also talked about "going to the cops, going to the FBI," Cappleman reminded jurors. "But nobody ever does that, that obvious thing, including this defendant. If you're innocent and a bad guy is trying to put your name in something, you go straight to the cops."

She next focused on Katie's reaction to Charlie's statement, "You fuck with the king himself, you better kill him, because he's going to be a big problem." Cappleman paused, seemingly flabbergasted. "*My God,*" she said, "she continues to engage in the conversation… She doesn't say, "*Kill,* I'm not killing anybody. What are you talking about, *kill*?" Smiling ear to ear, her words laced with sarcasm, the seasoned prosecutor suggested, "Kill might be a word you might remember."

Yet when Katie had been asked about that particular clip on cross-examination, Cappleman noted, she'd professed to having no recollection whatsoever of the word "kill" coming out of Charlie's mouth. She then play-acted what she'd have done upon hearing someone talking about killing another human being—backpedaling from the lectern with deliberate steps, forming a mock phone with her right hand, and speaking the word "police" into the tip of her pinky finger. Why hadn't Katie Magbanua done precisely that after hearing what Charlie was telling her? "'Cause she's involved," the assistant state attorney said with a chuckle. "I mean, there's no other explanation."

She quoted Charlie's statement, "So help me God, if they fuck with my family, it's going to be fucking Nazi shit"— no price too high. And reminded jurors how the wealthy periodontist had then shifted the conversation to Garcia, asking Katie if everything was "kosher" with her "husband." Which further established that Charlie didn't have "an independent relationship with Garcia because *he's going through her.*"

Cappleman spent considerable time walking the jury through the wiretapped calls between Charlie, Katie, and Garcia, pointing out that the calls always traveled in that direction—or in reverse—without Charlie or Garcia ever "jumping the train car" to speak directly with one other. That was because Katie was "insulating Garcia and Charlie from each other," she argued. "She's walling them off. She was the glue in this conspiracy. It does not work without her." But at the same time, "She's playing both of these guys. She's lying. She's manipulating both sides of this conspiracy."

The lead prosecutor picked apart several of Katie's answers from the witness stand. If Charlie had "ghosted her" in August 2014, she asked rhetorically, "Why would he want her to become his personal assistant? She could not answer that question." She also couldn't tell jurors what services she'd actually performed for Charlie or why he'd done so many favors for her, but none of his other ex-girlfriends. "These are easy questions folks," Cappleman asserted. Yet trying to get answers from Katie was like "trying to nail Jell-O to a wall."

As she neared the end of her argument, she addressed the defense team's central theory, reminding jurors of Tara Kawass's promise that the defense would offer "definitive proof" of a direct link between Charlie and Garcia. But after seeing and hearing all of the evidence in the case, she declared, "We are no closer to proving the defense's theory than we were in the opening statement. What is the smoking gun? The fact that they both had the same auto mechanic?"

The defense theory was clearly belied by the evidence, Cappleman told jurors. After the double date at Yardbird in March 2014—when Garcia had been so angry he wanted to drive his truck through the outdoor patio—Rivera testified that he'd calmed his friend down and that they'd spent the rest of the evening together.

Katie herself told the jury "that there was no confrontation other than the jet ski incident that occurred on July 1." Garcia didn't even know Charlie's telephone number on that date—four months after spying on his "wife" and Charlie at Yardbird—which is why he mistakenly left a voicemail on Harvey's phone rather than on Charlie's. Furthermore, Cappleman asked, why would Garcia "be trying to fight the guy that he's in the process of trying to do a murder for? A guy that's about to pay him … his portion of $100,000?"

Despite how "clueless" Katie had acted on the witness stand,

Cappleman asserted, she "was not the pawn in someone else's scheme. She was not the pawn of two master manipulators. She herself was the stage manager in this thing. She was directing these guys. The defendant is guilty of everything she's charged with." With only ten of her allotted 90 minutes remaining, the two-time Florida State grad abruptly ended her argument, saving the rest of her time for rebuttal.

• • •

IN YET ANOTHER DEPARTURE from the script they'd followed at the 2019 trial, Katie's defense team opted to have Tara Kawass deliver their closing argument. Kawass was keenly aware that her words over the next 90 minutes could prove the deciding factor in whether her client walked out of the courtroom a free woman later that day or spent the remainder of her life in prison. The pressure resting on her slender shoulders was enough to prevent her from catching even a wink of sleep.

But with adrenaline coursing through her veins as she stood before the jury, the Jamaican-born attorney delivered her argument with her trademark fire and passion—as full-throated an advocate as any defendant charged with first-degree murder could possibly have wanted behind the lectern.

Rather than a PowerPoint presentation, the projection screen behind Kawass displayed one static image throughout the first 45 minutes of her argument—the one with photos of the Adelsons arrayed across the top row and the two hitmen at the bottom, with a vertical line connecting Charlie to Garcia and Katie nowhere to be found. Like a military mantra, the defense lawyer repeatedly drilled into jurors' heads the heavy burden the prosecution was required to satisfy to prove its case "beyond and to the exclusion of every reasonable doubt."

The entire case against Katie, she argued, was a "wrongful prosecution" of an "innocent woman" who "ended up having to fight for her life for something that she did not do." The prosecution's contention that there was no direct link between

Garcia and the Adelsons was "completely false," she declared, reminding jurors that "it was the call from Sigfredo Garcia directly to the Adelson family that cracked the case open for them" —a point she'd previewed in her opening statement. Yet jurors were now well aware from Sergeant Corbitt's testimony that the July 1, 2014 call she was referencing was actually a 37-second voicemail left on *Harvey* Adelson's phone, not Charlie's. Nevertheless, Kawass insisted that the existence of that call "goes directly against" the prosecution's theory of Katie's involvement. "That's the link."

The State was trying "to filter out all the facts that do not fit their theory," she asserted indignantly, "and then only present you with what they believe is important." As she proceeded deeper into her argument, Kawass broadened that theme, suggesting to jurors that it was the government's obligation to "show you everything," not just factual material supporting its case. "If they were that confident in their case, members of the jury, then why just not let you have *everything*?" she asked, gesticulating forcefully. By not sharing *all* of the evidence, "the prosecutors in this case are hiding things from you. Their act of hiding it, alone, proves that she's innocent."

The defense attorney offered two explanations for Katie's skyrocketing cash deposits, first pointing out that she'd worked several different jobs that paid in cash, "including the ultimate cash-making field—the service industry." Despite Ramzi Naber's testimony to the contrary, Kawass insisted that anyone who'd ever worked as a waitress or bartender, as she herself had, "knows it's an all-cash business." She lashed out at Agent Sanford for waiting until 2020 to investigate Katie's work at the nightclubs—four years after he'd first learned about those jobs. Because of his inexcusable delay, she told jurors, Katie's employment records had been lost forever due to the flooding at Club Fate.

The second explanation for the dramatic spike in cash deposits, she contended, was Garcia's payoff for the murder— Katie's "husband" sharing his bounty with her because she was the mother of his children. Though absolutely no evidence had been presented consistent with her contention—not even from Katie herself—Kawass made it seem as if that fact had been clearly established. She reminded jurors that Rivera had supplied his sister and his mother with cash he'd received for the homicide. Were they arrested and thrown in jail? But Katie, who'd done precisely the same thing, Kawass complained, that somehow meant "she's getting paid for a murder."

Plus, she argued, this "well-educated college woman" wouldn't have been stupid enough to deposit money into the bank if she'd known it had derived from a murder. "Why are you going to walk into the bank and deposit money from a homicide so that everybody knows that it's there?" Everything that Katie did, Kawass told the jury, "is evidence that she did not know." She applied the same logic to her client being placed on the Adelson Institute's payroll, noting how easy that made it for investigators to discover and track those payments. "Common sense alone tells you that that was not payment for a murder."

Kawass labeled as "just ridiculous" the notion that her client hadn't actually earned the $17,000 she'd been paid by the Adelson Institute. Katie had explained from the witness stand, she said, "that it's not a legitimate like nine-to-five job where she goes in. There are text messages that support that she is basically a personal assistant for him. He's doing a favor for her. And this is helping her get the insurance for her kids. *Why, why, why* would Katie get up on the stand and say those things if it wasn't true?" A very odd question for a criminal defense lawyer to ask about her own client's veracity—the answer "to beat a murder rap" apparently eluding her.

As she began transitioning to the undercover sting operation, Kawass stressed how law enforcement had "zoned in" on Katie and tried "to build the case around her" because there was no other logical connection between the hitmen and the Adelson family. But the entire operation was flawed, she insisted. Investigators knew that Garcia was the murderer, but inexplicably decided not to tap his phone, a decision she told jurors amounted to "willful blindness."

Kawass flipped the script on the importance of the Dolce Vita audio, telling jurors, "The fact that the State has to present a recording and constantly have to tell you what they think is happening is not proof beyond a reasonable doubt." She accused Dugan of "adding words and making up sentences … speculating about what is being said"—describing her approach as "masterful misinterpretation." Yet it was the prosecution's burden to supply "reliable, concrete evidence so that there's nothing to figure out." Her words tinged with disdain, Kawass told jurors, "It's not your job to make sense of the nonsense case that they have brought to you."

"Why is it," she asked, "that they're desperately trying to shove their interpretation of what is going on in that audio down all of your throats?" She reminded jurors that there'd been no mention in the audio of "Tallahassee, murder, Dan Markel, *something definitive,* so that you know" that is what Charlie was talking about. "It speaks more that he doesn't mention it. Because if he did, and she had no reaction, *that* would be strange." What was "more telling," the defense attorney argued, was Katie's 2019 testimony, before she even knew the audio would later be enhanced. "And there is not one thing in her prior testimony that contradicts what is going on in that Dolce Vita video."

More importantly, Kawass emphasized, it was impossible to know what Katie was saying in response to Charlie's ramblings. "How do you know she didn't say, 'Dude, what are you talking about? Like, what's going on?' You don't know that she didn't say that because they weren't able to record *her* voice." All the State was able to show, she stressed, was a "chopped up audio" of just Charlie talking which, in her view at least, "proves that she had no idea what was going on."

Kawass transitioned to the wiretapped calls, lambasting the prosecution for failing to play *all 400* recordings—as if the jurors had been conscripted into months of civic duty—implying that the "select few that they decided to play for you" deliberately omitted evidence of Katie's innocence. "The fact that they didn't want you to have all the recordings," she argued, "in and of itself, is reasonable doubt."

The Miami-based attorney briefly digressed to Wendi Adelson's testimony, describing her time on the stand as a "horrible performance," acting as if she'd been a victim, and disparaging her murdered ex-husband. "And then has the audacity to come in here and defend her family." More evidence existed against Wendi, Kawass asserted, "than there is against Katherine Magbanua. And they gave *her* immunity."

Halfway through her argument, Katie's lawyer began tearing into Luis Rivera, describing him as "the worst person, the most desperate person, to help with their investigation." Over and over again, she called the blue-uniformed witness "a liar. It's offensive that the State of Florida brought that man into this courtroom and is going to ask you with a straight face to find him credible. I don't even know where to begin with the inconsistencies in his testimony."

Even though he'd been asked about the events surrounding Dan Markel's murder ten times, Kawass argued his inconsistencies established that he was lying. "It's difficult to remember a lie," she declared, "but the truth, that remains the same." She couldn't resist reminding jurors how he'd changed the creature he recalled posting on Instagram from an owl to a lion. "He couldn't even pick another bird?" she asked with a smirk. "He went lion?"

Even the State, Kawass contended, "doesn't believe Mr. Rivera. Look at how many times he tried to give them Wendi Adelson." She told jurors he couldn't possibly have seen Wendi and the boys walking into her former residence as he'd testified. But if Rivera's testimony were so credible, she asked, "Why hasn't Wendi been arrested?" Why wasn't she in jail?

She shifted gears to the jailhouse meeting on the eve of the first trial between Katie, her and DeCoste, and Cappleman and Jason Newlin. "Any lawyer will tell you, that never happens, that you're gonna let the prosecutors, under no promise of immunity, nothing—that's how confident we were that she was innocent … And then Ms. Cappleman has the *audacity* to come up here and say that meeting was a joke," she snarled, her anger now bubbling to the surface. It wasn't a joke to Katie, she said. "None of this is a joke."

Kawass's next topic was her client's testimony from the witness stand. She explained that Katie desperately wanted to remember details, but was being asked about events "that happened so many years ago." She'd been "sitting in a jail cell for six years. She told you herself she had COVID twice." Katie didn't have to testify at all, "but she wanted you to hear it out of her mouth: 'I had nothing to do with the murder of Dan Markel.'"

Glaring at Dugan at the prosecution table, Kawass rebuked the assistant state attorney for attempting to "bully" her client during her cross-examination, "getting frustrated with Katie when she wouldn't agree with her *misinterpretation* of the evidence." Implying the prosecutor had done something underhanded, she noted how Dugan had tried to get Katie "to commit to what Charles Adelson was saying." What she neglected to point out, however, was how often her client had willingly complied.

Her agitation and annoyance mounting, Kawass told the jury that Dugan had misrepresented Katie's prior testimony. "She did it twice," the defense lawyer complained, pointing in Dugan's direction. "She literally misread Katherine's words to you. That is how desperate they are, members of the jury, to try and piece together this *nonsense of a theory*, to try and sell to you that this is evidence of guilt of Ms. Magbanua." Yet oddly, she didn't specify what testimony Dugan had supposedly misrepresented.

With less than 20 minutes of her allotted time remaining, Kawass finally shared with jurors the evidence she believed established the tight-knit conspiracy between Charlie and Garcia—which amounted to two text message exchanges from Charlie's iCloud account, each of which she projected onto the screen. The first was the day after the double date at Yardbird in March 2014. Katie had written Charlie, "He called me and said have a nice dinner and to never call him again. I'm like wtf." According to Kawass, that text somehow demonstrated that Charlie was "trying to see if Garcia told Katie anything about *their meeting*. And that response let him know, nope, he never told her. So now he was in the clear." Yet nothing in Katie's text referred to—or even implied—any sort of meeting between Garcia and Charlie the prior evening.

The second text exchange was from April 2014, when Katie asked Charlie, "Did Tuto call ur phone?" and "Is ur cell phone listed online?" Why would she ask him that? Kawass wondered aloud. Only one explanation made logical sense to her—that Katie had gotten ahold of her "husband's" phone and found Charlie's number among his contacts.

She wanted jurors to conclude that had occurred even though Katie herself never recounted any such event from the witness stand—and even though Garcia *didn't* have Charlie's number on July 1, when he left a voicemail for Harvey intended for Charlie. But Kawass went even further, telling jurors that Charlie's sarcastic response that Garcia had contacted him and invited him "deep sea fishing" was the periodontist's way of concealing that he and Garcia had in fact been in direct communications. Which was proof enough for Tara Kawass.

Her time beginning to run out, Katie's lawyer finally got to the money drop. The only evidence about that event, she told jurors, had come from Rivera and Rodriguez, who couldn't even "get their stories straight." She described Rodriguez's testimony as "nonsense," solely intended to help her baby daddy get a good deal for turning State's evidence. Rivera, she said, was simply a "walking contradiction."

Katie was "living the worst nightmare that anyone on this planet could imagine," Kawass lamented, "sitting in a jail for a crime you did not commit." She was starting to choke up, her voice catching with emotion. She challenged Cappleman to explain, during her rebuttal, "Why in the world would Katherine not cooperate if she were guilty. Why?" If the prosecutor refused to accept that challenge, she argued, "then it's 'not guilty' ladies and gentlemen."

"Justice for Dan Markel is not convicting an innocent person of this crime," Kawass asserted, now wrapping up with her final words. "In fact, it would be a travesty of justice to convict Ms. Magbanua of any of the charges in this case … Because if she didn't know, members of the jury, she's *not guilty*." The defense attorney implored jurors not to convict Katie "for having awful taste in men" or because "the father of her children is a *scumbag*. You cannot convict her because she ended up dating Charles Adelson, probably one of the worst human beings on the face of the planet."

Kawass expressed confidence that, as they studied the evidence, the men and women who'd committed two weeks of their lives to sit in judgment on her client would "see that she didn't do this." Choking up once again, her voice barely audible, she ended her argument telling the 12 decision-makers, "She's innocent. Find her not guilty."

•••

GEORGIA CAPPLEMAN WAS on her feet one final time, responding immediately to Kawass's challenge, offering jurors a litany of potential explanations for why Katie had decided to roll the dice at trial rather than cop a plea. "Maybe she thinks she has very talented lawyers," she speculated. "Maybe she thinks she has a good chance of walking out of here. Maybe she thinks if she gets convicted, she'll offer to do something for me then. We'll see how that goes," the State's lead counsel said, conveying through her facial expression that the defendant shouldn't be holding her breath over a possible deal. She also suggested that Katie could be receiving "a big payoff" or that "somebody had threatened to do something to her," two leading candidates case watchers had bandied about for years as possible explanations for why the Filipina immigrant had steadfastly refused to flip on Charlie.

Cappleman focused again on everything the defense was asking jurors to conclude was merely a coincidence, rather than evidence of Katie's involvement in the murder, starting with her phone pinging a tower nearby the rental car company at the precise moment Garcia was renting, and later returning, the car used for the June 2014 trip to Tally. Katie's surge in cash deposits immediately following the murder was also just a coincidence, according to the defense. The veteran prosecutor swatted away Kawass's contention that the spike in her client's deposits had resulted from Garcia sharing his portion of the murder payoff, reminding jurors of Yindra Mascaro's testimony that Katie had been forced to sue her "husband" for child support.

"Is it a terrible coincidence for her," Cappleman asked jurors, "that she got placed on the payroll of the Adelson Institute, and it just happened to be right after the murder?" Rivera flipping on Katie was yet another apparent coincidence, she said, his story supposedly concocted to frame her. "Why didn't I just have Luis Rivera, since I'm also a liar and a crook who's trying to pull the wool over your eyes," she asked sarcastically, "why didn't I just have Rivera say ... Charlie Adelson did it? Why didn't I just do that? I'm desperate to get Charlie Adelson, aren't I? I'm laying awake at night wanting to do this trial again. Why don't I just get Rivera to say whatever I want? That's what I'm doing, aren't I?"

The biggest coincidence of all, Cappleman asserted, was that Katie had "a baby daddy who killed Dan Markel and a boyfriend who hired the hit ... Her child's father, *having nothing to do with her*, happened to murder the brother-in-law of her boyfriend." She asked rhetorically, "How many coincidences does it take for it to no longer be a coincidence?"

She pointed to Katie's own words in text messages to Charlie: "next time don't be such a dick to someone that has done something for u"; "sorry we have problems sleeping n shyt, we do have a lot of weight on our shoulders."

"The weight of this crime is inescapable," Cappleman declared, "and it is squarely on this defendant's shoulders." Katie's own words, she stressed, were the most damaging pieces of evidence against her, as in the call in which she told Charlie, "It's getting too detailed," and "it's somebody that knows for sure." Her "own words hang her worse than anything y'all have seen."

"What Katherine Magbanua is going through is *not* the worst nightmare that anyone could imagine," Cappleman told jurors, now holding the photo of a smiling Dan Markel in her right hand, and of his bloody face in her left. "Her being compelled to answer for what she did in this case, for what she set into motion, that is not the worst nightmare that anyone can imagine." She set the picture of Dan's bloody face aside and held up high the photo depicting his friendly smile. "This is what this case is about," she said in a solemn tone. "Find her guilty."

With that emotional plea and those final words, Georgia Cappleman resumed her seat beside Dugan at the prosecution table, hopeful, this second time around, she'd done enough to convince all 12 jurors of Katie's guilt for her role in the cold-blooded killing of Dan Markel.

•••

JUST BEFORE 1:00 P.M., jurors began their deliberations while chowing down on lunch provided courtesy of the State of Florida, Courtroom 3G now inactive and silent for the first time in two weeks. Hours passed without the slightest indication of their progress. Then, at about 4:45 p.m., a note from the foreperson revealed that the group wanted to hear the entirety of the Dolce Vita recording one more time. Which was music to Cappleman's ears, the jury clearly focused on what she and Dugan considered the most critical piece of evidence in the entire case.

Once Katie, the lawyers, Judge Wheeler, and interested observers reassembled in the courtroom, the bailiff led jurors back to their familiar seats, where each donned a pair of headphones and—for a second time—soaked in Charlie Adelson's meandering, 41-minute stream of consciousness. With that exercise complete, they returned to the jury room, focused on completing their work and heading home.

For everyone awaiting the verdict, the next three hours crawled by at a snail's pace—without the slightest hint as to whether the jury was making any progress. Concerns over the possibility of yet another hung jury loomed large. But finally, after nearly eight hours of deliberations, the foreperson signaled that they had reached a unanimous verdict.

One final time, jurors took their seats in the jury box, the tension in the courtroom nearly thick enough to cut with a knife. That was especially true at the defense table, where the defendant and her lawyers were about to learn if she'd be walking out of the courtroom and returning home to her kids or spending the rest of her life behind bars. Her daughter Kaylee's tenth birthday was just three days away. Katie had missed every birthday celebration since her fourth and desperately wanted to be present for her baby girl's big day. Twelve complete strangers were about to let her know whether she would.

The foreperson handed the verdict form to the bailiff, who walked it over to Judge Wheeler. The judge studied the piece of paper for a moment and confirmed that it appeared to be in proper form. Before he revealed any of the jury's findings, Katie, seated between her lawyers, began sobbing, gasping for breath, her chest heaving in and out. She seemed to sense that the outcome wasn't going to be good. And she was right.

"We the jury find as follows as to Count One," Judge Wheeler read off the verdict form. "The defendant is *guilty* of first-degree murder." Upon hearing those words, Katie's whimpering grew deeper and louder. She and her attorneys listened as the judge read out the jury's findings on the conspiracy and solicitation counts—guilty as to those as well. DeCoste and Kawass didn't flinch, staring straight ahead in stunned silence, Kawass eventually tearing up herself. At their request, the judge polled the jurors individually, each of whom confirmed that the verdict as announced was their "true verdict."

From their seats in the gallery, Phil, Ruth, and Shelly Markel broke out into smiles—not borne of joy or happiness, but of satisfaction and relief. Finally, two-and-a-half years after the first jury had failed to reach a verdict, Katie Magbanua had been convicted for her role in the murder and would soon be sentenced to life in prison without the possibility of parole, just like her "husband." A punishment a retributivist legal scholar named Dan Markel, had he still been alive, would almost certainly have found appropriate for his killers' heinous crime.

When the judge announced that court was in recess, Georgia Cappleman made a beeline for the gallery, where Ruth Markel welcomed her with open arms and hugged the prosecutor tightly. "You did it," the grateful mother said, her face beaming with appreciation and delight.

For her part, Cappleman told reporters gathered in the hallway outside the courtroom how gratifying it was to finally obtain "some justice for Dan's family. They've been through hell and back and I'm just thrilled to be able to give them a piece of peace in their lives." Dan's father, Phil Markel, dwelled on the long, difficult journey he and his family had been on since his son's life was snatched from them by an assassin's gunshots. "The wheels of justice turn very, very slowly," he lamented, "but we're grateful they're still turning."

•••

IN JUST SIX WEEKS' TIME, the tide in the Markel family's quest for justice had turned rather remarkably. As of mid-April, only the two hitmen, Sigfredo Garcia and Luis Rivera, had been convicted for their roles in Dan's vicious slaying. The entire Adelson family was still living comfortably ensconced in their cushy South Florida homes—driving their luxury vehicles—seemingly beyond the reach of the law. At the time, justice seemed frustratingly elusive, an ideal whose time might never arrive. Yet as of late in the evening on May 27, 2022, four of Dan's killers were now behind bars—including Charlie Adelson—three convicted for their atrocious crimes and the playboy periodontist seemingly headed in that direction.

Even more significantly, of the four incarcerated defendants, three suddenly had a tremendous incentive to make a deal to turn State's evidence. Absent an agreement with prosecutors,

Katie and her "husband" would spend the remainder of their lives in prison, missing every milestone in their children's lives. Whereas Garcia had good reason not to spill his guts while Katie was fighting the charges against her—as any truthful information he could have shared would have harmed her more than anyone—that calculus changed the instant the jury found her guilty.

And by not testifying on her behalf during the trial—supporting a defense theory he knew wasn't true—he hadn't damaged his credibility in the slightest. Though he probably didn't have any useful information about Charlie Adelson, unlike Luis Rivera, Garcia had the potential to be a prosecution witness unblemished by prior inconsistent statements. Thus, if he was finally willing to cooperate, Cappleman had ample reason to offer Tuto a shorter prison term in exchange for his proffer and testimony at future trials.

For her part, Katie had taken her "wrongful prosecution" argument to its logical extreme—and was now paying the very high price associated with its failure. Not only had she given up a golden opportunity to receive either immunity or a very short prison sentence to gamble on her attorneys convincing a jury to set her free, she'd damaged her credibility badly by taking the stand twice and denying her involvement in the murder plot. Were she now to acknowledge her role and provide the goods on Charlie, as the State's star witness against him, she'd have to admit to telling dozens of lies in two prior trials.

Yet all that said, Katie was the only convicted defendant who could tell prosecutors what Charlie had been doing and saying in the weeks and months leading up to July 18, 2014. And also, what he'd been doing in the years following the murder to cover his tracks and keep her and Garcia placated. For that matter, she could even share information about things Charlie had told her following the April 2016 bump that weren't captured on the wiretaps, most significantly, what he'd said about his mother—beyond her being up all night with diarrhea. The information she possessed was valuable even if Cappleman decided not to have her testify at any upcoming trials.

And for all of those reasons, even though the State Attorney's Office opted against seeking the death penalty against him, Charles Jay Adelson had to be extremely nervous about the weeks and months ahead. At any given moment, he was apt to learn that Garcia had flipped, or that Katie had—or even worse, that his mother had been cuffed, read her rights, and taken into custody. The walls of his claustrophobic jail cell had to be closing in on him pretty rapidly.

For a man so accustomed to being in total control, the Maestro was now at the mercy of people he no longer had any ability to manipulate or influence—all of whom were ready to see him get his just deserts. Was that enough pressure to cause Charlie Adelson to cave and strike his own deal? One that would allow him to spend at least a few years, in the twilight of his life, breathing the air as a free man? Would he throw his own mother, or sister, under the bus to get an even better deal? For someone who didn't have the slightest hesitation to destroy the lives of others so he could live a better one, even that scenario didn't seem terribly far-fetched.

With so many possibilities, it was by no means certain that Georgia Cappleman and her colleagues would be back in Courtroom 3G for a third trial. With each passing day, the odds were increasing that everyone who'd played a role in Dan Markel's brutal murder—including those who provided aid and refuge to his killers afterward—would be brought to justice. Though eight grueling years had proven that the criminal justice system isn't pretty or perfect, they'd also established that those guilty of horrific crimes—no matter how rich, powerful, or well-connected they may be—are never beyond its reach. Full and complete justice for Daniel Eric Markel and his family may be just around the corner.

Epilogue

AS FATE WOULD HAVE IT, there were actually *two* super-secret, somewhat miraculous events occurring simultaneously the afternoon of April 20, 2022 directly related to the late Dan Markel. Fittingly, one was taking place in Tallahassee and the other in Miami, the two cities—and 500 miles of highways between them—that serve as the epicenter of this story.

While Georgia Cappleman and Pat Sanford were laying out their evidence against Charlie Adelson before the grand jury in Tallahassee the day before his arrest, Ruth and Phil Markel were working their way through the bustling Miami International Airport, having flown in from Toronto just for the day. It had been six excruciating years since they'd last seen their grandsons, Ben and Lincoln. Years in which they'd fought tirelessly for the expansion of grandparents' rights at the Florida legislature, ultimately garnering a near-unanimous vote for a bill—informally named the "Markel Act"—that was currently sitting on Governor Ron DeSantis's desk awaiting his signature.

With Wendi expecting to testify at the upcoming retrial of Katie Magbanua—and not wanting to appear as mean-spirited as she had at the previous trial, when she'd admitted to preventing Ruth and Phil from visiting with their grandsons for years—she reached out by email to invite them to Ben's upcoming *bar mitzvah*. Though his 13th birthday wasn't until late July, Wendi revealed that the family was accelerating the traditional Jewish ceremony to the Saturday before the May 16 trial.

But what her former in-laws wanted more than anything was time alone with Ben and Lincoln. Their proposal for a separate meeting the day before the *bar mitzvah* ultimately morphed into an after-school visit at a restaurant at an outdoor shopping plaza in South Beach on Wednesday, April 20. And it was there that Ruth and Phil stood at 3:30 p.m. that afternoon, at the eatery's outdoor patio, nervously awaiting the arrival of their deceased son's precious cubbies. The anticipation they felt as they first glimpsed Wendi and the boys walking toward them was almost unbearable.

Ben and Lincoln had been four and three that fateful July morning when their dad's life was snuffed out by bullets fired from an assassin's handgun. They were six and five when Dan's parents had last seen them in April 2016. Ben was now 12, Lincoln 11. Ruth and Phil marveled at Ben's height as he neared them, now 5'9", nearly as tall as his father had been as an adult. Lincoln was the spitting image of Dan at the same age, his lush blond hair flowing freely in the mid-afternoon breeze.

Ruth and Phil asked the boys if they could greet them with hugs, an invitation the pre-teens gladly accepted. The brothers took turns wrapping their arms around their grandmother and grandfather, their embraces seemingly warm and genuine. Wendi, who was accompanied by a male friend, hung back, ultimately claiming an adjacent table.

After ordering their food, the grandparents chatted with the boys about their schooling and activities, Ben proudly describing his diligent preparation for his upcoming *bar mitzvah*. Before long, Phil pulled out his iPad, on which he'd created an album of pictures of Dan and his children when they were mere toddlers. Together, they swiped through photo after photo, Ben and Lincoln taking keen interest in images they hadn't seen in years. It was evident to Ruth and Phil that the boys knew who they were, and that they still felt genuine affection for the father—their Abba—they'd know only through pictures for the remainder of their lives.

The 90 minutes they were together flew by, the visit surpassing every expectation the grandparents had when their plane touched down earlier that day. Ben and Lincoln smiled and hugged them again before following their mother out of the restaurant. As Ruth and Phil waved good-bye, for the first time in years, they felt a genuine sense of connection to them. Though they had grave doubts about how soon—or even whether—they'd get to see the boys again, in that amazing moment, their son Danny stirred in their hearts.

Acknowledgements

I'M A STRONG BELIEVER in fate and divine intervention. When the two conspire to lead me in a certain direction, my instinctive response is to place one foot in front of the other and sprint forward furiously. Which is precisely how this book project began. In my last book, *Evil at Lake Seminole*, I'd written about a lifelong Tallahassee resident named Mike Williams who was murdered as the result of a conspiracy between his wife and best friend, who for years had been lovers behind Mike's back. His crusading mother, Cheryl Williams, was the true hero of that story, and someone I came to know and respect tremendously. Our conversations continued long after the book was released.

While talking to her one evening, she pressed me on what I planned to write next. When I told her I didn't know, she urged me to write about Professor Dan Markel's murder. At that point, all I knew about this story was that Dan had been a Florida State law professor who'd been murdered in Tallahassee. Which was all I needed to know. I wasn't about to spend another year or more of my life writing about a crime that occurred in Tally. "Been there, done that," I thought to myself. Halfheartedly, I told Cheryl, "I'll think about it."

Miraculously, just a couple of days later, a *Dateline* episode mysteriously appeared on our family's DVR as if it had been recorded by magic. Or *divine intervention*. The episode was a two-hour documentary recounting the story of, you guessed it, Dan Markel's murder and the long march to justice that followed. I owed it to Cheryl to at least take a look with an open mind. Lo and behold, I found the story that unfolded on my TV screen mesmerizing.

One of the "talking heads" connecting the documentary's disparate segments was Matt Shaer, the same Matt Shaer whose kind words grace the front cover of this book. Matt was the creative genius behind—and the syrupy voice that narrated—the *Over My Dead Body* podcast that has now been downloaded more than 30 million times. Conducting my due diligence, I listened to all seven episodes. By that point, there was no turning back. Some 2,000 hours of research, interviews, and writing later, the pages you've just consumed emerged. So thank you Cheryl and thank you Matt for being part of God's plan for me to write this story, and Matt for giving me a running head start through your awesome podcast.

When my work on this project began, I had no idea how deeply enmeshed Dan Markel had become in so many different social circles. Or that I would end up interviewing more than 50 individuals who were connected with him in one way or another. Speaking with them and gathering their perspectives, anecdotes, and opinions allowed me to flesh out the essence of this unique individual in ways I otherwise couldn't have. I'm indebted to everyone who spoke with me about Dan and particularly those who read and commented on various drafts of my manuscript.

Though some preferred their contributions to remain anonymous, I'm able to express my heartfelt appreciation to Frank Apodaca, Dave Aronberg, Alejandra Berlioz, Doug Berman, Josh Berman, Paul Caron, Tracey and Jeremy Cohen, Tamara Demko, Ben Depoorter, Patrick Flemming, Brian Galle, Aaron Gott, Judge Michael Daly Hawkins, Adam Hirsch, Burt Hodge, Sam Kimmelman, Adam Kramarow, Orly Lorbel, Courtney and Darrin McMahon, Hannah Monroe, Clara Murga, Will Ourand, Gregg Polsky, Shaul Robinson, Paul Secunda, Zach Shrier, Jason Solomon, Howard Wasserman, Donald Weidner, and Hirschy Zarchi. I'm also thankful to my lawyer friends Mitchell Kelling, Katie Simon, and Judy Tseng, who provided helpful thoughts and comments on the manuscript and to writer Karen Cyphers, whose thorough commentary in *Florida Politics* during Katie Magbanua's retrial assisted me in crossing the finish line less than 30 days following her conviction.

I was very fortunate the lawyers involved in this case were gracious enough to help me flesh out their biographies and to provide details about this story I hadn't otherwise come across. My sincere appreciation goes out to prosecutors Georgia Cappleman, Sarah Kathryn Dugan, and Anna Norris as well as paralegal Lori Abbey for handling my incessant (at times annoying) records requests; to defense lawyers Chris DeCoste, Tara Kawass, and Sam Zangeneh; and Dan's family law attorneys, Thomas Duggar and Scott Snavely. Equally important, I couldn't have described the atmosphere and dialog from inside the jury room at the first trial without extensive interviews of two of the panel's members, both of whom have chosen to remain anonymous. I'm thankful for their recollections and insights.

I'm especially grateful to law professors Michael Cahill, Jack Chin, Ethan Leib, and Jim Rossi, who were extremely generous with their time and for allowing me to hound them relentlessly—in true Dan Markel fashion—for important details about his academic career. And to Jim Geiger for welcoming me into his charming Betton Hills home, where he provided his step-by-step recounting of the most harrowing morning of his life. I couldn't have hooked readers into this story without Jim's considerable assistance. My special thanks to David Lat for his continuous support and encouragement from the inception of this project all the way to the finish line and also for his elegant foreword—a moving tribute to Dan.

Most of all, I'm deeply indebted to Ruth, Phil, and Shelly Markel, who have experienced a loss so profound, and a march to justice so lengthy and excruciating, I had no reason to expect their cooperation or support. I'm overwhelmed by their courage and fortitude and immensely appreciative for their willingness to share with me so many intimate details—details that allowed me to breathe life and texture into their Danny. More than anything, I hope the story I've told rings true to them and serves as a lasting legacy for their extended family and friends across the globe.

I'm blessed to work for a wonderful law firm full of amazing people, Poyner Spruill LLP. Though I didn't ask my partners' permission when I stumbled into this side hustle five years ago, they've been fully supportive of my budding writing career ever since, in particular my managing partner Dan Cahill. I'm also fortunate to have an incredible assistant who helps me look good every day, Sandy Chrisawn, my biggest cheerleader in my law practice and my writing.

The words, paragraphs, and chapters of this book were made significantly better by three talented women I didn't even know when I took my first steps along this path in 2017, but who are each indispensable to my writing career now: Anne Blythe, who continues to help me find my voice and add sparkle to my words, Kerry McQuisten, who plucked me from obscurity by offering me my first publishing contract and who's now cranked out my first three books, and my new friend and partner in (true) crime, author C.J. Wynn, whose own debut effort, *Wilder Intentions*, continues to rock the true crime charts. This journey has been so much more rewarding because I've gotten to share it with Anne, Kerry, and C.J.

Last, but certainly not least, is my family, whose encouragement and support is vital not just to what I do, but to who I am: my beautiful, talented, and amazing wife Alétia Ferreira, who makes every day of my life special and meaningful, and our kids Benjamin, Madeline, Enzo, Tucker, and Thomas, all but one of whom have now departed the nest and are soaring in flight. My mother, Evelyn Epstein, *kvells* in having an author as a son. Though he's been gone nearly 20 years, my Papa, Morris Goldstein, is as much an inspiration to me today as he was when I was struggling to cobble together my very first words in elementary school. His pride in me meant—and continues to mean—more than I can possibly express in words.

• • •

PHOTO GALLERY

Photo Credits: Tamara Demko
Middle Left Photo Credit: Jeremy Cohen

Top Left: Dan and Wendi before marriage, circa 2005. Top Right and Bottom Left: "On top of the world" in San Francisco, October 2008. Middle Left: Wendi's 30th birthday celebration, April 2009. Middle Right: Attending *bat mitzvah* of friend's daughter in Tally, January 2010. Bottom Right: The expectant parents ready to welcome Lincoln into the world, October 2010.

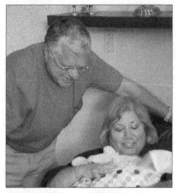

Top Left and Middle: Proud parents and grandparents at Ben's *bris*, August 2009. Top Right: Phil and Ruth doting on Baby Ben. Bottom Left: All smiles in Chicago, May 2010, Dan carrying Ben and Wendi "carrying" Lincoln. Bottom Right: Last trip to Canada as a family, August 2012. Unbeknownst to Dan, Wendi had already hired a divorce lawyer and taken a parenting course required to commence the process.

Harvey (Upper Left) and Donna (Upper Middle) raised their kids in Coral Springs, Florida. Upon graduation from dental school, Charlie (Upper Right) joined them at the Adelson Institute. Middle: Dan appeared most comfortable in his in-laws' midst at Ben's *bris*. Bottom: Charlie and Harvey reveling in their time with Lincoln following Dan's murder.

Dan was a well-known and highly regarded criminal law scholar, receiving tenure at Florida State in record time. Unlike Dan, Wendi was a member of Florida State's clinical law faculty, with a much lower rank and little job security. Professionally, she often found herself in Dan's shadow.

Ben and Lincoln were the light of Dan's life, occupying the center of his universe. Which is why he fought so hard to stop Wendi and her family from moving them to South Florida. And also why he sought to restrict Donna Adelson's visitation when she began disparaging him to his sons.

Following his separation from Wendi, Dan wanted to be with his "cubbies" as much as he possibly could. He ensured that they maintained close bonds with his mom and dad, his sister, and the boys' cousins in Canada. Those bonds, however, were irreparably broken two years after his murder.

Dan's intense love affair with Israel continued to his last days on earth. Top: At breakfast with his Israeli cousins on December 24, 2013 during his final visit to the Jewish homeland. Bottom: The epitaph on his tombstone at a Jewish cemetery in Toronto succinctly captures his essence: "His children were his world; His family, friends and community his pillars; His academic work his passion."

Top Left: Best friends since childhood, Sigfredo "Tuto" Garcia and Luis "Tato" Rivera were identified as the hitmen who assassinated Dan. Upper Right: As a foursome with their women, Katie Magbanua and Jessica Rodriguez. Lower Left: Garcia and his "wife" in Orlando just prior to the birth of their son. Lower Right: Proud parents with baby Ethan.

Top Left: By all outward appearances, Charlie and Katie seemed to be a normal, loving couple during the summer of 2014. Top Right: By early 2015, the Filipina immigrant had become a voluptuous blonde. Middle: All smiles sans kids on Father's Day 2014, Katie, Wendi, and Yindra Mascaro soaked in the sunshine near Harvey and Donna's South Beach condo. Bottom: Wendi couldn't even force a smile amid hours of questioning the afternoon of the shooting.

Photo Credits Top: Courtesy of Law & Crime Network
Photo Credits Bottom: 2nd Judicial Circuit State Attorney's Office

Craig Isom (Top Left) and Pat Sanford (Top Right) shed buckets of blood, sweat, and tears in their efforts to obtain justice for Dan Markel and his family. Bottom Left: The April 2016 bump between an undercover FBI agent and Donna. Bottom Right: Though Donna and Charlie carefully coordinated their next steps the following day, Charlie's own words at Dolce Vita later that afternoon would ultimately lead to his April 2022 arrest.

Photo Credits: Leon County Jail
Photo Credit Bottom Right: Broward County Jail

Rogue's Gallery: Four of Dan Markel's accused killers are now behind bars. Garcia (Top Left) and Katie (Bottom Left) have each been convicted of first-degree murder and are serving life sentences. Rivera (Top Right) is serving a 19-year sentence following his deal to turn State's evidence. Charlie (Bottom Right) faces possible life imprisonment once the case against him is tried.

Photo Credits: Courtesy of Law & Crime Network

Top Left: Judge James Hankinson ran a tight ship during the fall 2019 trial. Top Right: Judge Robert Wheeler proved a softer touch at Katie's May 2022 retrial. Bottom Left: Always calm and poised, Georgia Cappleman deftly stitched together the many disparate aspects of the evidence as lead prosecutor. Bottom Right: Prosecutor Sarah Kathryn Dugan played a significant role at the second trial, including her masterful cross-examination of Katie.

Photo Credits: Courtesy of Law & Crime Network

Top: Saam Zangeneh had by far the biggest challenge of the three defense lawyers. Though he wasn't successful in his defense of Garcia, he easily won the prize for the flashiest courtroom attire. Bottom Left: Chris DeCoste was spellbinding at times in Katie's defense, his questions and arguments delivered with a pleasing Boston accent. Bottom Right: Jamaican-born Tara Kawass brought her frenetic energy and fiery passion to what she labeled a "wrongful prosecution" of Katie.

Top Left: Wendi was undoubtedly the biggest media spectacle at both trials. Top Right: Her ex-boyfriend, Jeff Lacasse, shared his belief that Wendi had tried to frame him. Bottom Left: Though King Tato may have been an admitted killer and gang leader, his testimony came off as sincere and believable. Bottom Right: The well-dressed, demure woman who testified in her own defense contrasted sharply with the voice jurors had listened to on Katie's wiretapped calls with Charlie and Garcia.

For a trove of additional information, photos, and videos about this story, please visit **www.StevenBEpstein.com.**